2 Μακεδονίας· Ὅτι ἐν πολλῇ δοκιμῇ θλίψεως ἡ περισσεία τῆς χαρᾶς αὐτῶν, καὶ ἡ κατὰ βά-
3 θους πτωχεία αὐτῶν ἐπερίσσευσεν εἰς τὸν πλοῦτον τῆς ἁπλότητος αὐτῶν· Ὅτι κατὰ δύναμιν
4 (μαρτυρῶ) καὶ ὑπὲρ δύναμιν αὐθαίρετοι· Μετὰ πολλῆς παρακλήσεως δεόμενοι ἡμῶν, τὴν
5 χάριν καὶ τὴν κοινωνίαν τῆς διακονίας τῆς εἰς τοὺς ἁγίους, — δέξασθαι ἡμᾶς. Καὶ οὐ καθὼς
6 ἠλπίσαμεν, ἀλλ᾽ ἑαυτοὺς ἔδωκαν πρῶτον τῷ Κυρίῳ καὶ ἡμῖν, διὰ θελήματος Θεοῦ· Εἰς
τὸ παρακαλέσαι ἡμᾶς Τίτον, ἵνα καθὼς προενήρξατο, οὕτω καὶ ἐπιτελέσῃ εἰς ὑμᾶς καὶ
7 τὴν χάριν ταύτην· Ἀλλ᾽ ὥσπερ ἐν παντὶ περισσεύετε, πίστει, καὶ λόγῳ, καὶ γνώσει, καὶ
πάσῃ σπουδῇ, καὶ τῇ ἐξ ὑμῶν ἐν ἡμῖν ἀγάπῃ, ἵνα καὶ ἐν ταύτῃ τῇ χάριτι περισσεύητε.
8 Οὐ κατ᾽ ἐπιταγὴν λέγω, ἀλλὰ διὰ τῆς ἑτέρων σπουδῆς, καὶ τὸ τῆς ὑμετέρας ἀγάπης γνή-
9 σιον δοκιμάζων.
10 πτώχευσε
δίδωμι· τ

16. ἐν] — DE
Plantini, Bengelii,
Oecumenius, Theoph
culam ἐν igitur
ἐν posterius] —
1. γνωρίζομεν]
δὲ] — 37.
2. θλίψεως]
βάθους] βαθ
ἁπλότητος] χρ
ὑπὲρ] παρὰ DE
4. ἡμῶν] ἡμῶ
δέξασθαι ἡμᾶς] —
14. 19. 21. 23.
Syra utraque, Co
ctus, Photius ap.
5. ἀλλ᾽] ἀλλὰ
6. εἰς τὸ] ὥστε
ἐπιτελέσῃ] ἐπιτ
καὶ πάσῃ σπουδῇ]
ὑμῶν ἐν ἡμῖν] ἡμ
περισσεύητε] περ
ὑμετέρας] ἡμετ
ἡμῶν ἀγαπήσεως
9. ὑμᾶς] ἡμᾶς
ὑμεῖς τῇ ἐκείνου
πλούσιοι DEFG.
οὕτως] ὅτι FG.

τοῦ κελευθεὶς αὐτὸ
πέμψαι, αὐθαίρετος
ἔφησε. Constantius
ὑμῶν γένοι θεωρέ
κτῆμ κρίνω πρότερον
πολίτης ὁ προσαγορ
αὐθαιρέτως καὶ μὴ
οὗτος δ᾽ αὐθαίρετος

4. τοὺς ἁγίους] Su
5. ἑαυτοὺς ἔδωκαν]
κύπρεοι σφέας αὐτοὺς
13. οἱ δὲ οἱ ἔφραζον
αὐτοὺς. VI. 108.
τοῖσι Ἀθηναίοισι οἱ Πλαταιέες —— ἐδίδοσαν πρῶτα πα-
ρατυχοῦσι κλεομένεϊ τε τῷ Ἀναξανδρίδεω καὶ Λακεδαιμονίοι-
σι σφέας αὐτοὺς —— συμβουλεύομεν δὲ ὑμῖν, δοῦναι ὑμέας
αὐτοὺς Ἀθηναίοισι —— ἔδοσαν μὲν δὴ οἱ Πλαταιέες σφέας αὐτοὺς Ἀθηναίοισι. VII. 130. ταῦτα δὲ ἔχοντα ἔλεγε ἐς τοὺς
Ἀλεύεω παῖδας, ὅτι πρῶτοι Ἑλλήνων ἐόντες Θεσσαλοὶ ——
ἔδοσαν ἑωυτοὺς τῷ βασιλέϊ. 139. εἰ Ἀθηναῖοι —— ἔδοσαν
σφέας αὐτοὺς τῷ Ξέρξῃ. 132. ὅσοι τῷ Πέρσῃ ἔδοσαν σφέας
αὐτούς. *Libanius* D. XX. p. 515. D. Θηβαῖοι ——
μεθ᾽ ὑμῶν πολιτευόντες ἔδοσαν αὐτοὺς τῷ Μήδῳ καὶ συνεσ-
τράτευον. *Ter.* Andr. I. 1. 35. Sic vita erat, facile omnes perferre ac pati, Cum quibus erat cunque una,

οἷς θαυμάζουσιν οἱ πολλοὶ τοὺς κεκτημένους.
8. γνήσιον] *Strabo* VII. p. 414. A. Γνήσιοι γὰρ οἱ
γερμανοὶ κατὰ τὴν Ῥωμαίων διάλεκτον.
9. ἐπτώχευσε] *Plut.* Apophth. Lac. p. 235. D.
ἐπαινοῦντος ἤτουν Λάκωνα· ἀλλ᾽ εἰ δόμεν σοι, ἔφη, μᾶλλον
πτωχεύσεις.
πλούσιος ὤν] *Arrianus* Epictet. III. 26. οὐ παρέχει
μοι πολλὰ καὶ ἄφθονα, τρυφᾶν με οὐ θέλει· οὐδὲ γὰρ τῷ
Ἡρακλεῖ παρεῖχε τῷ υἱῷ ἑαυτοῦ. *Dio Chrys.* XIV. p. 234.
C. τὸν Ὀδυσσέα ἀκούοντες, ὅτι πτωχὸς ὤν, καὶ τὰς μνη-
στῆρας αὐτῶν, οὐδὲν ἧττον βασιλεὺς ἦν, καὶ τῆς οἰκίας κύριος.
10. ποιῆσαι] est dare, θέλειν ποιῆσαι, i. e. ποιεῖν
vel

hermeneia

Hermeneia
—A Critical
and Historical
Commentary
on the Bible

2 Corinthians 8 and 9

A Commentary
on Two Administrative Letters
of the Apostle Paul

by Hans Dieter Betz

Edited by
George W. MacRae

Fortress
Press Philadelphia

Library of Congress Catalog Card Number 83-48904
ISBN 0-8006-6014-5

Printed in the United States of America
Design by Kenneth Hiebert
Type set on an Ibycus System at Polebridge Press
K128G85 20-6014

TO
MARTIN CRESSEY
THEODOR LORENZMEIER
ARMIN SCHULZ
—FAITHFUL FRIENDS

NON IGNORAVIT PAULUS
ARTEM RHETORUM,
MOVERE LAUDANDO

Hugo Grotius,
***Annotationes in Novum Testamentum* II**
(Parisiis: Sumptibus Authoris, 1646)
p. 488

The Author

Hans Dieter Betz is Professor of New Testament at the Divinity School and Chairman of the Department of New Testament and Early Christian Literature at the University of Chicago. Born in 1931 in Lemgo, Germany, he served as a pastor of churches in the Reformed Tradition before he came to the United States in 1963. From 1963 to 1978 he taught at the School of Theology and the Claremont Graduate School in Claremont, California. The author's lengthy list of published works shows his major interests to be the epistles and theology of the apostle Paul (*Nachfolge und Nachahmung Jesu Christi im Neuen Testament; Der Apostel Paulus und die sokratische Tradition; Paul's Concept of Freedom; Galatians*) and the Sermon on the Mount (*Essays on the Sermon on the Mount*). Another of his interests has been the investigation of the relationship of the New Testament to its religious environment; this is reflected in books and journal articles on the New Testament and Greco-Roman literature (*Lukian von Samosata und das Neue Testament; Plutarch's Theological Writings and Early Christian Literature; Plutarch's Ethical Writings and Early Christian Literature; The Greek Magical Papyri in Translation*).

Contents

The name *Hermeneia*, Greek ἑρμηνεία, has been chosen as the title of the commentary series to which this volume belongs. The word *Hermeneia* has a rich background in the history of biblical interpretation as a term used in the ancient Greek-speaking world for the detailed, systematic exposition of a scriptural work. It is hoped that the series, like its name, will carry forward this old and venerable tradition. A second entirely practical reason for selecting the name lies in the desire to avoid a long descriptive title and its inevitable acronym, or worse, an unpronounceable abbreviation.

The series is designed to be a critical and historical commentary to the Bible without arbitrary limits in size or scope. It will utilize the full range of philological and historical tools, including textual criticism (often slighted in modern commentaries), the methods of the history of tradition (including genre and prosodic analysis), and the history of religion.

Hermeneia is designed for the serious student of the Bible. It will make full use of ancient Semitic and classical languages; at the same time, English translations of all comparative materials—Greek, Latin, Canaanite, or Akkadian—will be supplied alongside the citation of the source in its original language. Insofar as possible, the aim is to provide the student or scholar with full critical discussion of each problem of interpretation and with the primary data upon which the discussion is based.

Hermeneia is designed to be international and interconfessional in the selection of authors; its editorial boards were formed with this end in view. Occasionally the series will offer translations of distinguished commentaries which originally appeared in languages other than English. Published volumes of the series will be revised continually, and eventually, new commentaries will replace older works in order to preserve the currency of the series. Commentaries are also being assigned for important literary works in the categories of apocryphal and pseudepigraphical works relating to the Old and New Testaments, including some of Essene or Gnostic authorship.

The editors of *Hermeneia* impose no systematic-theological perspective upon the series (directly, or indirectly by selection of authors). It is expected that authors will struggle to lay bare the ancient meaning of a biblical work or pericope. In this way the text's human relevance should become transparent, as is always the case in competent historical discourse. However, the series eschews for itself homiletical translation of the Bible.

The editors are heavily indebted to Fortress Press for its energy and courage in taking up an expensive, long-term project, the rewards of which will accrue chiefly to the field of biblical scholarship.

The editor responsible for this volume was George W. MacRae, S.J., of Harvard University.

July 1985

Frank Moore Cross
For the Old Testament
Editorial Board

Helmut Koester
For the New Testament
Editorial Board

A commentary on only two chapters of one of the letters of the apostle Paul requires special justification. The chapters 2 Corinthians 8 and 9, however, have not been arbitrarily selected from a given body of text. These chapters constitute the hinge on which everything else concerning 2 Corinthians turns, one way or the other. Anyone who wishes to tackle the fundamental problems of this letter must first come to terms with the hypothesis of Johann Salomo Semler, published in 1776. This hypothesis—truly one of the brilliant ideas for which Semler is known—has been under discussion by New Testament scholars since its publication, some two hundred years ago now, but it has never been successfully proved or disproved. To do either would thus appear quite a risky undertaking. Indeed, arguments for or against the literary unity of 2 Corinthians have become firmly established traditions in themselves, and opinions have usually been formed before the discussion begins. Listing the traditional arguments for or against, and aligning oneself with one side or the other, however, will not suffice.

Rather, in a fresh examination what is needed first is a detailed and careful analysis of the chapters in order to find out whether they in fact can be related to letter categories known from other ancient epistolary literature, that is, whether their literary form, internal composition, argumentative rhetoric, and function can be shown to be that of independent epistolary fragments. The present study provides such an analysis of 2 Corinthians 8 and 9. This analysis is in most respects the first such attempt, but it is certainly not intended to be the last word on the subject. Sufficient evidence is provided to support the conclusions, so that quick reactions of mere agreement or disagreement, a mere embrace or indignation, will be avoided. The challenge to the serious students of the New Testament is to sustain a developed scientific argument.

The methodology applied throughout the investigation is the so-called historical-critical method, a number of philological, literary, historical, history-of-religions, and theological approaches complementing and checking each other. This method does not differ from that used in other scholarly investigations of ancient texts, but its use does not exclude special emphases which may be necessary in view of the material under investigation. In this study, therefore, a great deal of attention is devoted to matters of epistolography and administrative language, matters often neglected in New Testament studies. These matters, however, must be discussed in connection with comparable literary evidence from antiquity. Otherwise, the danger of ending up in fancy and idle speculation can hardly be avoided. Readers who may feel that they are exposed to too much such evidence should be patient and be mindful of other readers who will be delighted just to have access to the material.

What is the benefit of undertaking the whole exercise? For the author, the difference before and after the research has simply been that of understanding what he did not understand before. The experience has been as fascinating as would be discovering two new letters of Paul, and it is hoped that readers will be able to share this excitement.

Chapter 1 reviews the history of research from Semler—and even before—to the present. The main reason for presenting this evidence in greater detail is that the problems can only be recognized and clarified by a serious encounter with past scholarship. There are many aspects of this scholarship which have been forgotten or misunderstood, or which have implications for other letters of the apostle. It is thus important to see precisely where scholarship stands at present, how it got there, and where one must begin a fresh examination.

Chapters 2 and 3 present the literary, historical, and theological analysis together with a full commentary of 2 Corinthians chapters 8 and 9. Chapter 4 sums up what can be inferred regarding the literary genre and function of the two letters that these chapters comprise. Chapter 5 describes briefly how the two letters can be related to the other parts of Paul's correspondence with the Corinthians, especially 1 Corinthians and the other letter fragments of 2 Corinthians, and to Romans. Much of this chapter is tentative, to the extent that the literary analyses of these letters have not yet been undertaken and that the final judgment will have to await their appearance.

A great deal of the research and writing was done during a very productive research leave at the University of Oxford, England, in the autumn of 1981. I am sincerely grateful for the hospitality and assistance extended to me by the faculty of Oxford University and especially by the Bodleian and Ashmolean Libraries. Professors James Barr and George D. Kilpatrick have discussed with me special problems of the investigation, and I owe to them a number of excellent suggestions. In addition, I have been much stimulated by discussing the work in progress with many colleagues and students in Europe and the United States. To all of them I express my sincere thanks.

Several other persons and institutions deserve recognition. The University of Chicago, through Professor Franklin I. Gamwell, Dean of the Divinity School, has supported my research in a generous way. Professor Gerhard Delling of the University of Halle/Wittenberg provided me with photocopies of otherwise inaccessible works of Semler and his student, Michael Weber. Professor Laurence Welborn translated substantial portions of the manuscript and assisted me with improving the English of the rest. Professor George W. MacRae served as the volume editor and did a work of love and care while plagued with grave illness, not long before his sudden death on September 6, 1985. Dr. Harold W. Rast, the director of Fortress Press, did all he could to expedite the publication of the book. Mr. Jeffrey A. Trumbower assisted in the proofreading and the composing of the indices. Ms. Martha Morrow-Vojacek took great care in the typing of the complicated final manuscript.

The two letters which emerge before the eyes of the reader show an apostle Paul deeply embroiled in church administration, fiscal problems, and ecumenical strategizing (if that horrible word can be admitted). Here the great theologian that he was reveals himself to be involved with the toughest parts of church leadership: the raising of money for the needy; the establishing of voluntary cooperation among very different people, despite distances and fragile communication; the reconciliation between churches in different lands and cultures; and last but not least, the preservation of the church as a *Christian* institution. It is only fitting that I dedicate this book to three friends of old who have for their entire lives been engaged in the same practical work under three entirely different circumstances in England, West Germany, and East Germany.

Chicago
September 1985

H. D. Betz

Reference Codes

1. Abbreviations

Abot R. Nat.	*Abot de Rabbi Nathan*
ad loc.	*ad locum*
Aeschines	Aeschines
Contra Ctesiph.	*Contra Ctesiphon*
AGJU	Arbeiten zur Geschichte des antiken Judentums und des Urchristentums
AJPh	*American Journal of Philology*
AKG	Arbeiten zur Kirchengeschichte
Anaximenes	Anaximenes
Rhet.	*Rhetorica*
AnBib	Analecta Biblica
ANET	*Ancient Near Eastern Texts Relating to the Old Testament*
ANRW	Aufstieg und Niedergang der römischen Welt
Anth. Pal.	*Anthologia Palatina*
APOT	R. H. Charles, ed., *Apocrypha and Pseudepigrapha of the Old Testament*
Aristotle	Aristotle
Ath. Pol.	'Αθηναίων Πολιτεία
EE	*Ethica Eudemia*
EN	*Ethica Nicomachea*
MM	*Magna Moralia*
Pol.	*Politica*
Rhet.	*Rhetorica*
Arrianus	Arrianus
Peripl.	*Periplus*
ARW	*Archiv für Religionswissenschaft*
Athenagoras	Athenagoras
Leg.	*Legatio*
ATR	*Anglican Theological Review*
Augustine	Augustine
De civ. dei	*De civitate dei*
BDF	F. Blass, A. Debrunner, and R. W. Funk, *A Greek Grammar of the New Testament* (Chicago: University of Chicago, 1961)
BDR	F. Blass and A. Debrunner, *Grammatik des neutestamentlichen Griechisch*, ed. F. Rehkopf (Göttingen: Vandenhoeck & Ruprecht, 1976)
BFCTh	Beiträge zur Förderung christlicher Theologie
BGU	Aegyptische Urkunden aus den Museen zu Berlin: Griechische Urkunden I–VIII 1895–1933
BHTh	Beiträge zur historischen Theologie
BJRL	*Bulletin of the John Rylands Library*
BKP	Beiträge zur klassischen Philologie
BT	Bibliotheca Teubneriana
BZ	*Biblische Zeitschrift*
BZNW	Zeitschrift für die neutestamentliche Wissenschaft und die Kunde der älteren Kirche, Beiheft
ca.	*circa*, approximately
CBQ	*Catholic Biblical Quarterly*
chap(s).	chapter(s)
Chrysostom	Joannes Chrysostomus
Hom. 51.1 in Jo.	*Homilia in Evangelium Joannis 51.1*
In epist. II. ad Cor. Hom.	*Homiliae XXX in Epistolam secundam ad Corinthios*
Cicero	Cicero
De inv.	*De inventione*
De nat. deor.	*De natura deorum*
De off.	*De officiis*
De orat.	*De oratore*
Ep. ad Attic.	*Epistulae ad Atticum*
Ep. ad Brut.	*Epistula ad Brutum*
Ep. ad Quint.	*Epistulae ad Quintum Fratrem*
Ep. Fam.	*Epistulae ad Familiares*
Part. orat.	*De partitione oratoria*
Top.	*Topica*
CII	*Corpus inscriptionum Iudaicarum*
CIL	*Corpus inscriptionum Latinarum*
1–2 Clem.	*1–2 Clement*
Clemens Alex.	Clement of Alexandria
Quis dives	*Quis dives salvetur*
Columella	Columella
De re rust.	*De re rustica*
Corp. Herm.	*Corpus Hermeticum*
CPJ	*Corpus papyrorum Judaicarum*
CQ	*Church Quarterly*
CSEL	Corpus scriptorum ecclesiasticorum latinorum
Cyril of Jerusalem	Cyril of Jerusalem
Catech.	*Catecheses Mystagogicae*
Demosthenes	Demosthenes
Ep.	*Epistulae*
Exord.	*Exordia*
Did.	*Didache*
Dio Chrys.	Dio Chrysostom
Or.	*Orationes*
ed(s).	editor(s), edited by, edition
e.g.	*exempli gratia*, for example
EKK	Evangelisch-katholischer Kommentar zum Neuen Testament
Epictetus	Epictetus
Diss.	*Dissertationes*

Epiphanius	Epiphanius
Adv. haer.	*Adversus haereses (Panarion)*
EPRO	Etudes préliminaires aux religions orientales dans l'empire romain
esp.	especially
ET	English translation
et al.	*et alii,* and others
EWNT	*Exegetisches Wörterbuch zum Neuen Testament,* ed. Horst Balz and Gerhard Schneider, vols. 1–3 (Stuttgart: Kohlhammer, 1980–83)
f(f)	(and the) following (pages)
Frag.	Fragment
FRLANT	Forschungen zur Religion und Literatur des Alten und Neuen Testaments
FS	Festschrift
GCS	Die griechischen christlichen Schriftsteller der ersten drei Jahrhunderte
Geop.	*Geoponica*
GGR	*Geschichte der griechischen Religion*
HAT	Handbuch zum Alten Testament
HAW	Handbuch der Altertumswissenschaft
Herm.	*Hermas*
Mand.	*Mandata*
Sim.	*Similitudines*
Vis.	*Visiones*
Hesiod	Hesiod
Erga	*Erga et dies*
Theog.	*Theogonia*
HKAW	Handbuch der klassischen Altertumswissenschaft
HNT	Handbuch zum Neuen Testament
HR	*History of Religions*
HThK	Herders theologischer Kommentar zum Neuen Testament
HUCA	*Hebrew Union College Annual*
ibid.	*ibidem,* in the same place
ICC	International Critical Commentary
IDB	*Interpreter's Dictionary of the Bible*
IDBSup	*Interpreter's Dictionary of the Bible—Supplementary Volume*
idem	the same (author)
i.e.	*id est,* that is
Ign.	Ignatius of Antioch, *Epistles to the*
Eph.	*Ephesians*
Mag.	*Magnesians*
Phld.	*Philadelphians*
Pol.	*Polycarp*
Rom.	*Romans*
Smyrn.	*Smyrnaeans*
Trall.	*Trallians*
Irenaeus	Irenaeus
Adv. haer.	*Adversus haereses*
Isocrates	Isocrates
Ep.	*Epistulae*
JAAR	*Journal of the American Academy of Religion*
JBL	*Journal of Biblical Literature*

JHS	*Journal of Hellenic Studies*
Jos.	Josephus
Ant.	*Antiquitates Judaicae*
BJ	*Bellum Judaicum*
C. Ap.	*Contra Apionem*
Vita	*Vita*
JQR	*Jewish Quarterly Review*
JR	*Journal of Religion*
JSJ	*Journal for the Study of Judaism in the Persian, Hellenistic and Roman Period*
JTS	*Journal of Theological Studies*
Justin	Justin Martyr
Apol.	*Apologia*
Dial.	*Dialogus cum Tryphone*
KEK	Kritisch-exegetischer Kommentar über das Neue Testament (Meyer)
KlP	*Der kleine Pauly*
KNT	Kommentar zum Neuen Testament
LCL	The Loeb Classical Library
LSJ	Liddell-Scott-Jones, *Greek-English Lexicon*
Lucian	Lucian
Peregr.	*De Morte Peregrini*
LXX	Septuaginta
Menander	Menander
Sent.	*Sententiae*
MGWJ	*Monatsschrift für Geschichte und Wissenschaft des Judentums*
MH	*Museum Helveticum*
MNTC	Moffatt New Testament Commentary
MPG	*Patrologia, Series Graeca,* ed. J.-P. Migne
MT	Masoretic (Hebrew) Text
n(n).	note(s)
n.d.	no date
NEB	*New English Bible*
NF	Neue Folge, new series
no(s).	number(s)
NS	New Series
NT	New Testament, Neues Testament
NT	*Novum Testamentum*
NTAbh	Neutestamentliche Abhandlungen
NTS	*New Testament Studies*
NovTSup	*Novum Testamentum.* Supplements
OGIS	*Orientis Graeci Inscriptiones Selectae,* ed. W. Dittenberger
op. cit.	*opere citato,* in the work cited
Origen	Origen
Expos. in Prov.	*Exposita in Proverbia*
OT	Old Testament
p(p).	page(s)
Pap.	Papyrus
Grenf.	I, *An Alexandrian Erotic Fragment and Other Greek Papyri, chiefly Ptolemaic,* ed. Bernard P. Grenfell (Oxford: Clarendon, 1896). II, *New Classical Fragments,* ed. Bernard P. Grenfell and Arthur S. Hunt (Oxford: Clarendon, 1897)

Hibeh	*The Hibeh Papyri* I, ed. Bernard P. Grenfell and Arthur S. Hunt
Oxy.	*The Oxyrhynchus Papyri,* ed. Bernhard P. Grenfell and Arthur S. Hunt
par(r).	parallel(s)
passim	in various places
PECL I	*Plutarch's Theological Writings and Early Christian Literature,* ed. Hans Dieter Betz, SCHNT 3 (Leiden: Brill, 1975)
PECL II	*Plutarch's Ethical Writings and Early Christian Literature,* ed. Hans Dieter Betz, SCHNT 4 (Leiden: Brill, 1978)
PGL	*Patristic Greek Lexicon,* G. W. H. Lampe (Oxford: Clarendon, 1968)
PGM	*Papyri graecae magicae,* ed. Karl Preisendanz, new ed. Albert Henrichs, 2 vols. (Stuttgart: Teubner, 1973–74)
Philo	Philo of Alexandria
Agr.	*De agricultura*
Decal.	*De decalogo*
Deus	*Quod deus sit immutabilis*
Ebr.	*De ebrietate*
Her.	*Quis rerum divinarum heres sit*
Jos.	*De Josepho*
Leg. all.	*Legum allegoriarum libri*
Leg. Gai.	*De legatione ad Gaium*
Mos.	*De vita Mosis*
Op.	*De opificio mundi*
Plant.	*De plantatione*
Sacr.	*De sacrificiis Abelis et Caini*
Spec. leg.	*De specialibus legibus*
Virt.	*De virtutibus*
pl.	plural
PL	*Patrologiae cursus completus. Accurante Jacques-Paul Migne. Series Latina*
Pliny	Pliny the Elder
N.H.	*Naturalis Historia*
Plato	Plato
Leg.	*Leges*
Plutarch	Plutarch of Chaironeia
Defect. orac.	*De defectu oraculorum*
Glor. Athen.	*De gloria Atheniensium*
Laud. ips.	*De se ipsum citra invidiam laudando*
Thes.	*Theseus*
Pol.	Polycarp
Phil.	*Epistle to the Philippians*
PRE	*Paulys Real-Encyclopädie der classischen Alterthumswissenschaft*
PRE.S	—Supplement
PVTG	Pseudepigrapha Veteris Testamenti graece
Quint.	Quintilian
RAC	*Reallexikon für Antike und Christentum*
RB	*Revue biblique*
RE	*Realencyklopädie für protestantische Theologie und Kirche*
rep.	reprinted
RGG	*Die Religion in Geschichte und Gegenwart*
Rhet. ad Her.	*Rhetorica ad Herennium*
RHR	*Revue de l'histoire des religions*
RSR	*Recherches de science religieuse*
RSV	*Revised Standard Version* of the Bible
SBL	Society of Biblical Literature
SBLDS	—Dissertation Series
SBLMS	—Monograph Series
SBT	Studies in Biblical Theology
sc.	*scilicet,* namely
SCHNT	Studia ad Corpus Hellenisticum Novi Testamenti
SEÅ	*Svensk exegetisk årsbok*
SEG	*Supplementum Epigraphicum Graecum*
Seneca	Seneca
De ben.	*De beneficiis*
Ep.	*Epistulae morales*
SGKA	Studien zur Geschichte und Kultur des Altertums
SHAW.PH	Sitzungsberichte der Heidelberger Akademie der Wissenschaften. Philosophisch-historische Klasse
SHT	Studies in Historical Theology
SJLA	Studies in Judaism in Late Antiquity
SNTSMS	Society for New Testament Studies Monograph Series
SO	Symbolae osloenses
StJud	Studia Judaica
StNT	Studien zum Neuen Testament
Str-B	[H. Strack and] P. Billerbeck, *Kommentar zum Neuen Testament aus Talmud und Midrasch*
StTh	*Studia Theologica*
SUNT	Studien zur Umwelt des Neuen Testaments
s.v.	*sub verbo* or *sub voce,* under the word (entry)
SVF	*Stoicorum Veterum Fragmenta,* ed. von Arnim
TDNT	*Theological Dictionary of the New Testament,* ed. Gerhard Kittel and Gerhard Friedrich, tr. Geoffrey W. Bromiley, 10 vols. (Grand Rapids: Eerdmans, 1964–76)
TDOT	*Theological Dictionary of the Old Testament,* ed. F. Johannes Botterweck and Helmer Ringgren, tr. John T. Willis (Grand Rapids: Eerdmans, 1974–80)
Theocritus	Theocritus
Thalys.	*Thalysia*
Theophrastus	Theophrastus
Char.	*Characteres*
ThF	Theologische Forschungen
ThHNT	Theologischer Handkommentar zum Neuen Testament
ThJ	Theologische Jahrbücher

ThLZ	*Theologische Literaturzeitung*
ThR	*Theologische Rundschau*
ThStKr	*Theologische Studien und Kritiken*
ThWNT	*Theologisches Wörterbuch zum Neuen Testament,* ed. Gerhard Kittel and Gerhard Friedrich, 10 vols. (Stuttgart: Kohlhammer, 1933–79)
tr.	translation, translated by
TU	Texte und Untersuchungen zur Geschichte der altchristlichen Literatur
TWAT	*Theologisches Wörterbuch zum Alten Testament,* ed. G. Johannes Botterweck and Helmer Ringgren (Stuttgart: Kohlhammer, 1970–)
UNT	Untersuchungen zum Neuen Testament
v(v)	verse(s)
Varro	Varro
De reb. rust.	*De rebus rusticis*
Vg	Vulgate
VigChr	*Vigiliae Christianae*
viz.	*videlicet,* that is to say
v.l.	*varia lectio, variae lectiones,* variant reading
VT	*Vetus Testamentum*
WMANT	Wissenschaftliche Monographien zum Alten und Neuen Testament
WUNT	Wissenschaftliche Untersuchungen zum Neuen Testament
Xenophon	Xenophon
Anab.	*Anabasis*
Cyr.	*Cyropaedia*
Hell.	*Hellenica*
Mem.	*Memorabilia*
Oec.	*Oeconomicus*
Symp.	*Symposium*
YJS	Yale Judaica Series
ZKG	*Zeitschrift für Kirchengeschichte*
ZNW	*Zeitschrift für die neutestamentliche Wissenschaft und die Kunde der älteren Kirche*
ZPE	*Zeitschrift für Papyrologie und Epigraphik*
ZThK	*Zeitschrift für Theologie und Kirche*
ZWTh	*Zeitschrift für wissenschaftliche Theologie*

2. Short Titles of Commentaries, Studies, and Articles Often Cited

Adamietz, *Liber III*
Joachim Adamietz, *M. F. Quintiliani Institutionis Oratoriae Liber III,* Studia et Testimonia Antiqua 2 (Munich: Fink, 1966).

Bachmann
Philipp Bachmann, *Der zweite Brief an die Korinther,* KNT 8 (Leipzig: Deichert, [4]1922).

Barrett
Charles Kingsley Barrett, *A Commentary on the Second Epistle to the Corinthians,* Black's New Testament Commentaries (London: Black, 1973).

Bauer
W. Bauer, W. F. Arndt, and F. W. Gingrich, *A Greek-English Lexicon of the New Testament and Other Early Christian Literature* (Chicago and London: University of Chicago, 1979).

Baur, "Beiträge zur Erklärung der Korinthierbriefe"
Ferdinand Christian Baur, "Beiträge zur Erklärung der Korinthierbriefe," ThJ 9 (1850) 139–85.

Bell, *Jews and Christians in Egypt*
H. Idris Bell, *Jews and Christians in Egypt: The Jewish Troubles in Alexandria and the Athanasian Controversy* (London: British Museum, 1924).

Betz, *Lukian*
Hans Dieter Betz, *Lukian von Samosata und das Neue Testament,* TU 76 (Berlin: Akademie-Verlag, 1961).

Betz, *Nachfolge*
Hans Dieter Betz, *Nachfolge und Nachahmung Jesu Christi im Neuen Testament,* BHTh 37 (Tübingen: Mohr, Siebeck, 1967).

Betz, "Cleansing"
Hans Dieter Betz, "The Cleansing of the Ten Lepers (Luke 17:11–19)," *JBL* 90 (1971) 314–28.

Betz, *Paulus*
Hans Dieter Betz, *Der Apostel Paulus und die sokratische Tradition: Eine exegetische Untersuchung zu seiner "Apologie" 2 Kor 10–13,* BHTh 45 (Tübingen: Mohr, Siebeck, 1972).

Betz, *Galatians*
Hans Dieter Betz, *Galatians: A Commentary on Paul's Letter to the Churches in Galatia,* ed. Helmut Koester, Hermeneia (Philadelphia: Fortress, 1979).

Betz, *Essays*
Hans Dieter Betz, *Essays on the Sermon on the Mount* (Philadelphia: Fortress, 1985).

Bleek, "Erörterungen"
Friedrich Bleek, "Erörterungen in Beziehung auf die Briefe Pauli an die Korinther," *ThStKr* 3 (1830) 614–32.

Bolkestein, *Wohltätigkeit*
Hendrik Bolkestein, *Wohltätigkeit und Armenpflege im vorchristlichen Altertum* (Utrecht: Oosthoek, 1939).

Borgen, *Bread from Heaven*
Peder Borgen, *Bread from Heaven: An Exegetical Study of the Concept of Manna in the Gospel of John and the Writings of Philo,* NovTSup 10 (Leiden: Brill, 1965, [2]1981).

Bornkamm, *Vorgeschichte*
Günther Bornkamm, *Die Vorgeschichte des sogenannten Zweiten Korintherbriefes,* SHAW.PH 1961, 2. Abhandlung (Heidelberg: Winter, 1961); rep. with an addendum in his *Geschichte und Glaube II, Gesammelte Aufsätze IV* (Munich: Kaiser, 1971) 162–94.

Bousset, *Kyrios Christos*
Wilhelm Bousset, *Kyrios Christos: A History of the Belief in Christ from the Beginnings of Christianity to Irenaeus,* tr. John E. Steely (Nashville and New York: Abingdon, 1970).

Brightman
F. E. Brightman, *Liturgies Eastern and Western,* vol. 1: *Eastern Liturgies* (Oxford: Clarendon, 1896).

Bultmann, *Stil*
Rudolf Bultmann, *Der Stil der paulinischen Predigt und die kynisch-stoische Diatribe* (Göttingen: Huth, 1910; rep. Göttingen: Vandenhoeck & Ruprecht, 1984).

Bultmann, *Theology*
Rudolf Bultmann, *Theology of the New Testament,* 2 vols., tr. Kendrick Grobel (London: SCM; New York: Scribner's, 1951–55).

Bultmann, *Exegetica*
Rudolf Bultmann, *Exegetica: Aufsätze zur Erforschung des Neuen Testaments,* ed. Erich Dinkler (Tübingen: Mohr, Siebeck, 1967).

Bultmann
Rudolf Bultmann, *Der zweite Brief an die Korinther,* ed. Erich Dinkler, KEK 6. Abteilung, Sonderband (Göttingen: Vandenhoeck & Ruprecht, 1976); ET: *The Second Letter to the Corinthians,* tr. Roy A. Harrisville (Minneapolis: Augsburg, 1985).

Burkert, *Homo Necans*
Walter Burkert, *Homo necans: Interpretationen altgriechischer Opferriten und Mythen* (Berlin and New York: de Gruyter, 1972); ET: *Homo Necans. The Anthropology of Ancient Greek Sacrificial Ritual and Myth,* tr. Peter Bing (Berkeley and Los Angeles: University of California, 1983).

Burkert, *Religion*
Walter Burkert, *Griechische Religion der archaischen und klassischen Epoche* (Stuttgart: Kohlhammer, 1977).

Busolt, *Staatskunde I*
Georg Busolt, *Griechische Staatskunde I* (Munich: Beck, [3]1920).

Candlish, *The Duty of Laying By*
Robert Smith Candlish, *The Duty of Laying By, for Religious and Charitable Uses, a Stated Proportion of Our Income: An Analysis of 2 Cor viii.ix* (London: Nisbet, 1862).

Chrysostom
John Chrysostom, *Homiliae XXX in Epistolam secundam ad Corinthios, MPG* 61.381–610.

Collange, *Enigmes*
J.-F. Collange, *Enigmes de la deuxième épître de Paul aux Corinthiens: Etude exégètique de 2 Cor. 2:14–7:11,* SNTSMS 18 (Cambridge: Cambridge University, 1972).

Conzelmann, *Apostelgeschichte*
Hans Conzelmann, *Die Apostelgeschichte,* HNT 7 (Tübingen: Mohr, Siebeck, ²1972).

Conzelmann, *1 Corinthians*
Hans Conzelmann, *1 Corinthians: A Commentary on the First Epistle to the Corinthians,* Hermeneia (Philadelphia: Fortress, 1975).

Cook, *Zeus*
A. B. Cook, *Zeus: A Study in Ancient Religion,* 3 vols. (Cambridge: Cambridge University, 1914–40).

Cotton, *Documentary Letters of Recommendation*
Hannah Cotton, *Documentary Letters of Recommendation in Latin from the Roman Empire,* BKP 132 (Königstein: Hain, 1981).

Danker, *Benefactor*
Frederick W. Danker, *Benefactor: Epigraphic Study of a Graeco-Roman and New Testament Semantic Field* (St. Louis: Clayton, 1982).

Deininger, *Der politische Widerstand*
Jürgen Deininger, *Der politische Widerstand gegen Rom in Griechenland 217–86 v. Chr.* (Berlin and New York: de Gruyter, 1971).

Deissmann, *Light*
Adolf Deissmann, *Light from the Ancient East* (Grand Rapids: Baker, 1978).

Delling, *Worship*
Gerhard Delling, *Worship in the New Testament* (Philadelphia: Westminster, 1962).

Delling, "Alexander der Grosse"
Gerhard Delling, "Alexander der Grosse als Bekenner des jüdischen Gottesglaubens," *JSJ* 12 (1981) 1–51.

Dibelius, *Geschichte*
Martin Dibelius, *Geschichte der urchristlichen Literatur* (Leipzig: Teubner, 1926; Munich: Kaiser, ²1975).

Dibelius and Greeven, *James*
Martin Dibelius, *James: A Commentary on the Epistle of James,* rev. Heinrich Greeven, Hermeneia (Philadelphia: Fortress, 1976).

Dihle, *Die Goldene Regel*
Albrecht Dihle, *Die Goldene Regel: Eine Einführung in die Geschichte der antiken und frühchristlichen Vulgärethik* (Göttingen: Vandenhoeck & Ruprecht, 1962).

Dihle, "Goldene Regel"
Albrecht Dihle, "Goldene Regel," *RAC* 11 (1981) 930–40.

Dittenberger, *OGIS*
Wilhelm Dittenberger, *Orientis graeci inscriptiones selectae,* 2 vols. (Leipzig: Hirzel, 1903–05).

Dittenberger, *Sylloge*
Wilhelm Dittenberger, *Sylloge inscriptionum graecarum,* 4 vols. (Leipzig: Hirzel, ³1915–24).

Döring, *Exemplum Socratis*
Klaus Döring, *Exemplum Socratis: Studien zur Sokratesnachwirkung in der kynisch-stoischen Popularphilosophie der frühen Kaiserzeit und im frühen Christentum,* Hermes: Einzelschriften 42 (Wiesbaden: Steiner, 1979).

Ehrenberg and Jones, *Documents*
Victor Ehrenberg and A. H. M. Jones, *Documents Illustrating the Reigns of Augustus and Tiberius* (Oxford: Clarendon, ³1976).

Erasmus
Desiderius Erasmus, *Paraphrasis in duas epistolas Pauli ad Corinthios* (Lovanii, 1519); also in his *Opera Omnia,* vol. 7 (Lugduni Batavorum: Petrus van der Aa, 1706).

Feine, *Einleitung*
Paul Feine, *Einleitung in das Neue Testament* (Leipzig: Quelle und Meyer, 1913).

Finkelstein, "The Birkat Ha-Mazon"
Louis Finkelstein, "The Birkat Ha-Mazon," *JQR* NS 19 (1928–29) 211–62.

Georgi, *Gegner*
Dieter Georgi, *Die Gegner des Paulus im 2. Korintherbrief: Studien zur religiösen Propaganda in der Spätantike,* WMANT 11 (Neukirchen-Vluyn: Neukirchener Verlag, 1964).

Georgi, *Kollekte*
Dieter Georgi, *Die Geschichte der Kollekte des Paulus für Jerusalem,* ThF 38 (Hamburg-Bergstedt: Reich, 1965).

Giraudo, *La struttura letteraria*
Cesare Giraudo, *La struttura letteraria della preghiera eucaristica: Saggio sulla genesi letteraria di una forma: Toda veterotestamentaria, bᵉraka giudaica, anafora cristiana,* AnBib 92 (Rome: Pontifical Biblical Institute, 1981).

Gnilka, *Das Evangelium nach Markus*
Joachim Gnilka, *Das Evangelium nach Markus,* 2 vols., EKK 2/1–2 (Zurich: Benziger; Neukirchen-Vluyn: Neukirchener Verlag, 1978, 1979).

Goldin, *The Fathers*
Judah Goldin, *The Fathers According to Rabbi Nathan,* YJS 10 (New Haven: Yale University Press, 1955).

Gradenwitz, *Einführung*
Otto Gradenwitz, *Einführung in die Papyruskunde,* 1. Heft: *Erklärung ausgewählter Urkunden,* nebst einem Konträr-Index und einer Tafel in Lichtdruck (Leipzig: Hirzel, 1900).

Grenfell and Hunt, *The Hibeh Papyri*
Bernhard P. Grenfell and Arthur S. Hunt, *The Hibeh Papyri I* (London: Egypt Exploration Fund, 1906).

Grese, *Corpus Hermeticum XIII*
William C. Grese, *Corpus Hermeticum XIII and*

Early Christian Literature, SCHNT 5 (Leiden: Brill, 1979).

Grotius, *Annotationes*
Hugo Grotius, *Annotationes in Novum Testamentum,* 3 vols. (Parisiis: Sumptibus authoris, 1641, 1646, 1650).

Grundmann, *Lukas*
Walter Grundmann, *Das Evangelium nach Lukas,* ThHNT 3 (Berlin: Evangelische Verlagsanstalt, [2]1961).

Haenchen, *Acts*
Ernst Haenchen, *The Acts of the Apostles: A Commentary* (Oxford: Blackwell, 1971).

Hagge
H. Hagge, "Die beiden überlieferten Sendschreiben des Apostels Paulus an die Gemeinde zu Korinth," *Jahrbücher für protestantische Theologie* 2 (1876) 481–531.

Halmel
Anton Halmel, *Der zweite Korintherbrief des Apostels Paulus* (Halle: Niemeyer, 1904).

Hands, *Charities*
A. R. Hands, *Charities and Social Aid in Greece and Rome* (Ithaca: Cornell University, 1968).

Hässler, *Kyria-Klausel*
Manfred Hässler, *Die Bedeutung der Kyria-Klausel in den Papyrusurkunden,* Berliner Juristische Abhandlungen 3 (Berlin: Duncker & Humbolt, 1960).

Hausrath, *Der Vier-Capitel-Brief*
Adolf Hausrath, *Der Vier-Capitel-Brief des Paulus an die Korinther* (Heidelberg: Bassermann, 1870).

Heiler, *Das Gebet*
Friedrich Heiler, *Das Gebet: Eine religionsgeschichtliche und religionspsychologische Untersuchung* (Munich: Reinhardt, [5]1923).

Heinemann, *Prayer*
Joseph Heinemann, *Prayer in the Talmud: Forms and Patterns,* StJud 9 (Berlin: de Gruyter, 1977).

Heinrici
Carl Friedrich Georg Heinrici, *Der zweite Brief an die Korinther,* KEK 6. Abteilung (Göttingen: Vandenhoeck & Ruprecht, [8]1900).

Hertzberg, *Geschichte*
Gustav Friedrich Hertzberg, *Die Geschichte Griechenlands unter der Herrschaft der Römer,* 2 vols. (Halle: Buchhandlung des Waisenhauses, 1866, 1868).

Holsten, "Einleitung"
Carl Holsten, "Einleitung in die Korintherbriefe," *ZWTh* 44 (1901) 324–69.

Holtzmann, "Das gegenseitige Verhältniss"
Heinrich Julius Holtzmann, "Das gegenseitige Verhältniss der beiden Korintherbriefe," *ZWTh* 22 (1879) 455–92.

Hyldahl, "Die Frage"
Nils Hyldahl, "Die Frage nach der literarischen Einheit des Zweiten Korintherbriefes," *ZNW* 64 (1973) 289–306.

Jewett, "The Redaction"
Robert Jewett, "The Redaction of I Corinthians and the Trajectory of the Pauline School," *JAAR* 44 (1978) 398–444.

Jewett, *Chronology*
Robert Jewett, *A Chronology of Paul's Life* (Philadelphia: Fortress, 1979).

Johnson, Coleman-Norton, Bourne, *Ancient Roman Statutes*
Allan C. Johnson, Paul R. Coleman-Norton, Frank C. Bourne, *Ancient Roman Statutes* (Austin: University of Texas, 1961).

Jülicher, *Einleitung*
Adolf Jülicher, *Einleitung in das Neue Testament* (Tübingen: Mohr, Siebeck, [1.2]1894, [5.6]1906, [7]1931).

Käsemann, *Romans*
Ernst Käsemann, *Commentary on Romans* (Grand Rapids: Eerdmans, 1980).

Kaser, *Das römische Privatrecht*
Max Kaser, *Das römische Privatrecht,* HKAW 10.3.3.1 (Munich: Beck, [2]1971).

Kautzsch, *De Veteris Testamenti Locis*
Aemilius Fridericus Kautzsch, *De Veteris Testamenti Locis a Paulo Apostolo allegatis. Dissertatio critica* (Leipzig: Metzger & Wittig, 1869).

Kennedy, *Classical Rhetoric*
George A. Kennedy, *Classical Rhetoric and Its Christian and Secular Tradition from Ancient to Modern Times* (Chapel Hill: University of North Carolina, 1980).

Kennedy, *The Second and Third Epistles*
James Houghton Kennedy, *The Second and Third Epistles of St. Paul to the Corinthians* (London: Methuen, 1900).

Kim, *The Familiar Greek Letter of Recommendation*
Chan-Hie Kim, *Form and Structure of the Familiar Greek Letter of Recommendation,* SBLDS 4 (Missoula: Scholars, 1972).

Klöpper, *Exegetisch-kritische Untersuchungen*
Albert Klöpper, *Exegetisch-kritische Untersuchungen über den zweiten Brief des Paulus an die Gemeinde zu Korinth* (Göttingen: Vandenhoeck & Ruprecht, 1869).

Klöpper, *Kommentar*
Albert Klöpper, *Kommentar über das zweite Sendschreiben des Apostel Paulus an die Gemeinde zu Korinth* (Berlin: Reimer, 1874).

Klostermann, *Markusevangelium*
Erich Klostermann, *Das Markusevangelium,* HNT 3 (Tübingen: Mohr, Siebeck, [4]1950).

Koester, *Synoptische Überlieferung*
Helmut Koester, *Synoptische Überlieferung bei den Apostolischen Vätern,* TU 65 (Berlin: Akademie-Verlag, 1957).

Koester, *Einführung*
Helmut Koester, *Einführung in das Neue Testament* (Berlin: de Gruyter, 1980).

Koester, *Introduction*
Helmut Koester, *Introduction to the New Testament,* 2 vols., Hermeneia: Foundations and Facets (Philadelphia: Fortress, 1982).
König, "Der Verkehr"
Karl König, "Der Verkehr des Paulus mit der Gemeinde zu Korinth," *ZWTh* 40 (1897) 481–554.
Krenkel, *Beiträge*
Max Krenkel, *Beiträge zur Aufhellung der Geschichte und der Briefe des Apostels Paulus* (Braunschweig: Schwetschke, 1890, ²1895).
Kühner and Gerth, *Grammatik*
Raphael Kühner, *Ausführliche Grammatik der griechischen Sprache,* 2 vols., ed. Friedrich Blass and Bernhard Gerth (Hannover: Hahn, ³1890–1904; rep. Darmstadt: Wissenschaftliche Buchgesellschaft, 1966).
Kümmel, *Introduction*
Paul Feine and Johannes Behm, *Introduction to the New Testament,* rev. Werner Georg Kümmel, tr. Howard C. Kee (Nashville: Abingdon, ²1975).
Kuenzi, ΕΠΙΔΟΣΙΣ
Adolphe Kuenzi, ΕΠΙΔΟΣΙΣ*: Sammlung freiwilliger Beiträge zu Zeiten der Not in Athen,* Mit einem Anhang: *Epidosis in den übrigen griechischen Städten* (Bern: Haupt, 1923).
Kypke, *Observationes sacrae*
Georg David Kypke, *Observationes sacrae in Novi Foederis Libros ex auctoribus potissimum Graecis et antiquitatibus,* 2 vols. (Wratislaviae: Ioh. Iacobi Kornii, 1755).
Lafoscade, *De epistulis*
Leon Lafoscade, *De epistulis (aliisque titulis) imperatorum magistratuumque Romanorum, quas ab aetate Augusti usque ad Constantinum Graece scriptas lapides papyrive servaverunt,* Thèse Paris (Insulis: Le Bigot, 1902).
Cornelius a Lapide
Cornelius a Lapide, *The Great Commentary of Cornelius a Lapide: II Corinthians and Galatians,* tr. and ed. W. F. Cobb (London: Hodges, 1897).
Larsen, "Roman Greece"
Jakob A. O. Larsen, "Roman Greece," Tenney Frank, *An Economic Survey of Ancient Rome,* vol. 4 (Baltimore: Johns Hopkins, 1938).
Lattimore, *Hesiod*
Richmond A. Lattimore, *Hesiod: The Works and Days* (Ann Arbor: University of Michigan, 1959).
Lausberg, *Handbuch*
Heinrich Lausberg, *Handbuch der literarischen Rhetorik: Eine Grundlegung der Literaturwissenschaft* (Munich: Hueber, 1960, ²1973).
Lietzmann, *An die Römer*
Hans Lietzmann, *An die Römer,* HNT 8 (Tübingen: Mohr, Siebeck, ⁵1971).
Lietzmann
Hans Lietzmann, *An die Korinther I/II,* HNT 9 (Tübingen: Mohr, Siebeck, 1909, ⁴1949 [ed. by Werner Georg Kümmel]).
Lohse, *Colossians and Philemon*
Eduard Lohse, *Colossians and Philemon: A Commentary on the Epistles to the Colossians and to Philemon,* tr. William R. Poehlmann and Robert J. Karris, ed. Helmut Koester, Hermeneia (Philadelphia: Fortress, 1971).
Lüdemann, *Paulus der Heidenapostel I*
Gerd Lüdemann, *Paulus der Heidenapostel I: Studien zur Chronologie,* FRLANT 123 (Göttingen: Vandenhoeck & Ruprecht, 1980).
McCrum and Woodhead, *Select Documents*
Michael McCrum and Arthur G. Woodhead, *Select Documents of the Principates of the Flavian Emperors Including the Year of the Revolution A.D. 68–69* (Cambridge: Cambridge University, 1961).
Malherbe, "Ancient Epistolary Theorists"
Abraham J. Malherbe, "Ancient Epistolary Theorists," *Ohio Journal of Religious Studies* 5 (1977) 3–77.
Mannzmann, *Stiftungsurkunden*
Anneliese Mannzmann, *Griechische Stiftungsurkunden: Studie zu Inhalt und Rechtsform* (Münster: Aschendorff, 1962).
Martin, *Rhetorik*
Josef Martin, *Antike Rhetorik, Technik und Methode,* HKAW 2.3 (Munich: Beck, 1974).
Mason, *Greek Terms*
Hugh J. Mason, *Greek Terms for Roman Institutions,* American Studies in Papyrology 13 (Toronto: Hakkert, 1974).
Matthews, "Gesandtschaft"
John F. Matthews, "Gesandtschaft," *RAC* 11 (1977) 635–85.
Mayser, *Grammatik*
Edwin Mayser, *Grammatik der griechischen Papyri aus der Ptolemäerzeit,* 2 vols. (Berlin: de Gruyter, ²1970).
Metzger, *Textual Commentary*
Bruce M. Metzger, *A Textual Commentary on the Greek New Testament* (London and New York: United Bible Societies, 1971).
Meyer, *Juristische Papyri*
Paul M. Meyer, *Juristische Papyri: Erklärung von Urkunden zur Einführung in die juristische Papyruskunde* (Berlin: Weidmann, 1920).
Michaelis, *Einleitung*
Wilhelm Michaelis, *Einleitung in das Neue Testament* (Bern: Haller, ³1961 [with Ergänzungsheft]).
Mitteis and Wilcken, *Grundzüge und Chrestomathie*
Ludwig Mitteis and Ulrich Wilcken, *Grundzüge und Chrestomathie der Papyruskunde* (rep. Hildesheim: Olms, 1963).
Mott, "The Power of Giving and Receiving,"
Stephen Charles Mott, "The Power of Giving and Receiving: Reciprocity in Hellenistic Benevolence," *Current Issues in Biblical and Patristic Interpretation, FS M. C. Tenney* (Grand Rapids:

Eerdmans, 1975) 60–72.
Moule, *Idiom Book*
C. F. D. Moule, *An Idiom Book of New Testament Greek* (Cambridge: Cambridge University, 1955).
Moulton and Milligan
James H. Moulton and George Milligan, *The Vocabulary of the Greek New Testament Illustrated from the Papyri and Other Non-literary Sources* (London: Hodder, 1930).
Mussies, *Dio Chrysostom*
G. Mussies, *Dio Chrysostom and the New Testament,* SCHNT 2 (Leiden: Brill, 1972).
Nestle-Aland
Novum Testamentum Graece, post Eberhard Nestle et Erwin Nestle commutiter ediderunt Kurt Aland, Matthew Black, Carlo M. Martini, Bruce M. Metzger, Allen Wikgren; apparatum criticum recensuerunt et editionem novis curis elaboraverunt Kurt Aland et Barbara Aland una cum Instituto studiorum textus Novi Testamenti Monasteriensi (Westphalia) (Stuttgart: Deutsche Bibelstiftung, [26]1979).
Nilsson, *GGR*
Martin P. Nilsson, *Geschichte der griechischen Religion,* HKAW 5.2.1–2 (Munich: Beck, [2]1955–61).
Norden, *Die antike Kunstprosa*
Eduard Norden, *Die antike Kunstprosa vom VI. Jahrhundert v. Chr. bis in die Zeit der Renaissance,* 2 vols. (Leipzig: Teubner, 1898).
Oepke, *Galater*
Albrecht Oepke, *Der Brief des Paulus an die Galater,* ed. Joachim Rohde, ThHK 9 (Berlin: Evangelische Verlagsanstalt, [3]1973 [[1]1937, [2]1957]).
Ollrog, *Mitarbeiter*
Wolf-Henning Ollrog, *Paulus und seine Mitarbeiter: Untersuchungen zu Theorie und Praxis der paulinischen Mission,* WMANT 50 (Neukirchen-Vluyn: Neukirchener Verlag, 1979).
Orth, "Getreide"
Ferdinand Orth, "Getreide," *PRE* 7.1 (1910) 1336–52.
Otto, *Die Sprichwörter*
August Otto, *Die Sprichwörter und sprichwörtlichen Redensarten der Römer* (Leipzig: Teubner, 1890; rep. Hildesheim: Olms, 1962); see, in addition: Reinhard Häussler, ed., *Nachträge zu A. Otto, Die Sprichwörter und sprichwörtlichen Redensarten der Römer* (Darmstadt: Wissenschaftliche Buchgesellschaft, 1968).
Papazoglou, "Quelques aspects"
Fauoula Papazoglou, "Quelques aspects de l'histoire de la province de Macedonie," ANRW 2.7.1 (1971) 302–69.
Pease, *M. Tulli Ciceronis*
Arthur Stanley Pease, *M. Tulli Ciceronis De natura deorum* (Darmstadt: Wissenschaftliche Buchgesellschaft, 1968).
Pesch, *Markusevangelium*
Rudolf Pesch, *Das Markusevangelium I,II,* HThK (Freiburg: Herder, 1976/77).
Piscator, *Analysis logica*
Johannes Piscator, *Analysis logica utriusque epistolae Pauli ad Corinthios;* una cum scholiis et observationibus locorum doctrinae, . . . (Herbornae Nassoviorum: Typis Christophori Corvini, 1593).
Plummer
Alfred Plummer, *A Critical and Exegetical Commentary on the Second Epistle of St Paul to the Corinthians,* ICC (Edinburgh: Clark, 1915).
Poland, *De legationibus*
Franciscus Poland, *De legationibus Graecorum publicis,* Dissertatio inauguralis Lipsiensis (Leipzig: Teubner, 1885).
Preisigke, *Fachwörter*
Friedrich Preisigke, *Fachwörter des öffentlichen Verwaltungsdienstes Ägyptens in den griechischen Papyrusurkunden der ptolemäisch-römischen Zeit* (Göttingen: Vandenhoeck & Ruprecht, 1915).
Preisigke, *Wörterbuch*
Friedrich Preisigke, *Wörterbuch der griechischen Papyrusurkunden mit Einschluss der griechischen Inschriften, Aufschriften, Ostraka, Mumienschilder usw. aus Ägypten,* vols. 1–3: 1924–31; vol. 4/1–4, rev. Emil Kiessling; *Supplement* 1.1–3: 1969–71 (Berlin and Marburg: Selbstverlag, 1924–71).
Richardson, *Homeric Hymn*
Neil J. Richardson, *The Homeric Hymn to Demeter* (Oxford: Clarendon, 1974).
Robinson and Koester, *Trajectories*
James M. Robinson and Helmut Koester, *Trajectories Through Early Christianity* (Philadelphia: Fortress, 1971).
Rostovtzeff, *The Social and Economic History*
Michael I.Rostovtzeff, *The Social and Economic History of the Roman Empire* (Oxford: Clarendon, [2]1957).
Saldarini, *The Fathers*
Anthony J. Saldarini, *The Fathers According to Rabbi Nathan (Abot de Rabbi Nathan): Version B,* SJLA 11 (Leiden: Brill, 1975).
Schenke and Fischer, *Einleitung*
Hans-Martin Schenke and Karl Martin Fischer, *Einleitung in die Schriften des Neuen Testaments,* Vol. 1: *Die Briefe des Paulus und die Schriften des Paulinismus* (Berlin: Evangelische Verlagsanstalt, 1978).
Schmiedel, *Hand-Commentar*
Paul Wilhelm Schmiedel, *Hand-Commentar zum Neuen Testament,* vol. 2 (Freiburg: Mohr, Siebeck, 1891, [2]1892).
Schmithals, *Gnosis*
Walter Schmithals, *Die Gnosis in Korinth: Eine Untersuchung zu den Korintherbriefen,* FRLANT 66 (Göttingen: Vandenhoeck & Ruprecht, 1956, [2]1965, [3]1969).

Schmithals, *Gnosticism*
Walter Schmithals, *Gnosticism in Corinth,* tr. John E. Steely (Nashville: Abingdon, 1971).
Schmithals, *Paul and the Gnostics*
Walter Schmithals, *Paul and the Gnostics,* tr. John E. Steely (Nashville: Abingdon, 1972).
Schmithals, "Briefsammlung"
Walter Schmithals, "Die Korintherbriefe als Briefsammlung," *ZNW* 64 (1973) 263–88.
Schubert, *Thanksgiving*
Paul Schubert, *Form and Function of the Pauline Thanksgiving,* BZNW 20 (Berlin: Töpelmann, 1939).
Sevenster, *Paul and Seneca*
J. N. Sevenster, *Paul and Seneca,* NovTSup 4 (Leiden: Brill, 1961).
Sherk, *Roman Documents*
Robert K. Sherk, *Roman Documents from the Greek East: Senatus Consulta and Epistulae to the Age of Augustus* (Baltimore: Johns Hopkins, 1969).
Siotis, ΘΕΟΛΟΓΙΑ
Markos A. Siotis, "Die Klassische und die Christliche Cheirotonie in ihrem Verhältnis," ΘΕΟΛΟΓΙΑ 20 (1949) 314–34, 524–41, 725–40; 21 (1950) 103–24, 239–57, 452–63, 605–17; 22 (1951) 108–18, 288–93.
Smallwood, *Documents*
E. Mary Smallwood, *Documents Illustrating the Principates of Gaius Claudius and Nero* (Cambridge: Cambridge University, 1967).
Spicq, *Notes de lexicographie*
Ceslas Spicq, *Notes de lexicographie néotestamentaire,* 2 vols. (Fribourg: Editions universitaires, 1978).
Staab, *Pauluskommentare*
Karl Staab, *Pauluskommentare aus der griechischen Kirche,* NTA 15 (Münster: Aschendorff, 1933).
Strachan
Robert Harvey Strachan, *The Second Epistle of Paul to the Corinthians,* MNTC (New York and London: Harper, 1935).
Suhl, *Paulus*
Alfred Suhl, *Paulus und seine Briefe: Ein Beitrag zur paulinischen Chronologie,* StNT 11 (Gütersloh: Mohn, 1975).
Tcherikover and Fuks, *CPJ*
Victor A. Tcherikover and Alexander Fuks, *Corpus Papyrorum Judaicarum,* 3 vols. (Cambridge: Cambridge University, 1957–64).
Tertullian, *De pudicitia*
Tertullian, *De pudicitia,* ed. Franciscus Oehler, *Quinti Septimi Florentis Tertulliani Quae Supersunt Omnia,* vol. 1 (Leipzig: Weigel, 1853).
Theobald, *Die überströmende Gnade*
Michael Theobald, *Die überströmende Gnade: Studien zu einem paulinischen Motivfeld,* Inaugural Dissertation (Bonn: Rheinische Friedrich-Wilhelms-Universität, 1980).
Thraede, *Brieftopik*
Klaus Thraede, *Grundzüge griechisch-römischer Brieftopik,* Zetemata 48 (Munich: Beck, 1970).
Thraede, "Gleichheit"
Klaus Thraede, "Gleichheit," *RAC* 10 (1979) 122–64.
Turner, *Grammatical Insights*
Nigel Turner, *Grammatical Insights into the New Testament* (Edinburgh: Clark, 1965).
van der Horst, *Pseudo-Phocylides*
Pieter W. van der Horst, *The Sentences of Pseudo-Phocylides,* Studia in Veteris Testamenti Pseudepigrapha 4 (Leiden: Brill, 1978).
Versnel, *Faith, Hope and Worship*
H. S. Versnel, ed., *Faith, Hope and Worship: Aspects of Religious Mentality in the Ancient World,* Studies in Greek and Roman Religion 2 (Leiden: Brill, 1981).
Vielhauer, *Geschichte*
Philipp Vielhauer, *Geschichte der urchristlichen Literatur* (Berlin: de Gruyter, 1975).
Volkmann, *Rhetorik*
Richard Volkmann, *Die Rhetorik der Griechen in systematischer Übersicht* (Stuttgart: Teubner, ²1885).
von Soden, *Untersuchungen*
Heiko Freiherr von Soden, *Untersuchungen zur Homologie in den griechischen Papyri Ägyptens bis Diokletian,* Graezistische Abhandlungen 5 (Cologne and Vienna: Böhlau, 1973).
Weber, *De numero epistularum Pauli*
Michael Weber, *De numero epistularum Pauli ad Corinthios rectius constituendo. Programmschriften I–XII* (Wittenberg: University of Wittenberg, 1798–1807).
Weiss, *Der erste Korintherbrief*
Johannes Weiss, *Der erste Korintherbrief,* KEK 5. Abteilung (Göttingen: Vandenhoeck & Ruprecht, ⁹1910; rep. 1970).
Weiss, *Das Urchristentum*
Johannes Weiss, *Das Urchristentum,* ed. Rudolf Knopf (Göttingen: Vandenhoeck & Ruprecht, 1917).
Welles, *Royal Correspondence*
C. Bradford Welles, *Royal Correspondence in the Hellenistic Period: a Study in Greek Epigraphy* (New Haven: Yale University Press, 1934).
Wenger, *Stellvertretung*
Leopold Wenger, *Die Stellvertretung im Rechte der Papyri* (Leipzig: Teubner, 1906).
West, *Hesiod, Works and Days*
Martin L. West, *Hesiod: Works and Days* (Oxford: Clarendon, 1978).
Wettstein
Johann Jacob Wettstein, Ἡ Καινὴ Διαθήκη *Novum Testamentum graecum . . . Tomus II, Continens epistolas Pauli, etc.* (Amsterdam: Ex officina Dommeriana, 1752).
Wilamowitz-Moellendorff, *Die griechische Literatur*
Ulrich von Wilamowitz-Moellendorff, *Die griechische Literatur des Altertums,* in *Die Kultur der Gegenwart,* Teil I, Abteilung VIII (Leipzig and

Berlin: Teubner, 1905, [2]1907, [3]1912).
Wiles, *Paul's Intercessory Prayers*
Gordon P. Wiles, *Paul's Intercessory Prayers,* SNTSMS 24 (Cambridge: Cambridge University, 1974).
Wilhelm, *Königsbriefe*
Adolf Wilhelm, *Griechische Königsbriefe,* Klio. Beiheft 48, NF 35 (Leipzig: Dieterich, 1943).
Wilpert, "Autarkie"
Paul Wilpert, "Autarkie," *RAC* 1 (1950) 1039–50.
Windisch
Hans Windisch, *Der zweite Korintherbrief,* KEK 6. Abteilung (Göttingen: Vandenhoeck & Ruprecht, [9]1924; rep. 1970).
Ziegler, *Theologische Abhandlungen*
Werner Carl Ludwig Ziegler, *Theologische Abhandlungen,* 2 vols. (Göttingen: Vandenhoeck & Ruprecht, 1791–1804).

The English translation of 2 Corinthians 8 and 9 was provided by the author; it reflects his exegetical decisions. Other biblical texts are usually quoted from the Revised Standard Version. Unless indicated otherwise, quotations from Greek and Latin authors follow the editions and translations of the Loeb Classical Library.

The endpapers of this volume reproduce the section of 2 Corinthians 8 and 9 in Johann Jakob Wettstein's famous 1751–52 edition of the *Novum Testamentum Graecum* with its textual apparatus and collection of philological and literary parallels from ancient literature. One of the founders of critical and historical New Testament scholarship, Wettstein (1693–1754) taught at the university of his hometown, Basel, and, after his dismissal because of his views on textual criticism, at the university of Amsterdam. The Hermeneia Commentary series, especially the present volume, is indebted to the tradition of scholarship symbolized by Wettstein and continues it in the twentieth century.

2 Corinthians 8 and 9

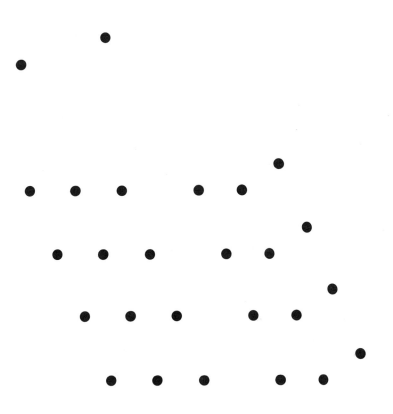

1. Semler's Discovery

Investigation of the literary problems of 2 Corinthians goes back to the beginning of historical-critical inquiry into the New Testament. In his 1776 commentary on 2 Corinthians, Johann Salomo Semler (1725–91), professor on the liberal theological faculty at Halle since 1753, proposed for the first time the hypothesis that Paul's Second Epistle to the Corinthians is composed of several distinct fragments. The importance of this insight for Semler lay in its use as an argument against the orthodox doctrine of the canon, and particularly against the prevailing theory of "the final perfection of Scripture," *perfectio finalis scripturae.*[1] Semler's historical investigations, only one of which was concerned with 2 Corinthians, demonstrated in case after case that the canon did not come into existence until a much later period, and that early Christianity neither knew of it nor was bound by it.[2] Semler's commentary on 2 Corinthians was only part of an ongoing debate which had begun prior to the writing of the commentary and did not end with it. Furthermore, at least one of the dissertations written under his supervision dealt with partition theories with regard to Romans. This dissertation was later reworked and included in Semler's commentary on Romans, but it has nothing to say on 2 Corinthians.[3]

The observations which were to bring about a decisive change in the course of scholarship on 2 Corinthians are found in the *Paraphrasis II: Epistolae ad Corinthios* of 1776. In the introduction, Semler proposed that the work is composed of two separate letters. The first letter consists of 2 Cor 1—8; Rom 16; 2 Cor 9, together with the conclusion in 13:11–13. This letter was sent to the Christians of Achaia, and was carried to them by Titus. A second letter was composed later, after distressing news about the situation at Corinth had arrived; this letter includes 2 Cor 10:1—13:10.[4]

Perhaps the most significant thing about Semler's hypothesis was that such a proposal was made at all. Its

1 See Gottfried Hornig, *Die Anfänge der historisch-kritischen Theologie: Johann Salomo Semlers Schriftverständnis und seine Stellung zu Luther* (Göttingen: Vandenhoeck & Ruprecht, 1961); Hans-Eberhard Hess, *Theologie und Religion bei Johann Salomo Semler: Ein Beitrag zur Theologiegeschichte des 18. Jahrhunderts* (Inaugural Dissertation, Kirchliche Hochschule Berlin, 1974; Augsburg: Blasaditsch, 1974). This dissertation has a large bibliography.

2 See especially Johann Salomo Semler, *Abhandlung von freier Untersuchung des Canon* (Halle: Hemmerde, 1771) Erster Theil; also Hermann Strathmann, "Die Krise des Kanons der Kirche. Joh. Gerhards und Joh. Sal. Semlers Erbe," *Das Neue Testament als Kanon* (ed. Ernst Käsemann; Göttingen: Vandenhoeck & Ruprecht, 1970) 41–61.

3 J. B. G. Keggemann, *Dissertatio historico-hermeneutica De duplici epistolae ad Romanos appendice capite XV, XVI* (Halae Magdeburgicae, 1767) 24 pp. This dissertation was suggested and supervised by Semler who then adopted and included it in his *Paraphrasis epistolae ad Romanos, cum notis, translatione vetusta, et dissertatione de appendice cap. XV, XVI* (Halae Magdeburgicae: Hemmerde, 1769) 277–311: "Dissertatio de duplici appendice huius epistolae C. XV. XVI.

4 *Praefatio* b 1: "ausus sum coniicere, forte istud Caput *nonum* fuisse schedulam seiunctam, quam alii, qui in alias Achaiae vrbes iam proficiscerentur, non Corinthum, acceperint a Paulo, vt traderent statoribus ecclesiarum; eam postea recte adiunxisse Corinthios huic Epistolae, isto loco, quo Paulus de eadem re egerat" ("I am venturing the conclusion that, in particular, the ninth chapter was [originally] a separate piece which others, who had already set out for the other towns of Achaia, not Corinth, were to receive from Paul, in order that they should hand it over to the officials of the churches. Later the Corinthians rightly connected this piece to the letter [to the Corinthians] at the very place at which Paul dealt with this very issue"). See also p. 238 n. 264: ". . . opinari et coniicere liceret, aliquas Epistolas serius demum sic quasi in vnum corpus compositas fuisse, ex varibus minoribus schedis, quae e.c. per *Achaiam,* in hanc illamve vrbem ab his legatis, a *Tito,* ab *altero,* a *tertio* afferebantur. Iam *colligebantur* et addebantur maiori parti, quam *Titus* secum ferebat; et sic in *unum* corpusculum tandem coierunt" (". . . the view and conclusion may be permitted that several letters of weighty business were put together in this way at the final stage as into one corpus which was [thus] made up of various smaller pieces. They were carried, perhaps through Achaia, to the city [of Corinth] by the envoy, be it Titus, be it the second or the third envoy. The smaller letters were then collected and added to the major part, which Titus carried with him. In this way they all came together finally into one literary corpus").

accuracy was a matter of secondary importance. With Semler the dam had broken, releasing a mighty flood which swept scholars of all persuasions and schools into the debate on partition theories of 2 Corinthians and other Pauline letters for the next two hundred years. Semler's hypothesis was first discussed in Germany, then in Holland and England. These debates were characterized by sharp polarization of the participants into two groups: on the one hand the more liberal scholars, who entertained partition theories of one kind or another, and on the other the more conservative, who tried to defend the unity of 2 Corinthians.[5]

There is good reason to question whether Semler was really the first to propose a partition theory for 2 Corinthians, and if so, how he may have managed to arrive at it. To be sure, Semler himself never mentioned predecessors, nor were any named by those who subsequently accepted or rejected his hypothesis. But our knowledge of scholarship of the period is incomplete, and the sources give one the impression that Semler was engaged in long, and largely undocumented, debates with students and colleagues.[6] Thus it is possible that discussion of the partition of the letter preceded the publication of Semler's hypothesis; but so far an extensive search has produced no evidence of actual predecessors, so that Semler must be regarded as the originator of the idea. Indeed it seems quite natural to attribute the idea to him, as he was one of the most creative minds of his time, and succeeded in setting the agenda for research for the nineteenth and twentieth centuries.

There can be no doubt, however, that the ground for Semler's hypothesis was prepared by his teacher Siegmund Jacob Baumgarten (1706–57),[7] whose excellent commentary on Paul's Epistles to the Corinthians Semler published posthumously, prefaced by his own *Vorrede*.[8] This commentary contains a detailed analysis of 2 Cor 8 and 9. In all probability it was this analysis that guided Semler's thought and led to the formulation of his hypothesis. In other words, Semler's partition theory was not merely the result of his own intuition, but a measured conclusion reached on the basis of Baumgarten's analysis.

Baumgarten's treatment of the Corinthian epistles is remarkable in several respects. In the first place, he employed categories which today would be called literary and rhetorical, though they are neither clearly identified as such nor sufficiently distinguished from considerations of sentence structure and internal logic. Regarding the whole of 2 Corinthians, Baumgarten included a section called "Partitioning of the Whole Letter" ("Zergliederung des ganzen Briefes") in the introductory chapter of his commentary.[9] In his brief analysis, he spoke of "an introduction" ("ein Eingang") in 2 Cor 1:1–11, and called 1:12—13:10 "the discourse" ("die Abhandlung"), which he divided into three sections ("Abschnitte"). Remarkably, these three sections correspond to the divisions of the letter that were to figure in later discussions of the partition theory. The first section, which includes 1:12—7:16, is called "a defense of his conduct and his doctrines" ("eine Vertheidigung seines Verhaltens und seiner Lehre"). The second is described as

5 For a survey of the hypotheses, especially those of the Dutch radical critics, see Carl Clemen, *Die Einheitlichkeit der paulinischen Briefe, an der Hand der bisher mit bezug auf sie aufgestellten Interpolations- und Compilationshypothesen geprüft* (Göttingen: Vandenhoeck & Ruprecht, 1894) 19–68; G. A. van den Bergh van Eysinga, *Radical Views about the New Testament* (tr. S. B. Black; London: Watts, 1912); idem, *Die holländische radikale Kritik des Neuen Testaments: Ihre Geschichte und ihre Bedeutung für die Erkenntnis der Entstehung des Christentums* (Jena: Diederichs, 1912).

6 Cf. Semler's caustic remark about the slavish application of the *principium auctoritatis*, the αὐτὸς ἔφα ("the principle of authority, the 'he himself has spoken'"), in his *Vorrede*, 47 (see below, n. 8).

7 On Baumgarten, see Johannes Herzog and Friedrich Bosse, *RE* 2^3 (1897) 464–66; Leopold Zscharnack, *RGG* 1^2 (1927) 814–15; Ernst Wolf, *RGG* 1^3 (1957) 934.

8 *D. Siegmund Jacob Baumgartens Auslegung der beiden Briefe St. Pauli an die Corinthier*, mit Anmerkungen und einer Paraphrasi M. Johann August Nösselts, . . . nebst einer Vorrede herausgegeben von D. Johann Salomon Semler (Halle: Gebauer, 1761).

9 Ibid., 611.

"an exhortation on the collection of alms" ("eine Ermanung zur Almosensteuer") and includes chapters 8 and 9. The third section is entitled "a defense of his apostolic office and authority" ("eine Vertheidigung seines Apostelamts und Ansehens"), comprising 10:1—13:10. The conclusion, 13:11–13, is treated separately as an appendix ("ein angehängter Beschlus").

Chapters 8 and 9 are analyzed in much greater detail in the commentary itself. Again, Baumgarten treated both chapters together as "an exhortation on the alms collection consisting of two parts" ("Eine Ermanung zur Almosensteuer, K. 8 und 9, so aus zwey Theilen besteht"),[10] but then proceeded to analyze the chapters as if they were separate entities. Chapter 8 is characterized as "an account of Paul's plans for the collection and the mission of Titus which it entailed" ("Eine Erzälung seines Vorhabens bey dieser Steuer und der deshalb geschehenen Abfertigung Titi").[11] Verses 1–5 are correctly identified as the *exordium* ("Ein Eingang und Vorbereitung"),[12] which introduces the main concepts of the grace of God (ἡ χάρις τοῦ θεοῦ) and the example of the Macedonians, which the Corinthians are encouraged to imitate.[13] The main portion of chapter 8 is treated as the actual "description of the plan for the collection" ("Die Erzälung solches Vorhabens selbst").[14] It opens with a brief summary report in vv 6–7,[15] which is then developed more fully in vv 8–24.[16] In vv 8–15, Baumgarten saw Paul defending his past efforts and anticipating possible objections. According to Baumgarten, there are three "apologies and defenses" ("Entschuldigung und Rechtfertigung") in this section: vv 8–9, 9–10, and 12–15, all demonstrating why Paul regarded the collection as so essential.[17] Baumgarten identified vv 16–24 as "the narrative proper on the sending of Titus and his companions" ("Die eigentliche Erzälung solcher Abfertigung Titi und seiner Gefärten, v. 16–24").[18] This section is subdivided into three reports: the sending of Titus (vv 16–17), the sending of another envoy (vv 18–21), and the sending of a third envoy (v 22). The conclusion is taken to be vv 23–24, consisting of "instructions to give the envoys a good reception" ("Eine Anbefelung dieser Abgefertigten zur guten Aufnam, v. 23.24").[19] Verse 23 is said to contain "still another presentation of the envoys' qualifications" ("Nochmalige Vorstellung ihrer Beschaffenheit, v. 23"),[20] while v 24 represents "the exhortation proper" ("Die eigentliche Ermanung zur geneigten Aufnam derselben, v. 24").[21]

Because 2 Cor 9 is treated separately from 2 Cor 8, an explanation of their relationship is required. According to Baumgarten, chapter 8 is largely narrative, while chapter 9 consists of exhortation; and the two chapters taken together constitute an exhortation. Thus chapter 9 is regarded as exhortation proper, containing the appeal for aid, together with three reasons that seek to justify its necessity.[22] The first such reason he found in vv 1–5, with μὲν γάρ in v 1 providing the connection to 8:24 and what has gone before. But this connection was already disputed. For though Baumgarten contended that γάρ

10 Ibid., 832.
11 Ibid.
12 Ibid.
13 Ibid., 833: ". . . dass solch Exempel einen starken Einfluss auf ihr Verhalten haben würde, sie zum Nacheifern zu reitzen; . . ." (". . . that such an example would have a strong influence on their conduct, so as to provoke them to do the same; . . .").
14 Ibid., 838.
15 Ibid.: "Ein kürzerer allgemeiner Bericht davon . . ." ("A shorter, more general account of it . . .").
16 Ibid., 840: "Die weitere Ausfürung dieser Erzälung . . ." ("The further elaboration of this account . . .").
17 Ibid., 841: "Eine Entschuldigung und Rechtfertigung dieser seiner gemachten Anstalt, v. 1–15, darin der Apostel manche mögliche Einwürfe, Vorurtheile und Misdeutungen aus dem Wege räumt, hingegen sehr nachdrückliche Bewegungsgründe zur willigen Annemung und Ausrichtung oder Beobachtung dieser Sache vorlegt, in drey Abschnitten" ("An excuse and justification for the measures he has taken [v. 1–15], in which the apostle clears away possible objections, prejudices and false interpretations; in addition, he presents very emphatic reasons for the willing acceptance and execution or consideration of this matter in three sections").
18 Ibid., 847.
19 Ibid., 853.
20 Ibid.
21 Ibid., 854.
22 Ibid., 855: "Die eigentliche Ermanung zum willigen und reichlichen Beitrag zu dieser Steuer, oder Vorstellung nachdrücklicher Bewegungsgründe, k. 9, deren drey hier vorkommen" ("The exhortation

indicates that 9:1 furnishes the proof for 8:24,[23] a footnote going back to Johann August Nösselt (1734–1807), who was a student, and later a colleague, of both Baumgarten and Semler,[24] offers another explanation: 9:1 should *not* be regarded as the proof of 8:24; rather, the particle γάρ should be taken in a wider sense, on the analogy of the way the Latin *nam* was used by Cicero whenever he wished to move on to another subject.[25] What the particle really indicates is that Paul now returns to the subject of the exhortation after an interruption in 8:16–24.[26] The importance of the discussion at this point becomes clear in light of subsequent debate, particularly that instigated by Johann Philipp Gabler.[27]

Baumgarten identified the Corinthians' own reputation and the expectations that others have of them as the theme of the first argument which Paul provided in support of his appeal to the church.[28] The second reason lies in the certainty of divine reward (vv 6–11),[29] while the final argument points to the glory of God and reminds the Corinthians of the thanksgiving which is his due (vv 11–15).[30]

On the whole it must be said that Baumgarten's

---

proper to contribute willingly and abundantly to this collection, or the presentation of the more important motivating reasons, chapter 9, of which three are present here").

23 Ibid.: "Γάρ zeigt an, es folge ein Beweis des nächstvorhergehenden, da denn eigentlich der 24ste Vers des 8ten Kapitels erwiesen wird: er selbst halte sich so gewis von ihrer Liebe versichert, dass er um seinetwillen solchen Erweis nicht verlange, sondern nur eine neue Erweisung desselben von ihnen um anderer willen erwarte, und um deswillen es überflüssig und unnötig zu seyn glaube ihnen viel Vorstellung zu thun. Mὲν zeigt an, dass er *concessiue* rede: er werde nicht alle Vorstellung um deswillen unterlassen" ("The word γάρ ["for"] indicates that a proof of what was previously stated will follow. This really means that the twenty-fourth verse of chapter 8 is provided with proofs: that he himself thinks so highly of their love; that he does not demand such proof for his own sake, but expects only a new proof of that love for the sake of others; that for this reason he believes it to be superfluous and unnecessary to make a great show of it. 'Yet' [Mὲν] indicates that he speaks by way of a concession: that he is not going to avoid all fuss about it altogether").

24 On the origin of the notes, see Semler's *Vorrede,* 46–47 (see above, n. 8): ". . . dass ich diesen meinen werthen Freund und nunmehrigen würdigen Collegen im öffentlichen theologischen Lehramt, dahin vermocht habe, hie und da seine eignen Anmerkungen und gesamleten Beobachtungen mit anzubringen. Ich habe auch zuweilen das Vergnügen gehabt, über dies und jenes Unterredung zu pflegen" (". . . that I was able to persuade this my esteemed friend and now also my worthy colleague in the public office of theological teaching, to contribute here and there his own comments and assembled observations. I also had the pleasure of having a conversation occasionally on this or that point").

25 *Auslegung,* 855 n. 227: "Man wird schwerlich diesen Worten des Apostels einen bequemen Verstand geben können, wenn man sie als einen Beweis von 8, 24 ansehen wil. Man hat es aber auch nicht nötig, an der gewöhnlichen Bedeutung der Partikel γάρ zu hängen. Wer den Cicero und andere alte gute Schriftsteller mit Aufmerksamkeit gelesen hat, der wird wissen, dass sie *nam* öfters alsdenn brauchen, wenn sie von einer Sache auf die andere kommen wollen" ("One will hardly be able to find a convenient interpretation of these words of the apostle, if one takes them to be a proof of 8:24. It is not necessary, to be sure, to cling to the usual meaning of the particle γάρ ["for"]. He who has read Cicero and other good ancient authors with diligence will know that they use *nam* ["for"] often when they want to move from one matter to the next").

26 Ibid.: "Eben so hatte Paulus beiläufig von k. 8, 16 an, Titum und seine Gefärten empfolen, jetzt kehrt er wieder zu seiner Ermanung zur Mildthätigkeit zurück" ("Thus, beginning in chapter 8, verse 16, Paul recommended Titus and his companions in passing, but now returns to his exhortation to be merciful").

27 See below, pp. 88–90.

28 *Auslegung,* 855: "Der erste Bewegungsgrund, v. 1–5, ist von ihrem Ruhm, anderer Hofnung und Erwartung von ihnen und ihrer Gutthätigkeit hergenommen" ("The first reason, v. 1–5, is derived from their fame, the hopes held by others and the expectations of their ability to do good").

29 Ibid., 860: "Der zweite Bewegungsgrund, v. 6–11, ist von der götlichen Belonung hergenommen" ("The second reason [v. 6–11] is taken from the idea of divine reward").

30 Ibid., 866: "Der dritte Bewegungsgrund, v. 11–15, besteht in Vorstellung der aus solcher Gutthätigkeit entstehenden Ehre Gottes und Danksagung gegen denselben" ("The third reason [v. 11–15] consists of the concept of God's honor which arises from doing good, and the thanksgiving due to him").

analysis of chapter 9 is less satisfying than that of chapter 8. He had some sense of the difficulty presented by the existence of parallels between the chapters, but had he realized the full extent of the problem, it would have proven impossible to conceive of both chapters as part of the same argumentative context. Yet Baumgarten paid attention to the relationship between the chapters. He recognized 9:15 as an appendix,[31] and pointed out the contrast between chapters 9 and 10.[32]

But for the most part, Baumgarten's analysis of chapters 8 and 9 can only be regarded as extraordinary, above all because of its sensitivity to literary and rhetorical dimensions of the text. Thus there can be no doubt that it was Baumgarten's work which gave rise to Semler's hypothesis. As Baumgarten's student and later as editor of his posthumously published commentary, Semler was naturally familiar with his teacher's analysis which, one may surmise, was also discussed in Baumgarten's seminars and lectures. Thus the step from Baumgarten to Semler was not so large as one might assume. It took only the kind of ingenuity of thought for which Semler was so justly famous.

Moreover there are indications that Baumgarten was not the only scholar at work on an analysis of 2 Corinthians at the beginning of the eighteenth century. In a brief study of 2 Cor 8:9 Semler[33] referred with praise to an English commentary by Matthew Henry which he had consulted. Matthew Henry (1662–1714) was among the nonconformist English theologians of whom both Baumgarten and Semler were so fond. It is of interest that Henry's commentary also contains an analysis of 2 Cor 8 and 9. Was Henry the author of this analysis, or had he obtained it from some other source? As authorities for his interpretation, Henry cited Hugo Grotius (1583–1654),[34] the well-known *Assembly's Annotations*,[35] Daniel Whitby (1638–1726),[36] William Burkitt (1650–1703),[37] and Samuel Clarke (1626–1701).[38] While these works occasionally provide some remarkable observa-

31 Ibid., 871: "Eine angehängte Lobeserhebung, v. 15" ("An added glorification [of God], v. 15").

32 Ibid., 871–72: "Paulus sucht in diesem letzten Hauptheil seines Briefes die feindselige Beschuldigung und Angriffe wider seine Würde und apostolische Gewalt von sich abzulenen, und verspart diese Abhandlung bis zu Ende des Briefs, theils seine Bescheidenheit damit zu bezeugen, dass dieses ihn insbesondere angehende Stück in seinen Augen nicht das vornemste sey; theils aber zu verhüten, dass die heilsame Wirkung der vorhergehenden Abhandlung durch diesen schärfern Theil nicht möchte gehindert werden; theils auch die gute Aufnam derselben bey den Lesern zu befördern" ("In the last main part of his letter Paul seeks to avert the hostile accusations and attacks against his dignity and apostolic authority. He saves this discussion until the end of his letter, in part to demonstrate his modesty, to indicate that this section dealing especially with himself is not the most important in his eyes; in part to prevent the wholesome effect of the preceding treatise from being undone by this harsher section of the letter; in part to promote the friendly acceptance of the preceding treatise by the readers").

33 Io. Salom. Semler, *Commentatio ad 2. Corinth. VIII, 9,* Nomine publico in natalium Domini nostri Iesu Christi memoriam prodita (Halae Magdeburgicae: Hendel, 1758) 4. (I am indebted to Gerhard Delling at Halle for providing me with a copy of the essay.) Semler refers to the fourth edition of Matthew Henry, *An Exposition of the Old and New Testament* (5 vols.; London: Knapton & others, ⁴1738) vol. 5. On Henry, see Alexander Gordon, *Dictionary of National Biography* 9 (1908) 574–75.

34 Hugo Grotius, *Annotationes in Novum Testamentum* (3 vols.; Parisiis: Sumptibus Authoris, 1641–50) 2.486–94, on 2 Cor 8—9.

35 See Matthaeus Polus [= Matthew Pole or Poole, 1624–79], *Synopsis criticorum aliorumque S. Scripturae interpretum* (4 vols. in 5; Londini: apud Carolum Smith, 1676) 4/2.610–25, on 2 Cor 8—9; furthermore, *Annotations upon the Holy Bible.* Wherein the sacred text is inserted, and various readings annex'd, Together with the Parallel Scriptures. The more difficult terms in each Verse are Explained. Seeming Contradictions Reconciled. Questions and Doubts Resolved. And the Whole Text Opened. Vol. II, Being a Continuation of Mr. Pool's Work by certain Judicious and Learned Divines (London: Thomas Parkhurst & others, 1688). On Poole, see Alexander Gordon, *Dictionary of National Biography* 16 (1909) 99–100.

36 Daniel Whitby, *A Paraphrase and Commentary on the New Testament* (2 vols.; London: Awnsham and John Churchill, 1703) 2.198, 223–28. On Whitby, see Alexander Gordon, *Dictionary of National Biography* 21 (1909) 28–30.

37 William Burkitt, *Expository Notes with Practical Observations on the New Testament* (2 vols.; London: Thomas Parkhurst & others, 1703). On Burkitt, see Alexander Gordon, *Dictionary of National Biography* 3 (1908) 371–72.

38 Samuel Clarke, *The New Testament of Our Lord and Saviour Jesus Christ* (London: Thomas Simmons,

tions, none of them contains a discussion like that found in Henry. It is always possible that Henry made use of works not named. Yet it must have been suggestive to many at the time when Hugo Grotius remarked in passing that Paul knew the art of rhetoric.[39] The *Annotations* of 1688 prefaces its treatment of 2 Corinthians with a section entitled "The Argument,"[40] in which Paul's motive for writing the letter is described as the need to defend himself against false teachers who have made accusations against him. The letter is divided into three sections: (1) "Apologetic or Exculpatory" (chaps. 1—7); (2) "Hortatory" (chaps. 8—9); (3) "Minatory or Threatening" (chaps. 10—13). The group of scholars responsible for the *Annotations* were apparently aware of Paul's knowledge of rhetoric, for on 2 Cor 8:7 they remarked: "Though the Apostle made little use of Oratory in his ordinary Discourses and Epistles, yet he knew how to use it when it might be of probable advantage to the Ends which he aimed at, *viz.* the Glory of God, and the good of the Souls that were under his care. He did not turn Divinity into mere words, and Rhetorical flourishes; yet he made use of these sometimes, as a waiting Maid to Divinity." In the introduction to his commentary on 2 Corinthians,[41] Burkitt also took the letter to be a defense against opponents; but when he came to 2 Cor 8—9 he treated the arguments of these chapters as those of a fund-raising letter, without explaining the apparent inconsistency.

There is some indication that new approaches to the analysis of the Pauline epistles were already being sought in the sixteenth century in the commentary of Johannes Piscator (1546–1625)[42] entitled *Analysis logica epistolarum Pauli*.[43] His treatment of 2 Cor 8 and 9 clearly takes into account the argumentative structure of the chapters. Chapter 8 is prefaced by an *argumentum* which shows the chapter to be made up of two sections: (1) vv 1–15, an exhortation to the Corinthians to bring the collection to completion; (2) vv 16–24, a commendation of Titus and two other brothers.[44] The exhortation of vv 1–15 employs six arguments: the example of the Macedonians, the judgment and hope of the Corinthians and the Macedonians, the Christian virtues, Christ's example, the fruit of praise, and the hope of reward.[45] The commendation of vv 16–24 describes the three envoys as Macedonians ("tres legatos Macedonum").[46] Piscator's analysis of chapter 9 assumes that it forms the sequel to chapter 8 and that it is composed of two sections: (1) vv 1–5, the statement of the cause of the collection; (2) vv 6–15, an exhortation to give generously.[47]

Still another attempt to ascertain the structure of 2 Corinthians is found in the commentary of Nicolaus Selnecker (1530–92).[48] Though far less useful than the commentaries discussed above, Selnecker's also points out that the exhortation of chapter 8 is supported by

1683). On Clarke, see Alexander Gordon, *Dictionary of National Biography* 4 (1908) 442–43.

39 *Annotationes* 2.488: "Non ignoravit Paulus artem Rhetorum, movere laudando" ("Paul was not ignorant of the art of rhetoric, to move people by praising them").

40 See above, n. 35. The work has no pagination numbers.

41 See above, n. 37. The work has no pagination numbers.

42 On Piscator, see E. F. Karl Müller, *RE* 15 (1904) 414–15.

43 (Londini: Impensis Georg. Bishop, 1591). The second edition, which is used here, was published under the title *Analysis logica utriusque epistolae Pauli ad Corinthios; una cum scholiis et observationibus locorum doctrinae,* etc. (Herbornae Nassoviorum: Typis Christophori Corvini, 1593).

44 Ibid., 323: "In hoc capite primúm hortatur Corinthios ad collectam quam superiore anno inchoarant, absolvendam: deinde commendat eis Titum et alios duos fratres, quos ad collectam illam ab ipsis accipiendam mittebat" ("In this chapter he first admonishes the Corinthians to complete the collection which they had started in the previous year. Then he commends to them Titus and two other brothers whom he sent to receive this collection from them").

45 Ibid., 325–26.

46 Ibid., 327.

47 Ibid., 331: "Pergit in eâdem quaestione, nempe de collecta; ac primúm causam exponit, cur tres illos fratres collectae absolvendae gratiâ ad eos miserit: deinde eos hortatur, ut liberaliter conferant" ("He proceeds to this question, surely about the collection. At first he explains the reason why he sent those three brothers for the purpose of completing the collection. Then he exhorts them that they contribute freely").

48 Nicolaus Selneccerus, *In omnes epistolas D. Pauli Apostoli Commentarius plenissimus* . . . Post auctoris obitum nun primum in lucem editus, studio filij Georgii Selnecceri (Leipzig: Sumtibus Iacobi Apelii Bibliop., 1595).

strong arguments ("rationes gravissimae").[49]

These early attempts to arrive at an understanding of the structure of the epistle, more examples of which may be brought to light by further research, suggest that Henry may have benefited from acquaintance with a long scholarly tradition devoted to discussion of the composition and rhetorical niveau of the Pauline epistles. Thus, in the introduction to his commentary on 2 Corinthians,[50] he identified two distinct causes for the writing of the letter: ". . . and there seem to be these two urgent occasions: l. The case of the incestuous person, who lay under censure, required that with all speed he should be restored and received again into the communion. . . . 2. There was a contribution now making for the poor saints at Jerusalem, in which he exhorts the Corinthians to join, ch. viii. ix."[51]

Even more astonishing is Henry's analysis of 2 Cor 8, included in a brief preface to the chapter: "In this and the following chapter Paul is exhorting and directing the Corinthians about a particular work of charity—to relieve the necessities of the poor saints at Jerusalem and in Judea. . . ." Henry divided chapter 8 into three sections: "In this eighth chapter he acquaints the Corinthians with, and commends, the good example of the Macedonians in this work of charity, and that Titus was sent to Corinth to collect their bounty (ver. 1–6). He then proceeds to urge this duty with several cogent arguments (ver. 7–15), and commends the persons who were employed in this affair (ver. 16–24)."[52] Henry made the following points with regard to the first section: (1) that Paul's purpose in making an example of the Macedonians was to encourage the Corinthians to imitate their liberality; and (2) that the section contains a narrative account of the part played by Titus in the collection.[53] In the second section Henry identified four "cogent arguments" used in vv 7–15 "to stir up the Corinthians to this good work of charity."[54] The "compliment" (vv 7–8) of "their eminence in other gifts and graces"[55] is stated so that they should "add this grace also, to abound in the charity to the poor."[56] The second argument appeals to the example of Christ (v 9). The third argument "is taken from their good purposes, and their forwardness to begin this good work"; thus it is an argument of expediency (vv 10–12).[57] The fourth and final argument "is taken from the discrimination which the divine Providence makes in the distribution of the things of this world, and the instability of human affairs, v. 13–15."[58] Henry identified the commendations of Titus and the two brothers as the third part of the letter. On v 23 he remarked as follows: "He concludes this point with the general good character of them all. . . ."[59] This argument leads on to v 24: "Wherefore, upon the whole, he exhorts them to show their liberality, answerable to the great expectation others had concerning them at this time, that these messengers of the churches, and the churches themselves, might see a full *proof of their love* to God and to their afflicted brethren, and that it was with good reason the apostle had even *boasted on their behalf,* v. 24."[60] Henry did not treat chapter 9 as if it were the continuation of chapter 8, but as a separate literary unit: "In this chapter the apostle seems to excuse his earnestness in pressing the Corinthians to the duty of charity (ver. 1–5), and proceeds to give directions about the acceptable way and manner of performing it, namely bountifully, deliberately, and freely; and gives good encouragement for so doing, ver. 6, to the end."[61]

Henry identified two distinct elements in the first part of the chapter: (1) the complimentary statements of vv 1–2, and (2) the apology for sending Titus and the other brothers (vv 3–5).[62] The second part of the chapter

49 Ibid., 907.
50 The edition quoted here is that of 1844, *An Exposition of the Old and New Testament,* A new edition, with a life of M. Henry, and of his father Philip Henry, by H. Davis (6 vols; London: Thoms, 1844).
51 4.606. The text is almost identical with the fourth edition used by Semler.
52 Ibid., 628.
53 Ibid., 628–29.
54 Ibid., 629.
55 Ibid.
56 Ibid., 630.
57 Ibid.
58 Ibid.
59 Ibid., 631.
60 Ibid., 632.
61 Ibid.
62 Ibid.

contains (1) "Proper directions to be observed about the right and acceptable manner bestowing charity. . . ."[63] It should be done bountifully, deliberately, and freely; (2) "Good encouragement to perform this work of charity in the manner directed." The Corinthians would be "no losers by what they gave in charity," and "the poor distressed saints would be gainers. . . . This would redound to the praise and the glory of God."[64]

Finally, Henry properly identified the conclusion of the passage (v 15), calling it a doxology: "Lastly, the apostle concludes this whole matter with this doxology. . . ."[65]

Henry's analysis is on the whole praiseworthy because of its clarity, precision, and perception. The argumentative structure that emerges reflects a striking sensitivity to rhetoric. The correct literary and form-critical categories are often employed. All this seems to reflect the refinement of a school tradition rather than Henry's own intuitions. This school tradition may have originated in the religious circles of the dissenters. From Henry and others it found its way to Baumgarten and Semler.

Subsequent scholars, however, whether in England or in Germany, do not seem to have pursued the insights of such a literary, rhetorical approach to the understanding of the epistle—at least not until Hans Windisch in the twentieth century.[66] Of course there may have been exceptions of which we are now ignorant; one has recently come to the attention of the present author.

Robert Smith Candlish (1806–73), one-time moderator of the Free Church of Scotland and a learned member of the clergy, published an analysis of 2 Corinthians in an essay entitled *The Duty of Laying By a Stated Proportion of Our Income: An Analysis of 2 Cor. VIII, IX* (London: Nisbet, 1852).[67] The essay was, in fact, a published address, delivered before the Systematic Beneficence Society, an interdenominational welfare organization which Candlish helped to establish in 1847.[68] The address is not provided with notes, but the analysis is quite detailed, and remarkably similar to that of Henry. Candlish did not say which commentaries he had consulted, but it would hardly be a surprise to learn that he had used Henry's. While no scholarly commentary refers to Candlish's essay, its very existence demonstrates, at least, that the kind of compositional analysis known to scholars of the eighteenth century was not entirely forgotten in the following era.

2. Partition Theories Following Semler

The history of partition theories on 2 Corinthians after Semler can be divided into a number of phases. The first phase runs from Semler to Adolf Hausrath, while a second reaches from Hausrath and James Houghton Kennedy to Hans Windisch. The third phase extends from Windisch to Walter Schmithals, who may be said to have inaugurated a new, fourth phase which also includes the work of Dieter Georgi and Günther Bornkamm.

a. From Semler to Hausrath

In a series of Programmschriften of the University of Wittenberg, Michael Weber[69] made public his accept-

63 Ibid., 633.

64 Ibid., 633–34. The argument is subdivided further.

65 Ibid., 634.

66 See below, pp. 16–18.

67 A copy is in the Bodleian Library at Oxford (G. Pamph. 2898 no. 14).

68 See Robert Cather, *The Origin and Objects of the Systematic Beneficence Society* (London: Nisbet, 1862). On Candlish, see W. G. Blaikie, *Dictionary of National Biography* 3 (1908) 857–60.

69 Michael Weber, *De numero epistolarum ad Corinthios rectius constituendo,* P. I. *Paulus, Apostolus non duas, sed quinque epistolas ad Corinthios scripsit, Programmschrift Easter 1798,* in *Neues Wittenbergisches Wochenblatt* 6 (1798) 143. Weber discussed and defended this thesis in twelve consecutive Programmschriften of the University of Wittenberg between 1798 and 1807. For information and copies of the relevant pages of this rare material, I am indebted to Professor Gerhard Delling of the University of Halle. For a review of Weber's thesis and its critique, see Johann Philipp Gabler, *Neues Theologisches Journal* 12/4 (1798) 405–10; Werner Carl Ludwig Ziegler, *Theologische Abhandlungen* (2 vols.; Göttingen: Vandenhoeck & Ruprecht, 1804) 2.107–14 (cf. Weber's defense against Ziegler in *Programmschrift* 11 [1806] 206–25).

ance of Semler's basic hypothesis, but with certain modifications. Weber now spoke of five letters to Corinth: (1) the one mentioned in 1 Cor 5:9; (2) 1 Corinthians; (3) 2 Cor 1—9 + 13:11–13; (4) Hebrews; (5) 2 Cor 10:1—13:10.

A new situation arose from the proposal of two hypotheses by Friedrich Bleek that had an indirect effect upon Semler's thesis.[70] On the basis of 2 Cor 12:14; 13:1, Bleek suggested that Paul must have been in Corinth twice before writing the Epistles to the Corinthians.[71] In fact the suggestion had been made before, as Bleek freely acknowledged,[72] but now it was supported by strong arguments. Bleek's second hypothesis asserted that Paul had written another letter to the Corinthians between the canonical epistles, a letter now lost.[73] Bleek reached this conclusion on the basis of announcements in 1 Cor 4:17; 16:10f that Timothy will soon visit Corinth, whereas in 2 Corinthians it is taken for granted that Timothy is with Paul (1:1), and no mention is made of a visit. Bleek concluded that the matter must have been discussed and finally resolved in a letter which is now lost, so that, in addition to the letter mentioned in 1 Cor 5:9, we must now speak of a second lost letter of Paul to the Corinthians.[74] Thus Bleek was the first to speak of an "intermediate letter" ("Zwischenbrief"). His hypothesis found many followers and has been part of the debate ever since.[75]

Following Bleek, attempts were made to reconstruct the content of the intermediate letter. Tertullian had already suggested that the evildoer of 1 Cor 5 and the "offender" (ἀδικήσας) of 2 Cor 2:5; 7:12 were not identical.[76] Thus Bleek[77] concluded that the incident mentioned in 2 Cor 2:3–4; 7:12 must have formed the subject of the intermediate letter. If, as Bleek and his followers assumed, the intermediate letter was written in response to an offense committed against Paul by a member of the Corinthian church at the instigation of Judaistic opponents, the offense must have been a grave one indeed and concerned Paul's apostolic authority.

The next stage in the discussion involved the painful incident in which Paul was insulted by a member of the Corinthian church. Bleek had placed Paul's second visit to Corinth before the writing of 1 and 2 Corinthians. Heinrich Georg August Ewald,[78] and others after him, moved the second visit into the space between 1 and 2 Corinthians, so that the intermediate letter became a

70 Friedrich Bleek, "Erörterungen in Beziehung auf die Briefe Pauli an die Korinther," *ThStKr* 3 (1830) 614–32; similarly, his *Einleitung in das Neue Testament* (ed. Wilhelm Mangold; Berlin: Reimer, ³1875) 469–70.

71 Bleek, "Erörterungen," 614–24.

72 The list of predecessors, ibid., 615 n. 1, traces it back to Erasmus and Chrysostom.

73 Ibid., 625–32.

74 Bleek believed that letter is mentioned in 2 Cor 2:3–4; 7:12, 14.

75 Among them are Olshausen, Credner, Billroth, Rückert, Neander, Beyschlag, Eylan, Ewald, Osiander, Maier, Krenkel, Hilgenfeld, Klöpper, and others. See Carl F. G. Heinrici, *Der zweite Brief an die Korinther* (KEK 6; Göttingen: Vandenhoeck & Ruprecht, ⁸1900) 14–18.

76 Tertullian *De pudicitia* 13–14, ed. Franciscus Oehler, *Quinti Septimi Florentis Tertulliani Quae Supersunt Omnia* (Leipzig: Weigel, 1853) 1.817ff.

77 Bleek, "Erörterungen," 629–31. Bleek, however, believed that the evildoer of 1 Cor 5 was also the one who attacked Paul according to 2 Cor 2:3–4; 7:12 (pp. 630–31).

78 Heinrich Ewald, *Die Sendschreiben des Apostels Paulus* (Göttingen: Dieterich, 1857) 226; "allein die dinge müssen sich só schlimm gestaltet haben dass Paulus, aufgebend den s. 220f. erwähnten weiteren plan, sich rasch entschloss auf dem nächsten wege über das Aegäische meer nach Korinth zu reisen, um durch einen kurzen überraschenden besuch selbst alles aus den fugen gegangene in sein geleise zu bringen" ("Certainly things must have become so bad that Paul, giving up the further plan [mentioned p. 220f], decided quickly to travel the shortest way across the Aegean Sea to Corinth, in order to use this short and surprising visit to put back on track all that had come undone"). As a reason, Ewald adds this remark in a note (p. 226 n. 1): "Wer die worte 2 Cor. 1,15. 2.1. 12,14.13,1 und dieses ganze sendschreiben gut versteht, kann über dieses alles keine zweifel hegen" ("He who understands the words of 2 Cor 1:15; 2:1, 12, 14; 13:1 and the entire letter in the right way can have no doubts about it all"). From 2 Cor 2:1ff (10:10; 13:3–4), Ewald concludes that during the visit, Paul was able to do far less than he had hoped: ". . . weit weniger zu thun vermochte als ér und seine nächsten Anhänger gewünscht hatten."

response to the "intermediate incident" ("Zwischenfall") which occurred during Paul's "intermediate visit" ("Zwischenbesuch"). The course of events was then reconstructed in the following way: after having written 1 Corinthians, Paul received distressing news, which prompted his decision to undertake an immediate journey to Corinth from Ephesus. During this visit he was attacked by the "offender" (ἀδικήσας) (2 Cor 7:12). Paul attempted to confront his opponent, but lost in the showdown. Following this distressing visit he wrote the intermediate letter, which is identical with the "tearful letter" mentioned in 2 Cor 2:4.

b. Hausrath's Thesis

When, a century after Semler, Adolf Hausrath of the University of Heidelberg published his short study *Der Vier-Capitel-Brief des Paulus an die Korinther*,[79] the time was ripe for a revision of Semler's thesis. Hausrath's aims were ambitious. Realizing that he was entering an exegetical "war of all against all," "bellum omnium contra omnes,"[80] he intended to settle the problem of the composition of 2 Corinthians by first deciding the question raised by chapters 10—13. Once that had been done, he expected that the rest of the epistle would fall into place more easily.[81]

Hausrath's study was received positively by a great number of scholars, yet one wonders why he was regarded as "the real founder of the modern hypothesis."[82] His investigation exhibits many of the same weaknesses that characterized earlier studies: a one-sided emphasis on 2 Cor 10—13, coupled with the belief that the problems of the rest of the epistle would become explicable by the separation of the four-chapter letter. Like earlier scholars Hausrath gave too much attention to the change of psychological mood ("Stimmung" and "Ton") between the sections of the letter. Furthermore his analysis was conducted without formal literary criteria.

Despite these liabilities, Hausrath made progress by examining four points at issue between Paul and the Corinthians: (1) the transgressor of 1 Cor 5:3–6; (2) the collection for Jerusalem; (3) Paul's change of travel plans; and (4) the agitators against Paul and their reception by the Corinthians. Hausrath was able to show that in every case the discussion in 2 Cor 10—13 reflects an earlier stage in the controversy when compared with 2 Cor 1—9, and concluded that chapters 10—13 preceded chapters 1—9. He believed that 2 Cor 10—13 was written by Paul from Ephesus not long after 1 Corinthians.[83]

What are the implications of Hausrath's thesis for 2 Cor 1—9? Here Hausrath's suggestions (pp. 27f) remain unfortunately vague and purely negative. He rejected theories which attempted to partition 2 Cor 1—9 further, mentioning the names of Johann Christian Karl von Hofmann and Heinrich Julius Holtzmann, but these theories are not discussed.

Meanwhile, Christian Hermann Weisse (1801–66),[84] a Leipzig philosopher, had in fact advanced a more interesting hypothesis. He believed 2 Corinthians to have been composed by a redactor out of three fragments. These fragments had been composed by Paul in the

79 (Heidelberg: Bassermann, 1870). The study has only twenty-eight pages, not counting the "Vorbemerkung." For an even shorter version, see Adolf Hausrath, *Neutestamentliche Zeitgeschichte* (4 vols.; Heidelberg: Bassermann, ²1875) 3.302–14.

80 See the "Vorbemerkung," III: "Der exegetische Krieg, in dem Jedermanns Ansicht gegen Jedermann ist, . . ." ("The exegetical war, in which everyone's opinion is against everyone else's").

81 Ibid., IV: "Ergibt sich aus ihnen ein überzeugendes Resultat über das Verhältnis der Theile des vorliegenden Schriftstücks, dann wird sich das Einzelne leichter zurechtlegen; . . ." ("If one gets from them a convincing result regarding the parts of the text before us, then the details can be accounted for in a better way . . .").

82 So Paul Feine, *Einleitung in das Neue Testament* (Leipzig: Quelle & Meyer, 1913): "Der eigentliche Begründer der modernen Hypothese." Feine, however, does not accept the thesis of Hausrath. Arguing that differences between sections can best be explained psychologically, he basically shares Hausrath's method but arrives at the opposite conclusion.

83 Hausrath, *Der Vier-Capitel-Brief*, 25–26.

84 Christian Hermann Weisse, *Philosophische Dogmatik oder Philosophie des Christenthums* (3 vols.; Leipzig: Hirzel, 1855–62) 1.145: "Aber der zweite Korintherbrief ist aus drei verschiedenen, zu verschiedenen Zeiten an die Gemeinde von Korinth gerichteten Sendschreiben zusammengesetzt, von denen das erste, welches den Anfang und die Hauptmasse der Urkunde nach ihrem gegenwärtigen Bestande hergegeben hat (Cap. 1—7), das späteste

following order: (1) chapters 10—13; (2) chapters 8 and 9; (3) chapters 1—7. Hausrath made use of the suggestion that chapters 10—13 were written earlier than the other chapters in the epistle, but failed to provide an adequate treatment of chapters 8 and 9 as well as 1—7.[85]

c. Kennedy's Thesis

At about the same time as Hausrath, but at first independently of him, James Houghton Kennedy developed his own partition theory in England.[86] As he himself told it, "my own attention was first called to the question . . . by a remark which was made in my hearing by the late Dr. Reichel, Bishop of Meath, to the effect that he was convinced that there were two Epistles in 2 Corinthians, and that the one which was written last had been placed before the earlier one."[87] Taking this remark as his starting point, Kennedy worked out his own hypothesis. When at length he learned of Hausrath's work, he found that they agreed on the composite nature of 2 Corinthians and on the observation that chapters 10—13 had been written before chapters 1—7. But he saw in addition that his own idea (that the sections incorporated in the present epistle represent no more than fragments of the original letters) provided a way out of some of the problems raised by Hausrath's thesis.[88]

Kennedy's study remains the most thorough discussion of the history of the complex of problems that lead up to the writing of 2 Corinthians and the literary composition of the epistle. His perceptive analysis is much to be preferred to that of Hausrath, though Kennedy went out of his way to let Hausrath be the first to introduce the idea.[89]

In short, Kennedy asserted that 2 Corinthians is a composite letter. Chapters 10—13, which he equated with the intermediate letter, contain the earliest material in the epistle. Unlike chapters 1—9, which were written from Macedonia, this intermediate letter was composed in Ephesus. Only the latter portion of the letter has been preserved; earlier parts must be considered lost. Kennedy named this letter "2 Corinthians." After Titus's successful visit to Corinth, Paul wrote "3 Corinthians" from Macedonia, of which chapters 1—9 are extant. In Kennedy's view chapters 8 and 9 are an integral part of 3 Corinthians, with the phrase "Thanks be to God for his unspeakable gift" (9:15) providing the break-off point of the fragment, after which "all is suddenly changed, and a torrent of mingled pathos and indignation is poured out. . . ."[90]

Kennedy's hypothesis was widely discussed by British and American scholars but did not receive as much attention in Germany.[91] There were many who accepted it, especially after it had received the endorsement of the distinguished scholar Kirsopp Lake.[92] Among major

ist" ("But the second Christian letter is put together from three different letters, sent at different times to the church of Corinth. The first one, and the one which makes up the major portion of the document in its present form [chaps. 1—7], is the latest"). Idem, *Beiträge zur Kritik der paulinischen Briefe an die Galater, Römer, Philipper und Kolosser* (ed. E. Sulze; Leipzig: Hirzel, 1867) 9, in a remark by Sulze: "Wahrscheinlich fand Weisse nach früheren Vorgängen in Cap. 10—13 das eine, in Cap. 8—9 aber das andere der ausserdem von ihm angenommenen selbständigen Sendschreiben" ("In all probability Weisse, following earlier attempts, found one letter in chapters 10—13, and the other independent letter he assumed to be in chapters 8—9").

85 Hausrath, *Der Vier-Capitel-Brief*, 6, mentions Weisse in a note: "Für Cap. 1—7 hat Weisse im Einklang mit Semler dasselbe behauptet, aber ohne irgend welche nähere Begründung. (Philos. Dogmat. I, p. 145)" ("Agreeing with Semler, Weisse claimed the same for chapters 1—7, but did not give any detailed reasons").

86 James Houghton Kennedy, *The Second and Third Epistles of St. Paul to the Corinthians* (London: Methuen, 1900).

87 Ibid., XII–XIII. Kennedy's careful description in the preface of the origin of his hypothesis is very helpful indeed.

88 Ibid., XIV.

89 Kennedy provides the best critical analysis of both Hausrath and his opponent Klöpper. See also his earlier article, "Are There Two Epistles in 2 Corinthians?" *The Expositor* 6 (1897) 231–38, 285–304. See also Marvin R. Vincent, "The Integrity of Second Corinthians," *Essays in Modern Theology and Related Subjects*, Gathered and Published as a Testimonial to Charles A. Briggs (New York: Scribner's, 1911) 185–89.

90 Kennedy, *The Second and Third Epistles*, 95.

91 It received a favorable review by Carl Clemen in *ThLZ* 25 (1900) 703–6.

92 Kirsopp Lake, *The Earlier Epistles of St. Paul: Their Motive and Their Origin* (London: Rivingtons, [2]1914) 144ff.

commentaries whose authors favored Kennedy's hypothesis were those of Alfred Plummer,[93] who provided an informative discussion of the problems involved, Gerald H. Rendall,[94] Robert H. Strachan,[95] Thomas W. Manson,[96] and Charles H. Dodd.[97] James Moffatt's statements in support of Kennedy in his *Introduction* were also of influence.[98]

Recent British scholarship has grown more skeptical of partition theories and has returned, for the most part, to the traditional view. The return has been characterized neither by strong convictions nor by convincing arguments.[99] Faced by uncertainties and weary of hypotheses, scholars have always been greatly tempted simply to take refuge in the tradition. Such a way out was already signaled by Allan Menzies in his commentary of 1912: "Surely it is better to try to read the whole as we have it than to plunge into such explanations."[100]

d. From Hausrath and Kennedy to Windisch

Hausrath's thesis met with both approval and disapproval. Among critical responses, that of Albert Klöpper was the most thoughtful and the most damaging. Klöpper had previously published a study of 2 Corinthians[101] and felt compelled to discuss Hausrath's thesis *in extenso* in the introduction to his commentary.[102] In the presentation of Hausrath's argument Klöpper could already point to an embarrassing degree of superficiality; but his main criticism was that Hausrath relied too much on psychology (p. 23), and that he failed to pay enough attention to 2 Cor 1—9. Singling out 2 Cor 6:14—7:1, Klöpper demonstrated that 2 Cor 1—9 is far from reflecting the mood of joy and tranquility which Hausrath claimed it displayed, and that the contrast of mood between 2 Cor 1—9 and 10—13 had been vastly exaggerated. But Klöpper himself had no new ideas to offer. He simply maintained that between 1 and 2 Corinthians there was an intermediate letter, now lost, and that 2 Corinthians is a literary unity.

More concessions are made to Hausrath's theory in Max Krenkel's *Beiträge zur Aufhellung der Geschichte und der Briefe des Apostels Paulus.*[103] Reviewing the contributions of Heinrich Julius Holtzmann,[104] Carl Holsten,[105] and Klöpper,[106] Krenkel considered Hausrath's thesis to have been disproved.[107] But Krenkel's own position shows Hausrath's influence. While he maintained the hypothesis of a lost intermediate letter, he allowed for

93 Alfred Plummer, *A Critical and Exegetical Commentary on the Second Epistle of St. Paul to the Corinthians* (ICC; Edinburgh: Clark, 1915) esp. XXII–XXXVI. Plummer argues against the separation of chapters 8 and 9, and against the theses of Semler and Halmel (pp. XXVI, 229ff, 252–53).

94 Gerald H. Rendall, *The Epistles of Paul to the Corinthians* (London: Macmillan, 1909).

95 Robert H. Strachan, *The Second Epistle of Paul to the Corinthians* (MNTC; New York and London: Harper, 1935) XIVff.

96 Thomas W. Manson, "St. Paul in Ephesus, (4): The Corinthian Correspondence," *BJRL* 26 (1941–42) 327–41, rep. as "The Corinthian Correspondence (2)," in his *Studies in the Gospels and Epistles* (ed. Matthew Black; Manchester: Manchester University, 1962) 210–24.

97 Charles H. Dodd, *New Testament Studies* (Manchester: Manchester University, 1953) 80–81.

98 James Moffatt, *An Introduction to the Literature of the New Testament* (New York: Scribner's, ³1918) 119ff.

99 See A. M. G. Stephenson, "Partition Theories on II. Corinthians," *Studia Evangelica* 2 (TU 87; Berlin: Akademie–Verlag, 1964) 639–46. Similarly also the most recent commentary by C. Kingsley Barrett, *A Commentary on the Second Epistle to the Corinthians* (London: Black, 1973) 12ff, 217–18, 232.

100 Allan Menzies, *The Second Epistle of the Apostle Paul to the Corinthians* (London: Macmillan, 1912) XXXVII.

101 Albert Klöpper, *Exegetisch-kritische Untersuchungen über den zweiten Brief des Paulus an die Gemeinde zu Korinth* (Göttingen: Vandenhoeck & Ruprecht, 1869).

102 Idem, *Kommentar über das zweite Sendschreiben des Apostel Paulus an die Gemeinde zu Korinth* (Berlin: Reimer, 1874) 1–28.

103 Max Krenkel, *Beiträge zur Aufhellung der Geschichte und der Briefe des Apostels Paulus* (Braunschweig: Schwetschke, ²1895) 153–378. The first edition was published in 1890.

104 Heinrich Julius Holtzmann, "Das gegenseitige Verhältnis der beiden Korintherbriefe," *ZWTh* 22 (1879) 455–92; Holtzmann agrees with Klöpper in rejecting Hausrath's thesis and defending the literary unity of 2 Corinthians.

105 Carl Holsten, "Einleitung in die Korinthierbriefe," *ZWTh* 44 (1901) 324–69. Also Holsten defends the unity of the letter against Semler and Hausrath (esp. pp. 348ff).

106 See above, nn. 101–2.

107 Krenkel, "Beiträge," 268ff.

the partition of 2 Corinthians: 2 Cor 1—9 and 13:11–13 form the letter taken to Corinth by Titus and the two brothers mentioned in 2 Cor 8 and 9; 2 Cor 10:1—13:10 is an appendix written by Paul and attached to a Macedonian letter to Corinth.[108]

In a careful, detailed study, Richard Drescher agreed that the differences between 2 Cor 1—9 and 10—13 are too substantial to allow for the unity of the letter.[109] Drescher divided 2 Corinthians into two letters, chapters 1—9 and 10—13. Over against Hausrath, he argued that chapters 10—13 are identical neither with the intermediate letter nor with the "letter of tears" (2 Cor 2:4). Drescher solved the dilemma by having Paul write chapters 10—13 as a separate letter during a three-month absence from Corinth, while traveling somewhere in Hellas. He placed this letter close in time to Romans; in fact, he asserted that it was written at the same time as Romans, with which it has many issues in common.[110]

Other scholars were quick to draw conclusions from Hausrath's thesis, which they accepted in principle. As 2 Cor 1—9 were further partitioned, chapters 8 and 9 began to pose difficulties. The Dutch scholar J. H. A. Michelsen[111] felt that 2 Cor 8 was more abrasive in tone than 2 Cor 9. Therefore, he reckoned chapter 8 to the same letter as chapters 10—13, putting chapter 9 together with chapters 1—7. Even more arbitrary is the thesis proposed by H. Hagge in an article entitled "Die beiden überleiferten Sendschreiben des Apostels Paulus an die Gemeinde zu Korinth."[112] Hagge divided 1 and 2 Corinthians into three distinct letters, an approach which was later to be taken up again by Schmithals.[113] In the course of his argument, Hagge returned to Semler's hypothesis that 2 Cor 8 was not originally a part of the epistle,[114] but the fragment of an independent community-letter included in 2 Corinthians by a later redactor. Thus Hagge attached chapter 9 to his letter C (2 Cor 1—7; 9; 13:11–13), with chapter 8 forming his letter D.

The essential point is not whether Hagge's hypothesis was better or worse than those of his predecessors, but that it succeeded in raising again the problem of 2 Cor 8 and 9. Against Semler, who sought to isolate chapter 9, Hagge argued that it was chapter 8 which was responsible for the problems. As 2 Cor 9:1 cannot form the continuation of 2 Cor 7:16, neither can it be the sequel to 2 Cor 8. Thus, 2 Cor 9:2 gives the impression that the latter work was written from Macedonia, but 2 Cor 8 points away from that locality.[115]

In response to Hagge, Paul Wilhelm Schmiedel took up the problem of the relationship between 2 Cor 8 and 9 in his commentary on 2 Corinthians.[116] He found Hagge's reasons for the separation of the chapters unconvincing and attempted to hold them together, constructing from 2 Cor 8 + 9 + 13:11–13 a single letter which he believed was after Paul's reconciliation with the Corinthians. This letter was therefore written after 2 Cor 10—13 and forms the conclusion of the Corinthian correspondence. On the whole, Schmiedel accepted Hausrath's thesis,[117] but went beyond it in recognizing that once the unity of 2 Corinthians had been given up, the arrangement of all the chapters, and not merely 10—13, needed to be reconsidered. Somewhat less sure

108 For a critique of Krenkel, see Adolf Jülicher, *Einleitung in das Neue Testament* (Tübingen: Mohr, Siebeck, [1.2]1894, [5.6]1906, [7]1931) 84ff.

109 Richard Drescher, "Der zweite Korinthierbrief und die Vorgänge in Korinth seit Abfassung des ersten Korinthierbriefs," *ThStKr* 70 (1897) 43–111.

110 Ibid., 111.

111 J. H. A. Michelsen, "'T Verhaal vaan Paulus' vlucht uit Damaskus, 2 Kor. XI:32,33; XII:1,7a een interpolatie," *Theologisch Tijdschrift* 7 (1873) 421–29, esp. 424.

112 *Jahrbücher für protestantische Theologie* 2 (1876) 481–531.

113 See below, pp. 18–20.

114 H. Hagge, "Die beiden überlieferten Sendschreiben des Apostels Paulus an die Gemeinde zu Korinth," *Jahrbücher fur protestantische Theologie* 2 (1876) 482ff. Hagge is right in defending Hausrath against the excessive criticism by Klöpper, suggesting that Klöpper, in order to defend the unity of 2 Corinthians, "approaches the letter with a kind of gnostic attitude" and follows what Klöpper himself calls "the old and well-tested principle of logic: 'bene noscit, qui bene distinguit' [he who distinguishes well, knows well]" (ibid., 482, citing Klöpper, *Kommentar,* 27).

115 Ibid., 484–85.

116 Paul Wilhelm Schmiedel, *Hand-Commentar zum Neuen Testament* (vol. 2; Freiburg: Mohr, Siebeck, [2]1892) esp. 226–27.

117 Ibid., 74ff.

of himself was Carl Clemen, who repeatedly changed his mind about how many letters there may have been. In his *Die Einheitlichkeit der paulinischen Briefe,*[118] he assumed that there were five Corinthian epistles, but in his later work on *Paulus,*[119] he reduced their number to four: (1) the precanonical letter mentioned in 1 Cor 5:9, of which a fragment has been preserved in 2 Cor 6:14—7:1; (2) 1 Corinthians; (3) the intermediate letter, containing 2 Cor 10—13; (4) 2 Cor 1:1—6:13; 7:2—9:15; 13:11–13. Thus, like Schmiedel, he placed 2 Cor 8 + 9 + 13:11–13 at the end of the Corinthian correspondence but did not see a point in separating these chapters from 1—7. However, Clemen also postulated the existence of a later letter: "that Paul could have given a letter of recommendation to Titus as well, who, according to 12:17f, was in Corinth again before the intermediate letter, or that he wrote to the congregation again at a later time, remains possible; nothing of that, however, has survived."[120]

Karl König,[121] a student of Richard Adelbert Lipsius, agreed with Hausrath and praised Schmiedel's commentary. Nevertheless, after all had been said, he admitted that 2 Corinthians remained for him an open question.[122]

The first era in the history of partition theories came to an end with the great work of Johannes Weiss, *Das Urchristentum.*[123] In 1910, Weiss published his commentary on 1 Corinthians[124] in which he attempted to justify not only his own theory but the plausibility of partition theories in general, in the face of the growing skepticism, and even hostility, toward such theories.[125] Weiss seems to have been the first participant in the debate to engage in careful methodological reflection. However, he postponed full discussion of these matters for his commentary on 2 Corinthians, which, unfortunately, never materialized.[126] *Das Urchristentum* began to appear in 1913 and was unfinished when Weiss died in 1914.

Weiss began the section devoted to the Corinthian correspondence[127] with an admonition to caution and even skepticism.[128] Many hypotheses have been proposed, but it remains doubtful whether any of them can be proven conclusively, or, for that matter, whether the letters were written in the form in which we now have them. In a footnote, he spoke of his intention to devote a separate work to the literary-critical problems of the Corinthian correspondence,[129] but death cut short his resolve.

In spite of these shortcomings, Weiss developed rather complex ideas on the partition of the Corinthian epistles, ideas which need not be discussed in detail here. Weiss separated 2 Cor 8 and 9, reckoning each chapter to a different letter: 2 Cor 8 was written not long after 1 Cor 16:1ff, while 2 Cor 9 was part of the final letter (2 Cor 1:1—2:13; 7:5–16; 9), written before Paul and the Macedonian delegation arrived in Corinth (Acts 20:2).[130]

e. Windisch's Thesis

With the death of Weiss, the assignment for the commentary on 2 Corinthians passed to Hans Windisch—a fortunate choice indeed.[131] As Windisch himself noted in the *Vorwort* to the commentary,[132] he had been among Weiss's students and was introduced by him to the

118 See above, n. 5.

119 Carl Clemen, *Paulus, sein Leben und Wirken* (Giessen: Ricker, Töpelmann, 1904) 1.75–85.

120 Ibid., 85.

121 Karl König, "Der Verkehr des Paulus mit der Gemeinde zu Korinth," *ZWTh* 40 (1897) 481–554.

122 Ibid., 549.

123 Johannes Weiss, *Das Urchristentum,* Nach dem Tode des Verfassers herausgegeben und am Schlusse ergänzt von Rudolf Knopf (Göttingen: Vandenhoeck & Ruprecht, 1917). ET: *Earliest Christianity* (2 vols.; tr. and ed. Frederick C. Grant; New York: Harper, 1959) 1.344ff.

124 Johannes Weiss, *Der erste Korintherbrief* (KEK 5; Göttingen: Vandenhoeck & Ruprecht, [9]1910; rep. 1970).

125 Ibid., XL–XLIII.

126 Ibid., XLIII.

127 *Das Urchristentum,* 245ff.

128 Ibid., 245.

129 Ibid., 245 n. 2: "die literarkritischen Probleme werde ich ausführlicher in einer besonderen Schrift erörtern."

130 Ibid., 269–72.

131 Hans Windisch, *Der zweite Korintherbrief* (KEK 6; Göttingen: Vandenhoeck & Ruprecht, [9]1924). According to his foreword, Windisch had worked on the commentary from 1917 to 1923. See the review by Erich Klostermann, *ThLZ* 52 (1927) 341–42. Cf. also Herbert Preisker, "Zur Komposition des zweiten Korintherbriefes," *Theologische Blätter* 5 (1926) 154–57.

132 Windisch, p. V.

problems of 2 Corinthians in a seminar in Marburg in the winter semester of 1901–2. In general, Windisch continued the methods of research of his teacher, but the commentary is his own achievement and confronts New Testament scholarship with new challenges even at the end of the twentieth century.[133]

Windisch emphasized that the problem of the literary unity of the epistle would receive major attention in his work. He found Krenkel's hypothesis of a four-chapter letter most persuasive and announced his intention of renewing it. But he also followed Weiss in doubting the literary unity of chapters 1—7 and 8—9.[134] Windisch did not propose yet another theory, but was content to present scholars with a renewed challenge to demonstrate the integrity of 2 Corinthians by means of *new* arguments.

There is no need to review the details of Windisch's masterly introduction here.[135] Based on a survey of research since Semler, Windisch came to the conclusion that three sections of 2 Corinthians had been isolated which must be treated separately: section A (chaps. 1—7) comprising Paul's friendly debate with the congregation, and in that context, a description of his office and an explanation of his conduct as an apostle; section B (chaps. 8 and 9) regarding the conclusion of the collection for Jerusalem; and section C (chaps. 10—13) containing "a sharp philippica against the leaders of the opposition in Corinth," including a censure of the congregation itself.[136] Furthermore, Windisch recognized that questions of literary unity were bound up with the historical assessment of events following the writing of 1 Corinthians[137] and the nature and activity of the opponents.[138] These observations were in themselves nothing new.

What was new in the commentary was Windisch's understanding of the term "literary" as referring not only to the unity of composition but also to style, genre, and forms of rhetoric. This increased awareness of the range of the term "literary" was acquired, as Windisch himself admits, from Weiss and Carl Friedrich Georg Heinrici.[139] But Windisch seems to have been the first to refer to letter-types as they were understood in ancient epistolography.[140] He recognized that in some respects the various sections of 2 Corinthians could be classified in those terms, while in others they went beyond what the letter-types envisioned. Thus the official pronouncement of 5:18f, the conduct of business in conjunction with exhortation in chapters 8 and 9, and the inclusion of information related to personal experiences in 1:8ff; 2:12f; 7:5ff; 11:23ff; 12:1ff are things which have no parallel in conventional types of letters. In other words, "No other Pauline letter has a character which, in this regard, is so strongly mixed."[141] In regard to the so-called four-chapter letter (2 Cor 10—13), Windisch[142] recognized the weakness of Hausrath's thesis, but emphasized that Hausrath's failure to make a convincing case did not in itself demonstrate the unity of 2 Corinthians. Thus Windisch supported Krenkel's version of the thesis,[143] a version according to which chapters 10—13 belonged to a separate letter and are not to be taken as part of the letter of tears (2:4). Rather, these chapters were part of a later epistle, written after Titus's depar-

133 It was reprinted without change (ed. Georg Strecker; Göttingen: Vandenhoeck & Ruprecht, 1970). See Strecker's introductory remarks, VIII–X.
134 Ibid., VI.
135 Ibid., 5–31.
136 Ibid., 5.
137 Ibid., 9ff.
138 Ibid., 23ff.
139 See ibid., V, where he mentions the names of Johann Jacob Wettstein's collection of classical parallels, Heinrici, and Weiss. See also the appendix in Heinrici's commentary, entitled "Zum Hellenismus des Apostels Paulus" (pp. 436–58); at the conclusion of this sharp rebuttal of Eduard Norden, Heinrici refers to Johannes Weiss, "Beiträge zur paulinischen Rhetorik," *Theologische Studien,* Bernhard Weiss zu seinem 70. Geburtstag dargebracht (Göttingen: Vandenhoeck & Ruprecht, 1897) 165–247.
140 Windisch, pp. 8–9. In 1910, Valentin Weichert's edition of *Demetrii et Libanii qui ferunt* ΤΥΠΟΙ ΕΠΙΣΤΟΛΙΚΟΙ *et* ΕΠΙΣΤΟΛΙΜΑΙΟΙ ΧΑΡΑΚΤΗΡΕΣ (Leipzig: Teubner, 1910) had been published; Windisch refers to the edition on p. 8. See also Abraham J. Malherbe, "Ancient Epistolary Theorists," *Ohio Journal of Religious Studies* 5 (1977) 3–77.
141 Windisch, p. 9.
142 Ibid., 12ff.
143 Ibid., 16ff. See also the new Anchor Bible commentary by Victor F. Furnish, *II Corinthians* (Garden City, NY: Doubleday, 1984).

ture and after a new attempt had been made by the opponents to use the collection as a means for spreading suspicions against Paul (cf. 12:16–18). Paul then wrote chapters 10—13 in reaction to this new crisis.

As Windisch saw it, if chapters 10—13 were not identical with the intermediate letter or letter of tears, they must have been part of a later letter in which Paul reacted to the conflict's newest turn for the worse. Thus he saw no need for an intermediate visit; the assumption of the arrival of new information from Corinth is enough to justify the sending of the letter.[144] Of course, this new outbreak in the crisis is entirely hypothetical and has no direct support in the sources.[145]

Windisch's doubts about the integrity of chapters 1—7[146] have important implications for the interpretation of chapters 8 and 9.[147] Windisch affirmed Semler's original hypothesis that chapter 9 was a separate letter, parallel to chapter 8. Thus he concluded that these two chapters must be kept apart from one another and should not be integrated into any of the other letters or fragments of letters.

These considerations were pursued further in the commentary itself, where chapters 8 and 9 were given a separate introduction[148] and conclusion.[149] According to Windisch, these two chapters have more in common with 1 Cor 16:1ff than with the rest of 2 Corinthians.[150] They deserve to be treated as fragments of two separate letters concerned with the final stages of the collection for Jerusalem. There can be no question about their epistolary character. Each appears to be a complete unit, comparable to Philemon. "Both letters are 'business letters'; but the way in which 'business' is conducted, the motivation for the appeal, the presentation of the 'business details', as well as the ethical-religious exhortation connected with it—all this lifts Paul's epistles far above the level of ordinary business letters. Even in the business letter, Paul remains a human being, a minister, an apostle, an educator and a witness."[151] These proposals carried Windisch beyond all previous research. Unfortunately, he did not reveal what led him to these considerations; he simply presented them as challenging possibilities.

Windisch concluded that 2 Cor 9:1 introduces an independent treatment of a new subject, not merely a new section of the previous letter.[152] Indeed, Anton Halmel had already demonstrated as much,[153] and was followed by Weiss.[154] The two letters are, therefore, literary units in themselves and not simply parts of other letters. "What follows from this is that chapters 8 and 9 contain two independent and complete presentations by Paul on the same theme."[155] The two letters were written at about the same time, but chapter 9 somewhat later than 8.[156] The address is also different. While chapter 8 must have been addressed to the church in Corinth, chapter 9 seems to have been a kind of accompanying letter sent to all the churches of Achaia.[157]

f. From Windisch to Schmithals

Rudolf Bultmann's work on 2 Corinthians represents the most important developments in exegesis following the commentaries of Windisch and Hans Lietzmann. Bultmann held lectures and conducted seminars on 2 Corinthians for many years, and some of the fruits of his research were eventually published. A short fascicle entitled *Exegetische Probleme des zweiten Korintherbriefes* appeared in the Symbolae Biblicae Upsalienses 9.[158] The work contains studies of 2 Cor 5:1–5; 5:11—6:10; 10—13; 12:21 which Bultmann presented on a visit to Uppsala in 1946.

The major portion of his work, however, went into the

144 Windisch, pp. 17–18.
145 This was pointed out by Schmiedel, *Hand-Commentar,* 82; Jülicher, *Einleitung,* 85.
146 Windisch, pp. 18–20.
147 Ibid., 20–21.
148 Ibid., 242–43, 268–71.
149 Ibid., 286–89.
150 Ibid., 242–43.
151 Ibid., 243.
152 Ibid., 268–69.
153 See pp. 26, 32 n. 312.
154 Weiss, *Das Urchristentum,* 268ff.
155 Windisch, p. 287.
156 Ibid.
157 Ibid., 288.
158 (Uppsala: Wretman, 1947), rep. in his *Exegetica* (ed. Erich Dinkler; Tübingen: Mohr, Siebeck, 1967) 298–322.

lecture notes on 2 Corinthians, written between 1940 and 1952. These quite sketchy notes were handed over to Erich Dinkler in 1954, in the hope that he would incorporate them into his own commentary on 2 Corinthians, to be written for the KEK. As Dinkler explained, though Bultmann's handwritten notes had been typed as early as 1955/56, his own work on the project remained unfinished. Upon Dinkler's retirement, he decided to publish Bultmann's notes, as incomplete as they were; thus Bultmann's exegesis was finally made public in 1976.[159]

In his brief *Vorbemerkung* (pp. 20–23), Bultmann expressed his agreement with Hausrath's thesis, although in a revised form. He assumed the existence of an intermediate visit, as well as an intermediate letter, but stopped short of a simple identification of the latter with chapters 10—13.[160] Chapter 8 was cautiously assigned to what Bultmann regarded as the last letter (1:1—2:13; 7:5–16; + 8),[161] while chapter 9 was considered part of the intermediate letter (2:14—7:4 [except 6:14—7:1 which he regarded as non-Pauline]; 10—13; + 9).[162]

There is clear evidence, however, that Bultmann's views with regard to chapters 8 and 9 remained tentative.[163] These chapters were treated separately at the end of the commentary in a section entitled "brief notes."[164]

In conclusion, one can say that, apart from certain shifts in critical perspective, the literary division of 2 Corinthians was pursued along the lines set out by Weiss and Windisch. Bultmann did not advance the matter any further, nor did he provide his own analysis of the literary composition.[165]

g. Schmithals's Thesis

Stimulated by Bultmann's lectures on the Corinthian correspondence, his student, Walter Schmithals, made the problem of Paul's opponents the subject of his 1954 Marburg dissertation.[166] His major thesis was that Paul's opponents were the same in 1 and 2 Corinthians, namely Gnostics. His thesis was thus diametrically opposed to that of Dieter Georgi[167] and Helmut Koester.[168] Consequently, Schmithals was not interested in the rigid separation of the two letters, as his "literary analysis" indicates.[169] He inserted 2 Cor 6:14—7:1 before 1 Cor 9:24,[170] at the beginning of his letter A; this means that the issues raised by Paul's opponents are in the picture

159 Rudolf Bultmann, *Der zweite Brief an die Korinther* (KEK 6; ed. Erich Dinkler; Göttingen: Vandenhoeck & Ruprecht, 1976). On the history of the work, see Dinkler's preface (pp. 9–12).

160 The "intermediate letter" was written shortly after the "intermediate visit" and is identical with the "letter of tears."

161 Consequently, Bultmann has Titus taking the letter to Corinth (p. 22).

162 Ibid., 22–23. On 2 Cor 1:14—7:1, see 176–82.

163 In *Exegetische Probleme* (see n. 158) 14 n. 6 (= *Exegetica,* 307 n. 17), Bultmann remarks in passing: "How chapters 8 and 9, which originally could not have belonged together, are to be distributed, I will not discuss" ("Wie die Kapp. 8 und 9, die ursprünglich nicht zusammengehört haben können, zu verteilen sind, will ich nicht erörtern").

164 Bultmann, pp. 255–60.

165 Dinkler himself does not follow Bultmann, as is evident from his article "Korintherbriefe," *RGG* 4 ([3]1960) 17–23, esp. 18. According to Dinkler, 2 Corinthians consists of a letter C (probably beginning with chapters 10—13; then 2:14—7:4 [excepting the non-Pauline interpolation 6:14—7:1]; 9; 13:11–13); and letter D (1:1—2:13; 7:5–16; 8). Chapter 9 is said to be older than 8 and is therefore attributed to letter C (col. 22).

166 Walter Schmithals, *Die Gnosis in Korinth: Eine Untersuchung zu den Korintherbriefen* (FRLANT 66 [NF 48]; Göttingen: Vandenhoeck & Ruprecht, 1956, [2]1965, [3]1969); ET: *Gnosticism in Corinth* (tr. John E. Steely from the 3d German edition; Nashville: Abingdon, 1971). See the review by Dieter Georgi, *Verkündigung und Forschung* 1958/59 (1960) 90ff.

167 See Schmithals's review of Georgi's book on the collection (see below, n. 179), *ThLZ* 92 (1967) 668–72, and the addenda to Schmithals, *Gnosis*[2], 309ff.

168 Helmut Koester, "Häretiker im Urchristentum," *RGG* 3 ([3]1959) 17–21; idem, *Einführung in das Neue Testament* (Berlin: de Gruyter, 1980) 485–86, 560–65, 570–72. Against Koester argues Schmithals, "Zur Abfassung und ältesten Sammlung der paulinischen Hauptbriefe," *ZNW* 51 (1960) 225–45, esp. 226; ET: "On the Composition and Earliest Collection of the Major Epistles of Paul," *Paul and the Gnostics* (tr. John E. Steely; Nashville: Abingdon, 1972) 239–74, esp. 240–41.

169 Schmithals, *Gnosis,* 84–94.

170 Ibid., 88.

from the very beginning. For the rest, Schmithals followed in the tradition of Weiss, Windisch, and Bultmann. With regard to chapters 8 and 9, he took the latter to have been written prior to chapter 8, while 8 forms the conclusion of the "letter of joy" (1:1—2:13 + 7:5–16 + 8).[171] In the appendix to the revised edition,[172] Schmithals essentially agreed with Bornkamm and Georgi, but did not change his mind on chapters 8 and 9.[173]

On the whole, Schmithals's literary operations were characterized by arbitrariness. Building rather uncritically upon the hypotheses of earlier scholars, which he tended to treat as proven facts, he simply rearranged the sections which had been isolated in terms of their content.[174] For example, the only reason that Schmithals offered for placing 2 Cor 6:14—7:1 before 1 Cor 9:24 was that this place seems best for an insertion. While this view was maintained in the first and second editions, Schmithals later altered his partition theory in response to criticism by Wolfgang Schenk,[175] so that the third German edition, from which the English translation was made, places 2 Cor 6:14—7:1 before 1 Cor 6:12 instead of 1 Cor 9:24.[176] Basic to Schmithals's and Schenk's methodology is the tendency to rearrange sections by content, as understood by the authors, until the place is found which "seems to fit best." No thought is given to the epistolary composition and rhetorical argument of individual sections, or to the macrostructures of the epistles.

h. Georgi's Thesis

At the same time as Schmithals, but independently of him, Dieter Georgi, a student of Bornkamm, was engaged in the investigation of 2 Corinthians. While concentrating on the question of the opponents in 2 Corinthians, Georgi, in his Heidelberg dissertation of 1958,[177] seems to adopt what must have been his teacher's theory of the literary partition of the letter. Georgi provided a convincing demonstration that the opponents encountered in 2 Corinthians represent a different theological perspective from those found in 1 Corinthians.[178] Though Georgi may not have devoted enough attention to the question of how changes in the opposition to Paul came about and how the different groups of opponents were related, he nevertheless demonstrated that real differences exist and thus

171 Ibid., 90–91.

172 Ibid., 312.

173 Cf., however, his later article, "Die Korintherbriefe als Briefsammlung," *ZNW* 64 (1973) 263–88, esp. 287–88.

174 *Gnosis*², 88 and also 89, and the summary 94 n. 2; cf. the addenda 311–12. Confusing is the fact that the English translations of earlier articles of Schmithals correct his theories according to the latest version, so that, e.g., the German version of "Zur Abfassung und ältesten Sammlung" (see n. 168, above) has 1 Cor 9:24, while the English version (p. 245) has 1 Cor 6:12. Readers of the English version cannot but be confused as to which passage Schmithals really has in mind.

175 Wolfgang Schenk, "Der 1. Korintherbrief als Briefsammlung," *ZNW* 60 (1969) 219–43.

176 Walter Schmithals, "Briefsammlung," 263–88; idem, *Gnosticism,* 94 and the summary 100 n. 30.

177 Dieter Georgi, *Die Gegner des Paulus im 2. Korintherbrief: Studien zur religiösen Propaganda in der Spätantike* (WMANT 11; Neukirchen-Vluyn: Neukirchener, 1964).

178 As soon as it was realized that the question of the "sinner" in 1 Cor 5:3–6 was no longer an issue in 2 Corinthians, and that the "evildoer" (ὁ ἀδικήσας) of 2 Corinthians pointed to someone else, the problem of the opponents emerged as the most pressing one. In particular since Hausrath, *Der Vier-Capitel-Brief,* 18ff, almost all discussions of the literary problem of 2 Corinthians include discussion of the nature of the opponents. This discussion was, of course, greatly enhanced by Ferdinand Christian Baur, *Paulus der Apostel Jesu Christi* (Stuttgart: Becher & Müller, 1845), who, however, had no interest in the literary problems of 2 Corinthians. See also Adolf Hilgenfeld, "Die Christusleute in Korinth," *ZWTh* 3 (1865) 241–42; Klöpper, *Exegetisch-kritische Untersuchungen,* 29–127; Holsten, "Einleitung," 324–69, esp. 332ff; Wilhelm Lütgert, *Freiheitspredigt und Schwarmgeister in Korinth* (BFCTh 12/3; Gütersloh: Bertelsmann, 1908); Weiss, *Das Urchristentum,* 253ff, Windisch, pp. 23ff; Günther Bornkamm, *Die Vorgeschichte des sogenannten Zweiten Korintherbriefs* (SHAW.PH 1961, 2. Abhandlung; Heidelberg: Winter, 1961) *passim.* For further references, see Georgi, *Gegner,* 7–16, where, however, no full account of the history of research on the problem is given.

provided further justification for the separation of the epistles. His thesis also furnishes a plausible explanation of the turn of events which, following the first epistle, led to the writing of a second letter.

Georgi dealt with a related problem in his *Habilitationsschrift* of 1962 on the history of the Pauline collection for Jerusalem.[179] On the whole, this work also confirms Bornkamm's thesis, but it includes more extensive discussion of the sending of the delegation of Titus and his companions to Corinth[180] and of the literary problems of 2 Cor 8 and 9.[181] These two chapters are regarded as fragments of two separate letters, chapter 8 being a "letter of recommendation for Titus and his companions,"[182] and chapter 9 a "circular letter to the churches of Achaia."[183] Georgi agreed with Windisch's classification of chapter 8 as a "business letter,"[184] but presented neither literary analysis nor comparative material to justify the classification. Georgi's careful exegesis of these two letters, which for the most part follows that of Windisch's commentary, goes a long way toward making their content more intelligible. With regard to formal analysis, Georgi added little to what Windisch had already done, apart from occasional reflections on Paul's language and sentence structure.

i. Bornkamm's Thesis

Considerable progress was made by Günther Bornkamm in his own study entitled "The Prehistory of the So-called Second Letter to the Corinthians," presented to the Akademie der Wissenschaften in Heidelberg on 6 May 1961.[185] We cannot discuss Bornkamm's work here in all its details, but it should be pointed out that basic progress was made at a number of points.

Bornkamm recognized that reconstruction of the course of events following the writing of 1 Corinthians depended in large measure upon an understanding of developments in the issues that had emerged in 1 Corinthians, which included both Paul's relationship to his congregation and the nature and activity of his opponents.[186] In a discussion of "literary problems," Bornkamm[187] defended Hausrath's thesis, contending that the arguments in its favor could be presented in a more forceful manner than had previously been the case, and that the objections which had been raised against it,[188] as summed up by Werner Georg Kümmel,[189] did not necessarily carry conviction. Thus Bornkamm returned to the original version of Hausrath's thesis. In his view, 2 Cor 10—13 belonged to the intermediate letter, which is identified with the letter of tears;[190] 2 Cor 2:14—7:4 (with the exception of the interpolated section 6:14—7:1) cannot have been a part of this letter,

179 Dieter Georgi, *Die Geschichte der Kollekte des Paulus für Jerusalem* (ThF 38; Hamburg-Bergstedt: Reich, 1965). See the review by Walter Schmithals, *ThLZ* 92 (1967) 668–72.

180 Georgi, *Kollekte,* 54–56.

181 Ibid., 56–58.

182 Ibid., 58–67.

183 Ibid., 67–79. See also Dieter Georgi, "Second Letter to the Corinthians," *IDBSup,* 183–86; Norman Perrin and Dennis C. Duling, *The New Testament: An Introduction* (New York: Harcourt Brace Jovanovich, ²1982) 181–82.

184 Ibid., 59.

185 Bornkamm, *Vorgeschichte.* The study was revised and reprinted, together with an addendum, in his *Geschichte und Glaube,* vol. 2 (= *Gesammelte Aufsätze,* vol. 4; Munich; Kaiser, 1971) 162–94. An abbreviated version appeared in English under the title "The History of the Origin of the So-called Second Letter to the Corinthians," *NTS* 8 (1962) 258–63; also in *The Authorship and Integrity of the New Testament* (Theological Collections 4; London: SPCK, 1967) 73–81.

186 Bornkamm, *Vorgeschichte* (= *Gesammelte Aufsätze* 4.165ff).

187 Ibid., 172–78.

188 He refers to Krenkel, Windisch, Jülicher (ibid., 175).

189 Paul Feine and Johannes Behm, *Einleitung in das Neue Testament* (12th ed. Werner Georg Kümmel; Heidelberg: Quelle & Meyer, 1963) 206–18; ET: *Introduction to the New Testament* (tr. Howard C. Kee; Nashville: Abingdon, ²1975) 279–93. Against Kümmel, see the addendum in Bornkamm, *Vorgeschichte* (= *Gesammelte Aufsätze* 4. 190–94); and again, against Bornkamm: Kümmel, *Introduction,* 292–93, defending the literary unity of 2 Corinthians (with the exception of 6:14—7:1).

190 On 2 Cor 10—13, see Hans Dieter Betz, *Der Apostel Paulus und die sokratische Tradition* (BHTh 45; Tübingen: Mohr, Siebeck, 1972) 1–42. With regard to the skepticism against the "letter of tears" being identical with chapters 10—13 (p. 42), one should consider the difference between the actual words of chapters 10—13 and Paul's later evaluation and

however, but constituted an earlier "first apology."[191] Consequently, Bornkamm divided 2 Corinthians in the following manner: 2:14—7:4 (except 6:14—7:1), an early apology, written after 1 Corinthians; 10—13, the intermediate letter (letter of tears); 1:1—2:13 and 7:5–16, the "letter of reconciliation."

Chapters 8 and 9 were treated separately in an excursus set off in small type.[192] Bornkamm agreed with Windisch and others that these two chapters must originally have belonged to different epistles. According to Bornkamm, chapter 8 is a letter of recommendation for Titus and his companions (whose names were omitted); either it formed the conclusion of the letter of reconciliation, in which case Titus carried the latter epistle to Corinth, or it formed a separate letter altogether. Bornkamm did not seem to favor the second solution, but raised it as a possibility nevertheless. Chapter 9 is certainly an independent letter, written later than chapter 8 and addressed to the churches of Achaia. Chapter 9 represents the last piece of Paul's Corinthian correspondence.

According to Bornkamm, the concluding verses 13:11–13 cannot be definitively ascribed to one of the letters thus identified. If, as he maintained, the redactor[193] used the letter of reconciliation as the frame for 2 Corinthians and inserted the other letter fragments into it, the best solution is to regard the final epistolary section 13:11–13 as the end of the letter of reconciliation. But it is by no means impossible that it formed the conclusion of the intermediate letter (10—13).[194]

j. Discussion Since Schmithals, Georgi, and Bornkamm

An important summary of the state of research following the works of Schmithals, Georgi, and Bornkamm was presented by Philipp Vielhauer in his *Geschichte der urchristlichen Literatur.*[195] Vielhauer had followed the discussion of partition theories since attending Bultmann's lectures on 2 Corinthians in the winter semester of 1935/36, the notes of which were used in his own work.[196] On the subject of partition, Vielhauer agreed for the most part with Bultmann and Bornkamm, but also kept constantly in mind the objections of Kümmel,[197] and in one instance, at least, attempted to answer them.[198]

Vielhauer assumed that following 1 Corinthians Paul wrote a letter C, the letter of tears (2:14—7:4 [except 6:14—7:1, which is regarded as a non-Pauline interpolation] + 10—13);[199] a letter D, the letter of reconciliation (1:1—2:13 + 7:5–16 + 9 [?]),[200] and the letter E, a "letter of recommendation for Titus and his companions" (8).[201]

2 Cor 8 and 9 are duplicates which cannot have belonged to the same letter. While Vielhauer regarded 8 as a separate letter, he remained unsure about 9. It could

description, including the rhetorical aspects, of what he had written.

191 Bornkamm, *Vorgeschichte* (= *Gesammelte Aufsätze* 4.177).

192 Ibid., 186–87.

193 A major contribution is Bornkamm's consideration of the possible concepts directing the operations of the redactor.

194 Bornkamm's literary analysis was taken over by Willi Marxsen, *Einleitung in das Neue Testament* (Gütersloh: Mohn, 1963) 73–77; ET: *Introduction to the New Testament* (tr. George Buswell; Oxford: Blackwell, 1968) 77–91. See also J.-F. Collange, *Enigmes de la deuxième épître de Paul aux Corinthiens: Etude exégètique de 2 Cor. 2:14—7:4* (SNTSMS 18; Cambridge: Cambridge University, 1972) 7–15.

195 (Berlin and New York: de Gruyter, 1975) 142–56. See my review in *SEÅ* 43 (1978) 128–32.

196 Vielhauer, *Geschichte,* 128 n. 1.

197 See ibid., 151: "Selbstverständlich lässt sich in beiden Fragen kein stringenter Beweis, sondern nur ein Wahrscheinlichkeitsbeweis führen. Aber auch die Verteidigung der Einheitlichkeit ist nicht besser dran, sie kommt nicht ohne Hypothesen aus und nicht über Wahrscheinlichkeiten hinaus. Es geht darum, welche Hypothese mehr Wahrscheinlichkeit besitzt" ("It is self-evident that in both questions no conclusive proof but only a probable proof can be supplied. Yet the defense of the literary unity is also no better off: it cannot do without hypotheses and does not get beyond probabilities. The question is merely which hypothesis has the greater probability"). On Kümmel, see below, pp. 31–32.

198 Ibid., 154–55. Vielhauer points to other collections of letters made in antiquity, which are comparable to 2 Corinthians.

199 Ibid., 153; so also Weiss and Bultmann (see above, pp. 16, 18–19).

200 Ibid., in disagreement with Bornkamm (see above, pp. 21–22) who contemplates adding chapter 8, not 9, to this letter.

201 Ibid., so also Bornkamm (see above, p. 22).

likewise have been a separate letter, written later than 8. But he regarded this as less likely than the possibility that 9 was a part of the letter of reconciliation.[202] The redactor put them both together because their content, the "exhortation for the collection," was the same.[203]

A major work which builds on Schmithals's theory of partition is Alfred Suhl's *Habilitationsschrift* of 1969, *Paulus und seine Briefe.*[204] As the subtitle indicates, Suhl was primarily concerned with the chronology of Paul's life, so that partition theories of 1 and 2 Corinthians functioned in his work as subarguments within an account of what he believed to be the three stages of Paul's conflict with the Corinthians. Stage I of this conflict begins with Timothy's visit to Corinth (cf. 1 Cor 4:17; 16:10f)[205] and ends with the writing of 1 Corinthians.[206] Stage II is inaugurated by Titus's initial journey to Corinth and brought to completion by Titus's meeting with Paul in Macedonia (cf. 2 Cor 7:5ff);[207] this stage includes the writing of the first apology 2:14—6:13 + 7:2–4 and the letter of tears, 10—13. Stage III "comprises the period of the collection-journey through Macedonia," where Paul meets with Titus, who is returning from Corinth.[208] This stage embraces the letter of reconciliation, which Suhl, in contrast to Georgi, did not wish to separate from chapter 8, and chapter 9.[209] Suhl's reasons for adopting Schmithals's theory rather than Georgi's were chronological rather than literary, but he did not share Schmithals's view that chapter 9 is older than chapter 8.[210]

The only formal criterion which Suhl provided for ascribing chapter 8 to the letter of reconciliation is the occurrence of the first-person plural. This is taken to indicate that Timothy is a co-sender (2 Cor 1:1).[211] Because chapter 9 is written in the first-person singular, it must have been written by Paul alone. From this Suhl concluded that Timothy must have preceded Paul to Corinth, carrying the letter of chapter 9 along with him. His departure took place "presumably several weeks, if not months"[212] after the sending of the letter of reconciliation and shortly before his arrival together with the Macedonian delegation in Corinth (mentioned in 9:4). Furthermore, Suhl rejected the notion that chapter 9 was a circular letter written to the churches of Achaia rather than to Corinth. In his view, Rom 15:26 proves that Achaia can only mean Corinth itself.[213]

A variation on the hypothesis of Schmithals and Bornkamm was proposed in the recently published introduction to the New Testament by Hans-Martin Schenke and Karl Martin Fischer.[214] Schenke and Fischer maintained that after 1 Corinthians,[215] which they divided into two letters, A and B, Paul wrote a letter C (2 Cor 2:14—6:13 + 7:2–4 + 9),[216] a letter D (the letter of tears 10—13),[217] and finally a letter E (the letter of reconciliation 1:1—2:13 + 7:5–16 + 8).[218]

202 Ibid., 153.
203 Ibid., 154.
204 Alfred Suhl, *Paulus und seine Briefe: Ein Beitrag zur paulinischen Chronologie* (StNT 11; Gütersloh: Mohn, 1975). Suhl names as his teachers at Münster Willi Marxsen, Günter Klein, and Ernst Haenchen.
205 Ibid., 141ff.
206 Ibid., 202ff.
207 Ibid., 233ff.
208 Ibid., 256.
209 Ibid., 260ff.
210 Ibid., 261 n. 20.
211 Ibid., 263; cf. 259 with n. 11.
212 Ibid., 262.
213 Ibid., 263 n. 28, against Windisch, p. 288; Georgi, *Kollekte,* 58.
214 Hans-Martin Schenke and Karl Martin Fischer, *Einleitung in die Schriften des Neuen Testaments,* vol. 1: *Die Briefe des Paulus und Schriften des Paulinismus* (Berlin: Evangelische Verlagsanstalt, 1978) 108–23.
215 Ibid., 93–94, 98ff.
216 Written probably from Ephesus before the "intermediate visit" and carried to Corinth "by Titus and brother X" (ibid., 111). Cf. below, n. 220.
217 Written from Ephesus after the "intermediate visit" and shortly before Paul's departure to Macedonia, and brought to Corinth presumably by Titus (ibid., 111).
218 Written from Macedonia not long before the departure to Corinth, taken to Corinth by Titus and the two brothers (ibid., 112). Schenke and Fischer agree that this letter became the frame-letter used by the redactor and that the original address is now found in 2 Cor 1:1b: *σὺν τοῖς ἁγίοις πᾶσιν τοῖς οὖσιν ἐν ὅλῃ τῇ Ἀχαΐᾳ* (so also Schmithals, *Gnosis*², 91 n. 1 (= *Gnosticism*, 97 n. 27). Schenke and Fischer, *Einleitung,* 117–18, also take 2 Cor 6:14—7:1 to be a later non-Pauline interpolation.

Schenke and Fischer held that chapters 8 and 9 are duplicates, written at different times. They agreed with Schmithals[219] that chapter 9 is the older of the two, written before the outbreak of the crisis at Corinth, while chapter 8 was written after the crisis had passed. Thus they attached chapter 8 to the letter of recommendation carried to Corinth by Titus.[220] Because chapter 9 seems closer in spirit to 1 Cor 16:1–4 (letter B), it is attached to letter C, a suggestion which, as Schenke and Fischer noted, is without predecessors.[221]

Reviewing the partition theories of Bornkamm, Schmithals, Schenke, and Suhl, Robert Jewett[222] followed Weiss and Bornkamm in emphasizing the importance of the redactor for division theories of 2 Corinthians, as well as for the collection of the Pauline corpus as a whole. He assumed that Paul's letters played an important role in the postapostolic conflict over "emergent Catholicism." Since some of Paul's letters proved to be useful tools in the hands of Gnostics, the redactor reedited the original epistles so that they were made to serve the purposes of the nascent Catholic church. It follows that this redactor must have been a representative of that church. Jewett found that the redactor's theology is similar to that of the pastoral epistles. He then reviewed recent scholarly studies of the so-called Pauline School, which he located in Ephesus, and made the redactor its representative.[223]

Jewett's method seems as arbitrary as that of Schmithals. He merely rearranged the parts of the Corinthian correspondence, making them into seven original letters. But he had learned from Bornkamm how to justify his rearrangement on the basis of the redactor's theology. In most instances, this approach simply results in speculation heaped upon speculation, though Jewett preferred to speak of evidence. His construction of a "trajectory"[224] from the original letters to the pastoral epistles, in whose vicinity he located the redactor, is never justified. More disturbing is the fact that Jewett never discussed the relationship of the "trajectory" to the so-called Deutero-Pauline letters (Colossians, Ephesians), and 2 Thessalonians.

Dealing mostly with 1 Corinthians, Jewett's essay only hints at implications for 2 Corinthians. He was more explicit about his conclusions, however, in the case of 2 Cor 9. Agreeing with Bornkamm that 2 Cor 9 should be placed "at the end of the frame letter,"[225] he was not satisfied with Bornkamm's explanation. "Its thematic and temporal relationship with 2 Cor 8:1–24 are presumably such that the reader could find no better place. This assumes that the redactor could apply the historical method to infer the original sequence of the letters, which seems rather unlikely. Moreover, the connection of 2 Cor 9:1–15 to the Jerusalem offering, which seems so obvious to the modern historian (Georgi, 1965:67–78), is not stated explicitly." The problem with this approach is twofold: (1) It takes for granted that we know what the redactor could and could not do, instead of explaining what he did and why he did it—if indeed that is possible. (2) Rather than remaining mindful of our ignorance and continuing to search for clues that might betray the method used by the redactor, it assumes that the redactor followed the method of rearrangement employed by Schmithals and Jewett—if in fact he had a method at all.

Heedless of these difficulties, Jewett proceeded with his own explanation: "The appropriate redactional question is what purpose the material in 2 Cor 9:1–15 would serve at the end of the first century, when Bornkamm suggests the editing took place. Compared with the specific instructions about the completion of the

219 Schenke and Fischer, *Einleitung,* 110, 120.

220 Schenke and Fischer, *Einleitung,* 110, harmonize the two brothers mentioned in 2 Cor 9:3, 5 with "Titus and the one brother" in 2 Cor 12:18. Being the same persons, they can be made the letter-carriers of letter C (see above, n. 216).

221 Ibid., 120. The reasons given are weak: Chapter 9 is early and cannot have been part of the "letter of tears" (10—13); there is only one possibility: it was part of letter C (ibid., 119-20, 110).

222 Robert Jewett, "The Redaction of I Corinthians and the Trajectory of the Pauline School," *JAAR* 44 (1978) 389–444.

223 Ibid., 429–32, referring to Hans-Martin Schenke, "Das Weiterwirken des Paulus und die Pflege seines Erbes durch die Paulusschule," *NTS* 21 (1974–75) 505–18.

224 The notion is borrowed from James M. Robinson and Helmut Koester, *Trajectories Through Early Christianity* (Philadelphia: Fortress, 1971).

225 Jewett, "The Redaction," 393.

offering in 2 Cor 8:1–24, including travel details for Titus and other unnamed representatives (8:18ff), which could have been hard for a later generation to follow, 2 Cor 9:6–15 provides pious reasons for generosity within a context that goes beyond a specific offering in the mid-fifties. 2 Cor 9:13 speaks of your contribution for them and for *all others.* This would be highly useful for the development of paid clergy, which was a major issue at the end of the century."[226] But for all his certainty about the questions which are appropriate to be addressed to the material, Jewett's explanation remains just another hypothesis for which no evidence has been, or can be, adduced. There is no evidence to suggest that the redactor of the Pauline epistles was interested in finding or highlighting "pious reasons" for supporting the interests of the clergy, a method which looks suspiciously modern.

The methodological problem in Jewett's work is evident in the one example which he provided: "The proximity of the Pastoral Epistles is particularly palpable in verse 13 (of chapter 9), whose succession of prepositional phrases, genitives, and datives is virtually impossible to translate. The combination of *hupotagē* ('subordination, obedience') and *homologia* ('confession') are unprecedented for Paul, but completely at home in the thought of the Pastorals."[227]

This explanation is beset by two problems: (1) The unwieldy sentences of which Jewett complained are not as obvious in the Pastorals as they are in Colossians and Ephesians, or, for that matter, in Paul's letters themselves. (2) The term *homologia* is not used here in the sense of "confession," but with the legal meaning, "contractual agreement."[228] Thus Jewett's decision to regard the redactor and his theology as close to that of the pastoral epistles merely leads to a mistranslation of the term.

Recent studies in the chronology of Paul's life raise the question of whether, and to what extent, partition theories have implications for problems of chronology. These studies show that the usefulness of such theories depends to a great extent on the attitudes of the authors concerned. Suhl, on the one hand, devoted attention to partition theories, particularly with regard to 2 Corinthians, but Jewett[229] neglected to mention them, and Gerd Lüdemann[230] contended that he could do without them. In his discussion of the resumption of the Jerusalem collection,[231] which he saw reflected particularly in 2 Cor 8—9, Lüdemann sharply rejected Windisch's and Georgi's separation of 2 Cor 8 and 9.[232] Referring to Nils A. Dahl[233] and Niels Hyldahl,[234] Lüdemann tended to favor the unity not only of 2 Cor 8—9 but even of 2 Cor 1—9.

3. Results

As has been shown in the previous sections, the debate on the literary composition of 2 Corinthians passed through a number of phases, concluding with the refinement of Hausrath's thesis by Georgi and Bornkamm. But throughout the debate, the literary unity of the letter continued to be maintained by conservative scholars. This serves as a reminder of the fact that even during its latest phase, the debate has not advanced beyond the hypothetical. Yet the same may be said of defenses of the unity of the epistle, for the unity of 2 Corinthians is also a hypothesis.

As one reads the many contributions to the debate, the complete lack of methodological reflection becomes more and more irritating. Thus from the methodological perspective, the debate has remained largely naive.[235] The contributors go about presenting their theories

226 Ibid., 393–94.

227 Ibid., 394.

228 Bauer's translation, to which Jewett, "The Redaction," 433 n. 1, refers, is wrong. Otto Michel, "ὁμολογέω," *ThWNT* 5 (1954) 201, lines 22–25, refers to the right rendering, but does not assume its presence in 2 Cor 9:13 (pp. 215–16). See also the discussion on the concept in 9:13 below, pp. 122–23.

229 Robert Jewett, *A Chronology of Paul's Life* (Philadelphia: Fortress, 1979).

230 Gerd Lüdemann, *Paulus, der Heidenapostel,* vol. 1: *Studien zur Chronologie* (FRLANT 123; Göttingen: Vandenhoeck & Ruprecht, 1980).

231 Ibid., 119–21.

232 Ibid., 120.

233 Ibid., 120 n. 150.

234 Ibid., 128 n. 165: "Im übrigen ist Hyldahls Aufsatz ein bemerkenswerter Versuch, 2 Kor als Einheit zu verstehen" ("In general, Hyldahl's essay is a remarkable attempt to understand 2 Corinthians as a unity"). On Hyldahl, see below, pp. 32–35.

235 It is remarkable that in the midst of the debates Heinrici, pp. 30–31, felt the need to define what is and what is not a scholarly hypothesis.

either in agreement or in disagreement with their predecessors, or modifying what they had proposed. Proponents of hypotheses of partition and of unity unconsciously employ the same types of arguments, turning them first to one purpose, then to another.

Three kinds of observations seem to underlie whatever proposals are found in these works: (1) breaks in the train of thought, (2) discontinuities in reports of events, (3) sudden changes in the tone of the presentation.

The counterarguments are equally speculative, based on deductions from (1) the underlying structure of Paul's thought, (2) reconstruction of the course of events, (3) Paul's psychological state at the time of composition. None of these arguments operates at the level of the text itself, but on hypothetical constructions lying beneath the text: the train of thought, the plan of the letter, the course of events, and psychology. One of the few scholars to have complained about the lack of methodological reflection in the debate was Anton Halmel.[236] He rightly observed that the debate was, from the beginning, too much determined by Semler, but no one took notice. Halmel was one of the few scholars who engaged in formal arguments pertaining to the text itself; by a meticulous investigation, he showed[237] that the introductory words of 2 Cor 9:1 (περὶ μὲν γὰρ . . .) must be distinguished from the formula περὶ δὲ . . . , so often used by Paul in 1 Corinthians[238] to introduce a new subject. Halmel maintained, against Karl Friedrich August Fritzsche,[239] that περὶ μὲν γὰρ . . . does not connect chapter 9 with chapter 8 in the manner of 1 Corinthians, but that 9:1 introduces a new letter and that the μέν in 9:1 is complemented by the δέ in 9:3.

But investigations of what modern text linguistics calls "Gliederungsmerkmale" (signs of demarcation)[240] remained the exception, and Halmel's methodological complaints went altogether unnoticed.

Windisch illuminated another dimension of the literary problem by referring to the letter-types employed by ancient letter-writers.[241] Windisch had, in fact, called attention to what today is known as genre research, a study belonging to the field of the comparative history of literature. Though Windisch hardly went beyond mentioning the importance of the subject, he correctly assigned chapters 8 and 9 of 2 Corinthians to the genre of business letters ("Geschäftsbriefe"), allowing for Paul's creative variation of the genre.

236 Anton Halmel, *Der zweite Korintherbrief des Apostels Paulus: Geschichtliche und literarkritische Untersuchungen* (Halle: Niemeyer, 1904) 3–4: "In allen Untersuchungen der literarischen und geschichtlichen Fragen des zweiten Korintherbriefes, auch in jenen, welche dessen Einheitlichkeit im engsten Sinne verteidigen, ist zur Zeit das treibende Motiv die Rücksicht auf die cc. 10—13. Die Sachlage ist im wesentlichen ein noch immer fortdauerndes Erbe der Kritik Semlers, die zuerst in diese Bahnen einlenkte und von deren Einfluss sich auch jene nicht losmachen können, die Semlers Kritik ablehnen. Das Phänomen der Schlusskapitel, das sich auch schon der oberflächlichen Betrachtung aufdrängt, und in weiterer Folge die Frage, wie sich diese Kapitel zu den Anfangskapiteln verhalten, gilt hiernach als *das* Problem des zweiten Korintherbriefes, und alle Einheits- und Teilungshypothesen zielen darauf ab" ("At the present time the driving force in all investigations of the literary and historical questions of 2 Corinthians, even in those which defend the unity of the epistle in the narrower sense, is consideration of chapters 10—13. This situation essentially represents the lasting heritage of the critique of Semler. It was this criticism which first paved the way, and not even those who reject his view can free themselves from its influence. The phenomenon of the concluding chapters which is apparent even to the superficial observer, and the question, moreover, of how these chapters are related to the first, must, therefore, be regarded as *the* problem of 2 Corinthians. All hypotheses with respect to unity and division must deal with it"). Halmel's work of 1904 supersedes an earlier one on 2 Cor 10—13: *Der Vierkapitelbrief im zweiten Korintherbrief des Apostels Paulus* (Essen: Baedeker, 1894). For a review, see Johannes Weiss, *ThLZ* 19 (1894) 513–15; cf. Adolf Jülicher, *Einleitung* ($^{5.6}$1906) 84–85.

237 Halmel, pp. 11ff.

238 1 Cor 7:1; 8:1; 12:1; 16:1.

239 Carl Friedrich August Fritzsche, *De nonnullis posterioris Pauli ad Corinthios epistolae locis dissertationes duae* (2 vols.; Leipzig: Reclam, 1824) 2.19–20.

240 See Elisabeth Gülich and Wolfgang Raible, *Linguistische Textmodelle* (Uni-Taschenbuch 130; Munich: Fink, 1977) 54.

241 See above, pp. 16–18; furthermore, Malherbe, "Ancient Epistolary Theorists" (see above, n. 140).

In an earlier study, I have pursued certain implications of Windisch's literary approach.[242] Since epistolography is a subcategory of rhetoric in ancient theory, and since 2 Cor 10—13 seems to conform to the description of an "apology," I concluded that these chapters ought to be treated as an apologetic letter, from the point of view of apologetic rhetoric. An investigation of the arguments used by Paul confirmed his extensive use of conventional rhetorical arguments and *topoi* found especially in the tradition of Socratic rhetoric. Bornkamm[243] advanced the debate a final step by focusing on the redactor of the composition known as 2 Corinthians, attempting to explain why he should have placed an earlier fragment at the end of the final composition.

a. Literary Options

The debate has resulted in the proposal of a number of literary hypotheses on 2 Cor 8 and 9, none of which has thus far been definitively proven or disproven.

1) Partition Theories

With respect to chapters 8 and 9 of 2 Corinthians, Semler's original observation still stands, that 2 Cor 9 may have been a letter by itself.[244] If this hypothesis is accepted, then we must ask whether chapter 8, because of its many parallels, did not also constitute an originally independent letter.

One option would be to assume with Georgi[245] that chapters 8 and 9 are fragments of originally independent letters dealing with the same subject matter, the collection to Jerusalem. This assumption raises the question of how the two letter fragments were originally related to one another. It has been argued that their difference is chronological. J. Weiss,[246] Bornkamm,[247] and Georgi[248] took chapter 8 to be older than 9, while Schmithals[249] and Dinkler[250] reversed the order. How much time passed between the composition of the letters? J. Weiss[251] assumed that chapter 8 was written before the Corinthian crisis, while chapter 9 was written afterward; but Schmithals[252] had it just the other way around. Bornkamm[253] and Georgi[254] took the difference to be not so much in time (according to them, the letters were written almost at the same time) as in the addresses: chapter 8 was sent to Corinth, chapter 9 to the churches of Achaia.

If one chooses not to accept Georgi's hypothesis of two separate letters, one of the chapters can be attached to another fragment. J. Weiss[255] wanted to assign chapter 9 to the letter of reconciliation, but Schmithals[256] and Dinkler[257] gave this place to chapter 8. Dinkler thought that chapter 9 belonged to the letter of tears, but Schenke and Fischer[258] assigned that chapter to their Apology C (2:14—7:4).

If one does not conceive of chapters 8 and 9 as originally independent letters which duplicate the same themes, one can follow Kennedy[259] and leave the chapters together, forming the conclusion of his Third Corinthians (2 Cor 1—9).

2) Theories of Literary Unity

Defenses of the literary unity of 2 Corinthians against theories of partition have been forthcoming from the time of Semler up to the present, and they generally correspond to the phases of the theories. Thus the first phase of the refutation was aimed at Semler himself and at Weber, while the second focused on Hausrath and Schmiedel. More recently, the target has been Schmithals, and subsequently Bornkamm and Georgi.

At each stage in the debate, it was believed that the exponents of partition theories had been dealt the final

242 Betz, *Paulus*.
243 See above, pp. 21–22.
244 See above, pp. 3–4.
245 See above, pp. 20–21.
246 See above, p. 16.
247 See above, pp. 21–22.
248 See above, pp. 20–21.
249 See above, pp. 19–20.
250 See above, p. 19 n. 165.
251 See above, p. 16.
252 See above, p. 20.
253 See above, p. 22.
254 See above, p. 21.
255 See above, p. 16.
256 See above, pp. 19–20.
257 See above, p. 19 n. 165.
258 See above, pp. 23–24.
259 See above, pp. 13–14.

blow. But the conclusion of one phase in the exchange merely served to introduce another, in which the arguments were refined and reformulated. Only recently[260] has it become apparent that the traditional view of the unity of the epistle represents nothing more than another theory in need of positive proof, and that its exponents cannot rely on the naive assumption that unity is the natural state of the letter.

Arguments against partition theories have been a regular part of New Testament introductions and commentaries ever since Heinrich August Wilhelm Meyer, the founder of the Meyer commentary series (KEK).[261] Since Heinrici,[262] these arguments have also included detailed surveys of the history of partition theories and their refutation.

At the close of the debate on Hausrath's theory, Eduard Golla[263] summed up developments in the period before J. Weiss and Windisch in his carefully argued dissertation, written under Roman Catholic scholar Johannes Sickenberger. As Golla saw it, these developments confirmed the theory of the unity of the epistle.

The most thorough critique of Semler's hypothesis came from Johann Philipp Gabler.[264] Gabler was not so much concerned with the dogmatic implications of Semler's work; rather, he intended to examine critically the problems which Semler, whom Gabler greatly admired, had pointed out and the conclusions which he had drawn from his observations.[265] As the title of his work indicates, Gabler did not believe that Semler's insights necessarily implied the disunity of the letter.

In his examination, Gabler concentrated on aspects of the epistle which Semler found problematic, above all on the transitions between the chapters. In section I of his work, Gabler discussed the connection between chapter 9 and the preceding chapters,[266] while in section II he investigated the relationship between chapters 10—13 and the rest of the epistle.[267] Gabler believed he had found a solution to the problems indicated by Semler.[268]

The first major attempt to refute Hausrath's thesis came from Albert Klöpper. Even before the appearance of Hausrath's work, Klöpper[269] had published studies on 2 Corinthians dealing with the issue of the intermediate letter. Taking his departure from Bleek, Klöpper provided substantial reasons for the existence of an "intermediate letter,"[270] which he believed to have been lost, then turned to a discussion of the "Christ party" in Corinth.[271] In his commentary of 1874, Klöpper explicitly defended the unity of 2 Corinthians against Hausrath.[272]

Klöpper recognized and fully exploited the weaknesses of Hausrath's proposal. The presentation of Hausrath's arguments alone sufficed, so he thought, to disprove the thesis. But Klöpper's arguments are equally weak, and he was quick to draw predictable conclusions. The tone of

260 See Hyldahl's hypothesis discussed below, pp. 34–35, and above, p. 22 n. 197.

261 Heinrich August Wilhelm Meyer, *Kritisch-exegetisches Handbuch über den zweiten Brief an die Korinther* (Göttingen: Vandenhoeck & Ruprecht, 1840). This commentary then became part of the KEK under the title, *Der Zweite Brief an die Korinther* (Göttingen: Vandenhoeck & Ruprecht, 1850, 1856, 1862, 1870). The first edition of 1840 argues against Semler, Weber, and Bleek.

262 See below, pp. 29–31.

263 Eduard Golla, *Zwischenreise und Zwischenbrief* (Biblische Studien 20/4; Freiburg: Herder, 1922).

264 Johann Philipp Gabler, *Dissertatio critica de capitibus ultimis IX–XIII posterioris epistolae Pauli ad Corinthios ab eadem haud separandis* (Göttingen: apud Vidvam Abr. Vandenhoek, 1782).

265 See on this point the *Praefatio,* V–XVIII, where also a full description of the various parts of the hypothesis of Semler can be found.

266 Ibid., 1–33.

267 Ibid., 34–98.

268 Agreeing with Gabler are, among others, Ziegler, *Theologische Abhandlungen* 2.107 (against Ziegler argues Weber, *Programm Wittenberg,* part X [1806] 206–25 [see also above, n. 69]); Hermannus Joannes Royaards, *Disputatio inauguralis De altera Pauli ad Corinthios epistola, et observanda in illa apostoli indole et oratione, . . .* (Trajecti ad Rhenum: J. Altheer, 1818) 48ff; Johann Friedrich von Flatt, *Vorlesungen über die beyden Briefe Pauli an die Corinthier* (2 vols.; Tübingen: Fues, 1827) 2.206ff; Christian August Gottfried Emmerling, *Epistola Pauli ad Corinthios posterior graece perpetuo commentario illustravit* (Leipzig: Barth, 1823) XXX–XXXIII.

269 Klöpper, *Exegetisch-kritische Untersuchungen.*

270 Ibid., 1–28.

271 Ibid., 29–127.

272 Klöpper, *Kommentar,* esp. the introduction, 1ff. For a learned defense of the unity of 2 Corinthians, see also Walther Weber, *Wieviele Briefe hat der Apostel Paulus an die Korinther geschrieben?* (Programm des Königlichen Gymnasiums zu Wetzlar; Wetzlar: Schnitzler, 1899).

indignation that pervades his discussion should not be confused with rational argumentation. His own method is clearly, if somewhat innocently, enunciated at the close of the polemic against Hausrath. The simple principle which might have resolved Hausrath's difficulties, and in which Klöpper himself indulged excessively, is this: "bene noscit, qui bene distinguit," "he who distinguishes well, knows well."[273] In other words, the problems earlier scholars had experienced with the unity of 2 Corinthians were at bottom self-deceptions;[274] it had been Hausrath's achievement to systematize the deceit.[275] This sort of apologetic, however embarrassing intellectually, became characteristic of subsequent attempts to defend the unity of 2 Corinthians.

Following Klöpper, the task of defending the unity of 2 Corinthians fell to Heinrich Julius Holtzmann.[276] In this, Holtzmann abandoned his earlier inclination toward partition theories.[277] The usefulness of his work lies in a clear presentation of the "plan of the labyrinth"[278] before grasping the "thread of Ariadne" which, in his view, provides the key to the continuity of the letter.[279] In agreement with Klöpper and Karl Heinrich von Weizsäcker, Holtzmann found the continuity of the epistle in the underlying structure of thought, according to which Paul sought to settle personal matters in the first part of the letter so as to turn to an apology for his apostleship in the latter part. Holtzmann believed one could show that the changes in subject matter and tone so often observed by earlier scholars could all be explained as part of the "comprehensive plan of the letter."[280]

The sharpest critique and the most unqualified rejection of partition theories came from Carl Friedrich Georg Heinrici, in the introduction to his commentary for the KEK series.[281] Previous publications had demonstrated Heinrici's penetrating intellect and his familiarity with ancient literature, so that his doubts represented more than a show of conservatism.[282] His analysis of the arguments, counterarguments, revisions, etc., connected with partition theories remains the best available.[283]

Heinrici's rejection of partition theories was based upon a careful study of the theories themselves. He demonstrated how a suggestive remark in Tertullian[284] gave rise to the first hypothesis, and how, in order to justify this hypothesis, others were soon proposed. The space which was thus created between 1 and 2 Corin-

273 Klöpper, *Kommentar,* 27.

274 Ibid., 15.

275 This kind of argument may best be illustrated by the following quotation (ibid., 28): "Haben nun schon früher Exegeten und Kritiker aus Mangel an Unterscheidungsvermögen Manches in unserem Briefe im unrichtigen und halbwahren Lichte gesehen: so bedurfte es nur der Systematisierung und Steigerung der schon vorhandenen Irrthümer durch eine mit der kelto-gallischen an leichtblütiger Kühnheit rivalisierende Phantasie, um nach der Zerstückelung des Sendschreibens ein Chaos an Selbstwidersprüchen zu hinterlassen, in welchem der letzte Rest von Verständniss unseres Briefes zu Grunde gehen musste" ("Even in earlier times exegetes and critics have seen things in our letter in a light that is false and only half-true, due to deficiencies in their ability to make the right distinctions. All that was needed was the systematization and heightening of the errors already on record, by a fantasy which rivaled the Celto-Gallic in its quick-tempered boldness. Having cut up the letter, what was left behind was a chaos of self-contradictions, in which the last remnants of the understanding of our letter had to collapse").

276 Heinrich Holtzmann, "Das gegenseitige Verhältniss," 455–92.

277 Ibid., 492; cf. 455: "Verfasser wenigstens hat, nachdem er die verschiedensten Wege beschritten, schliesslich nur wieder ein günstiges Vorurtheil für diejenige einfachste Auffassung der vorliegenden Sachlage gewinnen können, welche vor allen Hypothesen dagewesen ist. Ob es mehr als ein Vorurtheil ist, wagt er nicht zu entscheiden" ("This author at least, having explored the various paths, was able in the end to arrive again at a judgment in favor of the simplest view of the matter at hand, a view which existed prior to all hypotheses. Whether it is more than a prejudice, however, he does not venture to decide").

278 Ibid., 455.

279 Ibid., 492.

280 Ibid., 489: ". . . des dem Briefe zu Grunde liegenden Gesammtplanes."

281 Heinrici. The author had published an earlier work on 2 Corinthians: *Das zweite Sendschreiben des Apostels Paulus an die Korinther* (Berlin: Hertz, 1887).

282 The main evidence for this is Heinrici's controversy with Schmiedel (see the preface, IV–VI) and Norden (see above, n. 139).

283 Heinrici, pp. 5–32.

284 Tertullian *De pudicitia* 13–14 (see above, n. 76), who first acknowledged the incongruity between 1 Cor 5 and 2 Cor 2:5–6; 7:5–6. On Tertullian, see Heinrici,

thians was filled with more and more complicated theories, which explained less and less and had the tendency to "get lost more and more in novelistic exercise of fantasy."[285] Methodology was replaced by "calculation of the probable" or psychological speculation. The end of this process had been reached when a group of scholars[286] predictably compromised the enterprise as a whole by declaring the entire Pauline correspondence to be inauthentic.[287]

Heinrici argued that despite the complexity of the hypotheses they remained nothing more than possibilities which could be neither proven nor disproven. Partition theories contributed nothing to the solution of the difficulties, whose existence Heinrici was far from denying, but added new problems to those that were already on hand.

Thus, for largely negative reasons, Heinrici resigned himself to what has ever been the surest position of the historical critic, the *ars nesciendi,* "the art of not knowing." In the face of acknowledged difficulties, it must be the task of the historian "to establish what can be secured, and if the letters, as they are transmitted, provide a basically clear picture of Paul's struggles for the salvation of the souls of his congregation, the authority of his apostolic office, and the integrity of his character, to be restrained with regard to the ambiguities and possibilities of secondary importance."[288]

The attitude of restraint in the face of ignorance enabled Heinrici to maintain the same position through all the editions of his commentary.[289] Despite his rejection of partition theories, however, Heinrici's introductory remarks to chapters 8 and 9 contain valuable observations.[290] Heinrici underscored the peculiar tone and language of these chapters.[291] The exhortations in chapters 8 and 9 are not taken to refer in any way to chapters 10—13, which neither preceded nor followed them.[292] But Heinrici did not conclude from these observations that chapters 8 and 9 were once independent entities.

Chapter 9 is regarded as a supplement to chapter 8 in which Paul offered additional incentive for completing the work already begun by the congregation. In a note to chapter 9, Heinrici again discussed theories of partition as regards chapters 8 and 9. He admits that at first sight the chapters seem to be parallel, even duplicates. "But the first impression is not always correct."

pp. 11ff.

285 Heinrici, p. 26: "Die Hypothesen sind dadurch vermehrt, aber das Dunkel ist nicht gelichtet; ja, bei jedem Versuch, auf Grund der veränderten Combinationen der Quellen die Geschichte zu erzählen, verliert sich die Discussion mehr und mehr in novellenartigen Phantasiestücken" ("The number of hypotheses has been increased, but the darkness has not been illuminated. Indeed, with every attempt to relate the history on the basis of new and different combinations of sources the discussion gets more and more lost in novelistic tales generated by fantasy").

286 For a critique of the theories of Bruno Bauer and the Dutch radical critics, see Heinrici, pp. 28ff.

287 Cf. the result of his assessment, ibid., 30: "Daher werden die hypothetischen Wiederherstellungsversuche immer verwickelter; sie begnügen sich nicht allein mit immer gewagteren psychologischen Hilfslinien, sondern sie zertrennen auch die Einheit der Briefe, bis dann schliesslich der ermüdete Scharfsinn unter dem Eindruck des problematischen Werthes seiner Versuche die Unechtheit der Briefe selbst decretirt" ("Therefore the hypothetical attempts at reconstruction become more and more complicated. They are not satisfied with more and more daring psychological guidelines, but even disrupt the unity of the epistles, until in the end the mind's acuity is blunted under the impact of the questionable value of its own attempts, and even decrees the inauthenticity of the letters themselves").

288 Ibid.: ". . . das Sichere zu ermitteln, und wenn die Briefe, wie sie überliefert sind, in den Grundzügen ein klares Bild der Kämpfe des P. [*sc.* Paulus] um das Seelenheil seiner Gemeinde, um die Autorität seines Apostolats und die Lauterkeit seines Characters ergeben, sich in Bezug auf die Undeutlichkeiten und Möglichkeiten von secundärer Bedeutung zu bescheiden."

289 Heinrici was responsible for KEK 6, ^{6}1883, ^{7}1890, ^{8}1900.

290 Ibid. (^{8}1900) 264–67, 293–95.

291 Ibid., 265.

292 Ibid., 266: "Der Charakter ferner der Ermahnungen schliesst es aus, dass ihnen der 'Viercapitelbrief' . . . entweder vorangegangen oder nachgefolgt sei. Wäre jenes der Fall, so bleibt dann unbegreiflich, wie P. [*sc.* Paulus] nicht auf die dort berücksichtigten Ausbeuter und auf ihre Verläumdungen hier zu sprechen gekommen ist. Wie hätte er dann 8:6 schreiben können? Träfe dieses zu, so würde P. in der Beurtheilung der Lage sich gröblich getäuscht haben. Der Röm (15:27f.) zeigt aber, dass das nicht der Fall war" ("Moreover, the nature of the exhortations excludes the possibility that the 'four-chapter-

He enumerated six issues by which the chapters are related to one another. In every instance, the issues are either correlative, parallel, or supplementary, so that no literary separation is required. He did not seem to recognize that the existence of such relationships could also be used as an argument for the separation of the chapters. In any event, Heinrici's careful analysis will have to be taken into account in any attempt at a further investigation of the chapters.

In 1901, Oskar Herrigel published the notes he had taken from the lectures of his teacher, Carl Holsten, in the summer of 1896.[293] Owing to the fact that the section assigned to 2 Corinthians in Holsten's great work, *Das Evangelium des Paulus*,[294] was never published, Herrigel's notes represent Holsten's last ideas on the subject.[295] It is noteworthy that Holsten devoted less space to Hausrath than to Schmiedel, whose arguments seemed more convincing; even so, Holsten did not accept Schmiedel's views on the partition of the epistle. Like so many defenders of the unity of 2 Corinthians, he assumed that Paul wrote an intermediate letter which is now lost and which cannot be recovered from the existing version of 2 Corinthians.

Theories of partition were also summarily rejected by Hans Lietzmann in his influential commentary.[296] Lietzmann managed to overcome every difficulty by a little psychologizing. The transition between chapters 9 and 10 does not seem very bothersome. "As far as I am concerned, the assumption, for instance, of a sleepless night between chapter 9 and chapter 10 is sufficient as an explanation."[297] The shifts in mood and theme are "psychological" in nature. Paul's letter-writing must not be judged by "the normal yardstick."[298] Not surprisingly, Lietzmann explained the transition between chapters 7 and 8 in the same way, considering the beginning of chapter 8 "very prudently prepared" by the end of chapter 7.[299] A similar psychological explanation serves to bridge chapters 8 and 9.[300]

The first New Testament introduction to appear after World War II was that of Wilhelm Michaelis.[301] In his treatment of 2 Corinthians[302] he agreed with Paul Feine and Johannes Behm[303] in assuming that there had been both an intermediate visit and an intermediate letter, which is not to be identified with chapters 10—13.[304] Michaelis rejected all theories of partition and explained the lack of a transition between chapters 9 and 10 as an "interruption in the dictation of the letter" ("Diktat-pause"), the cure-all of traditionalists.[305] As for the rest, Michaelis was persuaded that the problems are only what one would expect of a letter written in a state of emotional turmoil.[306]

Among recent introductions to the New Testament, Werner Georg Kümmel's[307] revision of the old Feine-Behm has been most consistent in rejecting partition

letter' . . . either preceded or followed them. If the exhortations preceded, it remains inconceivable why Paul did not speak out about the exploiters and their slanderous defamations dealt with there. How could he have written 8:6? Had he done so, Paul would have gravely miscalculated the situation. Rom [15:27f], however, shows that such miscalculations did not occur").

293 Holsten, "Einleitung," 324–69.

294 Idem, *Das Evangelium des Paulus* (2 vols.; Berlin: Reimer, 1880, 1898).

295 Holsten, "Einleitung," 348ff.

296 Hans Lietzmann, *An die Korinther I/II* (HNT 9; Tübingen: Mohr, Siebeck, 1909, ²1921, ³1923, ⁴1949). Cited here is the 4th ed., ed. Werner Georg Kümmel.

297 Ibid., 139: "Mir genügt z.B. die Annahme einer schlaflos durchwachten Nacht zwischen c. 9 and c. 10 zur Erklärung." The statement became famous, if not infamous, and has often been quoted.

298 Ibid. Unavoidably, Georgi, *Gegner*, 18, concludes: "Eine seltsame Psyche! Das wäre doch eher ein Fall für die Psychopathologie" ("A strange psyche! It would rather be a case for psychopathology").

299 Lietzmann, p. 133.

300 Ibid., 137.

301 Wilhelm Michaelis, *Einleitung in das Neue Testament* (Bern: Haller, 1946, ²1954, ³1961 [mit Ergänzungsheft]). Cited here is the 3d ed.

302 Ibid., 176–82.

303 Paul Feine, *Einleitung in das Neue Testament* (rev. Johannes Behm; Leipzig: Quelle & Meyer, ⁸1936).

304 Michaelis, *Einleitung*, 176–79. The "intermediate letter" was, according to Michaelis (p. 178) carried to Corinth by Titus (2 Cor 2:13; 7:5ff).

305 Ibid., 180.

306 Ibid., 191, where he says about 6:14—7:1: "Doch ist solch sprunghafte Gedankenführung nicht unmöglich in einem offenbar rasch und in grosser Erregung geschriebenen Brief" ("Yet, such an erratic line of thought is not impossible in a letter written in an apparent hurry and in a state of great excitement").

307 Paul Feine and Johannes Behm, *Einleitung in das Neue*

theories of 2 Corinthians. Only in the case of 2 Cor 6:14—7:1 did Kümmel seem to waver for a moment, but even here he did not find his doubts strong enough.[308]

Kümmel did assume that Paul made an intermediate visit to Corinth,[309] followed by an intermediate letter which is identical with the letter of tears (2 Cor 2:4) carried to Corinth by Titus.[310] Since 10—13 are not to be separated from 2 Corinthians, these chapters cannot have been part of the intermediate letter which must therefore be considered lost.[311]

In Kümmel's view, there is no compelling reason for partition theories, "since they are all unprovable conjectures,"[312] and no convincing motive for such far-reaching redactional operations can be found.[313] Kümmel generally gave the tradition the benefit of the doubt: "Looking at the whole question, the best assumption is that II Cor as handed down in the tradition forms an originally unified letter."[314] But this simply begs the question of the form in which 2 Corinthians was handed down. Kümmel admitted that problems remain for the unity of the epistle but claimed that they are not serious. In fact, Kümmel had his own theory by which he silences questions: "Paul dictated the letter with interruptions, so the possibility of unevenness is antecedently present."[315] Changes in tone are explained psychologically: Paul was overcome by joy in one place and by concern for the future of the church in another.

Thus also with regard to chapters 8 and 9. "It is the subject matter itself that results in Chs. 8 and 9 having a tone of their own, in contrast to prior and subsequent statements. That Paul canvasses for the collection in tortured arguments and with a certain diffidence is thoroughly understandable in his position with regard to a newly reconciled community."[316] This sort of argument seeks to circumvent the observations of critical scholars by appealing to credulity and preference for the status quo.

The most explicitly programmatic attack on theories of partition with regard to 2 Corinthians has come from Niels Hyldahl, New Testament professor in Copenhagen, in his article entitled "Die Frage nach der literarischen Einheit des Zweiten Korintherbriefes."[317] Its programmatic aim was disclosed in the final sentence of the article when Hyldahl declared, "The time has come that exegesis stops creating its own preconditions and begins to interpret the two letters to the Corinthian churches on their own terms."[318]

Applying this principle to the issue of the literary unity of 2 Corinthians, Hyldahl tried to demonstrate that the problems perceived by scholars were actually the creations of scholarship and not of the text itself. The removal of these problems implies their solution or, better, makes both "problems" and "solutions" unnecessary. According to Hyldahl, the mistakes began with

Testament (12th ed. completely revised by Werner Georg Kümmel; Heidelberg: Quelle & Meyer, 1963) 206–18; ET: Kümmel, *Introduction,* 279–93. Kümmel's position is substantially the same as in the first edition of the work, Paul Feine, *Einleitung,* 37–38.

308 Kümmel, *Introduction,* 287–88, 291–92.

309 Ibid., 282.

310 Ibid., 286.

311 Ibid., 290.

312 Ibid., 291. Cf. Feine, *Einleitung,* 37: "Doch weichen die Lösungsversuche (Drescher, Lisco, Halmel, Völter) so stark von einander ab und beruhen trotz mancher richtigen und scharfsinnigen Beobachtungen zum Teil auf so anfechtbaren und unrichtigen Voraussetzungen, dass sie fast allgemeine Ablehnung erfahren haben" ("Yet, the attempted solutions [Drescher, Lisco, Halmel, Völter] differ so widely from one another and are based, in part, on such dubious and incorrect presuppositions that, despite many excellent and sharp-witted observations, they met with almost total rejection").

313 Kümmel, *Introduction,* 292. Against this argument, see Vielhauer, *Geschichte,* 154–55.

314 Kümmel, *Introduction,* 292. Cf. Feine, *Einleitung,* 38: "Man wird daher am besten tun, den Brief, wie er überliefert ist, zu nehmen."

315 Kümmel, *Introduction,* 292, basically agreeing with Feine, *Einleitung,* 38. Needless to say, this theory is unprovable as well and is not too different from Lietzmann's famous sleepless night (see above, n. 297).

316 Kümmel, *Introduction,* 293.

317 *ZNW* 64 (1973) 289–306.

318 Ibid., 306: "Es ist an der Zeit, dass die Exegese aufhört, sich ihre eigenen Voraussetzungen zu verschaffen, und anfängt, die beiden Briefe an die korinthische Gemeinde von den Bedingungen derselben her auszulegen."

Friedrich Bleek's assumption that the "letter written with many tears" (2:3ff; 7:8ff) could not have been 1 Corinthians, but must have been written between the canonical epistles.[319] Once this had been assumed, it was only natural to look for this letter among the extant writings rather than accepting that it had been lost. Hausrath took the next step by identifying 10—13 with the intermediate letter, or the letter of tears.[320] Once Hausrath's thesis had been accepted, if only in principle, the dismemberment of the rest of the epistle was a matter of course. As Hyldahl saw it, the theories proposed by J. Weiss, Bultmann, Bornkamm, Georgi, and others who are dependent on them, only refine Hausrath's thesis without questioning his basic premise.[321]

According to Hyldahl, a fundamental misunderstanding underlies Bleek's original thesis of an intermediate visit and an intermediate letter. On the basis of 2 Cor 2:l; 12:14; 13:1, Bleek concluded that Paul must have been in Corinth twice prior to the third visit announced in these passages. But the second visit, Bleek thought, took place before the writing of 1 Corinthians.[322] Scholars who followed Bleek soon made the second visit ("Vorbesuch") into an intermediate visit ("Zwischenbesuch"), thus filling the period between the composition of 1 and 2 Corinthians.[323] Since the wrongdoer mentioned in 2 Cor 2:5ff; 7:12 was no longer taken to be the same as the one found in 1 Cor 5:1ff, something else must have happened in the course of the intermediate visit which made Paul so unhappy. Hence an "intermediate incident" ("Zwischenereignis") was invented, an ugly confrontation between Paul and the Corinthian church involving the wrongdoer and resulting in Paul's sudden departure.[324] On the basis of a revised analysis of the letter's content, Hyldahl tried to show that Bleek's original assumption was unnecessary—and that therefore all partition theories are unnecessary. It is important to note that in this discussion Hyldahl began, somewhat cautiously, to make use of literary criteria such as "apology" and "digression."[325]

He showed that in 1:12 (following the prooemium 1:1–11), Paul began a "historical review, apologetic in character, on the relationship between the apostle and the congregation."[326] Such a historical review is nothing new in Paul's letters, but has parallels in 1 Thessalonians, 1 Corinthians, Philippians, and Galatians.[327] Part of this review consists of Paul's attempt to explain why he had altered his original travel plans, and that the changes did not mean that he was unreliable. In 1:23—2:2, Paul spoke of a visit which was planned but did not materialize, and in 2:3–11 of a letter (the tearful letter) which had been written to prevent trouble. In other words, the tearful letter was simply an ersatz for the visit that had not taken place.[328]

Referring to 1 Thessalonians, 1 Corinthians, and Romans, Hyldahl showed that these letters also served as ersatz for visits which either did not occur or, as in the last instance, for a visit which had not yet taken place. The result was that the intermediate visit which Bleek and his followers assumed to have taken place was based on the failure to recognize the nature of the epistles as ersatz compensating for visits planned but not realized.[329]

Hyldahl further concluded from 1:23[330] and 1:19 that, after founding the church, Paul "had since then never visited Corinth again,"[331] but instead of a visit had written the tearful letter which must, therefore, be identical with 1 Corinthians.[332] Turning to 2 Cor 10—13,[333] Hyldahl assumed that these chapters have the same function as the letter of tears: Paul was absent and wrote as if he were present; thus what he wrote is a

319 Ibid., 290. On Bleek, see above, p. 11.
320 Ibid.; on Hausrath, see above, pp. 12–13.
321 Ibid., 290–91. See above, pp. 16–28.
322 Ibid., 291. Bleek was supported in this view by Ferdinand Christian Baur, "Beiträge zur Erklärung der Korintherbriefe," *ThJ* 9 (1850) 139–85, esp. 139–65; idem, *Paulus, der Apostel Jesu Christi* (Stuttgart: Becker & Müller, ²1866) 1.337–38.
323 Hyldahl, "Die Frage," 291.
324 Ibid., 291–92. Hyldahl blames this turn of events mainly on Ewald (see above, n. 78).
325 Ibid., 293ff.
326 Ibid., 293.
327 Ibid., referring to 1 Thess 1:3–10 (prooemium); 2:1–12 (apology); 2:13–16, 17ff (persecution and travel plans); 1 Cor 2:1ff; Phil 4:15; Gal 4:13–14.
328 Ibid., 296–97.
329 Ibid., 297.
330 Ibid., interpreting the *οὐκέτι* in 1:23 as "not any more" instead of "not yet."
331 Ibid., 298.
332 Ibid., 299.
333 Ibid., 300ff.

substitute for the personal visit announced in 12:14; 13:1.[334] The "third visit" mentioned in 12:14; 13:1 was not "the third" in relation to the two which had already taken place, but the third of those which Paul had planned, none of which had actually occurred. What Paul announced in 2 Corinthians was his intention to visit Corinth a third time.[335] 2 Corinthians is a proleptic ersatz for the announced visit. Just as 1:23 refers to 1 Corinthians as the "tearful letter," so 12:14; 13:1–2 refer to 2 Corinthians. For this reason, Hyldahl concluded that chapters 10—13 must have belonged to the same letter as chapters 1—7, and thus that the literary unity of 2 Corinthians is established.[336]

The chapters on the collection (2 Cor 8—9) have, according to Hyldahl, a meaningful place in the letter. After having once mentioned the collection in 1 Cor 16:1ff, "he had sent Titus and perhaps also the brother" as part of the delegation to Corinth (2 Cor 8:6, 18);[337] when Paul and Titus met in Macedonia, what Titus had to report on the situation of the Corinthian church was partly encouraging, partly troubling. Those things which Paul found distressing are dealt with in 2 Cor 10—13.

> In this situation there was obviously only one thing to do: send a letter, which, while fully recognizing the zeal and the obedience of the congregation (2 Cor 7:5–16), serves to maintain the relationship with the congregation through the almost official completion of the collection by Titus, the brother trusted by the church, and another messenger (2 Cor 8:17, 18, 22, 23; cf. 12:18). On the other hand, the letter emphasized the essence of Christianity and its proclamation (2:14—7:4, except 6:14—7:1), and Paul's superiority over the false apostles (especially 11:1—12:10). Thus he forced the congregation to come to terms with itself, to decide whether the members were a church at all, or whether they wanted to risk being dissolved by Paul, just as he once brought them into the world. And this last suggestion was not an empty threat, because now finally Paul was about to arrive.[338]

Hyldahl's article is significant for several reasons.[339] As far as methodology is concerned, he has clearly dispensed with some of the major flaws of earlier attempts to defend the unity of 2 Corinthians: reliance on the tradition as the given state of the text and reliance on psychology to explain changes of tone and subject matter. He recognized that if the literary unity of the letter is to be maintained, it must be proven by evidence. On the positive side, Hyldahl employed arguments drawn from the study of rhetoric and from compositional or form-critical analysis.

Yet we must conclude that Hyldahl cannot be considered to have proven the literary unity of 2 Corinthians. In the first place, he conceded that 2 Cor 6:14—7:1 does not fit into the rest of the epistle and presents a special case.[340] Without entering into a discussion of every aspect of his hypothesis, it can be said that his thesis that the letters were substitutes for personal visits needs to be further analyzed in terms of epistolary *topoi;* Hyldahl never mentioned the existence of such *topoi* and

334 Ibid., 301–2.

335 Ibid., 303: "Die zwei vorigen Male, als Paulus nicht kam, sind 1. die Reise nach dem Plan I (2 Kor 1:15–16), der den Korinthern im ersten paulinischen Brief an sie (siehe 1 Kor 5:9) mitgeteilt worden war und innerhalb des Rahmens von 2 Kor 1—7 ausführlich erwähnt wurde, und 2. die Reise nach dem Plan II (1 Kor 16:5–9), über den die Korinther im 'Tränenbrief' Bescheid erhielten. Während es diese zwei Male zu nichts kam, wird es dies dritte Mal wirklich zu einem Besuch kommen" ("The two previous occasions on which Paul did not come are: (1) the journey of plan I [2 Cor 1:15–16], which was announced to the Corinthians in Paul's first letter to them [see 1 Cor 5:9] and which was discussed extensively in the context of 2 Cor 1—7; (2) the journey of plan II [1 Cor 16:5–9], about which the Corinthians were informed in the 'letter of tears'. While neither of these visits materialized, the third visit will really be carried out").

336 Ibid., 305.

337 Ibid. The problem is ignored here that both chapters 8 and 9 speak of this mission.

338 Ibid., 306.

339 Cf. also the remark by Lüdemann (see above, n. 234).

340 Hyldahl, "Die Frage," 293, 300. Hyldahl does not, however, discuss what this concession means for his hypothesis.

their relation to his theory of the letter as a substitute for personal presence.[341] Aside from his analysis of sections of the historical review, an important contribution which merits further investigation, Hyldahl provided no analysis of other units of the text, so that in the final analysis too much must be believed and too little has been shown. Many good observations made by earlier scholars were completely ignored. As far as chapters 8 and 9 are concerned, the thematic parallels and the problems regarding the delegation to Corinth were passed over without comment. Even if we accept that the sinner of 1 Cor 5:1ff and the "offender" (ἀδικήσας) of 2 Cor 7:12 are one and the same, in view of the critical observations made by earlier scholars, the notion that 1 Corinthians is the letter of tears remains simply too much to swallow. If partition theories are problematic, Hyldahl's theory of literary unity is even more so.

Nils Dahl seems to have been the most recent scholar to defend the unity of 2 Corinthians, supported by the work of his students at Yale Divinity School.[342] Dahl presented a number of arguments which bear consideration. First, he saw a thematic unity in the "joy" mentioned in 2 Cor 7:4, which is further elaborated in 7:15–16 and continued in chapter 8. But thematic connections hardly demonstrate literary unity; they can just as easily be explained as links between successive letters. The same is true of the expressions of confidence scattered throughout the epistles, and references to the wrongdoer. Although Dahl was certainly right in maintaining that the rhetoric of chapters 8 and 9 is deliberative or symbouleutic, this alone does not give literary unity to 2 Corinthians. Theoretically speaking, several fragments of the Corinthian correspondence could be deliberative in nature without belonging to one and the same letter. Finally, as was noted above, the beginning words of chapter 9 (περὶ μὲν γὰρ . . .) can hardly serve as the "transition from the recommendation of Titus and two brothers in 2 Cor 8:16–24 to the resumed treatment of the collection itself in chapter 9."[343] It should be said that Dahl was not in principle opposed to the idea of redactional changes; he acknowledged that "there is indeed a possibility that the document which we read as 2 Corinthians underwent some editorial redaction at an early stage."[344] Thus the question can only be, What sort of evidence can be adduced to demonstrate the extent and the kind of redaction in this letter?

b. Remaining Tasks

The history of research on 2 Cor 8 and 9 inspires little confidence in its results. Semler's initial hypothesis, proposed in 1776, marks a bright moment in the history of New Testament scholarship. Despite two hundred years of scholarly debate, it still awaits confirmation or refutation.

The investigation of the problem at hand attempted in the following chapters will include the following steps: first, a detailed literary analysis of the hypothetical letter fragments (chaps. 2 and 3). This will determine whether 2 Cor 8 and 9 constitute independent, self-contained textual units which can be interpreted in accordance with Greco-Roman rhetoric and epistolography. "Literary analysis" includes analysis of textual components and structures, argumentative techniques and structures, terminology and concepts, and theological presuppositions.

Chapter 4 discusses the question of the genre and

341 It should be a known fact that according to ancient epistolary theory, *all* letters were considered substitutes for personal presence. This does not mean, however, that personal presence becomes dispensable. References to this epistolary doctrine in both 1 and 2 Corinthians are far more complex than Hyldahl seems to assume. See on this Hans Dieter Betz, *Galatians: A Commentary on Paul's Letter to the Churches in Galatia* (ed. Helmut Koester; Hermeneia; Philadelphia: Fortress, 1979) 23ff, with further bibliography.

342 Nils A. Dahl, *Studies in Paul* (Minneapolis: Augsburg, 1977) 38–39.

343 Ibid., 39.

344 Ibid. Dahl assumes the later omission of the names of the two brothers and the interpolation of 2 Cor 6:14—7:1.

literary function of the letters. Finally, chapter 5 attempts to place the letters in the history of the Corinthian correspondence.

Semler's hypothesis can be regarded as proven if our analysis in chapters 2 and 3 yields positive results, if the literary genre and function can be identified (chap. 4), and if the letters thus reconstructed can be made understandable within the context of Paul's dealings with the Corinthian church.

8

Chapter II: 2 Corinthians 8, a Letter to the Church of Corinth

1 We call your attention, brothers, to the
grace of God that has been given in the
churches of Macedonia, 2/ because the
abundance of their joy [occurred] in a
terrible ordeal of distress, and their rock-
bottom poverty overflowed into the
wealth of their generosity. 3/ For [they
acted] according to [their] means, as I
can bear witness, and [even] beyond
their means, on their own initiative
4/ petitioning us in the form of a sincere
request for the favor of partnership in the
charitable gift [destined] for the saints.
5/ Not [only did they do this] as we had
hoped, but they [even] gave themselves,
first to the Lord and [then] to us, through
the will of God.
6/ As a result, we have appointed Titus, for
the purpose that as he had begun [it]
beforehand he should also bring this
charitable collection to completion for
your benefit.
7/ As you have abundance in everything, in
faith and eloquence and knowledge, as
well as in every kind of zeal and in that
love which came from us and dwells in
you, you should have abundance in this
gift of charity, too. 8/ I do not speak [to
you] in terms of a command but as one
who, through the zeal of others, conducts
a test of the genuineness of your love.
9/ For you know the grace of our Lord
Jesus Christ, that because of you, though
he was rich, he became poor, so that
through his poverty you might become
rich.
10/ On this point I am giving you my
advice: This is the expedient [thing to do]
for you who a year ago began [the
collection] ahead [of others] in regard not
only to action but also to determination.
11/ Now then, complete the action, so
that as there was your eager determination there may also be its completion—in
proportion to what you possess. 12/ For
if the willingness is present, [the gift is]
acceptable [when it is] in proportion to
what one possesses, not what one does
not possess.
13/ For the purpose [of the collection] is
not that there [should be] relief for others
and trouble for you, but [it should be] a
matter of equality. 14/ At the present
time your abundance should take care of
their deficiency, in order that their
abundance may take care of your deficiency, too, so that there may be equality. 15/ As it is written: "He who gathered much had not too much, and he who
gathered little had not too little."
16/ Thanks be to God who gave the same

zeal for you into the heart of Titus, 17/ for he has accepted the appointment; [indeed] being [even] more zealous [about it], he is about to depart to you on his own initiative. 18/ But we are sending with him the brother whose praise in the gospel has gone through all the churches. 19/ Not only this, but he was also elected by the churches as our traveling companion in association with this work of charity administered by us for the glory of the Lord [himself] and for our zeal. 20/ Acting in this way we avoid the possibility that someone should complain against us in view of the large sum of money being administered by us. 21/ For we take forethought for the good, not only before the Lord, but also before men.

22/ But we are sending with them our brother [as well] whom we have approved as being efficient in many matters at many times. Now he is more efficient than ever because of his great confidence in you. 23/ On behalf of Titus: my partner representing me, and a fellow worker assigned to you. Our brothers: envoys of the churches, glory of Christ.

24/ Therefore show to them, as to the person of the churches, the evidence of your love and our boast about you.

Literary Analysis of the Letter

a. Conspectus of the Analysis

omitted [I. Epistolary Prescript]
1–24 II. Body of the Letter

1–5 A. Exordium
1a 1. Opening formula: γνωρίζομεν δὲ ὑμῖν, . . . ("we call your attention, . . .")
2. Address: ἀδελφοί ("brothers")
1b–5 3. The example of the Macedonians
a. Description of their situation in general
1) The theological presupposition: the gift of God's grace
2 2) The paradoxical evidence of abundance
a) In terms of joy in distress
b) In terms of generosity in poverty
3–5 b. Their attitude toward the collection for Jerusalem
3 1) Oath
2) Four categories describing their attitude
a) In terms of power: adding up to abundance
(1) κατὰ δύναμιν ("according to their means")
(2) παρὰ δύναμιν ("beyond their means")
b) In terms of initiative: adding up to abundance
(1) αὐθαίρετοι ("on their own initiative")
4 (2) μετὰ πολλῆς παρακλήσεως δεόμενοι ("petitioning in the form of a sincere request")
5 3) Evaluation
a) In terms of expectation: contrary to Paul's own expectation
b) In terms of giving: giving themselves

(1) First, to Christ
(2) Second, to Paul
(3) Formula stating the theological rationale: διὰ θελήματος θεοῦ ("through God's will")

---

6 B. Narratio
6a 1. Conclusion by Paul: εἰς τὸ . . . ("as a result . . .")
2. Action taken by Paul: appointment of Titus
a. Authority for appointment: Paul
b. Name of appointee: Titus
6b c. Term specifying appointment: παρακαλεῖν ("appoint")
d. Assignment

7–8 C. Propositio
7 1. Points of agreement: existing abundance in Corinth
7a a. In general terms: ἐν παντί ("in everything")
7b b. In specific terms, first triad: πίστις, λόγος, γνῶσις ("faith, speech, knowledge")
7c 2. Points of challenge, second triad: σπουδή, ἀγάπη, χάρις ("zeal, love, grace")
3. Challenges specified
a. Regarding σπουδή ("zeal")
b. Regarding ἀγάπη ("love")
7d c. Regarding χάρις ("grace")
8 4. Nature of the challenge
8a a. Negatively: not an order (κατ' ἐπιταγήν)
8b b. Positively: a test (δοκιμάζειν)
1) Administrator: Paul
2) Method: imitation of the zeal of others
3) Goal: evidence of the genuineness of the Corinthians' love

---

9–15 D. Probatio
9 1. First proof: "the honorable" (*honestum*)
9a a. Introductory phrase: γινώσκετε γάρ . . . ("for you know . . .")
b. Statement of the doctrine of grace
1) General concept: ἡ χάρις τοῦ κυρίου ἡμῶν Ἰησοῦ Χριστοῦ ("the grace of our Lord Jesus Christ")
2) Specification
9b a) Christology
9c b) Soteriology
10–12 2. Second proof: "the expedient" (τὸ συμφέρον)
10a a. Type: γνώμη (*sententia*)
10b b. Statement of the principle of expediency
1) Presupposition: It is expedient to complete what one has begun
2) Application: It is expedient for the Corinthians to complete the collection begun a year ago
11 c. Proposal for present action
11a 1) Reference to time: νυνί ("now")
2) Action: completion of ποιεῖν ("doing")
d. Benefit to be gained
11b 1) Part already done: ἡ προθυμία τοῦ θέλειν ("the eagerness of willing")
11c 2) Part still to be done: τὸ ἐπιτελέσαι ἐκ τοῦ ἔχειν ("the completion in proportion to possession")
12 3) Conclusion: compliance with the rule for giving
12a a) Citation of the rule for the acceptability of a gift
12b (1) Positively
12c (2) Negatively
b) Inference
13–15 3. Third proof: "equality" (ἰσότης)
13 a. Statement of the principle of equality
13a 1) Negatively: a situation of inequality

a) Recipients (Jerusalem) alone enjoy relief
b) Donors (Corinth) have all the trouble
13b 2) Positively: equality implies mutuality
14 b. Proposal for present action
14a 1) Reference to time: ἐν τῷ νῦν καιρῷ ("at the present time")
2) Direction of donation required by principle
a) From abundance to deficiency
b) Conclusion: from Corinth to Jerusalem
14b c. Benefit to be gained
1) Direction of donation to be expected in the future
a) From abundance to deficiency
b) Conclusion: from Jerusalem to Corinth
2) Achievement of equality
15 d. Scripture proof
1) Quotation formula
2) Quotation of Exod 16:18 LXX

16–22 E. The commendation of the delegates
16–17 1. The commendation of the leader
16 a. Name: Titus
b. Qualification
1) Competence: σπουδή ("zeal")
2) Nature of Titus's σπουδή ("zeal")
a) Formula of thanksgiving: χάρις τῷ θεῷ ("thanks be to God")
b) Origin: inspiration of the heart (cf. 9:7)
17 3) Evidence
a) Acceptance of the appointment (cf. 9:6)
b) Increased zeal: σπουδαιότερος ("more zealous")
c) Having taken the initiative: αὐθαίρετος ("on his own initiative")
d) Imminent departure: ἐξῆλθεν πρὸς ὑμᾶς ("he is about to depart to you")
18–21 2. The commendation of the second delegate
18 [a. Name: name not given]
b. Qualification
1) Co-option by Paul
a) Inclusion in delegation: συμπέμπειν ("send with him")
b) Relationship to Paul: ἀδελφός ("brother")
19 2) Election by the churches
a) Standing and reputation in the churches
b) Formal election: χειροτονεῖν ("elect")
3) Assignments
a) Title expressing assignment in relation to Paul: συνέκδημος ("traveling companion")
b) Function in relation to the collection in Corinth
c. Reasons for the appointment
20 1) Prevention of future complaints
21 2) Citation of general administrative rule
22 3. The commendation of the third delegate
22a [a. Name: not given]
b. Qualification
1) Co-option by Paul
a) Inclusion in the delegation: συμπέμπειν ("send with him")
b) Relationship to Paul: ἀδελφὸς ἡμῶν ("our brother")
2) Competence: σπουδαῖος ("zealous")
3) Evidence
a) Past experiences: ἐν πολλοῖς πολλάκις ("in many matters at many times")
22b b) Present disposition
(1) Reference to time: νυνί ("now")
(2) Increased zeal: πολὺ σπουδαιότερος ("much more zealous")
(3) Reason: confidence in the Corinthians

23 F. The authorization of the delegates
23a 1. Of Titus
a. Formula of legal authorization
1) ὑπέρ-formula ("on behalf-formula")
2) Name
b. Official relation to Paul: κοινωνὸς ἐμός ("my partner")
c. Official relation to the church of Corinth: εἰς ὑμᾶς συνεργός ("fellow worker assigned to you")
23b 2. Of the two other delegates
a. Reference: ἀδελφοὶ ἡμῶν ("our brothers") (no names!)
b. Official title: ἀπόστολοι ἐκκλησιῶν ("envoys of the churches")
c. Official relation to the church of Corinth: δόξα Χριστοῦ ("glory of Christ")

24 G. Peroratio: appeal in view of the reception of the delegates in Corinth

omitted [H. Epistolary postscript]

b. Commentary

1) 8:1–15: The Advisory Section: The Commendation of the Collection for the Church in Jerusalem

■ 8:1–5: The Exordium (Introduction)

Verses 1–5 may be clearly identified as the introductory section of the letter, or the *exordium.*[1] When this is recognized, and when the purpose of the *exordium,* to gain the attention of the reader,[2] is borne in mind, the question naturally arises how, in this instance, Paul had achieved his goal. He began[3] the *exordium* with a phrase found elsewhere in his letters: "we make known to you, brothers . . ." (γνωρίζομεν δὲ ὑμῖν ἀδελφοί . . .).[4] What follows did not provide new information, but rather served to remind the Corinthians of what one may assume they already knew. The bare facts, at least, cannot have remained unknown to them. But Paul's words suggest that the full implications of the facts, particularly those pertaining to the present letter, had managed to escape them. What the facts imply is an embarrassment to the Corinthians; consequently, they may have been aware of them while hesitating to admit them. The *exordium* puts the cards on the table. Thus Paul's introductory words have a different nuance and shade of meaning from other introductory formulae; their import is: "we are reminding you of the fact that . . . ," or "we are making you aware of the implications. . . ." True to form, the *exordium* contains not only facts and information but a message, an appeal. How is this appeal made?

In the *exordium* to 2 Cor 8, Paul presented what ancient rhetoricians call an *exemplum* ("example"),[5] a genre commonly thought fitting for an *exordium.*[6] His example consists of a vivid description of the praiseworthy activities of the churches in Macedonia, praiseworthy because they have done so much on behalf of the collection for Jerusalem. Rhetorically, therefore, the

1 On the *exordium* generally, see Richard Volkmann, *Die Rhetorik der Griechen in systematischer Übersicht* (Stuttgart: Teubner, ^{2}1885) § 12; Heinrich Lausberg, *Handbuch der literarischen Rhetorik: Eine Grundlegung der Literaturwissenschaft* (2 vols.; Munich: Hueber, 1960, ^{2}1973) 1. §§ 263–88; Josef Martin, *Antike Rhetorik, Technik und Methode* (HKAW 2.3; Munich: Beck, 1974) 60–75; George A. Kennedy, *Classical Rhetoric and Its Christian and Secular Tradition from Ancient to Modern Times* (Chapel Hill: University of North Carolina, 1980) index, *s.v. Prooemium;* Betz, *Galatians,* 40–46.

2 See also on 2 Cor 9:1–2 below.

3 δέ sets the sentence off from the preceding section. Rather than 2 Cor 7, the preceding section must have originally been the epistolary prescript which the editor has omitted.

4 For this epistolary phrase which occurs often at the beginning of sections, see Gal 1:11; 1 Cor 12:3; 15:1. See Betz, *Galatians,* 56.

5 On the example (παράδειγμα, *exemplum*), see Lausberg, *Handbuch* 1, §§ 410–26; Martin, *Rhetorik,* 119ff; Adolf Lumpe, "*Exemplum,*" *RAC* 6 (1966) 1229–57; Marsh H. McCall, *Ancient Rhetorical Theories of Simile and Comparison* (Cambridge: Harvard University, 1969); Bennett J. Price, *Paradeigma and Exemplum in Ancient Rhetorical Theory* (Dissertation, University of California, 1975; Ann Arbor: University Microfilms, 1977).

6 So already Aristotle *Rhet.* 1.9.40, p. 1368a 29–30: τὰ δὲ παραδείγματα τοῖς συμβουλευτικοῖς ("Examples are most suitable for deliberative speakers"). Page, column, and line references for Aristotle are to Bekker's Berlin text (1831).

example is laudatory in character,[7] and thus an *encomium.*[8]

How does the example work? Paul first made some general observations on the paradoxical situation of the Macedonian churches. Like all Christian communities, including that of the Corinthians, the Macedonian churches had been granted the full measure of God's grace. The term introduced here is χάρις ("grace"); it embraces a whole range of meanings, all of which are important for the argument of the letter. In fact, it was part of Paul's strategy to play with the different meanings of the term. "The grace of God" (ἡ χάρις τοῦ θεοῦ) is an expression which virtually achieved the status of a *terminus technicus* in Paul's letters; as such, it describes God's salvation in Christ as a whole.[9] But the attributive participle τὴν δεδομένην ("which was given")[10] reminds us of the ordinary meaning of χάρις as "gift."[11] This aspect of the term brings to mind the enormous importance of gift-giving in the ancient world.[12] Today the giving of gifts is a wholly secular affair. In antiquity, however, the giving of gifts not only was a fundamental form of social conduct, but also had deep roots in religious practice. Among ancient peoples, gift-giving in all its forms was related to ritual sacrifice. Paul made use of such underlying connotations when he connected the grace of God, manifest in Christian salvation, to the gift of money expected of those who have participated in that salvation. This connection was in keeping both with Paul's theology and with religious notions and practices common to all antiquity.[13]

Significantly, Paul spoke first of God's grace as having been given to the churches of Macedonia, not Corinth. This indirect appeal is, of course, part and parcel of the function of the *exemplum.* The conduct of the Macedonian churches was, in effect, set up as a model for the Corinthians to imitate.

As the apostle presented it, the Macedonians had exhibited what in early Christian theology came to be

7 According to Quintilian (5.11.6), Paul's example in 8:15 is of the factual type and carries the force of immediate conviction: ". . . example, that is to say the adducing of some past action real or assumed which may serve to persuade the audience of the truth of the point which we are trying to make" (". . . exemplum, id est rei gestae aut ut gestae utilis ad persuadendum id quod intenderis commemoratio").

8 So correctly Chrysostom *In epist. II. ad Cor. Hom.* 16, *MPG* 61.553B, 4.

9 The variety of meanings of χάρις in 2 Corinthians was rightly pointed out by Johann Jacob Wettstein, Ἡ Καινὴ Διαθήκη *Novum Testamentum graecum,* Tomus II, Continens epistolas Pauli, etc. (Amsterdam: Ex officina Dommeriana, 1752) 2.96. See esp. 2 Cor 8:4, 6, 7, 9, 16, 19; 9:8, 14, 15. For further literature see Betz, *Galatians,* 41 n. 46.

10 The verb δίδωμι ("give") with the preposition ἐν ("in") looks unusual; it may refer to the divine gift as given *in* rather than *to* the churches (cf. phrases like "in the spirit" or "in Christ"). See also 1 Cor 1:4; 2 Cor 1:22; 8:16; Rom 15:5. For discussion, see Bauer, *s.v.* ἐν, I, 6; BDR, § 218 (BDF, § 218).

11 For χάρις as "gift," see 2 Cor 8:4, 6, 7, 19.

12 The social concept of the exchange of gifts is basic to both letters in chapters 8 and 9. For the general significance, see Marcel Mauss, "Essai sur le don; forme et raison de l'échange dans les sociétés archaiques," *Année sociologique* NS 1 (1925) 30–186; ET: *The Gift: Forms and Functions of Exchange in Archaic Societies* (tr. Ian Cunnison; New York: Norton, 1967); Gerardus van der Leeuw, "Die do-ut-des-Formel in der Opfertheorie," *ARW* 20 (1920) 241–53; René Maunier, "Recherches sur les échanges rituels en Afrique du Nord," *Année sociologique* NS 2 (1927) 11–97: Hendrik Bolkestein, *Wohltätigkeit und Armenpflege im vorchristlichen Altertum* (Utrecht: Oosthoek, 1939); Albrecht Dihle, *Die Goldene Regel: Eine Einführung in die Geschichte der antiken und frühchristlichen Vulgärethik* (Göttingen: Vandenhoeck & Ruprecht, 1962); idem, "Goldene Regel," *RAC* 11 (1981) 930–40 (lit.); Alfred Stuiber, "Geschenk," *RAC* 10 (1978) 685–703 (bibliog.). For modern sociological studies of exchange theory, see George C. Homans, *Social Behavior: Its Elementary Forms* (New York: Harcourt, Brace & World, 1961); Peter M. Blau, *Exchange and Power in Social Life* (New York: Wiley, 1964).

13 In 2 Cor 8 and 9, the word-field of terms denoting gifts is wide and diverse. The overarching term is certainly χάρις (see n. 9, above). Others are: δωρεά, "gift" (9:15), εὐλογία, "gift of blessing" (9:5,6), together with δίδωμι, "give" (8:5, 10, 16; 9:9); δότης, "giver" (9:7); ἁπλότης, "gracious giving" (8:2; 9:11, 13); χορηγέω and ἐπιχορηγέω, "provide" (9:10). More technical are the terms: διακονία, "service" (8:4; 9:1, 12, 13); διακονέω, "serve" (8:19, 20); κοινωνία, "partnership" (8:4; 9:13); λειτουργία, "public service" (9:12).

regarded as paradigmatic of Christian experience: the paradox of joy in the face of tribulation.[14] As Paul described it, "the abundance of their joy" (ἡ περισσεία τῆς χαρᾶς αὐτῶν) overflowed amidst "a terrible ordeal of affliction" (ἐν πολλῇ δοκιμῇ θλίψεως), the abundance[15] of their joy being contrasted with the severity of their afflictions. Other New Testament texts join in regarding this paradox as characteristic of the Christian experience. Paul referred to it in the first apology, in 2 Cor 4:7–18, and in the four-chapter letter, in 11:23, as a part of the catalogue of sufferings;[16] his sufferings are to be juxtaposed with the abundance of his boasting (10:8; cf. 12:9, 10; 13:9) and love (12:15). But it is the letter of reconciliation which takes the notion of joy in tribulation as its leading theme (see 1:3–7, 8–11, 12 [15 *v.l.*], 24; 2:3, 4, 7; 7:4, 7, 9, 13–16). Apart from Paul, the theme is found in early traditions in the Synoptic Gospels,[17] in particular in the Sermon on the Mount (Matt 5:12). In fact, the theme has its roots in Judaism.[18]

The apostle did not specify in what the affliction (θλῖψις) consisted. The term is used here in a general sense, a more specific meaning being supplied in v 2b. Both the Macedonians and the Corinthians were familiar with the general sense of the term. The letters to the Thessalonians[19] and the Corinthians[20] provide clear evidence of experiences of distress. That such sufferings were to be regarded as a kind of test (δοκιμή) was part of the doctrine of the nature and purpose of suffering. This doctrine was espoused not only by Paul,[21] but by early Christianity[22] and Judaism in general.[23] Moreover, the term δοκιμή points more to the positive outcome of such a test than to the test itself (which would be πειρασμός, "temptation").[24] Therefore Paul referred not only to the persecutions mentioned in 1 Thess 2:14,[25] but also to the early Christian theme of joy in affliction, of which theme 1 Thess 2:14 and other passages provide concrete examples.[26]

Whatever the affliction of the Macedonians may have been, their "abysmal poverty" (ἡ κατὰ βάθους πτωχεία) was a part of it. Ancient sources indicate that poverty was a way of life in Macedonia generally[27] and not only a result of their conversion to Christianity. Indeed, there must have been severe economic hardship in that part of the country, for Paul saw fit to mention it again in the central passage, 8:9.

In the context of Christian experience, however, the

14 Cf. the interpretation of Chrysostom, who stresses the miraculous nature of the experience, *In epist. II. ad Cor. Hom.* 16, *MPG* 61.554B: Διὸ καὶ πολὺ τὸ παράδοξον ἦν, ὅτι τοσαύτη ἡδονῆς περιουσία ἀπὸ θλίψεως αὐτοῖς ἐβλάστησεν. He refers as parallels to 1 Thess 1:6, 8; 2:14.

15 The word-field of terms describing abundance is also rich in 2 Cor 8 and 9: περισσεία and περίσσευμα, "abundance" (8:2, 14); περισσεύω, "have abundance" (8:2, 7; 9:8); περισσός, "abundant" (9:1); πλοῦτος, "wealth" (8:2); πλούσιος, "wealthy" (8:9); πλουτέω, "be wealthy" (8:9); πλουτίζω, "make wealthy" (9:11). All of these terms refer to general experiences of the Corinthians; cf. 1 Cor 1:5; 4:8; 8:8; 14:12; 15:58. On the whole subject, see the important dissertation by Michael Theobald, *Die überströmende Gnade: Studien zu einem paulinischen Motivfeld* (Bonn: Rheinische Friedrich-Wilhelms-Universität, 1980) esp. 301–34 on 2 Cor 8—9.

16 See also Rom 12:15; 1 Cor 7:30; 2 Cor 6:10. On the topic, see Hans Conzelmann, "χαίρω κτλ.," *TDNT* 9 (1974) 369–70 (D.3).

17 See, e.g., Luke 10:17–20; 15:5–7, 32, and for further references, ibid., 367–68 (D.2).

18 For references, see ibid., 368 n. 78.

19 See 1 Thess 1:6; 3:3, 4, 7. The first commentary on these passages is in 2 Thess 1:4–10.

20 The Corinthians seem to know of it through Paul's experiences rather than their own. See 1 Cor 7:28; the first apology 2 Cor 4:8, 17; 6:4; 7:4; the letter of reconciliation 1:4, 6, 8; 2:4; 7:5. Cf. Phil 1:17; 4:14.

21 See 1 Thess 2:4; Phil 2:22; Rom 5:4; etc.

22 See Matt 5:10–12; Jas 1:3, 12–15; 1 Pet 1:6–7. On the topic, see Leonhard Goppelt, *Der erste Petrusbrief* (KEK 12/1; Göttingen: Vandenhoeck & Ruprecht, 1978) 101–2; Norbert Brox, *Der erste Petrusbrief* (EKK 21; Neukirchen-Vluyn: Neukirchener, 1979) 59ff.

23 See Wolfgang Nauck, "Freude im Leiden. Zum Problem einer urchristlichen Verfolgungstradition," *ZNW* 46 (1955) 68–80; Lothar Ruppert, *Der leidende Gerechte und seine Feinde* (Würzburg: Echter, 1973); Theofried Baumeister, *Die Anfänge der Theologie des Martyriums* (Münsterische Beiträge zur Theologie 45; Münster: Aschendorff, 1980).

24 So also Chrysostom *In epist. II. ad Cor. Hom.* 16, *MPG* 61.554B.

25 See nn. 19 and 20, above.

26 Cf. Windisch, p. 244, who thinks that Paul speaks of the affliction mentioned in 2 Cor 7:4. But the distinction between the general doctrine and specific instances should be kept in mind.

27 See the excursus below on "Macedonia, Achaia, and Corinth."

misery of poverty had been transformed miraculously into something positive. This miracle, as we have explained, is basic to Christian experience. However remarkable it may seem, it is not based primarily on an interpretation of the crucifixion and resurrection of Jesus. In this, 2 Corinthians agrees with early traditions, like those found in the Sermon on the Mount. In these texts, the revaluation of poverty is accomplished in Jewish terms, so the whole theme must go back to Jewish Christian theology.[28] This notion is expressed most succinctly in the first Beatitude of the Sermon on the Mount (Matt 5:3):

> Blessed are the "poor in spirit,"
> for theirs is the kingdom of the heavens.
>
> *Μακάριοι οἱ πτωχοὶ τῷ πνεύματι,*
> *ὅτι αὐτῶν ἐστιν ἡ βασιλεία τῶν οὐρανῶν.*

In the view of the author of the Sermon on the Mount, the "poverty" of which the first Beatitude speaks (Luke 6:20, "Blessed are the poor . . .") had become "spiritual poverty," a virtue identical with humility, the source of spiritual wealth.[29]

Paul interpreted this teaching in 2 Cor 8 along different lines. His expression of it takes the form of an oxymoron: "their abysmal poverty has overflowed into the wealth of their liberality"[30] (*ἡ κατὰ βάθους πτωχεία αὐτῶν ἐπερίσσευσεν εἰς τὸ πλοῦτος τῆς ἁπλότητος αὐτῶν*). His statement circumscribes the miraculous change, without attempting to explain it.[31] This does not imply that Paul had no idea how the change had come about. Rather, what Paul left unsaid here emerges gradually in the course of the argument of 2 Cor 8, and 9 as well; in 2 Cor 8:2, it is present only at the level of presupposition.

An indication of the direction of Paul's thought appears in the term *ἁπλότης*, found here and in 9:11, 13.[32] The term is difficult to translate because it bears a range of meanings which are expressed in English by several different terms. In 2 Cor 8:2, the term is used to describe the Macedonians as people of "simplicity, sincerity, uprightness, frankness,"[33] as well as "generosity and liberality."[34] Together[35] these terms express the ancient ideal of the simple life.[36] According to this cultural ideal, people who live the simple life can be expected to show generosity in their giving and in their

28 See also Luke 6:20; Matt 11:2–6//Luke 7:18–23; Luke 4:18; Mark 12:41–44 par.; Jas 2:2ff; Rev. 2:9; 3:17; 13:16.

29 For the interpretation, see Hans Dieter Betz, "*Die Makarismen der Bergpredigt* (Matthäus 5,3–12). Beobachtungen zur literarischen Form und theologischen Bedeutung," *ZThK* 75 (1978) 3–19; ET: in Hans Dieter Betz, *Essays on the Sermon on the Mount* (Philadelphia: Fortress, 1985) 17–36. Chrysostom *In epist. II. ad Cor. Hom.* 16, *MPG* 61.554C observes the parallelism between *θλῖψις/χαρά* and *πενία/πλοῦτος ἐλεημοσύνης*. On the whole topic, see Ernst Bammel and Friedrich Hauck, "*πτωχός κτλ.*," *TDNT* 6 (1968) 885–915.

30 So Bauer, *s.v.* *περισσεύω*, 1.γ.

31 The phrase *κατὰ βάθους* in connection with poverty is proverbial and describes extreme conditions of "rock-bottom poverty" (Barrett, p. 219). For parallels to the expression, see Georg David Kypke, *Observationes sacrae in Novi Foederis Libros ex auctoribus potissimum Graecis et antiquitatibus* (2 vols; Wratislaviae: Ioh. Iacobi Kornii, 1755) 2.256; Wettstein 2.196; Bauer, *s.v.* *βάθος*, 2. Chrysostom *In epist. II. ad Cor. Hom.* 16, *MPG* 61.554C interprets as "in the extreme" (*μεθ' ὑπερβολῆς*).

32 See also 2 Cor 11:3; Rom 12:8; Col 3:22; Eph 6:5. The notion is important for Jewish Christianity; see Matt 6:22//Luke 11:34; Jas 1:5. For discussion, see Hans Dieter Betz, "Matthew vi. 22f and Ancient Greek Theories of Vision," *Text and Interpretation: Studies in the New Testament Presented to Matthew Black* (Cambridge: Cambridge University, 1979) 43–56; rep. in Betz, *Essays,* 71–87.

33 So Bauer, *s.v.* *ἁπλότης*, 1. See also Joseph Amstutz, ΑΠΛΟΤΗΣ: *Eine begriffsgeschichtliche Studie zum jüdisch-christlichen Griechisch* (Bonn: P. Hanstein, 1968).

34 So Bauer, *s.v.* *ἁπλότης*, 2; see also *s.v.* *ἁπλοῦς*, *ἁπλῶς* with many parallels; *PGL*, *s.v.*

35 As Bauer, *s.v.* *ἁπλότης*, 2, has pointed out, the meaning of "generosity" and "liberality" is disputed. But it can hardly be denied to exist. See *T. Issachar* entitled *Περὶ ἁπλότητος*, which defines the notion in 4:2: *ὁ ἁπλοῦς χρυσίον οὐκ ἐπιθυμεῖ, τὸν πλησίον οὐ πλεονεκτεῖ* ("The generous man does not crave for gold, he does not take advantage of his fellow man"). See also G. Mussies, *Dio Chrysostom and the New Testament* (SCHNT 2; Leiden: Brill, 1972) 177, referring to Dio Chrysostom 7.82; Pieter W. van der Horst, *The Sentences of Pseudo-Phocylides* (Studia in Veteris Testament Pseudepigrapha 4; Leiden: Brill, 1978) no. 50 and pp. 148–49; *PECL I,* 80, 81, 259; *II,* 505–6.

36 Frederick W. Danker, *Benefactor: Epigraphic Study of a*

hospitality.[37] Not that such people are naturally generous! Literary examples show that simple people may be fools[38] and even misanthropes, like the character whom Lucian described in his *Timon or the Misanthrope.*[39] But in many other instances in Greek and Latin literature, the popular ideal of the generosity of the simple folk is to be found.

These literary examples may, in turn, draw on folk tales which come from a variety of sources. The greatest of such tales is that of Philemon and Baucis in Ovid's *Metamorphoses* 8. 616–724,[40] but Callimachus's *Hecale*[41] also deserves to be mentioned.[42] The Bible itself, in both the Old Testament and the New,[43] bears witness to the popularity of these tales. Paul's language suggests that the Macedonians conformed to this cultural ideal when they demonstrated generosity in their situation of utter poverty. How were they able to do so? The answer is that they had been enabled by the gift of God's grace. In the view of the ancients, the generosity of the simple folk was always a response to divine grace. In Paul's theology, this general notion is specified: the divine gift is defined as salvation in Christ.

Verse 3 explains the matter further by means of a series of expressions designed to characterize the attitude of the Macedonians. They voluntarily contributed to the collection in a way that seemed incompatible with their poverty. The terminology Paul employed in this connection comes from the area of administration, in particular financial administration: they gave *κατὰ δύναμιν* ("according to ability"),[44] and even—as Paul emphasized through an oath (*μαρτυρῶ*, "I am the witness")—*παρὰ δύναμιν* ("beyond ability").[45] The term *αὐθαίρετος* ("of one's own accord") has an almost technical connotation in this

Graeco-Roman and New Testament Semantic Field (St. Louis: Clayton, 1982) 323–36. For this cultural ideal, see Heinrich Bacht, "Einfalt," *RAC* 4 (1959) 821–40; Rüdiger Vischer, *Das einfache Leben: Wort- und motivgeschichtliche Untersuchungen zu einem Wertbegriff der antiken Literatur* (Göttingen: Vandenhoeck & Ruprecht, 1965).

37 See esp. *Herm. Man.* 2.4–7, where the term *ἁπλότης*, etc., occurs several times. *Did.* 1.5–6; Matt 5:42; 7:7–11 seem to describe the same attitude without using the terminology. See also Rudolf Knopf, *Die Lehre der zwölf Apostel* (HNT, Ergänzungsband 1; Tübingen: Mohr, Siebeck, 1920) 9–10; Helmut Koester, *Synoptische Überlieferung bei den Apostolischen Vätern* (TU 65; Berlin: Akademie-Verlag, 1957) 230–36.

38 This is suggested in 2 Cor 8:13. Aristophanes' *Plutus* has been a most influential work on the subject. See Victor Ehrenberg, *The People of Aristophanes: A Sociology of the Old Attic Comedy* (Oxford: Blackwell, 1951) 219–52. Cf. also Prov 19:6: "Many seek the favor of a generous man, and every one is a friend to a man who gives gifts." Lucian, unsurprisingly, regards such generosity, which he observed in the Christians, as sheer stupidity (*Peregr.* 11ff; see Hans Dieter Betz, *Lukian von Samosata und das Neue Testament* [TU 76; Berlin: Akademie-Verlag, 1961] 9–11).

39 See on this work Franz Bertram, "Die Timonlegende" (Dissertation, Heidelberg, 1906).

40 See the commentary by Franz Bömer, *P. Ovidius Naso, Metamorphosen Buch VIII–IX* (Heidelberg: Winter, 1977) 190–232.

41 See the LCL edition of Callimachus's *Fragments,* tr. C. A. Trypanis, pp. 175–225.

42 The story is also told by Plutarch *Thes.* 14.

43 See Gen 18:1ff; 19:1ff; 1 Kgs 17:8ff; Luke 24:13ff; Acts 14:11–12. See furthermore *Did.* 11.3–12; *Herm. Man.* 11.

44 So Bauer, *s.v.* *δύναμις*, 2. LSJ, *s.v.* *δύναμις*, III.2, points out that the term can simply mean "worth or value of money." This meaning becomes stereotyped in the papyrus documents from Egypt, where, in marriage contracts in particular, *κατὰ δύναμιν* often means "in accordance with one's financial capability." For evidence, see James H. Moulton and George Milligan, *The Vocabulary of the Greek New Testament Illustrated from the Papyri and Other Non-Literary Sources* (London: Hodder, 1930) *s.v.;* Friedrich Preisigke, *Wörterbuch der griechischen Papyrusurkunden mit Einschluss der griechischen Inschriften, Aufschriften, Ostraka, Mumienschilder usw. aus Ägypten* (vols. 1–3, 1924–31; vol. 4/1–4 rev. Emil Kiessling; Supplement 1.1–3: 1969–71; Berlin and Marburg: Selbstverlag, 1924–71) 1, *s.v.* *δύναμις*, l; 4/4, *s.v.* *δύναμις*, 1. This special meaning fits 2 Cor 8:3 better than the more general one, which is of course common in the Greek language (since Herodotus 1.207; 3.142; 7.209). See also Wettstein 2.196.

45 So Bauer, *s.v.* *δύναμις*, 2. The expression is also technical (see n. 44, above). A good parallel occurs in the London Papyrus no. 196, lines 22–25 (the text is a letter of recommendation on behalf of a man in need, dated in the fourth century A.D.): Εἴ *τι καὶ εὑρήκαμεν παρεδώκαμεν αὐτῷ, ἀλλὰ καὶ ὑπὲρ τὴν*

context.[46] What the Macedonians undertook concretely is then reported in v 4, where the language is again of a technical nature, with close parallels in the papyri: *μετὰ πολλῆς παρακλήσεως* denotes the process of making a request ("in the form of an earnest request").[47] In this request the Macedonians "asked us for favor and partnership in the service to the saints."[48] The phrase "asked for favor" (*δεόμενοι τὴν χάριν*)[49] uses *χάρις* in the secular sense, as is common in administrative documents.[50] The favor sought is "partnership" (*κοινωνία*) in the collection for the church at Jerusalem. This term is also drawn from the language of administration and law. It is used in this sense elsewhere in Paul, and the legal meaning should not be ignored in favor of the personal or communal notion of fellowship.[51] The objective of their partnership is described by what seems to have been its official name: *ἡ διακονία τῆς εἰς τοὺς ἁγίους* ("the contribution meant for the saints").[52] The term *διακονία* has a Christian ring, but it remains in this context primarily an administrative term.[53]

Verse 5 constitutes the climax of the *exordium*. Beyond what Paul had hoped, the Macedonians had given

---

δύναμιν ἡμῶν ἐποιήσαμεν ("Whatever we could find we have given him; yea, we have done even beyond our means"). Citation is according to H. Idris Bell, *Jews and Christians in Egypt: The Jewish Troubles in Alexandria and the Athanasian Controversy* [London: British Museum, 1924] 76–80).

46 So Bauer's translation, *s.v.* The same term occurs in 2 Cor 8:17, but nowhere else in the New Testament (the adverb is found in Ign. *Mag.* 5.2). LSJ gives as the basic meaning "self-chosen," "self-elected," or, more general, "by free choice," "independent." The meaning can also be more specific, like "undertaking a duty at one's own expense" (see LSJ, *s.v.*). In the documentary papyri, the adverb appears often as a common formula together with *ἑκουσίως* ("voluntarily"). See for references Moulton and Milligan, *s.v.;* Preisigke, *Wörterbuch* 1, *s.v.;* 4/2, *s.v.;* Sup. 1, *s.v.;* furthermore, Wettstein 2.196–97; Friedrich Preisigke, *Fachwörter des öffentlichen Verwaltungsdienstes Ägyptens in den griechischen Papyrusurkunden der ptolemäisch-römischen Zeit* (Göttingen: Vandenhoeck & Ruprecht, 1915) *s.v.;* Paul M. Meyer, *Juristische Papyri: Erklärung von Urkunden zur Einführung in die juristische Papyruskunde* (Berlin: Weidmann, 1920) nos. 52,9; 93,36; Dittenberger, *OGIS* no. 583, lines 8 and 14. Cf. also the Latin terminology in Cicero's letters which seems to be parallel to the Greek, e.g., "libenter" ("readily"), *Ep. Fam.* 13.1.2; 1.6; and often; "peto in maiorem modum" ("I beg with greater earnestness"), 13.2; "cum multi a me petant multa" ("though many ask me for many things"), 13.5.1.

47 Bauer, *s.v.* *παράκλησις*, 2, translates "beg earnestly" and seems to miss the official, legal meaning which occurs only here in the New Testament (cf. 8:17); similarly Johannes Thomas, *EWNT* 3, *s.v.* See also LSJ, *s.v.* *παράκλησις* I, 4, and for more references, Bauer, *s.v.;* Moulton and Milligan, *s.v.;* Preisigke, *Wörterbuch* 1, *s.v.;* idem, *Fachwörter, s.v.*

48 The construction is a hendiadys, one idea expressed by two conjoined terms. See on this point Heinrici, p. 271; Plummer, pp. 235–36; Windisch, p. 246, who refers to Plutarch *Numa* 4.3 as a parallel.

49 The unusual construction of *δέομαι* has often been discussed (see Windisch, p. 246). The term itself is technical in official petitions, for which see Moulton and Milligan, *s.v.;* Preisigke, *Wörterbuch* 1, *s.v.* 3; 4/3, *s.v.* 3. Common are the pairs *παρακαλέω καὶ δέομαι*, *παράκλησις καὶ δέησις*. See also Terence Y. Mullins, "Petition as a Literary Form," *NT* (1962) 46–54.

50 Cf. Acts 25:3 and Bauer *s.v.* *χάρις*, 3; Heinrici, p. 271; Windisch, p. 246. The term is frequent in the papyri, for which see Moulton and Milligan, *s.v.;* Preisigke, *Wörterbuch* 1, *s.v.* 2.

51 See esp. Gal 2:9; Phil 1:5; 4:14–15; 2 Cor 9:13; Rom 15:26. Unclear are Bauer, *s.v.* 1; 4; Windisch, p. 246; Josef Hainz, "*κοινωνία*," *EWNT* 2 (1981) 749–55; correct is Friedrich Hauck, "*κοινωνός κτλ*," *TDNT* 3 (1965) 809 (D.2). For the technical meaning, see also LSJ, *s.v.;* Moulton and Milligan, *s.v.;* Preisigke, *Wörterbuch* 1, *s.v.;* Sup. *s.v.;* J. M. McDermott, "The Biblical Doctrine of KOINΩNIA," *BZ* 19 (1975) 64–77, 219–33.

52 See Bauer, *s.v.* 4. Cf. the usage in this sense in 1 Cor 16:15; 2 Cor 9:1; 12:13; Rom 15:31. See Georgi, *Kollekte,* 59–60.

53 Bauer rightly refers to Acts 6:1 (cf. 11:29; 12:25); *Acts of Thomas* 59; from the secular literature to Arrianus *Peripl.* 3.1. Secular usage is also found in Aeschines *Contra Ctesiph.* 3.13: *ὅσα τις αἱρετὸς ὢν πράττει κατὰ ψήφισμα, οὐκ ἔστι ταῦτα ἀρχή, ἀλλ' ἐπιμέλειά τις καὶ διακονία* ("Whatever a man is called on to do under special enactment, this is not an 'office,' but a sort of 'commission' and 'public service'"). Citation is according to Charles Darwin Adams, *The Speeches of Aeschines,* LCL.

themselves—as a living sacrifice. The construction of the sentence seems elliptical: "not as we had hoped" (οὐ καθὼς ἠλπίσαμεν) lacks its sequel and must be supplemented by the expression "they contributed."[54] In fact, given the poverty of the Macedonians, Paul could hardly have hoped for substantial financial assistance from them, but he had expected to receive some.[55] To his surprise, their gifts exceeded every reasonable expectation.[56]

How did this miracle come about? As extraordinary as it may seem, the action taken by the Macedonians was entirely commensurate with standards of ancient religion: having received the gift of divine grace, the greatest gift that could be bestowed on human beings, they had given themselves to God in return as a living sacrifice.

At this point, Paul introduced a concept which was not only basic to his own theology but to ancient religion in general. In Paul's theology, God's gift of grace (χάρις) involves Christ's self-sacrifice[57] as well as God's sacrifice of his own son.[58] While 8:9 contains no more than an implicit reference to Christ's sacrifice, it is certainly presupposed in v 5, though not explicitly stated.[59] It is understood that the only proper response to God's grace and sacrifice is the complete dedication of oneself to God. The idea that the Christian life is, in its entirety, a self-sacrifice to God is stated programmatically at the beginning of the paraenetic section of Rom in 12:1–2.[60] What is made explicit there is implicit in 2 Cor 8:9, and elsewhere in Paul.[61]

Interestingly, these theological concepts build on notions of sacrifice commonly held in antiquity. The sacrificial cult, so widely practiced in the ancient world, was regarded as a symbolic substitute for human self-dedication;[62] as such, it was the only proper response to the beneficence of the deity.[63]

It is at this point in the letter that the theological substructure appears for the first time. This substructure has a number of aspects: (1) the connection between the

54 Cf. the discussion in Heinrici, p. 271; Plummer, p. 236; Windisch, p. 247, who suggests that Paul had on his mind 2 Cor 12:14 with its contrast of τὰ ὑμῶν ("your property") and ὑμῶν ("yourselves").

55 Cf. the similar theological statements in the letter of reconciliation 2 Cor 1:8–11, where Paul admits he had given up hope altogether, but then to his surprise, God had saved him and his party from death. See also Phil 1:20; Rom 5:5; 12:12; 15:4. On the other hand, it should be noted that expressions like "beyond belief" are often merely epistolary clichés (see, e.g., Cicero *Ep. Fam.* 13.6.3 and often, using *incredibilis* and *incredibile).*

56 It should also be pointed out that references to self-sacrifice occur often in letters and are simply a *topos.* See Acts 15:26; Rom 16:4; 1 Thess 2:8; 1 Pet 4:19; 1 John 3:16. For further evidence, see Gustav Karlsson, *Idéologie et cérémonial dans l'épistolographie byzantine* (Acta Universitatis Upsaliensis: Studia Graeca 3; Uppsala: Almqvist & Wiksell, ²1962) 129. On self-sacrifice, see H. S. Versnel, "Self-Sacrifice, Compensation and the Anonymous Gods," *Le Sacrifice dans l'Antiquité* (Entretiens sur l'Antiquité Classique 27; Vandoeuvres-Genève: Fondation Hardt, 1981) 135–85.

57 See Gal 1:4; 2:20: 3:13; cf. Eph 5:2, and on the subject matter, Betz, *Galatians,* 41–42, 125–26, 149ff.

58 See also Rom 8:3, 32.

59 This has been suggested by Windisch, p. 247.

60 See also the use of παρίστημι ("present," "offer"), in Rom 6:13, 16, 19. See Ernst Käsemann, *Commentary on Romans* (Grand Rapids: Eerdmans, 1980) 183–84, 325ff (bibliog.).

61 Cf. also Phil 2:17; 4:18; 1 Cor 4:13. Chrysostom, *In epist. II. ad Cor. Hom.* 16, *MPG* 61.555C, comments on the passage by using the language of votive offerings. See also Wettstein 2.197.

62 There are affinities to be noted at this point between the self-dedication of the Macedonians told by Paul and their portrait in the Book of Acts (16:9—17:15; 18:5; 19:21–22, 29; 20:1–4; 27:2). In both the letter and Acts, they serve as *exempla,* showing the literary relationship between epistolography and historiography. In turn, both are also related to the inscriptions on monuments, on which see Helmut Häusle, *Das Denkmal als Garant des Nachruhms: Eine Studie zu einem Motiv in lateinischen Inschriften* (Zetemata 75; Munich: Beck, 1980); Danker, *Benefactor,* 321–23, 349–51. Moreover, Paul's own self-dedication should be mentioned; it is part of his portrait in Acts (20:22–24; 21:10–14) and the Pauline pseudepigrapha (Col 1:24–29; Eph 3:1–13; 2 Thess 3:2; 1 Tim 1:12–17; 2 Tim 1:7–14). For parallels to self-dedication, see also Wettstein 2.197; Kypke, *Observationes sacrae* 2.257–58.

63 For recent discussion and bibliography about the rituals of sacrifice, see F. T. van Straaten, "Gifts for the Gods," *Faith, Hope and Worship: Aspects of Religious Mentality in the Ancient World,* ed. H. S. Versnel (Studies in Greek and Roman Religion 2; Leiden: Brill, 1981) 65–151; *Le Sacrifice dans l'Antiquité* (Entretiens sur l'Antiquité Classique 27; Vandoeuvres-Genève: Fondation Hardt, 1981).

divine gift of salvation and the human response of self-sacrifice; (2) the connection between the charitable giving expected of Christians and God's beneficence; (3) the common ancient understanding of the nature and function of gifts;[64] (4) the connection of gift-giving with the cult.[65]

Appropriately, the Macedonians have "dedicated themselves first to the Lord." The term Lord (κύριος) must refer to God, as P⁴⁶ and other witnesses make clear.[66] "First" (πρῶτον) means first in importance, and not in time, and thus implies: "before I asked them," or "before they made their contribution."[67] In the view of the ancients, human self-dedication as a form of sacrifice could be addressed properly only to God.[68] The next statement reveals Paul's own place in the scheme of salvation: "and [they dedicated themselves] to us through the will of God." The formula "through the will of God" (διὰ θελήματος θεοῦ)[69] is usually found in connection with Paul's call to the apostleship,[70] so that the words "and [then] to us" point to himself as God's representative on earth.[71] As an apostle, Paul was, of course, merely an intermediary[72] between the Macedonians and other Christians, in this case those of the church at Jerusalem.

How did the self-dedication of the Macedonians manifest itself? Alfred Plummer suggests: "It is possible that this means no more than a general disposition to do all that was within their power; but it may refer to 'personal service in the work of spreading the Gospel, such as was given by Sopater of Beroea, Aristarchus and Secundus of Thessalonica, and Epaphroditus of Philippi' (J. H. Bernard). To these we may add Jason and Gaius, who were Macedonians, and perhaps Demas."[73] One can assume that the Macedonians' self-dedication coincided with the establishment of the church, which, in turn, included their own missionary activity. But in the present context, Paul was aiming at one specific target, the collection for Jerusalem. Thus here, self-dedication means the Macedonians' desire to take part in the collection (cf. 8:4). If 8:5 is the climax of the encomiastic *exordium,* the formula "through the will of God" is a fitting conclusion.

How does the *exordium* function? There can be little doubt about the reason for Paul's praise of the Macedonians: he hoped that the Corinthians would take it to heart and emulate it.[74] We may also assume that the choice of the Macedonians was not coincidental. Paul must have known of the rivalry, both ethnic and political, between the Macedonians and the Corinthians.[75] It is interesting to observe that he did not hesitate to make use of such rivalry.[76] By contrasting the Macedonians and the Corinthians in this way, Paul made use of the rhetorical figure of *syncrisis,* a technique used widely in ancient rhetoric and historiography[77] to stimulate competition between rivals by means of comparison.

---

64 See the bibliography above, p. 42 n. 12.

65 This connection is important for the relationship between the letter of chapter 8 and that of chapter 9. See below, pp. 120–28.

66 See *Novum Testamentum Graece,* post Everhard Nestle et Erwin Nestle commutiter ediderunt Kurt Aland, Matthew Black, Carlo M. Martini, Bruce M. Metzger, Allen Wikgren; apparatum criticum recensuerunt et editionem novis curis elaboraverunt Kurt Aland et Barbara Aland una cum Instituto studiorum textus Novi Testamenti Monasteriensi (Westphalia) (Stuttgart: Deutsche Bibelstiftung, ²⁶1979) in the *apparatus criticus ad loc.*

67 So correctly Plummer, p. 236.

68 See Rom 12:1; 14:18; Phil 4:18; Eph 5:2; 1 Pet 2:5.

69 See esp. 1 Cor 1:1; 2 Cor 1:1; Eph 1:1; Col 1:1; 1 Tim 1:1; cf. Gal 1:1, 4, 15; Rom 1:1–7. See also Betz, *Galatians,* 42–43.

70 On the concept of apostleship, see ibid., 74–75.

71 Therefore Windisch, p. 247, is not correct when he says that Paul thought he could place himself beside God: "P. [*sc.* Paul] war berechtigt, sich gleich neben Gott zu stellen, . . ." (cf. p. 248: "die etwas kühne Gleichordnung seiner Person mit Gott"). Windisch's statements reflect his peculiar ideas of Paul as a θεῖος ἀνήρ. See his later work, *Paulus und Christus* (UNT 24; Leipzig: Hinrichs, 1934); also Karl Prümm, "Zur Früh- und Spätform der religionsgeschichtlichen Christusdeutung von H. Windisch," *Biblica* 42 (1961) 391–422; 43 (1962) 22–56; Hans Dieter Betz, "Gottmensch II (Griechisch-römische Antike u. Urchristentum)," *RAC* 12 (1982), esp. 291–92, 296–300, 303, 305.

72 Not incidentally, Rom 12:1–2 is followed by statements concerning Paul's apostleship (12:3) and the church as the body of Christ (12:4ff). Cf. also Paul's apostleship as interpreted in Colossians and Ephesians (see above, n. 62).

73 Plummer, p. 236.

74 So correctly Robert Smith Candlish, *The Duty of Laying By, for Religious and Charitable Uses, a Stated Proportion of Our Income: An Analysis of 2 Cor. viii.ix* (London: Nisbet, 1862) 4; "Emulation is appealed to . . ." (see also p. 17).

Paul's literary technique is also related to the *agōn* motif; thus he proposed a contest between the Macedonians and the Corinthians to determine who would be first in generosity.[78]

Excursus: Macedonia, Achaia, and Corinth

The letters of 2 Cor 8 and 9 provide evidence of an extraordinary relationship between Paul and his churches in Macedonia (8:1), Achaia (9:2), and Corinth (cf. 1 Cor 1:2; 2 Cor 1:1, 23; 6:11). Apparently, Paul was related to these churches in different ways, though the nature of the sources prevents us from knowing exactly how the relationships had developed and how the churches were organized in the beginning. Certain observations, however, can still be made.

1) No doubt the apostle Paul was closest to the churches of Macedonia, for whom he had the greatest trust. In his letters, he expressed his admiration for their dedication, integrity, courage, and efficiency. In respect to 2 Cor 8 and 9, it should be pointed out that the delegation sent to Corinth had two members from Macedonia (8:18–22, 23b; 9:3–5). The delegation sent to Jerusalem also consisted largely of Macedonians (see below).

2) Paul always seems to have enjoyed good relations with the Christians of Achaia. From the Corinthian correspondence, it appears that the crisis in Corinth did not affect the other churches of Achaia. In 2 Cor 9, the apostle appealed to the Achaians for help in bringing the Corinthian collection for Jerusalem to a conclusion, particularly as regards its spiritual aspects.

3) The church in Corinth constitutes a special case. On the one hand, it belonged to Achaia, but in Paul's letter it is always treated separately. From the beginning, the church was a source of problems. When Paul wrote 2 Cor 8 and 9, the great crisis reflected in 2 Cor 10—13 was past, but the aftershocks are still felt in the letter of reconciliation (2 Cor 1:1—2:13; 7:5–16; 13:11–13). And an air of caution remains even in 2 Cor 8 and 9. It seems that not only the apostle, but the other churches as well, believed that the situation was still somewhat delicate, and that caution in dealing with Corinth was the better part of prudence. This led to the inclusion of the two envoys in the delegation to Corinth (8:18–22, 23b; 9:3–5). The image of the Corinthians which emerges in the letters is one of shallowness and immaturity (cf. 1 Cor 3:1). They make hasty commitments, and then fail to carry them out. They are disorganized and confused, so that they are in constant need of outside help to maintain congregational order. If anything, this picture is reinforced by 2 Cor 8 and 9.

The question must now be raised whether the differences we have observed in the relationships between Paul and his churches were dependent upon—among other factors—differences in the political and economic histories of the provinces of Macedonia and Achaia, and the city of Corinth. Without entering in detail here upon the complex history involved, we may affirm immediately that this was the case: as regards political history, status in the

75 See the excursus below.

76 See also 2 Cor 9:2–4; 11:9; in 9:13–15, the apostle applies the same strategy to the relationship between the Greek churches and the Jewish Christians at Jerusalem. According to 1 Thess 1:7–8, the Thessalonians have become models for the Macedonians and Achaians (cf. also 1 Thess 4:10). The underlying doctrine seems to be old; cf. Deut 32:21, where God says in view of the disobedience of Israel: "So I will stir them to jealousy with those who are no people; I will provoke them with a foolish nation." In Rom 9—11, Paul applies the same idea to the problem of coexistence between Christians and Jews (see esp. 10:19; 11:11, 14). Cf. Ignatius's notion of the ἐξεμπλάριον τῆς ἀγάπης ("example of love") and its connection with the notion of imitation (Ign. *Eph.* 2.1; *Trall.* 3.2; *Smyrn.* 12.1).

77 See Karl Jost, *Das Beispiel und Vorbild der Vorfahren bei den attischen Rednern und Geschichtschreibern bis Demosthenes* (Rhetorische Studien 19; Paderborn: Schöningh, 1936); Friedrich Focke, "Synkrisis," *Hermes* 58 (1923) 327–68; Hartmut Erbse, "Die Bedeutung der Synkrisis in den Parallelbiographien Plutarchs," *Hermes* 84 (1956) 398–424; Barbara Bucher-Isler, *Norm und Individualität in den Biographien Plutarchs* (Noctes Romanae 13; Bern and Stuttgart: Haupt, 1972) 62ff; Betz, *Paulus,* 119–20; Danker, *Benefactor,* 437–38.

78 See on this motif Victor C. Pfitzner, *Paul and the Agon Motif* (NovTSup 16; Leiden: Brill, 1967). Pfitzner, however, does not recognize the contest between the ethnic groups in 2 Cor 8 and 9. See also Ingomar Weiler, *Der Agon im Mythos: Zur Einstellung der Griechen zum Wettkampf* (Impulse der Forschung 16; Darmstadt: Wissenschaftliche Buchgesellschaft, 1974).

Roman Empire, composition of population, economic situation, and cultural and religious development, these provinces were very different indeed.[79]

When under Roman rule Greece was reordered, it was divided into two provinces, Achaia and Macedonia.[80] Achaia included the greater part of Greece: the Peloponnesus, Attica, Boeotia, and perhaps Epirus. The administration of the two provinces proved to be very difficult, however. Under Octavian, they were ruled by one governor, whose main preoccupation was the defense of the northern border of Macedonia. In 27 B.C., it became necessary to divide the administration and to create two senatorial provinces, Achaia and Macedonia.[81] Achaia also included Thessaly and most of Epirus, while Macedonia, which had the responsibility of guarding the Via Egnatiana, included southern Illyricum. Still later, the protection of the northern frontier was made the responsibility of the governor of Moesia. Responding to complaints, Tiberius merged the provinces once again in A.D. 15, making them into one large province, with the addition of Moesia. Then Claudius divided them up again in A.D. 44, establishing two senatorial provinces. This was the situation at the time of Paul.

These changes reflected an uneasy relationship between the provinces, which must have been due not only to external but also to internal pressures.[82] How these pressures arose is not always clear, but a glance at the political and economic structures shows at once that there were great differences between the political entities involved.[83]

Macedonia had been a Roman province since 146 B.C. The population was mostly Greek, largely rural, more or less Hellenized,[84] and organized along tribal lines. Michael I. Rostovtzeff has summed up the conditions in this way: "The . . . province of MACEDONIA . . . was never a land of intensive urbanization, apart from its Eastern coast. The strength of the Macedonian kingdom was based on the Macedonian peasantry, on the villages. During the Macedonian wars, the country suffered heavy losses. Under the rule of the Roman Republic, it experienced many disastrous invasions of barbarians. Then it became, with Thessaly, the main battle-field of the Roman generals during the civil wars. It was no wonder that this fertile land was less densely populated than it had been under its kings."[85]

To make up for the loss of population, Augustus decided to establish Roman colonies in the province, thus introducing a Roman element. Roman veterans and civilians settled in the major cities (Dyrrhachium, Philippi, Dium, Pella, Cassandrea, Byblis), while other urban centers were given the status of Roman *municipia* (Beroea, Thessalonica, Stobi).[86] It is easy to understand why Paul called the Macedonians' economic situation one of "rock-bottom poverty" (8:2) because such was, proverbially, the condition of the country.[87] On the other hand, it is noteworthy that the churches known to have been founded by the apostle were located precisely in the Romanized cities of Philippi, Thessalonica, and Beroea. Could it be that the membership of these churches consisted in part of Roman settlers?

The names of Paul's co-workers who came from

79 See Michael I. Rostovtzeff, *The Social and Economic History of the Roman Empire* (Oxford: Clarendon, ²1957) 253–54 with notes; Jacob A. O. Larsen, "Roman Greece," in Tenney Frank, *An Economic Survey of Ancient Rome* (5 vols.; Baltimore: Johns Hopkins, 1933–40) 4.259–498; Carl Schneider, *Kulturgeschichte des Hellenismus* (2 vols; Munich: Beck, 1967–69) 1.211ff, 313ff.

80 For the following, see Larsen, "Roman Greece," chap. 3 (pp. 436ff): "Greece and Macedonia from Augustus to Gallienus."

81 See Fanoula Papazoglou, "Quelques aspects de l'histoire de la province de Macedoine," ANRW 2.7.1 (1979) 302–69.

82 See Frank W. Walbank, "Polybius and Macedonia," *Ancient Macedonia, Papers read at the First International Symposium held in Thessaloniki, 26–29 August 1968* (Thessaloniki: Institute for Balkan Studies, 1970) 291–307.

83 For the background, see also Jürgen Deininger, *Der Politische Widerstand gegen Rom in Griechenland 217–86 v. Chr.* (Berlin and New York: de Gruyter, 1971).

84 Cf. the description by Dio Chrysostom *Or.* 33.26–27: "For the Macedonians, although they had but lately shed their rags and were known as shepherds, men who used to fight the Thracians for possession of the millet-fields, vanquished the Greeks, crossed over into Asia and gained an empire reaching to the Indians; yet when the good things of the Persians came into their possession, the bad things also followed in their train. Accordingly both sceptre and royal purple and Median cookery and the very race itself came to an end, so that to-day, if you should pass through Pella, you would see no sign of a city at all, apart from the presence of a mass of shattered pottery on the site." So also the report by Strabo 7.322.

85 *The Social and Economic History,* 253.

86 See Edward T. Salmon, *Roman Colonization Under the Republic* (London: Thames & Hudson, 1969); Robert K. Sherk, "Roman Imperial Troops in Macedonia and Achaea," *AJPh* 78 (1957) 52–62; Papazoglou, "Quelques aspects," 356ff.

87 Dedicatory epigrams in Book 6 of the *Anthologia*

these churches provide additional evidence in support of such a possibility. The list of names in Acts 20:4 appears to be old and may contain the names of the envoys who carried the money to Jerusalem:[88] Sopater, the son of Pyrrhus,[89] is from Beroea; Aristarchus[90] and Secundus[91] come from Thessalonica, Gaius from Derbe (but D* gig make him come from Doberos in Macedonia);[92] then there is Timothy,[93] along with Tychicus[94] and Trophimus,[95] from Asia. One can hardly overlook the fact that some of the names are Latin, which implies that their bearers were Roman. A similar picture emerges from a study of the list of names in Rom 16:21–23, which overlaps somewhat with that found in Acts 20:4. Rom 16:21–23 names Timothy[96] first, then Lucius,[97] Jason,[98] and Sosipater,[99] all fellow Jews; after that, the secretary Tertius[100] and Gaius,[101] Paul's host in Corinth; and finally Erastus[102] and Quartus.[103] The origin and purpose of this list are obscure. Is this another list of the envoys sent to Jerusalem? This possibility should not be dismissed too quickly.

At any rate, the Roman names indicate Romanized or Roman bearers. Some of them were Jews ethnically, not Macedonians. This information provides insight into the composition of a Roman settlement, which in turn has implications for the establishment of Jewish

Palatina, which are attributed to Macedonians, usually stress their poverty. Of special interest is *Anth. Pal.* 6.40, because of the contrast between the Macedonian and Corinthian harvests: "The two oxen are mine and they helped to grow the corn. Be kind, Demeter, and receive them, though they be of dough and not from the herd. Grant that my real oxen may live, and fill thou my fields with sheaves, returning me rich thanks [χάρις]. For the years of thy husbandman, who loves the truth [φιλαλήθης], are already four-score and four. He never reaped rich Corinthian harvests, but never tasted bitter poverty, stranger to corn." The man was grateful because he was spared the normal poverty of the Macedonian peasant (see also no. 36). Common is also the small donation as corresponding to poverty, as in no. 25: "If the gift is but a small one, it is not his [i.e., the donor's] fault, ye Nymphs, for this was all Cinyras had to live on." See also nos. 77, 98, 105, 164, 199, 209, 288, 355. Or the promise is made, as in no. 152: ". . . a small gift from small earnings; but if thou give him [i.e., the donor] something greater, he will repay thee with far richer gifts than these." See for this promise also nos. 190, 191, 300. Many of the epigrams are dedicated to Demeter and reflect the piety of the peasants (see nos. 36, 40, 41, 95, 98, 104, 258). (The translations are taken from the LCL edition of *The Greek Anthology,* by William Roger Paton.)

88 See on this list Hans Conzelmann, *Die Apostelgeschichte* (HNT 7; Tübingen: Mohr, Siebeck, ²1972) *ad loc.;* for the names and bibliography, see the dissertation by Wolf-Henning Ollrog, *Paulus und seine Mitarbeiter: Untersuchungen zu Theorie und Praxis der paulinischen Mission* (WMANT 50; Neukirchen-Vluyn: Neukirchener, 1979), 52–58, and *passim.*

89 He is probably identical with Sosipatros, Rom 16:21. See Bauer, *s.v.;* Ollrog, *Mitarbeiter,* 1, 54, 58.

90 He is mentioned as a Macedonian from Thessalonica in Acts 19:29; 27:2. See also Phlm 24; Col 4:10; and Ollrog, *Mitarbeiter,* 44–46.

91 The name is mentioned only here.

92 He is mentioned as Macedonian also in Acts 19:29 and probably in Rom 16:23; 1 Cor 1:14. Several scholars have suggested that the *varia lectio* Δουβέριος is original. See Bruce Metzger, *A Textual Commentary on the Greek New Testament* (London and New York: United Bible Societies, 1971) 475–76. Δερβαῖος seems an emendation for Δουβέριος due to scribes who were familiar with Derbe (Acts 14:6, 20; 16:1), while Doberos, a Macedonian township, sounded improbable.

93 Ernst Haenchen, *The Acts of the Apostles: A Commentary* (Oxford: Blackwell, 1971) 52–53, 581, believes that Timothy was included because he was from Lystra, near Derbe. But the more likely reason was that he was widely known as Paul's fellow worker. He is frequently mentioned: 1 Cor 4:17; 16:10; 2 Cor 1:1, 19; Phil 1:1; 2:19; 1 Thess 1:1; 3:2, 6; Phlm 1; Rom 16:21; Acts 16:1; 17:14, 15; 18:5; 19:22; etc. On Timothy, see Ollrog, *Mitarbeiter,* 20–23.

94 Probably from Ephesus. Cf. Col 4:7; Eph 6:21; 2 Tim 4:12; Tit 3:12.

95 From Ephesus. Cf. Acts 21:29; 2 Tim 4:20.

96 See above, n. 93.

97 A Lucius of Cyrene is named in Acts 13:1, but he does not seem to be the same as the Lucius in Rom 16:21. Cf. Bauer, *s.v.*

98 Perhaps he is the same as Paul's host in Thessalonia (Acts 17:5–7, 9).

99 See above, n. 89.

100 The man is mentioned only here; cf. the *subscriptio* to Romans.

101 See above, n. 92.

102 Perhaps the man is identical with the one named in Acts 19:22; 2 Tim 4:20. See Bauer, *s.v.*

103 He is named only here. Cf. the *subscriptio* to 1 Corinthians.

synagogues[104] and Christian churches. If these churches had Roman settlers among them, this may explain why Macedonians were chosen as envoys and travel-companions. Perhaps these men were chosen because they had served previously in the military or in civilian administration, and had experience in international travel and the transport of money. Unfortunately, the sources allow us to do nothing more than raise the possibility.

Paul also seems to have had an exceptionally good relationship with the Christians of Achaia. So far as we can tell, the Corinthian crisis was limited to Corinth, while the other Achaian churches maintained an untroubled and loyal relationship to the apostle. For this reason, Paul turned to them when he needed assistance in bringing the collection for Jerusalem to a conclusion. He trusted that the Achaians would be wise enough to ensure that the collection would be not only a financial, but also a spiritual success (see below on chapter 9).

Paul's estimation of the Achaians has an interesting parallel in Polybius's description of the creation of the Achaian League, an act which he ascribed not to military force, but to the political wisdom and maturity of the Achaians:

> One could not find a political system and principle so favourable to equality and freedom of speech, in a word so sincerely democratic, as that of the Achaean league. Owing to this, while some of the Peloponnesians chose to join it of their own free will, it won many others by persuasion and argument, and those whom it forced to adhere to it when the occasion presented itself suddenly underwent a change and became quite reconciled to their position. For by reserving no special privileges for original members, and putting all new adherents exactly on the same footing, it soon attained the aim it had set itself, being aided by two powerful coadjutors, equality and humanity.[105]

A vivid picture of the Achaians is provided in connection with the political crisis in southern Italy: "Embassies arrived from most parts of Greece offering their services as peacemakers, but it was the Achaeans on whom these cities placed most reliance and to whom they committed the task of putting an end to their present troubles . . .";[106] and in connection with the war between the Lacedaemonians and the Thebans: "They, however, referred the points in dispute to the Achaeans alone among all the Greeks, not taking their power into consideration, for they were then almost the weakest state in Greece, but in view of their trustworthiness and high character in every respect [τὴν πίστιν καὶ τὴν ὅλην καλοκἀγαθίαν]. For indeed this opinion of them was at the time, as is generally acknowledged, held by all."[107]

The province of Achaia had retained under Roman rule much of the federal structure of the Hellenistic period, in particular the leagues.[108] Social and economic conditions were similar to those in Macedonia: "The general picture is familiar. It is a picture of poverty and gradual depopulation. The famous description of Euboea by Dio Chrysostom is, of course, a fiction. His general statement in the Tarsian speech is rhetorical exaggeration. Yet the essential features of his description, the depopulation and the existence of large tracts of waste land, are certainly true."[109]

While the people of Achaia were largely Greek, Roman influence was concentrated in the vicinity of the residence of the proconsul, in Corinth. When the Corinthian church was founded, the city was only about one hundred years old. In 44 B.C., C. Julius Caesar had given orders that it be rebuilt, and that the

104 Synagogues have been excavated in Macedonia, and inscriptions have also been found. Most of the material is from the third/fourth century A.D., but the roots of the synagogues of Stobi and Thessalonica may go back to the first century A.D. For the inscriptions, see *Corpus Inscriptionum Iudaicarum* (ed. Jean-Baptiste Frey; vol. 1; New York: Ktav, ²1975), with new material by Baruch Lifshitz. See esp. the *Prolegomena,* 70–78 and nos. 693 and 694. In Stobi, two synagogues were found, one above the other; see Martin Hengel, "Die Synagogeninschrift von Stobi," *ZNW* 57 (1966) 145–83; Dean L. Moe, "The Cross and the Menorah," *Archeology* 30 (1977) 148–57; A. Thomas Kraabel, "The Diaspora Synagogue: Archeological and Epigraphic Evidence since Sukenik," ANRW 2.19.1 (1979) 494–97; Djordje Mano-Zissi et al., eds. *Studies in the Antiquities of Stobi* (4 vols.; Beograd: Narodni Muzej, 1973, 1981, 1982). For Thessalonica, see *CII* no. 693a; for Beroea, no. 694a and b. For advice at this point, I am indebted to Professor Thomas Kraabel.

105 Polybius 2.38.6–8. For the Polybius references, I am indebted to Walter Burkert.

106 Ibid., 39.4.

107 Ibid., 9–10. See the commentary by F. W. Walbank, *A Historical Commentary on Polybius* (3 vols.; Oxford: Clarendon, 1957–79) 1.221ff. The great model of Achaian patriotism and wisdom was Philopoemen (see Plutarch, *Philopoemen,* whom he compares with Titus Flamininus on the Roman side).

108 See Larsen, "Roman Greece," 441ff.

109 *The Social and Economic History,* 253–54, referring to Dio Chrysostom *Or.* 33.25 (on Thessaly and Arcadia), 26 (on Macedonia), and Plutarch *Defect.*

period of destruction which began with the razing of the city in 146 B.C. be brought to an end. Caesar brought in some eighty thousand Roman settlers, consisting mainly of freedmen from a variety of backgrounds. The result was that after one hundred years, the city had a rather mixed ethnic population. Life in Corinth was distinctly cosmopolitan, and contrasts with the traditional Greek way of life were obvious. Many of its citizens were wealthy. In fact, wealth and its ostentatious display became the hallmark of Corinth.[110] While Achaia as a whole suffered poverty and neglect, Corinth enjoyed prosperity; while Achaia led a quiet life remote from the noise and the press of the city and its politics, Corinth teemed with commerce and intrigue.[111] While the Greeks tried as best they could to preserve their traditional culture, the Corinthians indulged new attitudes and ways of life fueled by the new wealth and unbridled by ancestral tradition. Thus, the province and its capital were in many respects worlds apart. Their feelings about each other were, at best, ambiguous.[112] What may have been the prevailing sentiment with regard to the Corinthians was expressed succinctly by a Delphic oracle which Strabo[113] read at the temple of Apollo at Tenea. Strabo reported that an Asian had asked the oracle whether he should carry out his plan to move to Corinth or remain at home. The oracle's answer was as follows:

> Happy is Corinth, but I would rather be a Teneate.[114]
>
> Εὐδαίμων ὁ Κόρινθος, ἐγὼ δ' εἴην Τενεάτης.

Bibliography:

Macedonia

Gustav Friedrich Hertzberg, *Die Geschichte Griechenlands unter der Herrschaft der Römer* (2 vols.; Halle: Buchhandlung des Waisenhauses, 1866, 1868); Theodor Mommsen, *Römische Geschichte* (Berlin: Weidmann, ³1886) 5:230ff, 274ff; Fritz Geyer and Otto Hoffmann, "Makedonia," *PRE* 14.1 (1928) 638–771; Günther Neumann, "Makedonia," *KlP* 3 (1975) 910–19; Nicholas G. L. Hammond, *A History of Macedonia* (2 vols.; vol. 2 co-authored with G. T. Griffith; Oxford: Clarendon, 1972, 1979); Fanoula Papazoglou, "Quelques aspects de l'histoire de la province de Macedoine," ANRW II.7.1 (1979) 302–69.

Achaia

Hertzberg, *Geschichte* 2:56ff; Johannes Töpfer and Carl G. Brandis, "Achaja 2," *PRE* 1 (1894) 190–98; Joseph Keil, "The Greek Provinces: Achaea," *CAH* 11 (1936) 556–65; Bengt E. Thomasson, "Achaia," *KlP* 1 (1975) 32–38.

Corinth

Thomas Lenschau, "Korinthos," *PRE.S* 4 (1924) 991–1036; Ferdinand J. de Waele, *PRE.S* 6 (1935) 182–99, 1350–51; Jack Finegan, "Corinth," *IDB* 1 (1962) 682–84; Cynthia L. Thompson, "Corinth," *IDBSup* (1976) 179–80; Ernst Meyer, "Korinthos," *KlP* 3 (1975) 301–5; James Wiseman, *The Land of the Ancient Corinthians, Studies in Mediterranean Archeology* 50 (Göteborg: Åström, 1978); Winfried Elliger, *Paulus in Griechenland: Philippi, Thessaloniki, Athen, Korinth* (Stuttgart: Katholisches Bibelwerk, 1978) 200ff; James Wiseman, "Corinth and Rome, I: 228 B.C.–A.D. 267," ANRW II.7.1 (1979) 438–548.

■ 8:6: The Narratio (Statement of Facts)

The *exordium* concluded in v 5; v 6 turns to another matter: Paul's report of what he had done in response to the example of the Macedonians. The words εἰς τὸ sum up the consequences of the actions taken by the Macedonians: they had culminated in the appointment of Titus by the apostle.[115] Unfortunately, we are permitted to see only the outcome of what must have been a long series of careful deliberations, for it is not clear at first sight what the Macedonians' request had to do with the

Orac. 8, p. 414.

110 See Gustav Friedrich Hertzberg, *Die Geschichte Griechenlands unter der Herrschaft der Römer* (2 vols.; Halle: Buchhandlung des Waisenhauses, 1866, 1868) 2.81.

111 So ibid., 56.

112 For the background, see Deininger, *Der politische Widerstand*, esp. 23ff, 40ff, 220ff; James Wiseman, "Corinth and Rome, I: 228 B.C.–A.D. 267," ANRW 2.7.1 (1979) 438–548.

113 See Strabo 8.6.22–23; Polybius 2.39.2.

114 My translation. Cf. also Joseph Fontenrose, *The Delphic Oracle* (Berkeley and Los Angeles: University of California, 1978) 347 (question no. 242). As Fontenrose points out, the oracle is a proverb (p. 86).

115 The rendering of εἰς τό remains difficult. Windisch, p. 248 n. 1, takes it to mean "with the effect that." Plummer, p. 237, paraphrases "I was so encouraged by the generosity of the Macedonians that I thought I would send Titus to you." But Paul does not say that! See also BDF, § 402 (2); BDR, § 402 n. 3.

Corinthians.

With regard to the compositional analysis of this passage, several observations can be made: v 6 employs a different form of narrative from that found in the *exordium.* The *exordium* consists of an *exemplum* in the form of an account of the conduct of the Macedonians; implicit in this account is an appeal to the Christians of Corinth to imitate their Macedonian brethren. By contrast, v 6 is a report of Paul's action prior to the composition of the letter. In fact, the action reported in v 6 led directly to the decision to write once again to Corinth, for the letter was meant to accompany the envoys, bearing their commendation and authorization (8:16–24). For this reason, v 6 must be designated the *narratio* (statement of facts).[116]

What Paul had to report was that he had appointed Titus as his delegate to Corinth. The term used to describe the appointment is peculiar. The verb παρακαλεῖν is found frequently in Paul's writings, but it occurs here with the technical meaning "to summon," or even "to appoint."[117] Translators have frequently sought to render the term in harmony with the meaning found elsewhere in Paul, and thus have proposed to translate the phrase: "so that we entreated Titus."[118] But such a translation makes little sense in this case, and illustrates how questionable it is methodologically to impose a single meaning on a term every time it occurs. In fact, the verb which Paul used here is commonly found in administrative writings, where it refers to the appointment of legal or political representatives.

The purpose of Titus's appointment is given in the ἵνα-clause in v 6b: "so that as he had begun beforehand he should also bring to a conclusion among you this gift of charity."[119] The explanation of the verb "to begin beforehand," προενάρχομαι,[120] is no doubt found in vv 8–10, which imply that Titus had been in Corinth "a year ago" and had started the work of the collection. But up to the time this letter was written, the work had remained unfinished. Therefore it was the purpose of this mission "to bring it to a conclusion" (ἐπιτελεῖν).[121] It should be noted that the verb is again derived from the language of administration, where ἐπιτελεῖν occurs time and again to denote the "carrying out" of governmental orders by envoys.[122] The expression εἰς ὑμᾶς may simply mean "among you," or may refer to the departure of Titus (cf. v 18); it may even anticipate the formula of

116 For the nature and function of the *narratio,* see Volkmann, *Rhetorik,* § 13; Lausberg, *Handbuch* 1, §§ 289–347; Martin, *Rhetorik,* 75–89; Betz, *Galatians,* 58–62.

117 See also 1 Cor 16:12; 2 Cor 9:5; 12:18; παράκλησις 8:17; 1 Thess 2:3. Bauer does not list this special meaning; Otto Schmitz and Gustav Stählin, "παρακαλέω κτλ.," *TDNT* 5 (1967) 774–75 (A.1), discuss it but do not assume its occurrence in the New Testament. For the correct interpretation, see Carl J. Bjerkelund, *Parakalô: Form, Funktion und Sinn in den paulinischen Briefen* (Oslo: Universitetsforlaget, 1967) esp. 27–28. For the administrational term see LSJ, *s.v.* II; Moulton and Milligan, *s.v.;* Preisigke, *Wörterbuch* 1, *s.v.;* Meyer, *Juristische Papyri,* nos. 84, 33; 91 I, 7,11; C. Bradford Welles, *Royal Correspondence in the Hellenistic Period: A Study in Greek Epigraphy* (New Haven: Yale University, 1934) 396, index *s.v.;* Victor Ehrenberg and A. H. M. Jones, *Documents Illustrating the Reigns of Augustus and Tiberius* (Oxford: Clarendon, ³1976) no. 299, line 21, cf. lines 37ff; Dittenberger, *OGIS* no. 339, line 54. An example from literature is the conclusion of Aeschines' speech *On the Embassy* (*Or.* 2.184): Παρακαλῶ δὲ Εὔβουλον μὲν ἐκ τῶν πολιτικῶν καὶ σωφρόνων ἀνδρῶν συνήγορον . . . "I now call Eubulus as a representative of the statesmen and all honourable citizens . . ."). Text and translation according to the LCL edition by Charles D. Adams.

118 Plummer, p. 237; similarly Heinrici, p. 272.

119 χάρις refers to the collection again. See above, nn. 10–13.

120 The word is a *hapax legomenon,* found only in 2 Cor 8:6 and 10. See Bauer, *s.v.;* Windisch, p. 246; cf. Gal 3:3; Phil 1:6.

121 See also 2 Cor 8:11; Gal 3:3; Phil 1:6; Rom 15:28. See Bauer, *s.v.* 1; Gerhard Delling, "συντελέω," *TDNT* 8 (1972) 62–63.

122 See LSJ, *s.v.* I; Moulton and Milligan, *s.v.;* Preisigke, *Wörterbuch* 1, *s.v.,* where the close connection with the legal and financial contexts is to be noted; Meyer, *Juristische Papyri,* nos. 5,27; 24,4–5; 41,26; 49,17; 53,20; 72,2; Welles, *Royal Correspondence,* nos. 54,11; 65,11; 67,11. LXX shows that the terminology was common in Hellenistic Judaism: see Esth 8:14; 2 Macc 3:8, 23; 12:8; 14:29; 15:5; Philo *Leg. Gai.* 218. See Gerhard Delling, "συντελέω," *TDNT* 8 (1972) 62.

authorization in v 23a: "in relation to you, a fellow worker" (εἰς ὑμᾶς συνεργός). Paul has provided us with nothing more than the barest facts, so that important questions remain unanswered. It is also worth noting that at this point in the letter, the apostle made no mention of two other envoys who were sent. This can only indicate that these envoys were appointed by a separate action (see on vv 18–22). The matter is carried over into the letter of chapter 9, where Paul explained the sending of additional envoys but failed to mention Titus (9:3–5). Does this mean that Titus's appointment was not regarded as a matter of controversy, but the sending of "the brethren" required a special explanation? Indeed, their appointment comes as something of a surprise and leaves us wondering why it was necessary.

But the text raises still another question: When did Titus begin the collection in Corinth?[123] His relationship to the collection for Jerusalem went back to the conference, at which he was present.[124] Did he have a role to play in the plan for the collection even then? It seems strange that in 1 Cor 16:1–4, where Paul described in detail the methods to be employed in collecting the money, Titus's name is not mentioned. Paul spoke as if the collection was already under way. It may be that there was no need to mention Titus at this point. Perhaps his visit, during which the collection was begun, had taken place prior to the writing of 1 Corinthians, so that Paul's proposals in chapter 16 are of a supplementary nature.[125] Furthermore, the announcement of Timothy's visit (1 Cor 16:10–11) was not connected by Paul with the collection or with Titus's visit. These puzzling facts may simply represent gaps in our knowledge.

In the first apology (2 Cor 2:14—6:13; 7:2–4), Titus is not mentioned, but in the second (2 Cor 10—13), he plays an important part. In 12:18, Paul described him as his representative, sent to Corinth together with an unnamed brother (παρεκάλεσα Τίτον καὶ συναπέστειλα τὸν ἀδελφόν). Since the delegation with which 2 Cor 8 and 9 is preoccupied involved two brothers[126] in addition to Titus, 12:18 would seem to refer to the first visit to Corinth, on which the collection had been begun, for here Paul spoke of Titus and only one other brother.[127] The letter of reconciliation (2 Cor 1:1—2:13; 7:5–16; 13:11–13) speaks of a second visit by Titus to Corinth (2:13; 7:5–7, 13–14). This visit seems to have been undertaken in conjunction with or as a consequence of the sending of the four-chapter letter (2 Cor 10—13), because Paul spoke of this visit as preceding the writing of the letter of reconciliation (2:3–4, 9; 7:8, 12).[128] Titus's message for Paul—that reconciliation had been accomplished (7:6–7)—was delivered in Macedonia, where the two men met. After this, it was only logical that Titus's third visit to Corinth would be devoted to the resumption and completion of the collection. This mission seems to have been a success as well, for otherwise Paul could not have reported in Rom 15:25–32, a passage written from Corinth, that the collection was now completed (v 28) and that he himself was going to lead the delegation to Jerusalem in order to hand over the money to the church. The decision personally to lead the delegation to Jerusalem must have been made after 1 Corinthians, for in 1 Cor 16:4 it is discussed as nothing

123 For the various options, see Windisch, p. 249.

124 See Gal 2:1–10, where Titus is mentioned in v 1, and the collection in v 10. See C. Kingsley Barrett, "Titus," *Neotestamentica et Semitica: Studies in Honour of Matthew Black* (Edinburgh: Clark, 1969) 1–14; rep. in his *Essays on Paul* (Philadelphia: Westminster, 1982) 118–31; Betz, *Galatians,* 84; Ollrog, *Mitarbeiter,* 33–37.

125 See for this view Plummer, p. 237: "The rare verb προενήρξατο implies that Titus has been at Corinth before he took the severe letter alluded to in vii.12. This is some confirmation of the view that he, rather than Timothy, was the bearer of I Cor. But he *may* have been in Corinth before I Cor to start the collection." Similarly, Hans Conzelmann, *1 Corinthians: A Commentary on the First Epistle to the Corinthians* (Hermeneia; Philadelphia: Fortress, 1975) 295: "From the sequel it emerges that preparations for the collection have already been made in Corinth." Cf. Bultmann, p. 256 n. 1, who raises the question whether Timothy, not Titus, began the collection in Corinth.

126 2 Cor 8:18–23; 9:3–5 (see below, pp. 72–82; 93–96).

127 So Bultmann, pp. 237–38. This interpretation is supported by 12:14–18, an argument in the preceding four-chapter letter (10:1—13:10), in which Titus's mission is cited as evidence that Paul's envoys did not exploit the Corinthian church (cf. also 11:7–11). Such evidence would certainly be the first visit of Titus because it preceded the present controversy to which the four-chapter letter responds.

128 See below, p. 142. Cf. Plummer, p. 237.

more than an option, but in 2 Cor 9:4 and Rom 15:25 it is repeated as fact (see also Acts 19:21; 20:22). Remarkably, Titus does not seem to have been among the delegates on the final journey; at least his name does not occur in the lists in Acts 20:4 and Rom 16:21–23. Was he excluded because he had become a figure of controversy following the Jerusalem conference?[129] Would his inclusion in the delegation have constituted a diplomatic affront or, at the least, an act of imprudence? If so, why were the other envoys thought to be uncontroversial? Were they all Jews, like Paul? We can do no more than raise these questions here because of the general state of the evidence.

■ 8:7–8: The Propositio (Proposition)

The conjunction ἀλλά in v 7 marks the introduction of a new section in the argument. Paul no longer reported on his own actions in the past, but advised the Corinthians on what they should do in the future. He did not simply issue orders, however. Rather, he set forth a carefully constructed argument intended to lead them to an understanding of what they ought to do. Thus vv 7–8 constitute, rhetorically, the proposition, or *propositio*, which, as we would expect, immediately follows the *narratio*.[130] The purpose of the *propositio* is to set forth the points of agreement and disagreement; in keeping with this, v 7a corresponds to the Corinthians' self-understanding, while it remains to be seen whether they will accept or reject the thoughts expressed in v 7b.

With the statement in v 7a, "you have an abundance of everything" (ἐν παντὶ περισσεύετε), no one in Corinth would have disagreed.[131] Paul lists six virtues in particular, arranged in two groups of three. The first triad includes "faith [or faithfulness], eloquence, and knowledge" (πίστις καὶ λόγος καὶ γνῶσις). There are difficulties with the translation of these concepts. As there is reason for assuming that the triad is conventional, and not merely Pauline, πίστις may refer initially to faithfulness in the broadest sense, rather than to faith in terms of Pauline theology. Such a general meaning would be in keeping with the other terms used to praise the virtues of the Corinthians. This triad certainly corresponds to the Corinthians' own self-understanding, a fact which is underscored by the recurrence of two of the terms in a similar statement in 1 Cor 1:5: "in every kind of speech and every kind of knowledge" (ἐν παντὶ λόγῳ καὶ πάσῃ γνώσει).

The parallel between these two passages raises the question of the relationship between the letters. In 1 Corinthians, Paul conceded that the Corinthians were indeed wealthy in every way, especially with respect to the intellectual gifts of speech and knowledge (1 Cor 1:5). This wealth had given rise to a number of problems, which were the occasion of the letter, especially the strife which the people of Chloe had reported to be rampant in the Corinthian church (1 Cor 1:10ff). This situation not only ran counter to the intended purpose of their wealth, which was regarded as a gift of God in Christ (1:4–5), but also contradicted the fundamental theological assumptions upon which the church had been built. The goal of the apostle's arguments and recommendations in 1 Corinthians was to bring the abuses under the control of a theologically responsible faith.[132]

The situation presupposed in 2 Cor 8 and 9 is similar, though not identical. Here, too, the wealth of the Corinthians is taken for granted, but failure to make proper use of their wealth is represented as nothing more than a dark possibility of the future. Paul admitted that the Corinthians had failed thus far to bring the collection to completion. But they had made a start, and

129 Georgi, *Kollekte*, 16–17, agreeing with Albrecht Oepke, *Der Brief des Paulus an die Galater* (ed. Joachim Rohde; ThHK 9; Berlin: Evangelische Verlagsanstalt, ³1973 [¹1937, ²1957]) 73, points out that the appearance of an uncircumcised Gentile Christian would have constituted a provocation in the eyes of the anti-Pauline opposition in Jerusalem. Cf. differently Ollrog, *Mitarbeiter*, 37. See also Betz, *Galatians*, 84 n. 252.

130 On the *propositio*, see Volkmann, *Rhetorik*, § 15; Lausberg, *Handbuch* 1, § 346; Martin, *Rhetorik*, 91–95; Betz, *Galatians*, 114.

131 The Corinthians' abundance and wealth is a standing theme in the entire correspondence, esp. in 2 Cor 8 and 9. See above, pp. 42, 53. The *encomium* was noted by Chrysostom *In epist. II. ad Cor. Hom.* 17, *MPG* 61.558B.

132 The composition and function of 1 Corinthians cannot be discussed here. See, however, what may be the *exordium*, 1:4–9, and what may be the *peroratio*, 15:58.

would fall short if they reacted with indifference to the letter of 2 Cor 8 and the mission of the delegates. Thus the letters differ in an important respect, and this gives rise to yet another question. Why is faithfulness or faith (*πίστις*) added to the virtues listed in 2 Cor 8:7, in contrast to 1 Cor 1:5? The term is obviously meant to express something positive, an achievement of some kind. Can it be that it is only in 2 Cor 8 that Paul granted the Corinthians faith and faithfulness? The answer to this question is complicated by the fact that no further discussion of the notions is to be found in 2 Cor 8 and 9. But other portions of the Corinthian correspondence provide us with some clues.

Elsewhere in 2 Corinthians, Paul granted the Corinthians their eloquence and knowledge,[133] but his judgment on their faithfulness or faith (*πίστις*) differs from that found in 2 Cor 8. The Corinthians are repeatedly exhorted to examine their faith critically in 1 Corinthians. The same exhortations are found in 2 Corinthians in the first (2:14—6:13; 7:2–4) and second apologies (10—13).[134] All this changes when we come to the letter of reconciliation. Now Paul spoke of the strength and independence of the Corinthians' faith as though they had greatly matured.[135] 2 Cor 8:7 seems to confirm this judgment, recognizing the maturity of the Corinthians' faith, along with their other virtues. Such a recognition of their progress in faith is certainly appropriate after the successful resolution of the great crisis.[136] Even if *πίστις* refers to the Christian faith specifically, other connotations should not be excluded. These are suggested by the important role *πίστις* plays in administrative letters and documents. Thus when Paul spoke of faith, he may have had in mind the virtues of loyalty and mutual trust which were constitutive of the relationship between the congregation and their apostle. In this sense, *πίστις* is often found in language of the epistles,[137] sometimes in connection with other virtues.[138]

While thus far there had been little cause for disagreement between Paul and the Corinthians, the second triad presents more of a problem. The Corinthians may have wanted to claim these virtues as well, but whether they were justified in doing so would be determined by their future course of action in regard to the collection. The second triad seems to be constructed on the pattern of the first, but its concepts are drawn from the context of the present letter.[139] They include the notions of zeal, love, and charity. The first term (*καὶ πάσῃ σπουδῇ*) introduces the issue at hand. The term *σπουδή* designates

133 The terminology plays a decisive role in the controversies. See the use of *λόγος* in the first apology 2:17; 4:2; 5:19; 6:7; in the second apology 10:10, 11; 11:6 (see Betz, *Paulus,* 57ff); in the letter of reconciliation 1:18. The term *γνῶσις* is used in the first apology 2:14; 4:6; 6:6; in the second apology 10:5; 11:6. Of course, the terms are frequent already in 1 Corinthians: for *λόγος* see 1:5, 17–18; 2:1–16; 4:19–20; 12:8; 14:9, 19, 36; 15:2, 54; for *γνῶσις* see 1:5; 8:1, 7, 10, 11; 12:8; 13:2, 3; 14:6.

134 For *πίστις* ("faith"), see the first apology 4:13; 5:7; the second apology 10:15; 13:5. In 1 Corinthians, see 2:5; 12:9; 13:2, 13; 15:14, 17; 16:13.

135 In 2 Cor 1:24, Paul can assure the Corinthians that there is no need for him to dominate their faith, "for you stand firm in your faith" (*τῇ γὰρ πίστει ἑστήκατε*). In other words, the goals of 1 Cor 1:4–7; 15:58 have been reached.

136 Cf. by contrast 1 Cor 3:1: "And yet, my brothers, I cannot speak to you as 'men of the spirit' [*πνευματικοί*], but only as 'men of the flesh' [*σάρκινοι*], that is, as 'infants in Christ' [*νήπιοι ἐν Χριστῷ*]. My translation. Cf. also 1 Cor 13:11.

137 See Dietrich Schäfer, "Pistis 2," *PRE* 20 (1950) 1812–13; Walter Schmitz, *Ἡ πίστις in den Papyri* (Inaugural Dissertation, Cologne, 1964); Danker, *Benefactor,* 352–54.

138 See, e.g., Welles, *Royal Correspondence,* no. 67, lines 12–13: *εὐσεβείαι κα[ὶ] καλοκαγαθίαι . . . καὶ . . . πίστει* ("in piety and excellence and . . . in faith"). See also no. 44, line 1: *τιμὴ καὶ πίστις* ("honor and trust" [the reading is, however, not certain]); no. 63, line 8: *πίστις καὶ εὔνοια* ("faithfulness and good will"); no. 66, line 11: *εὐσέβεια . . . καὶ εὔνοια καὶ πίστις* ("piety . . . and good will and faith"); Dittenberger, *OGIS,* nos. 339, line 46; 441, line 43. In the Latin epistles, the important term is *fides,* merging with the Roman virtue just as easily as with the Christian notion of faith in Paul's letters. See, e.g., the triad of *fides, iustitia, bonitas* ("good faith, justice, goodness") in Cicero *Ep. Fam.* 13.4.3; also 5.1; 10.3; 16.2; and often. See Carl Becker, "Fides," *RAC* 7 (1969) 801–39.

139 The three notions are also quite common in the

"zeal"[140] in general as well as, more specifically, the aggressiveness and efficiency needed to get things done, a virtue one would expect of a good administrator.[141] The terms σπουδάζω, σπουδαῖος, and σπουδή occur frequently in this sense in administrative letters, and thus in 2 Cor 8, where the terms play an important role in reference both to the Corinthians and to the envoys.[142] The encouragement of the Corinthians' zeal may also go back to the letter of reconciliation, where it was mentioned by Paul in 7:11–12.

The next virtue, "love" (ἀγάπη), seems even more difficult, and Paul prefaced it by qualifications. If the Nestle-Aland text is taken to be correct, the phrase should be translated "which comes from us and dwells in you"[143] (καὶ τῇ ἐξ ἡμῶν ἐν ὑμῖν ἀγάπῃ). It may be that Paul interjected here a reminder to the Corinthians that in contrast to their other virtues, that of love was owed to his efforts. There is ample evidence in the Corinthian correspondence to suggest that the apostle had considerable difficulty in making them understand the notion of love (ἀγάπη). It may be that Paul made reference to the problem here. If that is so, then what the qualification implies is that their love is one "which came from us to you."[144]

The real test which lay before the Corinthians, however, was whether their gifts would manifest themselves in an abundant collection for Jerusalem. Verse 7b appears to be an anacoluthon,[145] the ἵνα-clause indicating the direction of Paul's thought: "so that you may have abundance in this work of charity also." The term χάρις connotes a variety of things: it refers, as in v 6, to the collection for Jerusalem, but it also implies that the collection, if successfully completed, would be evidence of the abundance of grace among the Corinthians—"grace" both in the theological sense of 8:1[146] and in the general attitudinal sense of "graciousness." In conclusion, we may say that there was full agreement between Paul and the Corinthians on the first triad of faith (or faith-

epistolary literature. In the Latin, they correspond to *studium* (see n. 137, above), *amor, amicitia,* and *gratia.* See, e.g., Cicero *Ep. Fam.* 13.1.5: "Sed ne plura (dicendum enim aliquando est), Pomponium Atticum sic amo, ut alterum fratrem. Nihil est illo mihi nec carius nec iucundius" ("But to waste no more words [I must say it sooner or later], I love Pomponius Atticus as a second brother. He is to me the dearest and most delightful man in the world"). On *gratia,* see *Ep. Fam.* 13.5.3 and often. On the whole notion, see Heinrich Dörrie, Herbert Dittmann, Otto Knoch, and Alfred Schindler, "Gnade," *RAC* 11 (1979) 313–446.

140 On the concept generally, see Bauer, *s.v.;* Günther Harder, "σπουδάζω κτλ.," *TDNT* 7 (1971) 559–68; Ceslas Spicq, *Notes de lexicographie néotestamentaire* (2 vols.; Fribourg, Suisse: Editions universitaires, 1978) 2.816–25.

141 For this meaning, see LSJ, *s.v.* II,1,a; Moulton and Milligan, *s.v.;* Preisigke, *Wörterbuch* 1, *s.v.* 2; Welles, *Royal Correspondence,* nos. 1, line 24; 14, line 2; 15, lines 10, 37; 25, line 43; 31, line 11; 32, line 11; 33, line 18; 44, line 26; 52, lines 10–39 (cf. σπουδάζω nos. 3, line 85; 71, line 12); Ehrenberg and Jones, *Documents,* no. 301, III, line 84; E. Mary Smallwood, *Documents Illustrating the Principates of Gaius, Claudius and Nero* (Cambridge: Cambridge University, 1967) nos. 370, lines 25, 34, 52; 371, lines 4–5; 374, line 23. Some classical parallels are also noted by Wettstein 2.197; Danker, *Benefactor,* 320–21. In the Latin epistles, the range of equivalent terms includes *studium (studiosus, studiosissimus), observantia (observans, observantissimus), officiosus (officiosissimus).* See, e.g., Cicero *Ep. Fam.* 13.3; 6.2–3; 8.1; Pliny *Ep.* 7.30.1. See also *Oxford Latin Dictionary, s.v.*

142 See 2 Cor 8:7, 8, 16; cf. σπουδαῖος 8:17, 22.

143 So following Plummer, p. 238, who also discusses other options based on different readings in manuscripts. See also Windisch, p. 250.

144 Cf. also 1 Cor 4:21; 8:1; 13:1–13; 14:1; 16:14, 24; in 2 Corinthians in the first apology 5:14; 6:6; in the second apology 11:11; 12:15; 13:11, 18; in the letter of reconciliation 2:4, 8; furthermore 8:8, 24; 9:7. For the notion and bibliography on it, see Betz, *Galatians,* 263 n. 98.

145 So Windisch, p. 249; similarly, Plummer, p. 238. The ἵνα with the subjunctive expresses a form of the imperative (see BDR, §§ 387, 3a with n. 4; 388 n. 2; BDF, §§ 387 (3) with n. 3; 388), which Paul at once corrects in v 8. Nigel Turner, *Grammatical Insights Into the New Testament* (Edinburgh: Clark, 1965) 147, thinks that "more than simple imperatival force is intended" and renders: "*See that [hina]* ye abound in this grace also."

146 See above, p. 42.

fulness), eloquence, and knowledge. With regard to the second triad—zeal, love, and charity—agreement depended upon the future actions of the Corinthians. What is implied in Paul's argument is that the last virtue, that of charity, would determine whether they could legitimately claim anything at all, or whether all their claims would be shown to be false.

Verse 8 supplements what has been said in v 7 by further clarification. Paul at once corrected himself, that is to say, he qualified the preceding imperatival expression, introduced by ἵνα, with the statement: "I do not speak in terms of command" (οὐ κατ' ἐπιταγὴν λέγω). The phrase "in accordance with a command" (κατ' ἐπιταγήν) is interesting in itself because of its connection with votive offerings in Greek religious texts.[147] But why did Paul make this correction? Several reasons can be given at this point.

In 1 Corinthians, Paul also hesitated to give orders (see 4:21; 7:6, 25). The case is different with the second apology and its harsh threats (see 2 Cor 10:4–6, 8; 12:14; 13:1–2, 10), which hurt the Corinthians' feelings. But in the letter of reconciliation (1:24)[148] he assured them that he had not intended to act as their lord in matters of faith, a sign that both sides are aware of the offense which his words had given.

But beyond this, another reason for Paul's self-correction may lie in the fact that in deliberative rhetoric—and that is what we have in 8:1–15—commands are out of order. Paul was offering advice to the Corinthians, nothing more. Furthermore, a collection of this sort depends by nature on the voluntary cooperation of the contributors, and this can only be the result of their personal insights and decisions. Ancient thought on public fund raising exhibited particular concern to maintain the voluntary nature of subscriptions. This had its cause in the frequent abuse of putting pressure on the contributors.[149] Hence, Paul's self-correction may reinforce a social convention that has a history of its own.

Finally, Paul's statement is an epistolary *topos* found frequently in letters of commendation, of which Cicero, *Ep. Fam.* XIII.1.2 is a good example: "And first of all I shall make this request of you—to do nothing for my sake against your will; but if you perceive that what I ask is of importance to me, while of no great importance from any point of view to yourself, not to grant me even that favour unless you have previously persuaded yourself to do so with your whole heart."[150]

Verse 8b states what Paul had in mind: he regarded the collection as a real test for the Corinthians, on the assumption that the continual test of faith is not the sign of a lack of trust but part of the life of faith itself.[151] By proposing yet another test of the Corinthians, Paul did not revoke anything that had already been granted, but only made sure that nothing with regard to the Christian

147 See for further references Moulton and Milligan, *s.v.* ἐπιταγή.

148 See above, n. 132; cf. also Paul's explanations in 2 Cor 2:4; 7:8–11; Phlm 14; and furthermore 1 Pet 5:2.

149 See the basic study by Adolphe Kuenzi, ΕΠΙΔΟΣΙΣ: *Sammlung freiwilliger Beiträge zu Zeiten der Not in Athen.* Mit einem Anhang: *Epidoseis in den übrigen griechischen Städten* (Bern: Haupt, 1923) esp. 2, 23ff; Andreas M. Andreades, *A History of Greek Public Finance* (rev. C. N. Brown; Cambridge: Harvard University, 1933) 1.131–32, who pictures things rather idyllically: "In fact, while only the wealthiest citizens were forced to assume these burdens, even those who were relatively poor were glad to contribute to them, and the rich willingly paid more than their share, all being inspired by a noble rivalry."

150 "Ac te illud primum rogato, ne quid invitus mea causa facias; sed id, quod mea intelleges, tua nullam in partem multum interesse, ita mihi des, si tibi, ut id libenter facias, ane persuaseris." The matter is repeated in the *peroratio:* "But I shall return to what I said at first. Before persuading yourself to do this at all, I would have you persuade yourself to do it readily, as a kindness to myself" ("Sed redeo ad prima. Prius velim tibi persuadeas, ut hoc mea causa libenter facias, quam ut facias"). Cf. Shackleton Bailey, *Cicero: Epistulae ad Familiares* (2 vols.; Cambridge: Cambridge University, 1977) 359 *ad loc.* Another example is *Ep. Fam.* 13.16.4: "Here then is the considered expression of my opinion; but such is your extraordinary penetration that you will far more easily decide the matter on your own account" ("Habes opinionis meae testimonium; sed hoc tu facilius multo, pro tua singulari prudentia, indicabis").

151 See 1 Cor 3:13; 11:28; 16:3; 2 Cor 13:5; furthermore Gal 6:4; Phil 1:10; 1 Thess 2:4; 5:21; Rom 1:28; 2:18; 12:2; 14:22. Cf. also δόκιμος ("genuine," "tested") 1 Cor 11:19; 2 Cor 10:18; 13:7; Rom 14:18; 16:10. See Betz, *Galatians,* 301ff.

faith was taken for granted. The method for conducting the test was simple: "through the zeal of others" (διὰ τῆς ἑτέρων σπουδῆς), a reference to the conduct of the Macedonians. So Paul hoped that their zeal would stimulate the Corinthians to do likewise (see 8:1–5). The object of the test was to prove the genuineness (τὸ γνήσιον)[152] of their love, which would only be manifested by the successful completion of the collection.

■ 8:9–15: The Probatio (Proofs)

The section 8:9–15 forms the *probatio*, or proofs, of a deliberative argument. In terms of composition, one would expect this section to follow the *propositio* (8:7–8). Section 8:9–15 can be interpreted without difficulty according to the rules and conventions of deliberative oratory as set forth by ancient rhetoricians. Since there was no firm consensus on these rules and conventions, however, the section must be dealt with in terms of the range of possibilities allowed in theory and practice.[153]

One would expect the *probatio* of a deliberative argument, concerned with the raising of money,[154] to employ a number of points for consideration. The number of such points may vary, along with the names they are given.[155] Cicero and the sources he employed in his *De inventione* spoke for many other orators in favor of three *res expetendae* ("things to be sought"): the *honesta* ("things honorable"), the *utilia* ("things advantageous"), and *honestas* ("honor") of a somewhat higher order.[156] Quintilian also discussed the widely held view that there were three parts: the *honestum* ("honor"), *utile* ("expediency"), and *necessarium* ("necessity"), but rejected the last one[157] in favor of τὸ δυνατόν ("possibility").[158] Reviewing the options, Quintilian believed that three general points would suffice: "Most writers, however, say that there are more than three. But the further considerations which they would add are really but *species* of the three general considerations just mentioned."[159]

Paul also employed three points of consideration in his *probatio*, two of which he identified properly by name, calling the second (vv 10–12) that of "expediency" (τὸ συμφέρον, Latin *utile*), and the third (vv 13–15) that of "equity" (ἰσότης, Latin *aequitas*). In view of the fact that two of the points are named, the question naturally arises whether the first and most important point belongs to the category of *honestum* (the "honorable"). Does Paul's first point (v 9) exemplify the honorable?

According to Cicero, the honorable can be defined as follows: "anything that is sought wholly or partly for its own sake."[160] Under the heading of "justice" (*iustitia*), Cicero included matters pertaining to religion as part of the "law of nature": "The law of nature is that which is not born of opinion, but implanted in us by a kind of innate instinct: it includes religion, duty, gratitude, revenge, reverence, and truth."[161] Religion is defined as

152 The term, in this sense, is a *hapax legomenon* in the New Testament. See Bauer, *s.v.* 2; Friedrich Büchsel, "γνήσιος," *TDNT* 1 (1964) 727; also Wettstein 2.197; Moulton and Milligan, *s.v.;* Preisigke, *Wörterbuch* 4/2, *s.v.* 2, 3; Dittenberger, *OGIS* no. 339, line 7. Cf. the discussion by Plummer, p. 240; Windisch, p. 251; BDR, § 263 n. 5.

153 On the *probatio*, see Lausberg, *Handbuch* 1, §§ 233–36; Martin, *Rhetorik*, 169–74; Joachim Adamietz, *M. F. Quintiliani Institutionis Oratoriae Liber III* (Studia et Testimonia Antiqua 2; Munich: Fink, 1966) 180ff; Betz, *Galatians*, 128–30.

154 According to Anaximenes *Rhet.* 2.2, p. 1423a26; 2.33–35, p. 1425b19–35, the raising of money (περὶ πόρου χρημάτων) is a proper subject for this kind of oratory. See also Cicero *De inv.* 2.52.157: "pecunia."

155 See Martin, *Rhetorik*, 169–70.

156 Cicero *De inv.* 2.52.157–58. See Martin, *Rhetorik*, 172–73.

157 Quintilian 3.8.22.

158 Ibid., 25.

159 Ibid., 26: "Tamen apud plerosque earum numerus augetur, a quibus ponuntur ut partes, quae superiorum species sunt partium."

160 Cicero *De inv.* 2.53.159: "Quod aut totum aut aliqua ex parte propter se petitur, honestum nominabimus." See also Cicero's discussion of the virtues which make up the "honorable" (ibid., 2.53.159–2.54.165).

161 Ibid., 161: "Naturae ius est quod non opinio genuit, sed quaedam in natura vis inserit, ut religionem, pietatem, gratiam, vindicationem, observantiam, veritatem."

"that which brings men to serve and worship a higher order of nature which they call divine."[162] Similarly, Quintilian argued that honor must come before expediency[163] and that honor primarily consists of honor due to the gods (*honor deorum*).[164] For Quintilian, as for Cicero, the honorable was therefore a comprehensive term: "Right, justice, piety, equity, and mercy (for thus they translate τὸ ἥμερον), with any other virtues that anyone may be pleased to add, all come under the heading of that which is honourable."[165] Since issues of religion fall into this category, 2 Cor 8:9 can be interpreted as an example of the rhetorical concept of the honorable.[166]

8:9: The First Proof

If Paul's first proof in v 9 belongs to the category of the honorable, what constitutes its persuasive force? The statement is doctrinal in nature, a concise formulation of the christological and soteriological concept of grace. As we indicated above, this doctrine is one of the underlying presuppositions of the letter.[167] The initial verb which Paul employed, "you know" (γινώσκετε), indicates that the doctrine was already known to the readers. Thus the statement functions rhetorically as a reminder, and as such is an authoritative example of the highest order.[168]

Formally, v 9 consists of a pair of lines which exhibit a chiastic structure. The first line enunciates the christological dogma; the second line draws its soteriological consequences. The statement presents in narrative form a summary of the myth. Because its content is known to the readers, the story can be told briefly.

It is hard to say whether Paul composed the statement ad hoc, or whether it was derived from some other context.[169] In this passage, at least, the statement is meant to function as an example (*exemplum*).[170] If, as Paul expected, the readers accepted the example of Christ as authoritative for their own lives, then honor was due to God. The result, as Cicero had said, is to produce the virtues of duty and gratitude: "Duty is the feeling which renders kind offices and loving service to one's kin and country. Gratitude embraces the memory of friendships and of services rendered by another, and the desire to requite these benefits."[171] Translated into the terms of Paul's theology, the force of the argument is clear: the Jerusalem collection presented the perfect opportunity to respond appropriately to the example of Christ.[172]

Though the lines of the argument are generally clear, questions nevertheless remain. Whence did the Corin-

162 Ibid.: "Religio est, quae superioris cuiusdam naturae, quam divinam vocant, curam caerimoniamque affert. . . ."

163 Quintilian 3.8.30. "Saepe vero et utilitatem despiciendam esse dicimus, ut honesta faciamus. . . ."

164 Ibid., 29.

165 Ibid., 26: "Nam fas iustum, pium, aequum, mansuetum (sic enim sunt interpretati τὸ ἥμερον) et si qua adhuc adiicere quis eiusdem generis velit, subiici possunt honestati."

166 Ibid., 29. See Adamietz, *Liber III,* 183–84.

167 See above on 8:1.

168 On the *commemoratio,* see Lausberg, *Handbuch* 1, §§ 415–18.

169 The passage has often been discussed for its Christology. See Heinrici, pp. 275ff; Windisch, pp. 251ff; Wilhelm Bousset, *Kyrios Christos: A History of the Belief in Christ from the Beginnings of Christianity to Irenaeus* (tr. John E. Steely; Nashville and New York: Abingdon, 1979) 180, 209; Rudolf Bultmann, *Theology of the New Testament* (2 vols.; tr. Kendrick Grobel; London: SCM; New York: Scribner's, 1951–55) 1.175; idem, *Exegetica,* 77, 450; Barrett, pp. 222ff; Ethelbert Stauffer, "ἵνα," *TDNT* 3 (1965) 328–29; Ernst Bammel, "πτωχός κτλ.," *TDNT* 6 (1968) 910; Hans Dieter Betz, *Nachfolge und Nachahmung Jesu Christi im Neuen Testament* (BHTh 37; Tübingen: Mohr, Siebeck, 1967) 144, 156, 178, 185.

170 Cf. Quintilian's remark about such examples (5.11.16): "On the other hand in certain cases it will be sufficient merely to allude to the parallel. . . . Such parallels will be adduced at greater or less length according as they are familiar or as the interests or adornment of our case may demand."

171 *De inv.* 2.53.161, immediately following the statement on religion (cited above, n. 157): ". . . pietas, per quam sanguine coniunctis patriaeque benivolum officium et diligens tribuitur cultus; gratia, in qua amicitiarum et officiorum alterius memoria et remunerandi voluntas continetur."

172 Cf. *Rhet. ad Her.* 3.4.7.: "The Praiseworthy is what produces an honourable remembrance, at the time of the event and afterwards" ("Laudabile est quod conficit honestam et praesentem et consequentem

thians have the knowledge[173] which he attributed to them in v 9? Was he merely referring to the present letter in which the doctrine of the "grace of our Lord Jesus Christ" is treated? But thus far only the grace of God has been mentioned (8:1), not the grace of Christ. Therefore the doctrine of which Paul reminded his readers must have been taught them before. If that is the case, then ὅτι ("that") at the beginning of v 9b–c functions as a quotation mark, introducing a statement taken from another context. There is, however, no other passage in the New Testament from which v 9b–c could have been derived. The closest parallel is no doubt the Christ-hymn in Phil 2:6–11, with its juxtaposition of Christ the divine and the human being. But the contrast between wealth and poverty is not found in the Christ-hymn.[174] 1 Cor 1:26–31 also bears a close resemblance, but here, too, the contrast between wealth and poverty goes unmentioned. In fact, Christ's economic status plays no decisive role in the New Testament,[175] except in 2 Cor 8:9 and in the infancy narratives.

The infancy narratives provide a legendary description of Jesus' life as a life lived in circumstances of poverty.[176] We may surmise that these legends have their doctrinal basis in a Christology similar to that of 2 Cor 8:9. But no direct connection between the passages can be demonstrated. If one assumes a relationship of some sort, 2 Cor 8:9 must be taken to precede the infancy narratives. In any event, the Pauline statement stands, so far as we can tell, at the beginning of an important christological development, the doctrine of the poverty of Christ (*paupertas Christi*). This doctrine came to the fore only in the period subsequent to the New Testament and should not therefore be read back into 2 Cor 8:9. The later, developed doctrine of the *paupertas Christi* played a special role in the Middle Ages and the Reformation. It was beautifully summed up by Cornelius a Lapide: "Christ, the King of kings, for your sakes became poor when He was born in the stable, because there was no room for Him in the inn. Instead of His royal throne He had a manger; for bedding, hay; for fire, the breath of ox and ass; for curtains, spiders' webs; for sweet perfumes, stable ordure; for purple, filthy rags; for His stud, ox and ass; for a crowd of nobles, Joseph and Mary. So, too, His whole after-life was stamped with poverty, or, as Erasmus renders the Greek here, with beggary. From this it appears that Christ was not merely poor, but was also an actual beggar."[177] By contrast, the concepts of wealth and poverty found in 2 Cor 8:9 are metaphorical, and must be interpreted by analogy to Phil 2:6–11 and similar passages.

This makes it likely that v 6b–c was formulated ad hoc, as part of an ongoing argument.[178] But these options are by no means mutually exclusive. What was known to the Corinthians may have been doctrines and concepts,

commemorationem").

173 γινώσκετε is present tense, not the imperative (contra Chrysostom).

174 See also the passages considered by Windisch, p. 252; Lietzmann, p. 134. See also above, n. 164.

175 Commentators in the past have often introduced the notion of Jesus' poverty during his life on earth as an illustration, referring especially to Matt 8:20 par. But the fact is that nowhere in the Gospels, not even in Matt 8:20, does one read anything about Jesus having given up his wealth. Because of this lack of evidence, commentators have then turned to Jesus' "inner" wealth, his consciousness of being God's son, as having been given up by him (see for the references, Heinrici, pp. 276ff; Plummer, p. 241). The strange fact is to be noted, however, as Windisch, pp. 252–53, points out, that the notion of Jesus' poverty plays no important role in the Synoptic Gospels.

176 See especially the adoration of the infant Jesus (Matt 2:1–12//Luke 2:8–20) and the flight to Egypt (Matt 2:13–21). The contrast of poor and rich is found in the Magnificat (Luke 2:53), but without apparent reference to Jesus. See for further references, Walter Bauer, *Das Leben Jesu im Zeitalter der neutestamentlichen Apokryphen* (Tübingen: Mohr, Siebeck, 1909; rep. 1967) 316.

177 Cited according to the translation by W. C. Cobb, *The Great Commentary of Cornelius a Lapide, II. Corinthians and Galatians* (London: Hodges, 1897) 114. Cf. Fridericus Balduinus, *Apologia apostolica: hoc est, S. Apostoli Pauli epistola posterior ad Corinthios* (Wittenberg: Sumtibus haeredum Samuelis Selfichi, 1620) 429ff, 442ff. As already Wettstein, 2.197–98, has shown, this interpretation has significant parallels in Epictetus *Diss.* 3.31–36; Dio Chrysostom 14.22, commenting on the examples of Heracles and Odysseus (see also Mussies, *Dio Chrysostom,* 178). These passages reflect the ideals of the Socratic and Stoic traditions. See Klaus Döring, *Exemplum Socratis: Studien zur Sokratesnachwirkung in der kynisch-stoischen Popularphilosophie der frühen Kaiserzeit und im frühen Christentum* (Hermes, Einzelschriften 42; Weisbaden: Steiner, 1979) 2, 17, 25, 33, 59, 96, 98, 117, 121–

rather than the exact wording of the present text. An analogous situation seems to exist in other Pauline texts, such as 1 Cor 1:18–31; 2 Cor 10:1; Rom 15:1–6.

The statement that Christ became poor "on your account" (δι᾽ ὑμᾶς) introduces the soteriology of v 9c. This statement, with its ἵνα-clause, is again to be taken metaphorically.[179] The "poverty" of the Corinthians stood in stark contrast to their pride in their economic status. Yet the statement that they had become rich conformed more closely to their own estimation of themselves.[180] For the moment, for the sake of the argument, Paul left the matter of whether he considered the Corinthians rich both spiritually and economically completely open. In comparison with the Macedonians, not to mention the poor saints in Jerusalem, the Corinthians are certainly rich economically. But it remained to be seen whether they regarded themselves merely as rich, or as "spiritually" rich, that is, as having been made rich by the grace of God. The answer to this question depended upon their response to the example of Christ.

8:10–12: The Second Proof

The second point (vv 10–12) differs from the first both in form and in content. Instead of appealing to christological and soteriological doctrine, Paul alluded to a common-sense *sententia* (γνώμη)[181] on expediency, a stock argument in deliberative oratory.[182] Accordingly, a particular course of action may be recommended if its expediency can be demonstrated.[183] The basic presupposition of this argument is that it is more expedient to finish what one has begun than to leave it unfinished. Yet this commonplace remains at the level of a presupposition. It is not elaborated, but is at once applied to the situation at hand: the Corinthians have begun "not only to do but also to desire." It remains only for them to complete their action.

But the argument is somewhat more involved than this. It moves through three stages: (1) the past situation, as it bears upon the present (v 10c); (2) the present situation, as it determines what is to be done (v 11); and (3) a concluding *sententia,* cited as a proof text (v 12). Unlike the *sententia* employed in v 10, the commonplace of v 12 is stated in full.[184] We must be especially attentive at this point to the distinction between what is stated and what is presupposed. In addition, Paul made use of the special meaning of language drawn from the realms of business and law.

What Paul applied to the situation in Corinth in v 10 was not merely his own opinion but a commonplace which he believed would make sense to the Corinthians.[185] Though it remains at the presuppositional level, it is nevertheless present in the words that follow (ἐν τούτῳ).[186] The force of the argument proceeds by way of three steps: (1) Since the greatest part of the task

22, 132; Betz, *Lukian,* 75–76.

178 So Windisch, p. 252.

179 For the soteriological ἵνα, see Ethelbert Stauffer, "ἵνα," *TDNT* 3 (1965) 323–33; Betz, *Galatians,* 122 n. 81.

180 See above, p. 43 n. 15. Even in 1 Cor 1:26ff, poverty is not mentioned.

181 See Quintilian's definition (8.5.3): "Although all the different forms are included under the same name, the oldest type of *sententia,* and that in which the term is most correctly applied, is the aphorism, called γνώμη by the Greeks. Both the Greek and the Latin names are derived from the fact that such utterances resemble the decrees or resolutions of public bodies. The term, however, is of wide application. . . ." On the whole subject, see Lausberg, *Handbuch* 1, §§ 872–79; Martin, *Rhetorik,* 122, 124, 257ff; Betz, *Galatians,* 291–93.

182 See Lausberg, *Handbuch 1,* § 375; Martin, *Rhetorik,* 169ff.

183 The rhetorical force of the argument has been under discussion since Aristotle *Rhet.* 1.3, p. 1358b22; 1.6.1, p. 1362a18; 1.7.1, p. 1363b5; etc.; *Rhet. ad Her.* 3.3; Cicero, *De inv.* 2.51.156; 2.55.166–68; *De orat.* 2.82.334; *Part. orat.* 83; *Top.* 91; Quintilian 3.8.1. See furthermore Lausberg, *Handbuch* 1, §§ 234–36; Martin, *Rhetorik,* 160ff; Adamietz, *Liber III,* 170, 185ff.

184 Heinrici, p. 283, correctly defines v 12 as a *gnome.*

185 Commentators often emphasize correctly that Paul gives here more than his personal opinion. See Heinrici, p. 279; Windisch, pp. 253–54. Plummer, p. 242, refers to the Vulgate translation as *consilium* (so also Desiderius Erasmus, *Paraphrasis in duas epistolas Pauli ad Corinthios* [Lovanii, 1519]; also in his *Opera Omnia* [Lugduni Batavorum: Petrus van der Aa, 1706], vol. 7, *ad loc.;* cf. Theodorus V. Beza, *Annotationes Majores in Novum Testamentum* [n.p., 1594] 283: *sententia*). The term stands juxtaposed to ἐπιταγή ("command") in 8:8. See also 1 Cor 1:10; 7:25, 40; Phlm 14. See also Danker, *Benefactor,* 362.

186 Cf. Windisch, p. 253, who takes ἐν τούτῳ to mean "in this matter" (par. 1 Cor 11:22), or "with these words." Cf. also Plummer, p. 242: "ambiguous."

has already been accomplished, it is only expedient to complete the collection rather than leaving it undone. (2) To leave a small portion of the task incomplete is to jeopardize the whole, since only the delivery of the collection assures that anything has been accomplished at all. (3) Initial enthusiasm is praiseworthy, but goes to waste unless the final goal is attained.

As regards the past (v 10c), the Corinthians have already done what was "expedient" (*τὸ συμφέρον*),[187] for they "were first in the field, not merely in doing something but also in cherishing a desire to help, and that was as far back as last year."[188]

The language of vv 10c–12 poses special problems. The verbs "to do" (*ποιεῖν*) and "to will" (*θέλειν*) seem to be used simultaneously in a general and in a special sense. In both senses, the verbs play important roles in administrative language. The potential disparity between doing and willing was a commonplace in antiquity, as was the statement or the necessity of combining action and will to achieve a goal.[189] More specifically, administrative writings employed these terms to speak of getting things done (*ποιεῖν*)[190] and of being motivated toward certain accomplishments (*θέλειν*).[191] Paul spoke first of doing and then of willing, and joined the terms by the phrase "not only, but also" (*οὐ μόνον, ἀλλὰ καί*). This would seem to indicate that he regarded pure activism as easier to accomplish than sincere motivation. Nevertheless, he maintained that the Corinthians had achieved both when they started the collection a year before. The verb "to begin before" (*προενάρχομαι*) had already been used by Paul in v 6; now in v 10 he provided further details. Though Titus (v 6) had inaugurated the collection, the Corinthians were fully involved themselves in the initial phases (v 11), which transpired "a year ago" (*ἀπὸ πέρυσι*).[192] The adverbial expression *ἀπὸ πέρυσι* implies no doubt about the actual facts known to the readers;[193] the time-span intended can have been anywhere from one to twenty-three months, but it is likely that at least

187 For the usage of *τὸ συμφέρον* as an argument in Paul, see also 1 Cor 6:12; 10:23; 12:7; 2 Cor 12:1. Cf. *σύμφορος* 1 Cor 7:35; 10:33. See Moulton and Milligan, *s.v.* *συμφέρω*; Bauer, *s.v.* *συμφέρω*; Konrad Weiss, "*συμφέρω κτλ.*," *TDNT* 9 (1974) 71–80, who, however, denies the common-sense aspects of Paul's argument.

188 Plummer's paraphrase seems to catch the meaning of Paul's untranslatable sentence.

189 It is reflected also elsewhere in the New Testament; see esp. Mark 14:38; Rom 7:15ff; 9:16; 1 Cor 4:36; Gal 5:17; Phil 2:13; Phlm 14. See Herbert Braun, "*ποιέω κτλ.*," *TDNT* 6 (1968) 480–81(b).

190 This special meaning of the terminology is usually not treated in the commentaries. In fact, it is rare in the New Testament, occurring only here and 2 Cor 8:11. But it is found often in the Greek documentary papyri. See Preisigke, *Wörterbuch* 1, *s.v.* *ποιέω*, 1. A circular letter by a high official (A.D. 184[?]) contains the order *ποίησον* (*Pap. Oxy.* 474, 20), probably with the meaning "make a payment" (cf. Preisigke, *Wörterbuch* 1, *s.v.* 4). In another document (2d century A.D.), the king or his secretary authorizes a document by adding *ποιῆσαι* ("to carry out"); see Paul Meyer, *Griechische Texte aus Ägypten* (Berlin: Weidmann, 1916), no. 1, line 29.

191 For this special meaning, see Preisigke, *Wörterbuch* 1, *s.v.* *θέλω*. 1. In official letters, *θέλειν* often occurs in formulaic expressions. See, e.g., *Pap. Hibeh* 79, lines 2–6, in a letter from ca. A.D. 260: *εἰ ἔρρωσαι καὶ ὧν πρόνοιαν ποιεῖ καὶ τἆλλα σοι κατὰ λόγον ἐστὶν εἴη ἂν ὡς ἐγὼ θέλω καὶ τοῖς θεοῖς πολλὴ χάρις* . . . ("If you are well, and if the objects of your care are in order as I wish, much gratitude would be due also to the gods . . ."). The text is cited according to Bernhard P. Grenfell and Arthur S. Hunt, *The Hibeh Papyri* (Vol. 1; London: Egypt Exploration Fund, 1906) 235. In a letter of Isidora to Asclepiades (first century A.D.), a formula occurs: *ὡς θέλετε ποιεῖτε* ("Do as you wish"), BGU no. 1205, line 13. Another formula, used also in connection with financial transactions, is found in *Pap. Oxy.* no. 653, line 31, in an account of a trial: *θέλων καὶ μὴ θέλων, ἀποκαταστήσεις αὐτῷ. ὅπερ ἐὰν μὴ ποιήσῃς* . . . ("If you want, or don't want, you will pay up; if you do not carry that out . . ."). The translations of the passages are mine. For further references, see Dittenberger, *Sylloge* 4 (^{3}1920), index p. 378, *s.v.* *θέλω*; Welles, *Royal Correspondence*, nos. 32, line 17; 44, line 16; 53 I A, line 6; 60, line 12. This evidence also shows that Lietzmann's suggestion (p. 135) of a confusion in the text is unwarranted. See also Bultmann, p. 256.

192 On this expression, see Windisch, p. 255, with more references; Bauer, *s.v.* *πέρυσι*; Moulton and Milligan, *s.v.*; Preisigke, *Wörterbuch* 1, *s.v.* *πέρυσι*; 4/1, 222–23. cf. Plummer, p. 243: "'From last year,' i.e., 'as long ago as last year.' Not 'a year ago' which implies twelve months ago."

193 Cf. also 2 Cor 9:2 (see below, pp. 91–92).

three, and no more than eighteen, months have passed.[194] This was the period within which the crisis, Titus's second visit to Corinth, the reconciliation, and the writing of the letters now included in 1 and 2 Corinthians must have occurred.[195]

In v 11, Paul formulated his proposal in respect to the present situation (*νυνί*). All that was lacking was the accomplishment (*τὸ ποιεῖν*) of what they had desired, and this was what the apostle urged upon them (v 11a). The term "to finish up," or "to complete" (*ἐπιτελεῖν*) is used here, as in v 6, in the specific sense of completing an administrative act.[196] The comparison between Titus and the Corinthians is obvious. Titus had received an oral commission to go to Corinth and complete the collection (v 6); the Corinthians would receive written advice (not an order, v 8!) from their apostle to the same effect. They were admonished to help Titus finish the collection, just as a year ago they had helped to get it started.

Verse 11b supplies the rationale for what Paul recommended in v 11a:[197] ". . . just as there [was] readiness to will, there may also be completion."[198] Again Paul employed language from the realm of business and law. The phrase *ἡ προθυμία τοῦ θέλειν* seems redundant and untranslatable ("the willingness to be willing"), but the expression had been current since Plato *Leg.* III.697d.[199] The term "willingness" (*προθυμία*) occurs with surprising frequency in 2 Cor 8 and 9, and is also found elsewhere in the New Testament.[200] Its use as a business term is well attested in classical sources,[201] inscriptions,[202] and the papyri.[203] Thus it is unnecessary, and even mistaken, to look for a special Christian meaning at this point.[204]

Still another unusual phrase in v 11c must be related to what has gone before: "so also the completing in accordance with what you possess" (*οὕτως καὶ τὸ ἐπιτελέσαι ἐκ τοῦ ἔχειν*). No doubt, the completing refers to the doing mentioned in v 11a; but the phrase *ἐκ τοῦ ἔχειν* presents us with problems because it occurs nowhere else, and the meaning is ambiguous.[205] Does it mean "out of what you have" (*RSV;* cf. Vg: *ex eo, quod habetis*) or "in proportion to what you possess"?[206]

The use of the preposition *ἐκ* in the sense of "in accordance with" is not uncommon in the Greek language.[207] The papyri use it in this sense, especially in connection with financial matters.[208] The verb *ἔχειν* commonly has the meaning "to possess," even in the New

194 So Windisch, p. 255.

195 This time period has, of course, implications for the chronology of Paul, a problem which cannot be discussed here. See Philipp Bachmann, *Der zweite Brief an die Korinther* (KNT 8; Leipzig: Deichert, [4]1922) 318–19; Plummer, p. 243; Windisch, pp. 255–56; Lüdemann, *Paulus der Heidenapostel I,* 119–21, 133–35; Jewett, *Chronology.*

196 See above on 8:6.

197 On this sentence introduced by *ὅπως*, see Bauer, *s.v.* *ὅπως*, 2, a, α: "here *γένηται* or *ᾖ* is to be supplied as the predicate of the *ὅπως*-clause." Cf. 2 Cor 8:14.

198 So the rendering of Plummer, p. 243. Cf. Vg: *promptus est animus voluntatis.*

199 See Windisch, p. 265; Bauer, *s.v.* *προθυμία.*

200 For *προθυμία*, see also 2 Cor 8:12, 19; 9:2; cf. *πρόθυμος* Mark 14:38//Matt 26:41; Rom 1:15; *προθύμως* 1 Pet 5:2. See also Bauer, *s.v.*, with references; Spicq, *Notes de lexicographie* 2.746–51; Danker, *Benefactor,* 321.

201 LSJ, *s.v.;* Kuenzi, ΕΠΙΔΟΣΙΣ (see n. 149, above) 5.

202 See Dittenberger, *Sylloge* 4, index, 532–33 *s.v.;* Welles, *Royal Correspondence,* nos. 11, line 14; 15, line 11.

203 See Moulton and Milligan, *s.v.;* Preisigke, *Wörterbuch* 1, *s.v.*

204 This is done by Karl Heinrich Rengstorf in his article on "*πρόθυμος, προθυμία*," *TDNT* 6 (1968) 699–700.

205 See Bauer, *s.v.* *ἐκ*, 3, i: "of the underlying rule or principle 'according to, in accordance with'"; Bauer refers to 2 Cor 8:13 *ἐξ ἰσότητος* ("on the basis of equality") as a parallel. See also BDR, § 403, 3; BDF, § 403. Cf. the formula *ἐκ τῶν ἰδίων* ("from one's own property"), which occurs frequently on votive inscriptions and once in the New Testament (John 8:44). See Gerhard Naumann, *Griechische Weihinschriften* (Halle: Klinz, 1933).

206 So Plummer, p. 244, who bases his conclusion on v 12 and v 13 (*κατὰ δύναμιν*, "in accordance with ability"). Cf. *NEB:* "according to your means."

207 See Raphael Kühner, *Ausführliche Grammatik der griechischen Sprache* (2 vols; ed. Friedrich Blass and Bernhard Gerth; Hannover: Hahn, [3]1890–1904; rep. Darmstadt: Wissenschaftliche Buchgesellschaft, 1966) 1.461(g).

208 See Preisigke, *Wörterbuch* 4/4, 717–18, *s.v.* *ἐκ, ἐξ* (6–8), where close parallels are given. A direct parallel is Tob 4:8: *ἐξ αὐτῶν* (see below, n. 209).

Testament.[209] Furthermore, what Paul wished to say can be inferred from parallel passages within the present epistle.[210] He laid down a rule which recalled what he had recommended in 1 Cor 16:2: "he may save in accordance with his gains" (*θησαυρίζων ὅ τι ἐὰν εὐοδῶται*) (so Bauer, *s.v.* *θησαυρίζω*, 1).

Carl Friedrich Georg Heinrici gave expression to important insights into this passage. He recognized that v 12 constitutes a concluding *sententia,* in which "willingness" (*ἡ προθυμία*) is the subject. He also pointed to the importance of personified abstracts elsewhere in Paul's theology:[211] in this instance, willingness actively presents itself (*πρόκειμαι*).[212] The second part of the *sententia* specifies the terms for the giving of gifts. Though willingness is basic to the act of gift-giving, even more important is the matter of the gift's acceptability (*εὐπρόσδεκτος*) to the recipient. An acceptable gift, then, is measured by what one possesses, and not by what one does not possess. Indeed, it is absurd to think of giving what one does not possess, though such giving is often done. But more than this is at stake.

The term "acceptable" or "welcome" (*εὐπρόσδεκτος*) points beyond the ordinary realm to that of sacrificial gifts.[213] With regard to sacrificial gifts in particular, antiquity upheld the rule that such must be acceptable to the deity. Again, the above rule applies in determining what constitutes acceptability: the one who offers the gift gives in proportion to what he has.[214] If one is poor, and thus offers a small sacrifice, it is just as acceptable to the deity as the rich gifts of a wealthy man. The deity has no regard for the size of the sacrifice, but whether one is willing to give what he or she has. To be sure, there is nothing specifically Christian about these ideas; they were common to the religious thought of all antiquity.[215]

There may be a connection, in addition, between the *sententia* of v 12 and the mention of the Macedonians having given themselves to God in v 5. If the sacrifice of things is to symbolize the sacrifice of oneself, the only adequate gift is the gift of all one has.[216] Thus willingness to give all is what counts in the eyes of God.[217]

Heinrici[218] rightly called attention to the story of the poor widow's sacrifice in Mark 12:41–44 par. as a Gospel commentary on the *sententia* of 2 Cor 8:12. This text has its own history,[219] of course, but story and *sententia* do, in fact, express the same idea, a general rule on the giving of gifts, and in particular on sacrificial gifts to God.

209 See esp. 2 Cor 8:12; 6:10; and Bauer, *s.v.* *ἔχω*, I, 2.

210 See above, n. 200.

211 Heinrici, p. 283, referring to 1 Cor 13:4–7 as an example.

212 Heinrici, p. 283, refers to the Vulgate, Erasmus, and others as predecessors. See also Windisch, p. 257; Bauer, *s.v.* *πρόκειμαι*, 2; Moulton and Milligan, *s.v.;* Kypke, *Observationes sacrae* 2.259.

213 See also Rom 15:31, a statement made in the same context of the collection for Jerusalem; 15:16; 2 Cor 6:2. On the term, see Bauer, *s.v.* 1; Windisch, p. 257; Walter Grundmann, "*δεκτός κτλ.*," *TDNT* 2 (1964) 58.

214 *καθὸ ἐὰν ἔχῃ*. The meaning is identical with *ἐκ τοῦ ἔχειν* (v 11). See also Bauer, *s.v.* *καθό*, 2.

215 In Tob 4:8, the rule is stated in the context of Jewish almsgiving (4:7–11): "If you have many possessions, make your gift from them in proportion [*ἐξ αὐτῶν*]; if few, do not be afraid to give according to the little you have." See also Prov 3:27–28; Sir 4:31; also the texts listed in Str-B 1.45–46, 3.523; on the Greek side, see esp. Xenophon *Mem.* 1.3.3, quoting Hesiod *Erga* 336: *καδδύναμιν δ' ἔρδειν ἱέρ' ἀθανάτοισι θεοῖσι* ("According to thy power render sacrifice to the immortal gods." Translation by Edgar C. Marchant, LCL). See also the discussion in Aristotle *EN* 4.2, p. 1122a18ff, on the vices opposed to liberality. The same ideas were part of the Delphic piety and found expression in some characteristic stories, for which see Wolfgang Schadewaldt, "Der Gott von Delphi und die Humanitätsidee," in his *Hellas and Hesperien* (2 vols.; Zurich: Artemis, 1970) 1.677–78.

216 In his commentary, Cornelius a Lapide, p. 117, refers to stories told by church fathers to illustrate this point. Augustine *De civ. dei* 1.10.57–69 tells the story of Bishop Paulinus of Nola, who spent all his possessions on the poor and then gave himself up to the Vandals to become a slave in place of the son of a widow. He was rewarded by God, for the Vandals recognized who he really was. They treated him well and sent him home. Even further goes the legend of St. Paula, who had given all her belongings to the poor and had only one wish which God granted her as a reward: to be buried at the expense of others, and in someone else's clothes.

217 For other rules concerning receiving and giving, see Matt 10:8; 14:19–20 par.; Acts 20:35; 1 Cor 4:7; etc.

218 See Heinrici, p. 283n.

219 Erich Klostermann, *Das Markusevangelium* (HNT 3; Tübingen: Mohr, Siebeck, [4]1950) 130–31; Rudolf Pesch, *Das Markusevangelium* (2 vols.; HThK; Freiburg: Herder, 1976–77) 2.260–64; Joachim Gnilka, *Das Evangelium nach Markus* (2 vols.; EKK 2/1–2; Zurich: Benziger; Neukirchen-Vluyn: Neukirchener, 1978–79) 2.175–78.

It should also be noted that this rule is the key to the much-discussed story in Mark 10:17–22 par.[220] The rich would-be disciple fails because he cannot live up to the rule, while Peter states the approved standard of discipleship in Mark 10:28: "See, we have left everything and followed you."[221]

8:13–15: The Third Proof

As Paul himself said (v 13), the third and final proof is that of equality (*ἰσότης*; Vg: *aequalitas*), another stock argument in deliberative oratory.[222] It is based on the well-known principle of *suum cuique,*[223] about which the *Rhetorica ad Herennium* remarks, by way of example:

> . . . if we say that we ought to pity innocent persons and suppliants; if we show that it is proper to repay the well-deserving with gratitude; . . . if we urge that faith ought zealously be kept; . . . if we contend that alliances and friendships should scrupulously be honoured; if we make it clear that the duty imposed by nature toward parents, gods, and fatherland must be religiously observed; if we maintain that ties of hospitality, clientage, kinship, and relationship by marriage must inviolably be cherished; if we show that neither reward nor favour nor peril nor animosity ought to lead us astray from the right path; if we say that in all cases a principle of dealing alike with all should be established.[224]

Beyond rhetoric, the concept of "equality" (*ἰσότης*; *aequalitas*) is also at home in the field of ancient law.[225]

In v 13a, Paul first stated the relation of inequality. The entire purpose of the collection would be missed if it resulted in a situation in which relief and rest (*ἄνεσις*) were enjoyed by others, namely the recipients of the collection, while the Corinthian donors had to endure affliction (*θλῖψις*).[226] Then in v 13b, the key term is introduced: their relationship should rather be "a matter of equality" (*ἐξ ἰσότητος*).[227] The concept of equality (*ἰσότης*) is also numbered among the virtues, as Col 4:1 reminds us.[228] What Paul had in mind in v 13 was no doubt the Greek virtue which played such a large role in

220 The passage must be interpreted first of all in sacrificial terms, then in ethical terms, but not in terms of the ascetic ideal of poverty alone. See Betz, *Nachfolge,* 29–30; differently Pesch, *Markusevangelium,* 2.135–47; Gnilka, *Das Evangelium nach Markus,* 2.83–91.

221 Gerd Theissen's interpretation of this statement as expressing the social attitude of the wandering charismatic is at least one-sided because he fails to pay attention to the sacrificial connotations. See, e.g., Matt 5:23–26, 40–42. For Theissen's interpretation, see his essay, "'Wir haben alles verlassen': Mc X 28," *NT* 19 (1977) 161–96; idem, *Sociology of Early Palestinian Christianity* (Philadelphia: Fortress, 1977) 12, 78. For a critique of Theissen which, however, does not pay attention to the sacrificial aspects, see Wolfgang Stegemann, "Wanderradikalismus im Urchristentum? Historische und theologische Auseinandersetzung mit einer interessanten These," in Willy Schottroff and Wolfgang Stegemann, *Der Gott der kleinen Leute* (2 vols.; Munich: Kaiser, 1979) 2.94–120, esp. 107–10.

222 See Aristotle *Rhet.* 1.9, p. 1366b9; *Rhet. ad Her.* 3.2.3: "Justice is equity, giving to each thing what it is entitled to in proportion to its worth" ("Iustitia est aequitas ius uni cuique rei tribuens pro dignitate cuiusque"). Similarly Cicero *De inv.* 2.53.160. For further passages, see Caplan's note e (pp. 162–63) of his LCL edition of the *Rhet. ad Her.;* Lausberg, *Handbuch* 1, § 375; Martin, *Rhetorik,* 174.

223 See Leopold Wenger, "Suum Cuique in antiken Urkunden," *Aus der Geisteswelt des Mittelalters, FS Günter Grabmann* (Münster: Aschendorff, 1935) 1.1415–25; Klaus Thraede, "Gleichheit," *RAC* 10 (1979) 122–64; Albrecht Dihle, "Goldene Regel," *RAC* 11 (1981) 930–40 (lit.).

224 *Rhet. ad Her.* 3.3.4.

225 The principle is also cited or presupposed in other New Testament passages. See esp. Mark 12:17; Luke 6:34; Acts 11:17; Rom 13:7.

226 As Bauer rightly sees, the terms *ἄνεσις* and *θλῖψις* are used here in the common secular sense (*s.v. ἄνεσις,* 2). Cf. the complaints of the workers in Matt 20:12, and of the older son, Luke 15:29–30; furthermore 1 Cor 16:18; 2 Cor 2:13; 7:5.

227 So Bauer, *s.v. ἰσότης,* 1.

228 Col 4:1 combines "justice and equality" (*τὸ δίκαιον καὶ τὴν ἰσότητα*) in accordance with Greek thought (see also Philo *De rer. div. heres* 161ff). See Gustav Stählin, "*ἴσος κτλ.,*" *TDNT* 3 (1965) 345–48(3); Eduard Lohse, *Colossians and Philemon: A Commentary on the Epistles to the Colossians and to Philemon* (tr. William R. Poehlmann and Robert J. Karris; ed. Helmut Koester; Hermeneia; Philadelphia: Fortress, 1971)

law, politics, and morality.[229] According to Aristotle,[230] equality is the foundation of the city and the society, that is, it is the basis of their concord (ὁμόνοια)[231] and peace (εἰρήνη);[232] its opposite is greed (πλεονεξία).[233]

A financial contribution which involved Greeks as donors and Palestinian Jews as recipients was certainly a political matter, though in this instance a matter of ecclesiastical politics. As the apostle explained in greater detail in 2 Cor 9:6–15, he regards the collection for the poor in Jerusalem as a means of bringing about unity within the church between Jews and Greeks.[234] In chapter 8 these ideas remain largely at the presuppositional level. Yet 8:14 provides one example of how the collection could bring about equality. Since equality consists in reciprocity, there must be give-and-take on both sides. Thus "at the present time" (ἐν τῷ νῦν καιρῷ, v 14a)[235] the Corinthians' abundance (περίσσευμα)[236] should be used to alleviate[237] the want (ὑστέρημα)[238] of the saints in Jerusalem. At the literal level, Paul certainly intended the material abundance of the Corinthians and the material poverty of the Jerusalem church.[239]

Verse 14b is more difficult to understand: "so that also their abundance may go to your want" (ἵνα καὶ τὸ ἐκείνων περίσσευμα γένηται εἰς τὸ ὑμῶν ὑστέρημα). The construction ἵνα . . . γένηται εἰς . . . can point either to the future or to the present.[240] The choice in this instance depends on how the terms "abundance" and "want" in v 14b are to be interpreted. It is hard to imagine that Paul would ever have expected a material shortage in Corinth to be relieved by the material affluence of the church in Jerusalem. Rather, Paul must have used these terms metaphorically, to speak of the spiritual wealth of the Jerusalem Christians to which the Corinthians were deeply indebted. In other words, he seems to have employed here the same thought found in Rom 15:27.[241]

But talk of the "spiritual want" of the Corinthians in the present context raises difficulties, for, strictly speaking, it should have been a matter of the past. At present, they were spiritually wealthy, both in their own regard and in that of Paul.[242] As a result, 2 Cor 8:14b cannot be harmonized completely with Rom 15:27. Thus it is understandable that Dieter Georgi[243] thought that Paul looked to a future messianic kingdom to produce spiritual equality. This option is less likely, however, because v 14 refers to the present time (ὁ νῦν καιρός).

ad loc.; Georgi, *Kollekte,* 62–65.

229 See the basic study by Rudolf Hirzel, *Themis, Dike und Verwandtes: Ein Beitrag zur Geschichte der Rechtsidee by den Griechen* (Leipzig: Hirzel, 1907) 228–320, 421–23; Engbert J. Jonkers, "Aequitas," *RAC* 1 (1950) 141–44; Klaus Thraede, "Gleichheit," *RAC* 10 (1979) 122–64; Max Kaser, *Das römische Privatrecht* (HAW 10.3.3.1; Munich: Beck, ²1971) 1. § 48; 2. § 61, with further literature.

230 Aristotle *Pol.* 2.1, p. 1261a30–31: τὸ ἴσον τὸ ἀνεπιπονθὸς σῴζει τὰς πόλεις ("Reciprocal equality is the preservative of states." Translation by H. Rackham, LCL).

231 See also Ps. Aristotle *De mundo* 5, p. 397a3–4: τὸ ἴσον σωστικὸν ὁμονοίας ("Equality is the preservative of concord").

232 See Philo *Her.* 162: εἰρήνην ἰσότης (ἔτεκε) ("Equality gave birth to peace"). See on this point also Erwin R. Goodenough, *The Politics of Philo* (New Haven: Yale University, 1938) 87ff.

233 Cf. Menander *Monostichoi* 259 (ed. Siegfried Jaekel, *Menandri Sententiae* [BT; Leipzig: Teubner, 1964): Ἰσότητα τίμα, μὴ πλεονέκτει μηδένα ("Honor equality, do not act greedily toward anyone"). Cf. 366: Ἰσότητα δ᾽ αἱροῦ <καὶ> πλεονεξίαν φύγε ("Choose equality and flee greediness"). My translations.

234 See below, pp. 122–28.

235 Cf. the νυνί ("now") in v 11.

236 See on this term 2 Cor 8:2 (above, p. 43 n. 15).

237 The sentence may be elliptic; cf. v 14b. The usage of the preposition εἰς is sometimes peculiar in 2 Cor 8 and 9 and may refer specifically to payments to be made on behalf of Jerusalem (see also 1 Cor 16:1; 2 Cor 8:4; 9:1, 13; Rom 15:26; Acts 24:17). See Moulton and Milligan, *s.v.* εἰς; Bauer, *s.v.* εἰς 4,g.

238 The opposite term is περίσσευμα. See also 2 Cor 9:12; Phil 2:30. For further discussion see Bauer, *s.v.;* Ulrich Wilckens, "ὕστερος κτλ.," *TDNT* 8 (1972) 598–600 (C.4).

239 See also 2 Cor 9:12–13; Rom 15:25–28; 1 Cor 16:17; Phil 2:30. Parallel is again (see above, p. 66) Mark 12:44//Luke 21:4: ὑστέρημα meaning poverty.

240 For the meaning of γίνομαι εἰς, see Bauer, *s.v.* γίνομαι 4,c. Some manuscripts (P⁴⁶ 630 1175 1739 1881 *pc*) solve the problem by dropping γένηται, thereby making v 14b conform to v 14a and having both refer to the present.

241 Cf. Stählin, "ἴσος κτλ.," *TDNT* 3 (1965) 349; Wilckens, "ὕστερος κτλ.," *TDNT* 8 (1972) 597; Georgi, *Kollekte,* 67.

242 See 1 Cor 1:7, where Paul spells out the promise of the salvation in Christ "so that you are not lacking in any spiritual gift" (ὥστε ὑμᾶς μὴ ὑστερεῖσθαι μηδενὶ χαρίσματι).

There is no alternative but to assume that the church at Jerusalem, though poor economically, had spiritual wealth, while the church of Corinth, while rich in every respect, nevertheless had its shortcomings.[244] The saints in Jerusalem were, then, in a situation not unlike that of the Macedonians (8:2), while the deficiency of the Corinthians consisted in the fact that thus far they had not been able to bring the collection to a conclusion. In this sense, the Corinthians' deficiency was real and present, and gave rise to Paul's admonition.

Verse 14c confirms this interpretation: "that there may be equality" (ὅπως γένηται ἰσότης). Once the collection had been completed and delivered, the church at Jerusalem would indeed have helped to eliminate the present want of the Corinthians.

It is noteworthy that Paul could speak at both the material and the spiritual level of the Corinthians' lack. When he spoke of the deficiency of the Corinthians, he had something spiritual in mind. Yet a material deficiency is implied as well: despite their wealth, the Corinthians had not yet been able to raise the money. By contrast, Paul could speak of the spiritual abundance of the church at Jerusalem in spite of their material poverty. Thus give-and-take should occur at a number of levels, and this is the meaning of equality.

Paul concluded his argument in 8:15 with a proof text from Exod 16:18, introduced by a quotation formula, "as it is written" (καθὼς γέγραπται):[245] "He who gathered much had not too much, and he who gathered little had not too little"[246] (ὁ τὸ πολὺ οὐκ ἐπλεόνασεν, καὶ ὁ τὸ ὀλίγον οὐκ ἐλαττόνησεν). The text as quoted here differs only slightly from the LXX.[247] It seems to have occupied a traditional place in Jewish Haggadah on the miracle of the manna in Exod 16. This much can be concluded from the fact that *Targum Onqelos* and *Targum Jerushalmi I*[248] comment on the passage. Of special interest is the fact that Philo proved this very passage in his rather lengthy treatise, "On equality" (περὶ ἰσότητος), included in his *Quis rerum divinarum heres sit* 191[249] (quoted in accordance with the LXX).[250] In Philo's interpretation, the miracle of Exod 16 was twofold: all were fed, and the collection of what remained did not lead to excess on the part of those who gathered too much, or to shortage for those who gathered little. Apparently the tradition was conscious of the ethical implications of the exodus

243 Georgi, *Kollekte,* 65, 74–75. See also other options discussed by Windisch, pp. 259–60.

244 Paul seems to have this kind of deficiency (ὑστέρημα) in mind when he attributes it to the Corinthians in 1 Cor 16:17; cf. also Phil 2:30. In other words, it is also the function of the apostle's letters to eliminate spiritual deficiencies.

245 On this formula see below on 2 Cor 9:9.

246 My translation.

247 Exod 16:18 LXX reads: οὐκ ἐπλεόνασεν ὁ τὸ πολύ, καὶ ὁ τὸ ἔλαττον οὐκ ἠλαττόνησεν. Cf. also Aemilius Fridericus Kautzsch, *De Veteris Testamenti locis a Paulo apostolo allegatis* (Leipzig: Metzger & Wittig, 1869) 19–20; and the critical apparatus in Alan E. Brooke and Norman McLean, *The Old Testament in Greek* (3 vols.; Cambridge: Cambridge University, 1906–40) 1.208.

248 According to Str-B 3.523. Strangely, some works on targumic traditions in the New Testament do not comment on 2 Cor 8:15; see Bruce J. Malina, *The Palestinian Manna Tradition: The Manna Tradition in the Palestinian Targums and Its Relationship to the New Testament* (AGJU 7; Leiden: Brill, 1968); Peder Borgen, *Bread from Heaven: An Exegetical Study of the Concept of Manna in the Gospel of John and the Writings of Philo* (NovTSup 10; Leiden: Brill, 1965, [2]1981) 141–42, commenting on Exod 16:18 but not on 2 Cor 8:15. The passages are, however, discussed in Anthony T. Hanson, *Studies in Paul's Technique and Theology* (London: SPCK, 1974) 174–77; Theobald, *Die überströmende Gnade,* 307–15. See furthermore Louis Ginsberg, *The Legends of the Jews* (Philadelphia: Jewish Publication Society, 1911) 3.45ff.

249 The section includes all of *Quis rerum divinarum heres* 141–206. See Georgi, *Kollekte,* 62–65, 97–98; Borgen, *Bread from Heaven,* 141–42; Theobald, *Die überströmende Gnade,* 313–14.

250 This was pointed out by Windisch, p. 259. The interpretation by Philo uses terminology similar to Paul's. See especially expressions like ἐξ ἴσου ("in equal portions"), for which cf. 2 Cor 8:13, and ὡς μηθ' ὑστερῆσαι μήτ' αὖ περιττεῦσαι ("that there was neither shortcoming nor superabundance"). Cf. also Philo's interpretation of πλεονεξία ("greediness") in *Leg. all.* 3.166; *Decal.* 155.

Haggadah. Paul seems to have appropriated this tradition here in order to apply it to the situation at hand.[251]

2) 8:16–23: The Legal Section: Commendation and Authorization of the Envoys

■ 8:16–22: The Commendation of the Delegation

As scholars have previously noted, Paul changed both the form and the content of his presentation in the second part of the chapter: from arguments (vv 9–15), he proceeded to official business in vv 16–23.[252] In sum, vv 16–22 contain the commendation of the delegation to be sent to Corinth. First Titus, then the two envoys of the churches (vv 18–22), are commended to the Corinthians (vv 16–17). These commendations are followed by Paul's official authorization (v 23), and the conclusion of the letter (v 24).

■ 8:16–17: The Commendation of Titus

Paul's commendation of the envoys begins with Titus (vv 16–17), whom he had already mentioned in v 6. The commendation gives his name and a description of his qualifications for the task at hand, that is to say, his "zeal" or *σπουδή*. It is of interest for our analysis of the composition of the letter that the commendation of Titus in vv 16–17 is formulated without regard to v 6, as if v 6 had not been written. Thus what looks like repetitiveness is in fact a manifestation of the formal requirements of the commendation.

Two things may be said with respect to the qualifications of zeal which Paul ascribed to Titus: (1) zeal (*σπουδή*) is commonly found in Hellenistic administrative letters as the most important qualification of the administrator;[253] (2) Paul's somewhat elaborate manner of presentation is out of the ordinary.

Paul first pointed out that Titus's zeal was not simply a matter of natural ability, but was due to divine inspiration. Because such inspiration is ipso facto miraculous in nature, Paul offered a prayer of thanksgiving, adopting performative language. The opening phrase is an introductory formula conventional for such thanksgiving prayers: "Thanks be to God" (*χάρις τῷ θεῷ*).[254]

The following phrase, "who gave the same zeal for you into the heart of Titus" (*τῷ δόντι τὴν αὐτὴν σπουδὴν ὑπὲρ ὑμῶν ἐν τῇ καρδίᾳ Τίτου*), picks up a liturgical formula and applies it directly to Titus. God has given the same zeal to Titus by inspiration[255] that he has given to the Corinthians (v 7) and the Macedonians (v 8).[256]

Verse 17 goes on to provide evidence of Titus's zeal. Three items are mentioned: (1) "He accepted the appointment" (*τὴν παράκλησιν ἐδέξατο*). The language Paul employed here is of a technical nature: *παράκλησις* is a noun form of the verb *παρακαλεῖν* found in v 6. To accept such an appointment was to accept a legal mandate (*mandatum*).[257] (2) Titus's attitude was such that it met the necessary prerequisites: he was "utterly sincere" about the collection (*σπουδαιότερος*),[258] and took the initiative himself (*αὐθαίρετος*).[259] (3) In keeping with his zeal, he is about to depart for Corinth: *ἐξῆλθεν πρὸς ὑμᾶς*.[260] From this we may also conclude that Titus was

251 Cf. also Irenaeus *Adv. haer.* 1.10.2; Chrysostom *In epist. II. ad Cor. Hom.* 17, *MPG* 61.561A–B; Cornelius a Lapide, pp. 118–19, who has further references to the church fathers.

252 See the commendation for envoys in Welles, *Royal Correspondence,* no. 15, lines 36–39: . . . οἱ] *πρεσβευταί, οὓς διά τε τὰ ἄλ [λα ἃ ἔπραξαν, ἐπαινοῦμεν καὶ δ] ιὰ τὴν σπουδὴν ἣν ἐποιοῦν [περὶ τῶν συμφερόντων τῶι δήμωι]* (". . .] envoys whom [we praise for their conduct] in general and especially for the concern they have shown [for the interests of your people]"). See also nos. 31, line 11; 32, line 11; 33, line 18; 44, line 26; 52, lines 10, 39; Robert K. Sherk, *Roman Documents from the Greek East: Senatus Consults and Epistulae to the Age of Augustus* (Baltimore: Johns Hopkins, 1969) nos. 38, line 5; 58, line 84.

253 For further references, see above on 8:7.

254 See 1 Cor 15:57: "Thanks be to God, who gives us the victory through our Lord Jesus Christ" (*τῷ δὲ θεῷ χάρις τῷ διδόντι ἡμῶν τὸ νῖκος διὰ τοῦ κυρίου ἡμῶν Ἰησοῦ Χριστοῦ*). For further discussion see below on 2 Cor 9:15.

255 Cf. also Rom 5:5; 11:8; 1 Cor 12:8; 2 Cor 1:22; 5:5; 1 Thess 4:8; etc. See also 2 Cor 9:7.

256 Cf. Plummer, pp. 246–47, who thinks of Paul's own zeal as being the same as Titus's. Windisch, p. 261, thinks of the Macedonians only.

257 This was not recognized by Bauer, *s.v. παρακαλέω*. The New Testament translations usually follow the Vulgate, which has *exhortatio.* The technical usage of the term is indeed unique in the New Testament. See the excursus on "The Mandate (mandatum)" below, p. 71.

258 See also 2 Cor 8:22.

the bearer of the letter. An explicit statement to this effect is lacking; but this is often the case in letters of recommendation,[261] and its omission here does not weigh against Titus as the bearer of the epistle.

Excursus: The Mandate (mandatum)

The technical use of *παράκλησις* (8:17) and *παρακαλεῖν* (8:6; 9:5) indicates that the appointment of Titus and the two "brothers" is to be regarded as an instance of the operation of the Greek and Roman legal institution of the mandate (*mandatum*). The institution was well established, though it could take many forms, depending on whether the case belonged to private, civil, or state law. A "mandate" was understood to be a binding declaration in which one person (*mandans, mandator*) commissioned another (*mandatar, is qui mandatum suscepit, procurator, . . .*) to carry out tasks (*negotia*) on his behalf. The term mandate derives from *manum dare* ("give a hand," see Kaser, *Das römische Privatrecht* I, 577 n. 1), referring to the handshake which concluded the contract (see, e.g., Gal 2:9 and Betz, *Galatians,* 100). Under Roman law, the acceptance of a mandate was regarded as an *officium,* that is to say, a public obligation of a citizen in good standing, to be discharged without financial compensation. A mandate could be delivered to perform a business or administrative act of any kind, provided that such acts were within the law and in conformity to the provisions of the contract. For this reason, the terms of the contract had to be quite specific. The persons authorizing and accepting the mandate had to be named, and the nature and limits of the assignment, its date of termination, etc., had to be stipulated.

Paul's appointment of Titus is such a mandate. The document containing the contract is identical with chapter 8, with its designation of Titus in v 6 and the commendations and authorizations in vv 16–23. The description of Titus's personality, the statement of his qualifications and standing in the community, and the account of his specific assignment correspond to the legal formulae included in such documents. Presumably the completion of the collection would terminate the mandate.

The fact that not only Titus but two other brothers were appointed is unusual and had to be justified by Paul. As we shall note below, the appointment of the two brothers came about at the insistence of the churches, who were concerned about the implications of the collection for future relations between the communities. In addition, the amount of money that was involved made supervision of the *mandatar* advisable (see on 8:20–21). Moreover, it seems to have been the common practice to mandate groups of two and three in the early church, especially in connection with the work of the missionaries and the apostles. At the conference in Jerusalem (see Gal 2:1–10), the delegation from Antioch consisted of Paul, Barnabas, and Titus; they entered into negotiation with the three "pillars," Peter, James, and John. We are familiar with the practice of sending out missionaries in groups of two from the instructions found in the Gospels (Mark 6:7; Luke 10:1; cf. Mark 11:1 par.; 14:13; Luke 24:13; etc.). When John the Baptist encountered Jesus, John was in the company of two disciples (John 1:35; cf. Acts 10:23b). The purpose may have been, among other things, to provide for witnesses (see Matt 18:16; 2 Cor 13:1 [Deut 19:15]; John 18:17; 1 Tim 5:19; Heb 10:28).

Bibliography:

Leopold Wenger, *Die Stellvertretung im Rechte der Papyri* (Leipzig: Teubner, 1906); Hans Kreller, "Mandatum," *PRE* 27. Halbband (1928) 1015–25; Max Kaser, *Das römische Privatrecht,* vol. I (Munich: Beck, ²1971), esp. 577–80; Alan Watson, *The Contract of Mandate in Roman Law* (Oxford: Clarendon, 1961). Of interest are excerpts from a protocol book which states the requirements for the mandate, published by Hubert Metzger, "Zur Stellung der liturgischen Beamten Ägyptens in frührömischer Zeit," *MH* 2 (1945) 54–62. See, in addition, Ernst Rabel, "Systasis," *Archives d'Histoire du Droit Oriental* 1 (1937) 213–37; Johannes Herrmann, "Interpretation von Vollmachtsurkunden," *Akten des 13. Internationalen Papyrologenkongresses Marburg / Lahn, 2.–6. August 1971, Münchener Beiträge zur Papyrusforschung und antiken Rechtsgeschichte* 66 (Munich: Beck, 1974) 159–67.

259 See also 2 Cor 8:3. The verb *ὑπάρχω* seems to belong to both adjectives, the second of which is even stronger than the first.

260 *ἐξῆλθεν πρὸς ὑμᾶς* is epistolary aorist like *συνεπέμψαμεν* in vv 18 and 22. So correctly Heinrici, p. 287; Windisch, p. 262. See BDR, § 334; BDF, § 334. For the technical meaning of *ἐξέρχομαι* ("depart"), see also 2 Cor 2:13; Phil 4:15.

261 Letters of recommendation often identify the names of the person as being the same as the bearer of the letter. See Chan-Hie Kim, *Form and Structure of the Familiar Greek Letter of Recommendation* (SBLDS 4; Missoula, MT: Scholars, 1972) 37ff; Hannah Cotton, *Documentary Letters of Recommendation in Latin from the Roman Empire* (BKP 132; Königstein: Hain, 1981) 5 with n. 26.

■ **8:18–22: The Commendation of the Two Brothers**

The commendation of the two other delegates (vv 18–22) is clearly treated separately from that of Titus (cf. also v 23a and b). These envoys were no doubt of a lower rank. Though their appointments resulted from different procedures, they nevertheless are treated together as a group. The appointment of these two brothers raises questions which are intriguing not only for us today, but no doubt at the time when 2 Cor 8 and 9 were written. Paul's repeated defense of the appointments raises more questions than it answers (cf. also 9:3–5). The epistolary aorists[262] (vv 18 and 22) make clear Paul's decision to accept the two envoys and assume the responsibility for the delegation as a whole. The verb συμπέμπω[263] ("send someone with someone") has a technical meaning in the context of the sending of envoys.[264]

An interesting example of the sending of letters with additional envoys is found in Welles's collection. Letter no. 60[265] was sent by Eumenes II and Attalus II to Attis, priest of the temple of Cybele at Pessinus. Welles dated the letter to the late first century B.C. The content of the letter is obscure, but it must have dealt with some kind of intrigue. So much is indicated by the words: ". . . after opening and resealing the letter, I have sent it to you. For they said that you would not be able to open it, if I sent it as it was. Do you take it then, and send what men you wish as they invite you to do, assured that we know that whatever you do you will do to our advantage. By all means, therefore, summon the bearer of this letter, for he wishes to speak with you. It is, you see, useful for our other projects that you hear from him what he says he wants to tell you, and that there be sent some one from you with him[266] into the upper districts to accept what is given—and to report more carefully to us the disposition of the people there. . . ."

The subject of the intrigue is unknown. Yet it is clear that envoys bearing letters had functions apart from those related to the letters themselves. The envoy served as observer, trusted agent, and bearer of messages not entrusted to the letters. Here, the envoy who bore the letter was authorized to conduct certain business, while the other envoy served as witness and exercised control over the negotiations.

Since a delegation of two or three seems to have been the rule,[267] there is nothing in the sending of a three-man delegation to Corinth which would have given cause for surprise. But the appointment of the two brothers did not occur at the same time as the appointment of Titus, but only after some negotiation. It is the belatedness of their appointment which gives rise to questions.

In the first place, we must examine what seems to be a rather inconspicuous matter, the title "brother" given to the two envoys. The term "brother" (ἀδελφός), as it is used here and elsewhere in the New Testament, stands simply for "fellow Christian."[268] But the term also occurs frequently in Greek and Roman correspondence, where it was used, apparently, with little concern for a precise meaning. It was applied to blood relations and to those named in the honorary declarations[269] commonly made by Hellenistic rulers.[270] Thus Paul's use of the term in reference to the envoys[271] may have been influenced by such administrative language. In that case, those whom

262 See above, n. 260.

263 In the New Testament, the term occurs only in 2 Cor 8:18, 22; cf. Acts 15:25: πέμπω σύν; Ign. *Phld.* 11.2; *Smyrn.* 12.1.

264 For parallel references, see LSJ, *s.v.;* Bauer, *s.v.;* Preisigke, *Wörterbuch,* 2, *s.v.; Sup.* I, p. 528 *s.v.;* Dittenberger, *Sylloge,* nos. 116, line 20; 409, line 5; 696 B; 697 B; idem, *OGIS,* nos. 309, line 12; 315, line 79. See also Philo *Jos.* 184; Josephus *C. Ap.* 1.48.

265 In Welles, *Royal Correspondence,* it is no. 60, whose translation is given here; see also his commentary, pp. 249–50.

266 The term here is συμπέμπω.

267 Cf. the delegation of Stephanas, Fortunatus, and Achaicus in 1 Cor 16:17. See the excursus on "The Mandate (mandatum)" above, p. 71; also Welles, *Royal Correspondence,* nos. 31, lines 3–4; 32, lines 2–3. Welles also refers to Otto Kern, "Magnetische Studien," *Hermes* 36 (1901) 500–503, and Paul Boesch, ΘΕΩΡΟΣ*: Untersuchung zur Epangelie griechischer Feste* (Dissertation, Zurich, 1908; Göttingen: Dieterich, 1908) 22, 30–35. See for the number of delegates also Franciscus Poland, *De legationibus Graecorum publicis* (Inaugural Dissertation, Lipsiensis; Leipzig: Teubner, 1885) 53–70: *De numero legatorum.*

268 The term occurs in 2 Cor 8:1, 18, 22, 23; 9:3, 5. See also the second apology 11:9; 12:18; and the letter of reconciliation 1:1, 8; 2:13; 13:11.

269 Welles, *Royal Correspondence,* nos. 41, line 1; 45, line 5; 56, line 5; 57, line 2; 59, line 4; 61, line 15; 65, lines 2, 5, 14; 71, line 2; Dittenberger, *OGIS,* nos. 138, line 2; 168, lines 26, 36; 257, line 2. Cf. Cicero *Ep. Fam.* 13.1.5: "Pomponium Atticum sic amo, ut

Paul referred to as "brothers" were considered not only as fellow Christians, but also as church-political allies.

Another problem is presented by the fact that the names of the two brothers are not given in the text. Commentators have long found the omission of the names puzzling.[272] Were the names originally in the letter and later removed by the redactor? But why should they have been removed? Did they become an embarrassment? Hans Lietzmann and Hans Windisch assumed that the names were later excised because they had, for some unknown reason, become undesirable.[273] The redactor would then have followed Ignatius's practice of refusing to name certain heretics so as not to increase their notoriety.[274] The question which must be raised, however, is whether Paul could have omitted the names himself. It is surely odd to recommend people without giving their names, as Lietzmann has rightly observed, though examples of this practice are known.[275] It is true that elsewhere Paul gave the names of those whom he recommended.[276] When names were omitted, they were those of his adversaries (1 Cor 3:10ff; 2 Cor 2:5ff; 7:12) or of the wrong doer in 1 Cor 5:1, 5. In an effort to be consistent, Lietzmann maintained that the brother whose name is omitted in 2 Cor 12:18 is the same as the envoy of 8:22.[277] But there is no evidence to support the hypothesis that the names were later removed. If, on the other hand, Paul himself had omitted the names, what could have been his motive for doing so?

Did the apostle intend to play down the role of the brothers? One can argue that he agreed to the inclusion of these envoys in the delegation only after considerable negotiation. The brothers were not really *his* envoys, but, as v 23b says, the "envoys of the churches" (ἀπόστολοι ἐκκλησιῶν). This implies that Paul did not nominate or appoint them himself, but took them over when he assumed final responsibility for the delegation. By omitting their names, Paul avoided giving them more status than was due. Obviously, Paul did not wish to diminish the authority of Titus in any way. Since the brothers had the title "apostle" and Titus did not, a conflict of authority could easily have arisen. By neglecting to mention their names, in effect, Paul created two levels of authorization within the delegation. Titus alone was authorized in the full sense, while the brothers derived their authority from him. The brothers were not authorized as individuals. Their role could be played by any suitable person, while without Titus the letter had no legal force at all. Thus, had the brothers arrived in Corinth without Titus, or had they sought to pursue an independent course of action, they would have done so without the authorization of the letter. In fact, the role of the brothers was limited to that of attendants (ἀκόλουθοι).[278]

One should also note the discrepancy between the titles given the envoys by the churches ("apostles of the churches") and the less dignified manner in which they were spoken of by Paul. This discrepancy may have its origin in the discussions which preceded the appointment of the brothers. It may also indicate that an element of caution was involved on Paul's part. Paul may have sought to avoid creating a basis for possible conflict once the delegation has arrived in Corinth.

alterum fratrem" ("I love Pomponius Atticus as a second brother").

270 See Bauer, *s.v.* ἀδελφός, 5 with references.

271 2 Cor 8:18, 22, 23; 9:2, 5; 12:18.

272 See Heinrici's survey of the various hypotheses (pp. 287–88). Many would agree with Plummer, p. 248: "Luke seems to be the best guess."

273 Lietzmann, pp. 136–37; Windisch, p. 262; cf. Plummer, p. 248, who has misunderstood Lietzmann. The hypothesis is old; see already Michel Mauduit, *Analyse des Epîtres de Saint Paul* (Lyon: A. Briasson, [3]1710) 369ff.

274 Ign. *Smyrn.* 5.3: "Their names, however, being unbelieving names, seemed best to me not to write down. But be it far from me to even remember them . . ." (τὰ δὲ ὀνόματα αὐτῶν, ὄντα ἄπιστα, οὐκ ἔδοξέν μοι ἐγγράψαι. ἀλλὰ μηδὲ γένοιτό μοι αὐτῶν μνημονεύειν . . .). My translation. See also Betz, *Galatians,* 49 n. 65.

275 Lietzmann, p. 136: ". . . es ist geradezu selbstverständlich, nicht bloss höflich, dass man keine Anonymi vorstellt und empfiehlt." However, Kim, *The Familiar Greek Letter of Recommendation,* 40, has four letters without names (nos. 32, 60, 68, 78).

276 Plummer, p. 248, mentioning 1 Cor 16:10–15: Timothy and Stephanas; Rom 16:1: Phoebe; Col 4:7–10: Tychicus, Onesimus, Mark; Tit 3:12–14: Zenas and Apollos. See also Acts 15:22, 25, 27.

277 Lietzmann, p. 137; so also Windisch, p. 262.

278 In terms of the diplomatic rank of envoys, the role of the brothers in Paul's view amounts to nothing more than to that of ἀκόλουθοι (Latin: *legatorum comites*). These persons were attached to a delegation but had no authority to negotiate on their own. See, e.g.,

That such caution was in order can be seen from a remark in Claudius's letter to the Alexandrians, which forms an interesting parallel to our text.[279] The emperor complained that the Jews of Alexandria had sent two delegations to Rome, a fact which clearly created confusion and frustration. He exhorted them not to do this again, "and not in future to send two embassies as if they lived in two cities, a thing which has never been done before . . ." (μηδὲ ὥσπερ ἐν δυσεὶ πόλεσειν κατοικοῦντας δύο πρεσβείας ἐκπέμπειν τοῦ λοιποῦ, ὃ μὴ πρότερόν ποτε ἐπράκθη . . .).[280] What Claudius meant by this remark is still a matter of discussion,[281] but so much is clear: sending two embassies from the same city representing opposite points of view gave rise to diplomatic confusion it would have been better to avoid. In light of this parallel, a further question suggests itself: did Paul agree to the inclusion of the two brothers in the delegation with Titus (συνέπεμψεν δὲ μετ' αὐτοῦ), so as to avoid a situation like that which arose in the case of the Alexandrian Jews? The matter must remain open, because the text as it stands does not allow us to do more than raise the question.

In Paul's defense, it must be said that once he had adopted the two additional envoys, he gave them his full support. With respect to the first of the churches' envoys, Paul allowed him the honor which he both enjoyed and deserved (cf. Rom 13:7). The phrase used to describe the envoys, "the brother whose fame in the things of the gospel has gone through all the churches" (ὁ ἔπαινος ἐν τῷ εὐαγγελίῳ διὰ πασῶν τῶν ἐκκλησιῶν),[282] is unique in Paul. It is a tribute to the reputation and standing of this man in the Christian churches, a fact which Paul simply reported. Again, Paul's language reflects the political practices of the larger society. In democratic elections in Greece, the good standing of the candidate in the community was considered a prerequisite for his nomination and election.[283] But this prerequisite had already come under attack in Greek political thought,[284] and we may wonder whether Paul would have simply endorsed it. What is such ἔπαινος really worth in light of Paul's theology? Does not God's praise alone count?[285] Is the apostle's description, therefore, slightly ironic? Even if no irony is intended, the discrepancy between the standing of this man within the churches[286] and the role he is given to play in Paul's disposition of the collection is remarkable. There can be no doubt that Paul did all he could to lower the man's profile in the context of the delegation.

Verse 19 adds a second, and more important, quality of the delegate: "he was chosen by the churches" (χειροτονηθεὶς ὑπὸ τῶν ἐκκλησιῶν). Χειροτονεῖν is a technical term and describes the process of electing envoys by the raising of hands in the assembly.[287] That such a process was known in the church at a later period is attested by

Xenophon *Hell.* 7.1.33, where the names of a delegation are given, to which is then added one unnamed Argive as an ἀκόλουθος. See also *Hell.* 6.3.2.; Thucydides 2.67.1; 4.118.6; 5.32.5; and Poland, *De legationibus,* 78–81.

279 This parallel was called to my attention by Professor George D. Kilpatrick (October 1981).

280 Quoted according to *CPJ* 2, no. 153, lines 90–92. The text can also be found in Smallwood, *Documents* (1967) no. 370.

281 Tcherikover and Fuks, *CPJ* 2.50–52, call the passage a *crux interpretationis* and discuss it at length. For further literature, see 36–37.

282 So the rendering by Bauer, *s.v.* ἔπαινος, 1, a, α.

283 In the Greek political assembly, the list of the candidates was contained in the προβούλευμα ("preliminary decree"), which was then presented to the membership for the χειροτονία ("election"). See on these procedures Carl Georg Brandis, "Ἐκκλησία," *PRE* 5 (1905) 2163–2200, esp. 2186g; Georg Busolt, *Griechische Staatskunde* (2 vols.; Munich: Beck, ³1920) 1.442ff.

284 Already Aristotle *Ath. Pol.* 2.8ff discusses the corruption of public applause by clever demagogues. In the New Testament throughout, public applause is viewed with skepticism. See Mark 11:1–9 parr.; 15:6–15 parr., 29–32 parr.; Acts 12:22; 14:11ff; 16:19ff; 17:8, 13; 19:23ff; 21:27ff, passages that show how early Christianity saw it as a result of the manipulation of the masses.

285 To be really valid, the praise must come from God, and this will not happen until the last judgment. See Rom 2:29; 1 Cor 4:5. See Betz, *Galatians,* 92–95, on Gal 2:6; also Jouette Bassler, *Divine Impartiality: Paul and a Theological Axiom* (SBLDS 59; Chico, CA: Scholars, 1981).

286 Windisch, p. 262, suggests he was a well-known evangelist and refers as parallels for the language to 1 Thess 3:2; Rom 1:9; 10:14ff; Eph 4:11; 2 Tim 4:5. There could also be polite exaggeration in Paul's words, as Windisch, p. 262 n. 2, implies (cf. 1 Cor 4:17; 16:10ff; Phil 2:19ff; Rom 16:1–2; Col 4:7–8; Acts 25:22, 25; 3 John 12; etc.).

287 See LSJ, *s.v.;* Dittenberger, *Sylloge* 4, index, *s.v.;*

the sources.[288] But it is surprising to see it at work in the time of Paul. Paul's treatment of the matter is remarkable, however, because of its conflicting nuances. On the one hand, the election is reported as a matter of course, but on the other hand, it is clear that this was not his own method of appointing envoys. His method, of which the appointment of Titus furnishes an example, seems to have been that of apostolic decree. By contrast, the churches in Greece seem to have operated in accordance with the democratic procedures employed in the society at large.

The difference in the manner in which the envoys were appointed naturally gives rise to the question whether Paul was really in favor of the election of ecclesiastical officials. Elections were, of course, characteristic of the political life of the Greek city, as it was carried on in the "assembly" (ἐκκλησία) of the people.[289] At a very early stage, the churches of Greece seem to have taken over these democratic procedures[290] and made use of them in the appointment of envoys and, it may be, other officials.[291] We should like to know what Paul's attitude was toward these procedures. Did he perceive the inherent contradiction between his apostolic authority and the democratic elections of church officials?[292] Unfortunately, the texts permit us to do no more than raise the question. The fact remains, however, that by accepting the churches' envoys, Paul endorsed the process of their selection. Moreover, since their appointment took place for the quite rational reasons described in vv 20–21, Paul had apparently been persuaded by these reasons. This implies that Paul had been brought to accept the advice of the churches, along with their manner of appointment. They must have convinced him that by sending only one man (Titus) to Corinth to accomplish the delicate task, he would be taking a risk that a committee representing different constituencies would not entail. Here, then, is an undeniable instance in which Paul's thinking underwent a process of Hellenization.

In v 19 we read that the envoy was appointed as a "traveling companion" (συνέκδημος) for Paul. This introduces another term with a technical meaning, which is found only here and in Acts 19:29.[293] What was the companion's function? Paul's somewhat indirect statements[294] make it clear that the envoy had a certain amount of control over the collections: he had been

idem, *OGIS*, index, *s.v.;* Moulton and Milligan, *s.v.;* Preisigke, *Wörterbuch* 1, *s.v. Suppl.* I, index, *s.v.;* Welles, *Royal Correspondence*, no. 53, I, C, line 16. On the election procedures, see Busolt, *Staatskunde* 1.454, 469; Cuthbert H. Turner, "χειροτονία, χειροθεσία, ἐπίθεσις χειρῶν," *JTS* 24 (1923) 496–504; Markos A. Siotis, "Die Klassische und die Christliche Cheirotonie in ihrem Verhaltnis," ΘΕΟΛΟΓΙΑ 20 (1949) 314–34, 524–41, 725–40; 21 (1950) 103–24, 239–57, 452–63, 605–17; 22 (1951) 108–18, 288–93.

288 See for this term also Acts 14:23; Tit 1:9 *v.l.;* 2 Tim, *subscriptio; Did.* 15.1; Ign. *Phld.* 10.1; *Smyrn.* 11.2; *Pol.* 7.2. For discussion, see Windisch, p. 263; Bauer, *s.v.;* Eduard Lohse, "χείρ κτλ.," *TDNT* 9 (1974) 426–27, with further material; *PGL, s.v.* Cf. also Acts 15:22, 25.

289 In fact, χειροτονία covers a range of procedures used by the *polis.* See Siotis, ΘΕΟΛΟΓΙΑ 20 (1949) 326ff, 524ff.

290 For the election of cultic officials in Greek religious organizations, see Siotis, ΘΕΟΛΟΓΙΑ 20 (1949) 332ff.

291 See Acts 14:23 for the appointment of presbyters by Paul and Barnabas; also 10:41.

292 Siotis, ΘΕΟΛΟΓΙΑ 21 (1950) 249, does not even consider the possibility that the envoys were actually elected, but he simply declares: "χειροτονία bezeichnet hier den Akt der Bevollmächtigung zu einem Auftrag, doch auch die Übertragung des Auftrags selbst." See also pp. 612ff. Hans von Campenhausen, *Kirchliches Amt und geistliche Vollmacht in den ersten drei Jahrhunderten* (BHTh 14; Tübingen: Mohr, Siebeck, 1953) 72, comments on the passage but overlooks the implications for his rather one-sided view that the early church had little, if any, organizational structure. See also G. H. R. Horsley, *New Documents Illustrating Early Christianity: A Review of the Greek Inscriptions and Papyri Published in 1976* (North Ryde, NSW, Australia: Macquarie University, 1981) no. 80 and p. 123.

293 On συνέκδημος (Latin: *comes*), see Bauer, *s.v.;* Moulton and Milligan, *s.v.;* Windisch, p. 263, with references; LSJ, *s.v.;* Dittenberger, *Sylloge* 4, index, *s.v.;* idem, *OGIS*, no. 494, line 13; Hugh J. Mason, *Greek Terms for Roman Institutions* (American Studies in Papyrology 13; Toronto: Hakkert, 1974) 89; Ollrog, *Mitarbeiter*, 63ff.

294 So rightly Lietzmann, p. 137.

appointed, "in this work of charity which is being administered by us for the glory of the Lord [himself] and our zeal" (*σὺν τῇ χάριτι ταύτῃ τῇ διακονουμένῃ ὑφ' ἡμῶν πρὸς τὴν [αὐτοῦ] τοῦ κυρίου δόξαν καὶ προθυμίαν ἡμῶν*). The language is certainly Pauline; the terms all occur elsewhere in the epistle.[295] But there is much which the apostle seems determined not to disclose. The commendation accomplishes two goals: (1) it compliments the envoy for his part in the work, and (2) it insists that the collection is Paul's work and not that of another. The collection was being made on account of Paul's zeal for the glory of the Lord. That is to say, it was Paul's undertaking, and not that of any particular ecclesiastical institution. On the other hand, the presence of the envoys meant that certain institutions were involved, namely, those whom the envoys represented. Again, one can hardly avoid the impression that Paul's words were carefully chosen to conceal the real or feared conflict of authority between himself and other church officials.

Why, then, was the envoy of the churches added? Verse 20 provides the answer: as a precautionary measure. This seems to have been the reason originally given by the churches for sending their envoy along with Paul. Subsequently, it was adopted by the apostle himself. The statement *στελλόμενοι τοῦτο, μή* . . . can be interpreted in a number of ways:[296] (1) *στέλλομαι* can mean the same as *φοβοῦμαι μή* . . . , "I am afraid, lest . . . ,"[297] or "I try to avoid this, lest . . .";[298] (2) Karl Heinrich Rengstorf[299] preferred the older, classical meaning, "I put myself in the position that I not . . ." or "I guard myself against. . . ." Plummer's interpretation is similar: "taking precautions about this, that no man blame us. . . ."[300]

Precaution is necessitated by potential or actual opposition: "that no man blame us in the matter of this bounty which is being administered by us" (*μή τις ἡμᾶς μωμήσηται ἐν τῇ ἁδρότητι ταύτῃ τῇ διακονουμένῃ ὑφ' ἡμῶν*).[301] The remark is interesting for several reasons:

1) It serves as a reminder of what has happened in the past. When Paul wrote 1 Thess 2:3–12, he was already obliged to draw a sharp distinction between himself and the religious charlatans who filled the Roman world. Such men had a reputation for raising funds for what were purported to be good causes, and then lining their own pockets.[302] The apostle provided a similar defense of his intentions in 1 Cor 4:1–13, as well as in the first apology in 2 Cor 6:3. But 2 Cor 8:20 looks back directly on the crisis that has just past. This is clear from 2 Cor 12:16–18, where Paul mentioned a previous mission of Titus and a certain brother as evidence that he had not embezzled any of the money collected. Meanwhile, another mission of Titus had taken place and resulted in reconciliation. The letter of reconciliation, in which the apostle expressed his joy over the resolution of the crisis

---

295 For *χάρις* see above, p. 42, on 8:1; for *διακονέω* see above, p. 46, on 8:4; for *δόξα* see below, pp. 81–82, on 8:23; for *προθυμία* see above, p. 65, on 8:11.

296 The term *στέλλω* with this meaning occurs only here in Paul. See Moulton and Milligan, *s.v.*; Bauer, *s.v.* 2; Karl Heinrich Rengstorf, "*στέλλω κτλ.*," *TDNT* 7 (1971) 588–99. In a text-critical note, George D. Kilpatrick has suggested that the variant reading *ὑποστελλόμενοι* in F G L may be original: "The tendency of Greek as of Latin was to develop compounds at the expense of simple verbs. Hence one of the features of Atticism was to replace compounds with the simple forms." Thus the simple form may be due to scribal tendency. ("The Text of the Epistles: The Contribution of Western Witnesses," *Text–Wort–Glaube: Studien zur Überlieferung, Interpretation und Autorisierung biblischer Texte, Kurt Aland gewidmet* [ed. Martin Brecht; AKG 50; Berlin and New York: de Gruyter, 1980] 47–68, esp. 58).

297 Cf. Hesychius, *Lexicon, s.v.*: *στέλλεται· φοβεῖται*. See also Wettstein 2.198–99.

298 Cf. Bauer, *s.v.* 2: "avoiding" or "trying to avoid this, lest someone."

299 Karl Heinrich Rengstorf, "*στέλλω κτλ.*," *ThWNT* 7 (1964) 590: "indem ich mich darauf einstelle bzw mich darauf rüste, dass ja nicht etwa . . ." (ET: "inasmuch as I see to it, or take steps, lest . . ."). Windisch, p. 265, admits that this meaning is possible.

300 Plummer, pp. 249–50.

301 Plummer's translation, p. 249.

302 The interpretation along these lines is found in the commentaries by Didymus of Alexandria and Severianus of Gabala. See Karl Staab, *Paulus-kommentare aus der griechischen Kirche* (NTA 15; Münster: Aschendorff, 1933) 35, 295; furthermore, Betz, *Lukian*, 8ff.

(1:1—2:13; 7:5–16; 13:11–13), states that the "one who committed the offense" (ὁ ἀδικήσας) is no longer a problem (7:12). Paul asked that the punishment of the man be brought to an end (2:5ff). Thus it would appear that the offense in question was a charge of fraud made by this man against the apostle.

2) Although reconciliation was accomplished, Paul and the churches of Greece remained on guard against a similar attack in the future. This indicates that despite all the positive things Paul had to say about the Corinthians, he still felt it wise to treat them cautiously. It was for this reason that Paul decided to accept the representative of the churches.

The mention of the large sums of money he expected to raise points in the same direction. The term "abundance" (ἁδρότης) is found only here in the New Testament;[303] and it is again a *terminus technicus.*[304] Was polemical use made of the term by those who appointed the brothers? In any case, the large sums of money called for strict supervision, particularly in the event that complaints might be made.

Paul concluded the commendation of the delegate in v 21 by citing a proverbial saying like that found in Prov 3:4 LXX:

> For we take forethought for the good not only before the Lord but also before men.
>
> προνοοῦμεν γὰρ καλὰ οὐ μόνον ἐνώπιον κυρίου ἀλλὰ καὶ ἐνώπιον ἀνθρώπων.[305]

The apostle cited the same rule in Rom 12:17, but there it is part of the paraenesis and contributes to the refutation of the *ius talionis:*

> Repay no one evil for evil,
> but take forethought for what is good before all the people.
>
> μηδενὶ κακὸν ἀντὶ κακοῦ ἀποδιδόντες,
> προνοούμενοι καλὰ ἐνώπιον τούτων ἀνθρώπων

Since the rule is found elsewhere in Jewish and Christian literature,[306] and since its text is sufficiently different from that of Prov 3:4,[307] it does not appear that Paul cited Scripture directly, but indirectly. That is to say, he knew and cited the saying as a proverb.[308] The proverb was of use to Paul because it contained language typically employed in administration. The terms προνοεῖν and πρόνοια occur frequently in official letters, often in stereotypical phrases which describe forethought as a quality of an able official: "exercising all zeal and forethought . . ." (ἅπασαν σπουδὴν καὶ πρόνοιαν ποιού[με]νος . . .).[309] This usage is also found in the speech of the orator Tertullus in Acts 24:2, who praises the fore-

303 For parallel references, see Windisch, p. 265; Bauer, *s.v.*

304 For references, see Wettstein 2.199; LSJ, *s.v.* ἁδρός, ἁδρότης; Preisigke, *Wörterbuch* 1, *s.v.* ἁδρός, 4/1, *s.v.* ἁδρός.

305 My translation.

306 See also Pol. *Phil.* 6.1; Ign. *Trall.* 8:1; Philo *Ebr.* 84; *'Abot* 2.1. Other rabbinic sayings are cited by Str-B 3.299. Cf. also Matt 5:11 par.; Acts 24:16.

307 The LXX reads quite differently from the New Testament: καὶ προνοοῦ καλὰ ἐνώπιον κυρίου καὶ ἀνθρώπων. As LXX so often does, it has replaced the Hebrew with the equivalent Greek proverb. See also below on 2 Cor 9:7.

308 Plummer, p. 250; Windisch, p. 266, referring to the parallel in Cicero *De off.* 2.21.75: "Caput autem est in omne procuratione negotii et muneris publici, ut avaritiae pellatur etima mimima suspicio" ("But the main thing, both in private business and in public affairs, is to avoid even the slightest suspicion of self-seeking." The translation cited is according to John Higgenbotham, *Cicero on Moral Obligation: A New Translation of Cicero's "De officiis" with Introduction and Notes* [Berkeley and Los Angeles: University of California, 1967] 128). For further references, see Wettstein 2.199; Plummer, p. 250; Cornelius a Lapide, p. 121.

309 Welles, *Royal Correspondence,* no. 52, line 10; see also nos. 53 II, A, line 2; 54, line 11 (for the noun); 37, line 11; 63, line 12 (for the verb); Leon Lafoscade, *De epistulis (aliisque titulis) imperatorum magistratuumque Romanorum, quas ab aetate Augusti usque ad Constantinum Graece scriptas lapides papyrive servaverunt* (Thèse Paris; Insulis: Le Bigot, 1902) nos. 93, line 3; 112 XG, lines 12–13; and pp. 81 n. 8; 94; Sherk, *Roman Documents,* nos. 63, line 9; 65 D, line 32; 67, line 38 (for προνοεῖν); 35, line 9; 65 D, line 32 (for πρόνοια); Ehrenberg and Jones, *Documents,* nos. 308, line 9; 312, line 38; Smallwood, *Documents* (1967) nos. 370, lines 103, 105; 384, line 31. See furthermore Dittenberger, *Sylloge* 4, index, *s.v.;* idem, *OGIS,* index, *s.v.;* Danker, *Benefactor,* 359–60; Moulton and Milligan, *s.v.;* Preisigke, *Wörterbuch, s.v.*

thought (πρόνοια) of Felix.[310] In the Egyptian government, there was an official who bore the title of "curator," or προνοητής, whose primary responsibility was the supervision of the fiscus.[311]

The commendation of the second brother (v 22) differs considerably from that of the first (vv 18–21). It is shorter; it lacks the caution and decorum of the former. Although Paul accepted responsibility for sending the man, it is clearly under different circumstances.[312] So much is indicated by the wording: "and we are sending together with them our brother whom we have proved to be in earnest many times in many things."[313] It should not be overlooked that Paul called the man, whose name he does not disclose, "*our* brother." This would seem to suggest that Paul nominated the man himself.[314] But why should Paul wish to add to the delegation when he had already appointed Titus?[315] Several conclusions may be drawn at this point: (1) The appointment of a second brother was clearly of importance to Paul. In the four-chapter letter (12:18),[316] which in our view preceded 2 Cor 8, Paul mentions a two-man delegation sent to Corinth, which included Titus and another brother. In 2 Cor 9:3–5, he justifies the appointment of a second brother to accompany the first. (2) The second brother seems to have been appointed after the first was elected by the churches. Perhaps the second appointment was made necessary by the first. In that case, the reason for the appointment of a second envoy can only have been that Paul wanted to make sure that his representatives were in the majority. At the same time, the appointment of a second brother had the effect of limiting the role of the first.

In sum, the delegation was carefully balanced. It consisted of (1) Titus as Paul's apostolic representative, appointed by him directly; (2) the representative of the churches, nominated and elected by them, and adopted by Paul; (3) another representative of the churches, of Paul's choosing, appointed by the churches. In the end, it was Paul who took final responsibility for the delegation.

With regard to the qualifications of the second brother, he is commended [317] as being zealous (σπουδαῖος)[318] and is said to have proven himself in many situations at many times.[319] Because of the confidence now placed in him, his zeal can only increase. Perhaps this is the same man mentioned in 12:18, who had proven to be a good worker even then.[320] In any event, this remark anticipates the theme of the *peroratio* (v 24).[321]

■ 8:23: The Authorization of the Delegates

The unusual statements found in v 23 have been a source of puzzlement to readers ever since they were written. Most commentators have chosen to regard them as summaries of the commendations in vv 16–22.[322] But

310 See also Rom 13:14; 1 Tim 5:8, and for more references, Bauer, *s.v.* προνοέω, 2; πρόνοια, 2.

311 See Friedrich Oertel, *Die Liturgie: Studien zur ptolemäischen und kaiserlichen Verwaltung Ägyptens* (Leipzig: Teubner, 1917) 231ff; Preisigke, *Wörterbuch, Suppl.* 1 (1971) 380, *s.v.* προνοητής; Mason, *Greek Terms,* pp. 80ff, *s.v.* προνοητής; 143; PGL, *s.v.* 1.

312 On συμπέμπω see above, p. 72, on 8:18.

313 Plummer's translation, p. 250.

314 Paul does not refer here to his physical brother, as it was sometimes assumed. See Heinrici, p. 291; Plummer, p. 250; Windisch, p. 266.

315 Windisch, p. 267, is right that this brother is not identical with Titus.

316 See above, p. 73.

317 δοκιμάζειν is another administrative term ("to consider qualified"). See above, pp. 56–60, on 2 Cor 8:8; 1 Cor 16:3; and for more references, Bauer, *s.v.* 2, b.

318 On σπουδή, σπουδαῖος see above, pp. 57–58, 70.

319 Note the *figura etymologica* and the π-alliteration in this sentence. For parallels, see Wettstein 2.199.

320 Possibly the brother of 8:22 is the same who went with Titus to Corinth before (cf. 12:16–18), but Paul does not say so. Differently Windisch, p. 266: "Dass der Betreffende schon einmal in Kor. [Corinth] war, ist nicht wahrscheinlich." Windisch takes it also as an argument against Hausrath's thesis: "Damit erweist sich die Hsr.sche [Hausrath's] Hypothese abermals als nicht angängig—wenigstens wenn der Bruder schon 12_{18} gemeint war." This conclusion is, however, not necessary.

321 This was noted by Windisch, p. 266: "ein kaum zu überhörender Appell an die Gemeinde: lasst dieses Vertrauen, das er zu euch hegt, ja nicht zu Schanden werden."

322 Heinrici, p. 292: "summarische Schlussempfehlung." Similarly Windisch, p. 266.

their conciseness,[323] their formulaic structure, and parallels in legal and administrative texts suggest that the verse contains a formula of authorization. Consequently, our interpretation will first have to identify the formulaic elements. In addition, the conciseness of the statement will make it necessary to pay careful attention to details.

The conditional particles "if . . . if" (εἴτε . . . εἴτε)[324] at the beginning of v 23a and b divide the sentence into two parts, distinguishing between the kind of authorization given to Titus and the kind given to the brothers.

■ 8:23a: The Authorization of Titus

Titus was superior in rank to the other envoys. So much is clear from the way he was treated by Paul throughout the epistle (see on vv 6 and 16–17). His esteem was only increased by his authorization in v 23a. The most important element in his authorization is the preposition ὑπέρ, apparently used in a special administrative and legal sense.[325] Such a use is found frequently in legal documents.[326] In business papyri, it can simply mean that payment has been made *à conto* of a certain party.[327] More generally, it refers to the rendering of a certain service, or to a legal statement on someone's behalf.[328] This last meaning is of special significance for 2 Cor 8:23a. In texts which have legal representation as their subject, the prepositional phrase ὑπέρ τινος designates the act of authorized representation ("instead of," "in representation of," "on behalf of").[329] Thus by means of this expression in 8:23a, Paul made an official statement on behalf of Titus, authorizing him to be his legal and administrative representative.[330]

In the papyri, this act is often expressed by the more complete formula, "I, NN, am writing on behalf of NN" (ὁ δεῖνα ἔγραψα ὑπὲρ τοῦ δεῖνα).[331] It is also related to the so-called *kyria*-clause, which was often used in order to certify documents. A good example of the *kyria*-clause is found in Hibeh Papyrus no. 84, lines 26–28: "This contract shall be valid whenever produced by Timocles or any other person on Timocles' behalf, executing it as aforesaid" (ἡ δὲ συνγρα[φὴ][ἥδε κυρία ἔστω ὅ] ταν [ἐπιφέ]ρη Τιμοκλῆς ἢ ἄλλος τ[ις] ὑπὲρ Τιμοκλέους πράσσων κα[τὰ] τ[α]ῦτα).[332]

In a special study of the *kyria*-clause, Manfred Hässler[333] has shown that it was widely used in Egypt in different forms.[334] Its function was to certify that the content of a given document, to which the clause was

323 There is no need for Plummer's suggestion: "The constr. is broken in dictating."

324 See BDR, § 454 n. 3 (BDF, § 454 n. 3).

325 Cf. BDR, § 231, 1; BDF, § 231; Bauer, *s.v.* 1, f.

326 See Moulton and Milligan, *s.v.;* Preisigke, *Wörterbuch* 1, *s.v.* ὑπέρ, 1; 4/1, *s.v.* ἀγράμματος; Edwin Mayser, *Grammatik der griechischen Papyri aus der Ptolemäerzeit* (2 vols.; Berlin: de Gruyter, ²1970) 2/2.2, p. 124; Archibald T. Robertson, "The Use of ὑπέρ in Business Documents in the Papyri," *Expositor* 18 (1919) 321–27. See also Kühner-Gerth, *Grammatik* 1.486ff.

327 See Mayser, *Grammatik* 2/2.2, pp. 458–59 (124, A, II, 3, c).

328 See ibid., p. 458 (124, A, II, 3, a).

329 Ibid., p. 460 (124, A, II, 5, a); Leopold Wenger, *Die Stellvertretung im Rechte der Papyri* (Leipzig: Teubner, 1906) 12.

330 So correctly the interpretation by Chrysostom *In epist. II. ad Cor. Hom.* 18, p. 567 B.

331 For passages, see Preisigke, *Wörterbuch, s.v.* ἀγράμματος.

332 Grenfell and Hunt, *The Hibeh Papyri* 1.242–45. The same formula occurs in line 11.

333 Manfred Hässler, *Die Bedeutung der Kyria-Klausel in den Papyrusurkunden* (Berliner Juristische Abhandlungen 3; Berlin: Duncker & Humblot, 1960). See also Hans Julius Wolff, *Das Recht der griechischen Papyri Ägyptens in der Zeit der Ptolemäer und des Prinzipats* (2 vols.; Munich: Beck, 1978) 2.82 n. 6; 145–46; 155ff.

334 See Hässler, *Kyria-Klausel,* 13–19, who (p. 19 n. 63) mentions authorizations in appointments of personal representatives, such as *Pap. Fouad* 1, 35 (A.D. 48); *Pap. Oxy.* 2, 261 (Ludwig Mitteis and Ulrich Wilken, *Grundzüge und Chrestomathie der Papyruskunde* [rep. Hildesheim: Olms, 1963] 346); *Pap. Oxy.* 1, 97 (Mitteis and Wilcken, *Grundzüge und Chrestomathie,* 347); *Pap. Oxy.* 4, 726 (A.D. 135); BGU 4, 1093 (A.D. 265); Bernhard A. van Groningen, *A Family Archive from Tebtunis (P. Fam. Tebt.)* (Papyrologica Lugduno-Batava 6; Leiden: Brill, 1950) no. 27, lines 24–25: . . . ἔγραψα καὶ ὑπὲρ αὐ(τῆς) μὴ εἰδυ[ίας γ]ράμματα ("... I have written on behalf of her who does not know how to write").

added, was correct and that the document was legally valid without further proof.[335]

If Paul's statement in v 23 is related to the *kyria*-clause, then the phrase "on behalf of Titus" (ὑπὲρ Τίτου) makes him the owner of the epistle to be presented in Corinth, charged with certifying its correctness and validity.[336] A connection between Paul's statement and the *kyria*-clause is justified by a number of close parallels, though the extreme brevity with which it is formulated in 8:23a is unexampled. The problem should not, however, be overestimated. After all, our knowledge of legal language depends to a great extent on Egyptian papyri, while legal processes in Greece and Asia Minor can only be approximated. The fact, therefore, that there is no precise parallel to the conciseness of the authorization formula of 2 Cor 8:23a is no reason to reject the hypothesis that here a *kyria*-clause lies to hand. Paul followed the mention of the name of Titus with a statement of his official titles and functions: (1) In relation to the apostle, Titus is "my partner" (κοινωνὸς ἐμός). This title[337] designates Titus as Paul's apostolic representative. (2) In relation to the Corinthians, Titus is "fellow worker among you" (εἰς ὑμᾶς συνεργός). This title is used of Paul's fellow workers in other passages as well.[338] The term "fellow worker" implies that Titus had no authority *over* the Corinthians such as Paul had:[339] he was Paul's representative *to* the Corinthians, but he worked *with* them on an equal basis. Titus was assigned to the Corinthians to work with them until the completion of the task described in 8:6.[340]

■ 8:23b: The Authorization of the Two Brothers

Surprisingly, the authorization of the two brothers in v 23b lacks the ὑπέρ-formula found in the authorization of Titus. They are merely referred to in the nominative, by means of the descriptive phrase "regarding our brothers" (εἴτε ἀδελφοὶ ἡμῶν). Consequently, the brothers were not authorized to represent Paul in the same way as Titus did. In fact, Paul did little more than recognize them as members of the delegation and fellow Christians of whom he had approved (see on vv 18 and 22). He referred to them as "our brothers" because this is the designation which corresponded to their official rank, which was by no means one of special distinction (see again on vv 18 and 22). No names are given which would identify the two men personally.

The legal consequences of Paul's treatment of the brothers are clear: the brothers were prohibited from using the letter as authorization in the event that Titus was not with them. If, for some reason, the two men had arrived in Corinth without Titus, the letter would have been worthless in terms of authorization. Only when Titus had been properly recognized by the Corinthians would the other envoys be allowed to exercise any

335 Hässler, *Kyria-Klausel,* 39: ". . . eine besondere, den Urkundeninhalt betreffende Beweiswirkung, indem sie die unwiderlegbare Vermutung der Richtigkeit des tatsächlichen Urkundeninhalts begründete und die Urkunde damit mit absoluter Beweiskraft ausstattete."

336 For the formula ὁ ὑπὲρ τοῦ δεῖνος see Hässler, *Kyria-Klausel,* 48.

337 See also Luke 5:10; Phlm 17. On κοινωνός see Bauer, *s.v.* 1, a, α; d; Moulton and Milligan, *s.v.;* Friedrich Hauck, "κοινωνός κτλ.," *TDNT* 3 (1965) 797–809; J. Y. Campbell, "Κοινωνία and Its Cognates in the New Testament," *JBL* 51 (1931) 352–80, esp. 362; against any "technical" meaning of the term in Paul, Ollrog, *Mitarbeiter,* p. 77 n. 86; Josef Hainz, "κοινωνία," *EWNT* 2 (1981) 749–55; Preisigke, *Wörterbuch* 1, *s.v.; Suppl.* 1, *s.v.;* Mason, *Greek Terms,* 61, *s.v.;* Dittenberger, *OGIS,* no. 603, line 5.

338 For συνεργός see also 1 Thess 3:2; Phil 2:25; 4:3; Rom 16:3, 9, 21; Phlm 1, 24. See Moulton and Milligan *s.v.;* Bauer, *s.v.;* Georg Bertram, "συνεργός κτλ.," *TDNT* 7 (1971) 871–76; Ollrog, *Mitarbeiter,* 63–72, 74–75, 90–92; Preisigke, *Wörterbuch* 2, *s.v.; Suppl.* 1, *s.v.*

339 Cf. Paul's humble statement in the letter of reconciliation, making himself the συνεργός ("fellow worker") of the Corinthians (2 Cor 1:24).

340 Some pertinent parallels of this language can be found in Plutarch *Eumenes* 12.1: Ἀντίγονος . . . ἐβούλετο τὸν Εὐμένη φίλον ἔχειν καὶ συνεργὸν ἐπὶ τὰς πράξεις. ("Antigonus . . . desired to have Eumenes as friend and helper in his undertakings"); Diodorus Siculus 18.50.4: . . . (Ἀντίγονος) . . . ἐξαπέστειλε πρεσβευτὴν πρὸς τὸν Εὐμένη, παρακαλῶν . . . γενέσθαι δὲ φίλον καὶ σύμμαχον αὐτῷ . . . πρωτεύοντα τῶν παρ' ἑαυτοῦ φίλον κοινωνὸν ἔσεσθαι τῆς ὅλης ἐπιβολῆς ("[Antigonus] . . . sent him as an envoy to Eumenes, urging the latter . . . to become his friend and ally . . . and in general to be the first of Antigonus' friends and his partner in the whole undertaking").

authority.

In what follows, Paul gave the official titles and functions of the additional envoys. Their title reflects their authorizing institution; they were "envoys [or apostles] of the churches" (ἀπόστολοι ἐκκλησιῶν). As has often been pointed out,[341] this concept of an apostle has little in common with Paul's use of the term, but refers simply to a messenger or envoy.[342] What the title means in effect is therefore "envoys representing the churches."[343] This title was bestowed upon them by the churches, not by Paul who, nonetheless, endorsed it. Again, one cannot fail to notice the discrepancy between the high rank given them by the churches and the somewhat lower rank granted them by Paul.[344] By calling them "our brothers," in effect, he avoided calling them "fellow apostles."[345]

Paul's description of the function the two brothers were to perform in Corinth is also somewhat unusual: they were to be the "glory of Christ" (δόξα Χριστοῦ). What can this strange expression mean?

Like many commentators, Windisch[346] assumed that the meaning of the term must be derived from 1 Cor 11:7, where man is said to possess the "image and glory of God" (εἰκὼν καὶ δόξα θεοῦ), and from 2 Cor 3:18, where the same notion is stated in a different way: "we all . . . reflect as in a mirror the glory of the Lord" (ἡμεῖς δὲ πάντες . . . τὴν δόξαν κυρίου κατοπτριζόμενοι). Furthermore, the doctrine is undoubtedly related to Gen 1:27,[347] and the idea of the creation of man in God's image.[348] Since this notion enjoyed widespread popularity in the Hellenistic era,[349] it is understandable that Paul developed an entire *doxa*-theology, presented in different ways in his epistles.[350] Though the theological background of the idea can be illuminated to a certain degree, the notion is not known to have been used often in administrative letters.

Welles's collection contains a letter (no. 15) from Antiochus II to Erytrae, granting the city autonomy and tax-exemption (dated after 261 B.C. [?]). In the letter, the king responded to a delegation of three men sent by Erytrae to deliver a decree stating that the city had voted the king honors, a wreath, and a gift of gold. Naturally, they attached a petition: "they asked with all earnestness and zeal that we should be friendly to you and should aid in advancing the city's interests in all that refers to glory and honor" (ἠξίουν μετὰ πάσης σπουδῆς τε καὶ προθυμίας φιλικῶς διακεῖσθαι ὑμῖν καὶ <ὁ>μοῦ πᾶσιν τοῖς ἀνήκουσι πρὸς τιμὴν καὶ δόξαν συναύξειν τὰ τῆς πόλεως).[351]

Welles's no. 25 is a letter from King Ziaelas of Bithynia to the council and the people of Cos, also in response to a delegation which had presented him with a petition. In his response, the king made the following remarks about his own conduct: "We do in fact exercise care for all the Greeks who come to us as we are convinced that this

341 See Bauer, *s.v.* 1, referring to 2 Cor 8:23 ("perh.[aps] missionary"); Phil 2:25; John 13:16; Karl Heinrich Rengstorf, "ἀπόστολος," *TDNT* 1 (1964) 407–45; for further bibliography, see the excursus "Apostle (ἀπόστολος)" in Betz, *Galatians*, 74–75.

342 See LSJ, *s.v.*, referring to Herodotus 1.21; 5.38; Moulton and Milligan, *s.v.;* Preisigke, *Wörterbuch* 1, *s.v.;* 4/1, *s.v.;* 2; *Suppl.* 1, *s.v.;* Rengstorf, "ἀπόστολος," *TDNT* 1 (1964) 407–8; Ollrog, *Mitarbeiter*, 79–84.

343 Cf. also Acts 15:22, 27, where Judas and Silas serve as envoys of the church of Jerusalem. See also Chrysostom *In epist. II. ad Cor. Hom.* 18, *MPG* 61.597C: . . . ἀπόστολοι ἐκκλησιῶν· τουτέστιν, ὑπὸ ἐκκλησιῶν πεμφθέντες. ("apostles of the churches, that means men sent by the churches").

344 See above, pp. 73–78.

345 For a different interpretation, see Theodore of Mopsuestia, who remarks that the εἴτε indicates that the difference does not matter: ἀδιαφορίαν πολλὴν ἐπὶ τῆς φράσεως ἐνδεικνύμενος (Staab, *Pauluskommentare*, 199).

346 Windisch, p. 267, referring to Weiss, *Der erste Korintherbrief*, 272–73.

347 See also Conzelmann, *1 Corinthians*, Excursus: "εἰκών 'image,'" 187–88; Horst Kuhli, "εἰκών," *EWNT* 1 (1980) 942–49, with further literature.

348 Windisch, p. 267, paraphrases: ". . . dass die (geistige) Glorie Christi sich auf ihnen spiegelt. Cf. Plummer, p. 251: "a glory to Christ."

349 See on this subject Hans Dieter Betz, "The Delphic Maxim 'Know Yourself' in the Greek Magical Papyri," *HR* 21 (1981) 156–81, esp. 166ff.

350 See Gerhard Kittel, "δοξάζω," *TDNT* 2 (1964) 253–54; Harald Hegermann, "δόξα," *EWNT* 1 (1980) 832–41.

351 Text and translation according to Welles, *Royal Correspondence*, no. 15, lines 10–12 (pp. 79, 80). As Welles notes, p. 82, the phrases are of the diplomatic stock; for τοῖς ἀνήκουσι πρὸς τιμὴν καὶ δόξαν see also nos. 42, lines 5–6; 44, lines 19–20; 52, lines 36–37; cf. 52, lines 19–20.

contributes in no small way to one's reputation" (ἡμεῖς δὲ πάντων μὲν τῶν ἀφικνουμένω[ν] πρὸς ἡμᾶς Ἑλλήνων τυγχάνομεν τὴν ἐπιμέλειαν ποιούμενοι, πεπεισμένοι πρὸς δόξαν οὐ μικρὸν συμβάλλεσθαι τὸ μέρος τοῦτο).[352]

Letter no. 34 in Robert K. Sherk's collection is similar. M. Valerius Messala, praetor of 193 B.C., wrote to the council and people of Teos, in response to the Teans' sending of the envoy Menippus (dated 193 B.C.):[353] "And we have received the man in a friendly manner, and because of the glory that had been bestowed on him before and because of his genuine goodness we have also given a favorable hearing to him with regard to the things he asked for"[354] (ἡμεῖς δὲ τόν τε ἄνδρα ἀπεδεξάμεθα φιλοφρόνως καὶ διὰ τὴν προγεγενημένην αὐτῶι δόξαν καὶ διὰ τὴν ὑπάρχουσαν καλοκαγαθίαν περί τε ὧν ἠξίου διηκούσαμεν εὐνοῶς).

These documents show that the concern for glory (δόξα) was firmly connected with the practice of sending and receiving envoys.[355] The authors were vague about what is meant in specific, but no doubt reference is made to certain privileges.[356]

If we apply these insights to the expression "glory of Christ" (δόξα Χριστοῦ) in 2 Cor 8:23b, the influence of secular diplomatic terminology cannot be excluded. Thus, the term is used in a somewhat different way than in 1 Cor 11:7 and 2 Cor 3:17. The secular expression has been Christianized by the addition of the genitive, "of Christ": as envoys, the two brothers ought to be representatives of a kind of glory (δόξα) consistent with that of Christ.[357] However vague the expression remains, it no doubt refers to the brothers' appearance, conduct, and speech, as well as to their privileges as guests in Corinth.[358] The very vagueness of the expression may reflect the language of diplomacy, where vagueness is a virtue.

3) 8:24: The Peroratio (Peroration)

The conclusion[359] of the letter, the *peroratio,* is signaled by the conjunction "therefore" (οὖν) in v 24. If we are correct in assuming that v 24 is the *peroratio,* we would expect it to contain the summary of the letter and a final statement of its purpose.[360] The verse is certainly concise, perhaps even elliptic.[361] With respect to the ellipsis, the manuscript evidence is divided as to whether the text should contain the participle ἐνδεικνύμενοι (B D*

352 Welles, *Royal Correspondence,* no. 25, lines 11–17 (p. 119).

353 Sherk, *Roman Documents,* no. 34, lines 8–11 (p. 214). See also Allan C. Johnson, Paul R. Coleman-Norton, and Frank C. Bourne, *Ancient Roman Statutes* (Austin: University of Texas, 1961) no. 20. Further references are to be found also in Dittenberger, *Sylloge* 4, index, *s.v.* δόξα; Moulton and Milligan, *s.v.* δόξα.

354 My translation.

355 See Cicero's definition *De inv.* 2.55.166: "Gloria est frequens de aliquo fama cum laude" ("Glory consists in a person's having a widespread reputation accompanied by praise"). The term has, of course, great importance in Roman political theory. See on this subject Horst-Theodor Johann, *Gerechtigkeit und Nutzen: Studien zur ciceronischen und hellenistischen Naturrechts- und Staatslehre* (Bibliothek der klassischen Altertumswissenschaften, *Reihe 2,* NF 68; Heidelberg: Winter, 1981) 379ff.

356 Cf. also in a similar context Phil 2:29: καὶ τοὺς τοιούτους ἐντίμους ἔχετε ("and honor such men"); Ign. *Phld.* 11.1; *Smyrn.* 10.1. Chrysostom *In epist. II. ad Cor. Hom.* 18, *MPG* 61.567E, rightly equates εἰς δόξαν with εἰς τιμήν and reflects at length on the implications for the power of the church.

357 Cf. Chrysostom *In epist. II. ad Cor. Hom.* 18, *MPG* 61.567C: . . . "Δόξα Χριστοῦ." Εἰς ἐκεῖνον γὰρ ἀναφέρεται, ἅπερ ἂν εἰς τούτους γένηται. Cf. also the royal letter in 2 Macc 9:21: τιμὴ καὶ εὔνοια.

358 Cf. also 2 Cor 8:18 (see above, pp. 73–74); 1 Pet 1:7: εἰς ἔπαινον καὶ δόξαν καὶ τιμήν ("unto praise and glory and honor"). For the formula τιμὴ καὶ δόξα ("honor and glory") in Hellenistic usage and in New Testament Christology, see Johannes Schneider, "τιμή," *TDNT* 8 (1972) 169–80, esp. 172 (lg), 173–74, (II and III), 174–76 (b).

359 So correctly Meyer, p. 166; differently Windisch, p. 293, who takes it to be the transition to the following. Plummer, pp. 251–52, thinks it is the conclusion to chapter 8. Cf. also Windisch, pp. 267–68; Kennedy, *Classical Rhetoric,* index, *s.v.* Epilogue.

360 For the purpose of the *peroratio,* see Volkmann, *Rhetorik,* § 27; Lausberg, *Handbuch* 1, §§ 431–42; Martin, *Rhetorik,* esp. 147–66; Betz, *Galatians,* 313.

361 Windisch, p. 267, however, goes too far when he calls it "ein abgerissener Satz."

F G 33 pc b ρ vg[ms]) or the imperative ἐνδείξασθε (ℵ C D[2] Ψ 0225 0243 𝔐 lat).[362] The participle certainly represents the more difficult reading, making the sentence lack a finite verb. Hence the imperative is more likely to be a correction.[363] But whoever made the correction did not seem to realize that the participle, in accordance with Semitic idiom, can also function as an imperative.[364] If the sentence is written in the imperatival mood, it constitutes in its entirety an appeal[365] to the Corinthians, which is precisely what one would expect of the *peroratio*. The appeal is given emphasis by means of a *figura etymologica*:[366] "demonstrate . . . the demonstration" (τὴν ἔνδειξιν . . . ἐνδεικνύμενοι).[367] As Plummer has rightly observed, it is "an appeal to facts."[368]

The appeal also sums up the content of the letter which, taken as a whole, was intended to give advice to the Corinthians on the reorganization and completion of the collection for the church in Jerusalem (see especially vv 6, 7–8, 9–15). The attainment of this goal remained the purpose of the delegation (vv 6, 16–23), for which the letter served as authorization. Appropriately, the *peroratio* looks into the future, to the moment when the delegation would arrive in Corinth.

The use of the term ἐνδεικνύεσθαι in the sense of "to demonstrate" or "to display" good will is attested in the papyrus letters.[369] A good example is furnished by Princeton Papyrus N. 74, which contains a fragment of a letter from A.D. 300. The writer asked his correspondent to display toward him the same good will which he had received from others. In the course of the fragmentary letter, the phrase, "display good will and honor" (ἐνδείξασθαι εὔνοιαν καὶ τειμήν), occurs twice.[370]

A Christian letter from Egypt is also worthy of note (ca. A.D. 330–40). It was co-authored by a certain Moses and his colleague Herieous and sent to the priest Heriêous and others. It contains a recommendation to lend support to a certain Pamonthius, who is described as being in great need. The letter, which shows many parallels to 2 Cor 8 without actually being dependent, has an interesting postscript:[371] "Show them the love and compassion that are native to you and the affection of your fatherliness" (Ἐνδίξασθε οὖν τὴν ἔμφυτον ὑμῶν ἀγάπην καὶ εὐσπ<λ>αγχνία[ν] καὶ τὴν στοργὴν τῆς ὑμῶν πατριότητος).

Other documents show that Christian writers of the time simply continued, with little variation, the epistolary conventions of an earlier period.[372] From these examples, and others which might easily be added, the connection between the term ἐνδείκνυμι and the sending and receiving of delegates is assured.[373] The place for such requests is clearly in the final part of the letter. This can be seen in a letter from Augustus to the Sardians, the *Epistula Augusti ad Sardianos* (5th cent. B.C.), lines 26–27: "I praise you, therefore, that you have demonstrated

362 So according to Nestle-Aland, 26th ed.

363 So Metzger, *Textual Commentary*, 582. Cf. Windisch, pp. 267–68; Plummer, p. 252.

364 See BDF, § 468; BDR, § 468, 2, b.: C. F. D. Moule, *An Idiom Book of New Testament Greek* (Cambridge: Cambridge University, 1955) 179–80; Turner, *Grammatical Insights*, 166; Metzger, *Textual Commentary*, 582, with further references.

365 Windisch, p. 267: ". . . noch einmal einen Appell an die Gemeinde."

366 The figure of speech is also found in Plato *Leg.* 12. 966B; Herodes Atticus *Pol.* § 16, ed. Engelbert Drerup [*Herodes*] Περὶ πολιτείας: *ein politisches Pamphlet aus Athen 404 v. Chr.* (SGKA 2/1; Paderborn: Schöningh, 1908) 11, line 4; see Windisch, p. 268.

367 Vg. translates "ostensionem . . . ostendite." See Plummer's attempts to preserve the rhetorical figure (p. 251).

368 Plummer, p. 251.

369 Preisigke, *Wörterbuch* 1, *s.v.* 4; 4/4 (1971) 791, *s.v.* 4, from where the following references are taken.

370 Edmund H. Kase, *Papyri in the Princeton University Collection* (Princeton: Princeton University, 1936) 2.71–72, no. 74.

371 Cited according to the edition and translation of Bell, *Jews and Christians in Egypt*, 76–80, no. 1916 (Inv. no. 2545), lines 31–32. See also no. 1924 (ca. A.D. 350), lines 7–8 (p. 105): . . . ἵν' ἐν τοῖς [δυ]νατοῖς τὴν παρ' ἐμοῦ σπουδὴν ἐνδείξω (". . . that so far as possible I may show my zeal").

372 See also *Pap. Oxy.* nos. 494, line 10 (2d century A.D.); 705, line 732 (3d century A.D.); 2106, line 10 (4th century A.D.), a letter to the authorities at Oxyrhynchus; and the letter in the Italian collection, *Pubblicazioni della società italiana: Papiri Greci e Latini* 7 (Florence: Ariani, 1925), no. 742, line 2 (5th/6th century A.D.). For further references, see Preisigke, *Wörterbuch* 1, *s.v.* 4; Dittenberger, *Sylloge* 4, index, *s.v.*; idem, *OGIS*, index, *s.v.*

373 See also Georg Friedrich Schömann, *De comitiis Atheniensium libri tres* (Gryphiswaldiae: Sumptibus Ernesti Mauritii, 1819) 112, 120, 175, 241, 289.

respect, and that in view of benefits given you by me, you are also grateful toward me as well as to all my people. Farewell."[374] (ἐπαινῶ οὖν ὑμᾶς φιλοτειμουμένους ἀνθ' ὧν εὐεργετῆσθε ὑπ' ἐμοῦ εὐχαρίστους ἀτοὺς εἴς τε ἐμὲ καὶ τοὺς ἐμοὺς πάντας ἐνδείκνυσθαι· ἔρρωσθε).[375]

Outside the realm of epistolography, demonstrations such as those mentioned in these letters are, of course, among the conventions of friendship and hospitality. Needless to say, these conventions are wholly stereotypical. How common and meaningless such displays of good will could actually be is evident from a description of false friends in Aristophanes: "displaying each some token of good will" (ἐνδεικνύμενος ἕκαστος εὔνοιάν τινα).[376] Moreover, the important role played by such terms as ἐνδείκνυμι and ἔνδειξις in oratory can be documented by countless examples. Demosthenes' use of the terms in his speech against Meidias is typical. Here the great orator listed the merits of Alcibiades: "displaying his patriotism, not by gifts of money or by speeches, but by his body," that is, by serving the cause of democracy by personally taking up arms (τῷ σώματι τὴν εὔνοιαν, οὐ χρήμασιν οὐδὲ λόγοις ἐνεδείξατο τῇ πατρίδι).[377]

Conventions such as these were especially important at receptions for official embassies. Again, an example must suffice. It is drawn from Philo's account in *Legatio ad Gaium.* The warm reception Gaius gave to the delegation of Alexandrian Jews proved illusory: "For he greeted us first in the plain beside the Tiber—he happened to be coming out of his mother's gardens. He returned our salutation, waved his right hand as an indication of his favour, and then sent the official in charge of embassies, one Homilus, to us with the remark, 'I will listen to your case in person when I am free.' At this, the bystanders all congratulated us as if we had already won our case, and so did those of our own number who were taken in by superficial appearances."[378] Philo's account of a later reception is also illuminating: "As soon as we came into Gaius' presence, we realized from his appearance and gestures that we were standing not before a judge but before an accuser more hostile to us than to our actual opponents."[379] The envoys were then brought to the gardens of Maecenas and Lamia:

> We were brought into Gaius' presence, and as soon as we saw him we bowed low to the ground with the greatest reverence and punctiliousness, and greeted him with the title 'Augustus Imperator.' His reply was so polite and kind that we despaired not only for our case but also for our lives. For with a sneering grin he said, 'So you are the god-haters, the people who do not believe that I am a god—I, who am acknowledged as a god among all other nations by this time but am denied that title by you?' And raising his hands to heaven he uttered a Name which it is a sin even to hear, let alone to pronounce. How overjoyed the envoys from the other party were at this, imagining that Gaius' first remark meant that their mission had already succeeded! They waved their arms about, danced up and down, and called him by the titles of all the gods.[380]

In the New Testament itself, the delegation sent to Jerusalem is said to have been given a friendly reception at first, in Acts 21:17: "When we had come to Jerusalem, the brothers received us gladly" (Γενομένων δὲ ἡμῶν εἰς Ἱεροσόλυμα ἀσμένως ἀπεδέξαντο ἡμᾶς οἱ ἀδελφοί). But it too proved to be an illusion, as did the initial reception at Rome (Acts 28:15).[381]

Other passages dealing with the reception of envoys are to be found in Paul's letters. In Phil 2:29, Paul asked

374 Author's translation.

375 The text is cited according to Sherk, *Roman Documents,* no. 68. The text is also cited in Ehrenberg and Jones, *Documents* (^{2}1976) no. 99. Cf. also Smallwood, *Documents* (1966) no. 444, line 7.

376 Aristophanes *Plutus* 785.

377 Demostenes *Or.* 21.145. See also Thucydides 4.126.6, the end of a speech by Brasidas; Aeschines *Or.* 3.219; Aelius Aristides *Or.* 46.2 (vol. 2, p. 363, line 3, ed. Keil).

378 Philo *Leg. Gai.* 181. The translation is that of E. Mary Smallwood, *Philonis Alexandrini Legatio ad Gaium* (Leiden: Brill, 1961) 100; cf. the commentary, 253–54.

379 *Leg. Gai.* 349; Smallwood, *Documents,* 140.

380 *Leg. Gai.* 352–54; Smallwood, *Documents,* 141–42, with the commentary, 317ff.

381 Cf. Acts 15:4; 18:27; 24:3; 28:30.

that Epaphroditus be given a friendly reception in Philippi: "Receive him, therefore, in the Lord with all joy and honor such men . . ." (προσδέχεσθε οὖν αὐτὸν ἐν κυρίῳ μετὰ πάσης χαρᾶς καὶ τοὺς τοιούτους ἐντίμους ἔχετε . . .). Similarly, in 1 Cor 4:17; 16:10–11, Paul appealed that Timothy be given a cordial reception in Corinth. In this connection, one should also mention Paul's commendation for Phoebe (Rom 16:1–2) and for Onesimus, the runaway slave (Phlm 8–14).[382]

Returning to 2 Cor 8:24, Paul's use of the *figura etymologica* ἔνδειξιν ἐνδεικνύομαι appears to be unique in the New Testament. Other passages use the terms in a different way.[383] However, certain passages in the Pauline pseudepigrapha come close to the meaning of 2 Cor 8:24.[384] That of which Paul desired that the Corinthians give proof is twofold: (1) "of your love" (τῆς ἀγάπης ὑμῶν). Love has been the theme of the letter throughout (see especially 8:7, 8).[385] For Paul asked that their love should be demonstrated in concrete action, first by the reception of the envoys, then by the collection for Jerusalem. (2) By so doing, the Corinthians would give Paul occasion to boast: "and of our boasting about you" (καὶ ἡμῶν καυχήσεως ὑπὲρ ὑμῶν). Having thus far boasted only of the Macedonians (8:15), he would now be able to boast about them as well, if they responded to his appeal. That this is no idle promise can be seen from 9:3, where Paul reported to the Achaians that he had been boasting about them to the Macedonians. We should also note that the discussion of boasting unites the *exordium* and the *peroratio,* as one would expect it to do.[386]

As we have mentioned once before, the final words of the epistle offer a preview of the future. Already intimated in the phrase "glory of Christ" (v 23b), the *peroratio* envisages the welcome that should take place at the time of the arrival of the delegates.[387] At that time, the letter (2 Cor 8) would be read to the assembly, and the community would respond through its leaders. Their response would determine whether the purpose for which the envoys were sent would be achieved. For this reason, Paul's final appeal calls upon the Corinthians to demonstrate their love "in the face of the churches" (εἰς πρόσωπον τῶν ἐκκλησιῶν). The latter phrase is found nowhere else in Paul, nor does it appear, for that matter, in the other writings of the New Testament. But on the other hand, 1 Thess 3:10 is acquainted with the idea of a group having a face: "praying to see your face" (δεόμενοι εἰς τὸ ἰδεῖν τὸ πρόσωπον ὑμῶν).[388] In the context of 2 Cor 8, the expression τὸ πρόσωπον must mean more than simply "before."[389] There is an undeniable connection here with the legal concept of *persona*.[390] Such a connection was contested by Eduard Lohse in his article on πρόσωπον in the *TDNT,* where he claimed that the legal meaning is not attested in the first two centuries of the Christian era, and that the technical sense of πρόσωπον as *persona*[391] emerged only under the influence of Roman

382 See also Phil 2:29; 1 Thess 5:13a; Phlm 17; cf. Col 4:7–9; Eph 6:21–22.

383 For the verb see also Rom 2:15; 9:17 (Exod 9:16), 22; Eph 2:7; for the noun see Rom 3:25, 26; Phil 1:28.

384 See for the verb alone 1 Tim 1:16; 2 Tim 4:14; Tit 2:20; 3:2; Heb 6:10, 11. See also Bauer, *s.v.;* Werner Georg Kümmel, "Πάρεσις und ἔνδειξις. Ein Beitrag zum Verständnis der paulinischen Rechtfertigungslehre," *ZThK* 49 (1952) 154–67; rep. in his *Heilsgeschehen und Geschichte* (Marburg: Elwert, 1965) 260–70, esp. 263; Henning Paulsen, "ἐνδείκνυμαι, ἔνδειξις," *EWNT* 1 (1980) 1098–99.

385 See also the letter of reconciliation 2 Cor 2:4, 8. For a good parallel, see also Pol. *Phil.* 1.1.

386 See on this point Betz, *Galatians,* 313.

387 For the political background of the reception of delegations, see Poland, *De legationibus,* 9.

388 Cf. also Mark 12:14; Matt 22:16; Ign. *Pol.* 2.2; *Herm. Vis.* 3.6.3.

389 Bauer, *s.v.* πρόσωπον, 1, b. See also *PGL, s.v.* VI, A.

390 See 2 Cor 1:11: ἐκ πολλῶν προσώπων ("by many persons"). For further references, see Bauer, *s.v.* πρόσωπον, 2; Eduard Lohse, "πρόσωπον κτλ.," *TDNT* 6 (1968) 768–79; Moulton and Milligan, *s.v.;* Preisigke, *Wörterbuch* 2, *s.v.; Suppl.* 1, *s.v.;* Dittenberger, *OGIS,* index, s.v.

391 *TDNT* 6 (1968) 771, lines 21–22, with the reference to the basic studies by Siegmund Schlossmann, *Persona und* ΠΡΟΣΩΠΟΝ *im Recht und im christlichen Dogma* (Kiliae: Lipsius & Tischer, 1906); Rudolf Hirzel, *Die Person: Begriff und Name derselben im Altertum* (Sitzungsberichte der Bayerischen Akademie der Wissenschaften, Heft 10 [1914]) esp.

law.[392] But there can be no doubt that the legal meaning was already present in 2 Cor 8:24. Those who were sent were the envoys of the churches (ἀπόστολοι ἐκκλησιῶν), v 23b. They were sent as representatives, so that whatever was done to them was done to the churches. This implies that the two brothers were the legal and political *persona* of the churches they represented.[393] This final statement reveals why Paul considered the mission of the two brothers so important. When the delegation was received, he thought it best that Titus not have to stand alone; in this way he hoped to put the collection on a broader legal and ecclesiastical basis.[394]

47–48, 51. See also Franz Altheim, "Persona," *ARW* 27 (1929) 25–52; Hans Rheinfelder, *Das Wort 'Persona': Geschichte seiner Bedeutungen mit besonderer Berücksichtigung des französischen und italienischen Mittelalters* (Halle: Niemeyer, 1928) 148ff; Manfred Fuhrmann, "Persona, ein römischer Rollenbegriff," *Identität* (ed O. Marquardt and K. Stierle; Munich: Fink, 1979) 83–106; Kaser, *Das römische Privatrecht* 1, §§ 64, 72; II, §§ 206, 214; Arthur Steinwenter, *Das Recht der koptischen Urkunden* (HAW 10.4.2; Munich: Beck, 1955) § 13.

392 So Lohse, "πρόσωπον κτλ.," lines 24ff. He therefore translates 2 Cor 8:24: "vor den Augen der (übrigen) Gemeinden" (ET: "before the eyes of the [other] churches").

393 The singular points to the churches as a legal *persona*. See Kaser, *Das römische Privatrecht* 1.307ff, where references to religious communities acting as legal persons can be found.

394 Plummer, pp. 251–52, has rightly pointed this out: "'To the face of the Churches'; i.e., as if the congregations to which they belong were present. They are representative men, delegates who will report to the Churches that elected them what they see and hear at Corinth, to which they are coming with high expectations; and the Corinthians must take care that there is no disappointment. This last clause is added with solemnity; it points to a host of witnesses, in whose presence the Corinthians will virtually be acting." See also Oecumenius of Tricca in Staab, *Pauluskommentare,* 445; Windisch, p. 268.

9

Chapter III: 2 Corinthians 9, a Letter to the Christians of Achaia

1 Now concerning the charitable collection
for the saints, it is redundant for me to
write to you. 2/ For I know your
willingness, of which I boast on your
behalf to the Macedonians, [telling them]
that Achaia has been prepared since a
year ago, and your zeal has stirred up a
good many of them.
3/ But I have sent the brothers so that our
boasting on your behalf may not be made
void in this particular point, so that, as I
have [just] said, you may be prepared.
4/ Or else, if Macedonians should come
with me and find you unprepared, we—
not to mention you—would be put to
shame in this project. 5/ Therefore we
considered it necessary to appoint the
brothers, so that they would go ahead to
you and get things ready in advance—
that is, your gift of blessing previously
pledged, that it be ready as indeed a gift
of blessing and not greed.
6/ Consider this: "He who sows sparingly,
sparingly will he also reap," and he who
sows bountifully, bountifully will he also
reap.
7/Everyone [gives] as his heart has
decided, not as a result of internal
distress or external pressure. For "God
loves a cheerful giver."
8/ But God is powerful [enough] to make
every benefit abundant for you, so that by
having full self-sufficiency in all things at
all times you may also have abundance
for [doing] every good work.
9/ As it is written: "He scattered, he gave
to the poor; his righteousness remains
into eternity." 10/ The one who provides
"seed for the sower and bread for
consumption" will provide and [indeed]
increase your seed and multiply the fruits
of your righteousness.
11/ [As a result] we are wealthy in every
respect [and] for every kind of generosity,
the very thing that generates through us
thanksgiving to God. 12/ For the
charitable act of this public service not
only supplies the wants of the saints but
also abounds through many thanksgivings to God.
13/ Through the evidence of this charitable
gift, they praise God for the submission
[expressed] by the contractual agreement for the [benefit of] the gospel of
Christ, and [for] the generosity of the
partnership benefiting them and all. 14/
In their prayer for you they also long for
you on account of the exceeding grace of
God [bestowed] on you.
15/ Thanks be to God for his indescribable
gift.

Literary Analysis of the Letter

a. Conspectus of the Analysis

omitted	[I. Epistolary Prescript]
1–15	II. Body of the Letter
1–2	A. Exordium
1a	1. Subject matter
1b	2. Statement of purpose: redundancy *topos*
2	3. *Captatio benevolentiae*
2a	a. Acknowledgment of the addressees' willingness
	b. Report about Paul's dilemma
	1) His boast to the Macedonians on behalf of the Achaians
2b	2) Quotation of the boast
2c	3) Effect on the Macedonians
3–5a	B. Narratio
3	1. The facts regarding the brothers
3a	a. The envoys in question
	b. Paul's responsibility for sending them
3b	c. Purpose of their mission
	1) Negatively: to prevent embarrassment to Paul
3c	2) Positively: to assure that the claims in Macedonia agree with the facts in Achaia
	a) Reference to the claim: καθὼς ἔλεγον ("as I have said")
	b) Repetition of quotation (cf. v 2b)
4	2. Considerations leading to the sending of the envoys
4a	a. Prevention of embarrassment to Paul
	1) A possible scenario of his forthcoming visit to Achaia
	a) Arrival with a group of Macedonians
	b) Discovery of the Achaians' unpreparedness
4b	2) The resultant embarrassment
	a) His being put to shame
	b) Failure of the project
	b. Prevention of embarrassment to the Achaians
5a	3. The measures taken
	a. Connection: οὖν ("therefore")
	b. Type of decision
	c. Type of measure
	1) Technical term: παρακαλεῖν ("appoint")
	2) Envoys in question
5b	d. Their assignment
	1) To form an advance team
	2) To get things ready in advance
5b–c	C. Propositio
5b	1. Points of agreement
	a. Collection has been pledged before
	b. It is to be called a "gift of blessing"
5c	2. Points of uncertainty
	a. Unfinished state of the collection
	b. Concern for the character of the gift
	1) That it turn out to be what its name indicates, a "gift of blessing" (εὐλογία)
	2) That it not become the opposite, "greediness" (πλεονεξία)
6–14	D. Probatio
6	1. Thesis in the form of a sententia

6a a. Citation formula
b. Citation of a proverb
6b c. Paul's interpretation by antithetical parallelism
7–14 2. Interpretation
7 a. First proof: the giver of a gift of blessing
7a 1) The common view
a) He is motivated by the heart
b) He makes a decision
2) Possible motivations
7b a) Improper motivations
(1) Internal distress
(2) External pressure
b) Proper motivation
7c 3) Scripture proof
a) Sign of quotation: γάρ ("for")
b) Quotation of Prov 22:8a LXX, including Paul's interpretation, substituting ἀγαπᾷ ("he loves") for εὐλογεῖ ("he blesses")
8 b. Second proof: a gift of blessing is a response to divine grace
8a 1) Presupposition: the Achaians understand themselves as being richly endowed with God's grace
8b 2) Conclusions
a) Their full self-sufficiency
b) Their ability to do good work
9–11 c. Third proof: God's gift of grace includes material and spiritual things
9 1) Common view: God is the primary provider
2) Scripture proof
9a a) Quotation formula
9b b) Quotation of Ps 111:9 LXX
10 3) Interpretation by the metaphor of "sowing" (v 6)
10a a) Of Ps 111:9a LXX by Isa 55:10
(1) Of "he scattered" by the divine epithet "the one who provides"
(2) Of "he gave to the poor" by the continuation of the divine epithet
(3) Exegetical conclusion regarding material benefits
10b b) Of Ps 111:9b by the metaphor of "fruit"
(1) Of "his righteousness" by "the fruits of your righteousness"
(2) Of "remains" by "he will multiply"
11 4) Conclusions for those who share the doctrine
11a a) They understand, being made rich in every respect
11b b) They are enabled to be generous
c) They will generate spiritual blessings
(1) Through Paul's mediation
(2) The "fruit": thanksgiving to God
12 d. Fourth proof: the gift of blessing is an act of "liturgy" (public service)
12a 1) Common view: the διακονία ("service") is a λειτουργία ("public service")
2) Conclusions:
a) The collection will take care of the financial needs of the Jerusalem saints
12b b) The collection will generate spiritual abundance: many thanksgivings to God
13–14 e. Fifth proof: the gift of blessing leads to mutual acceptance
13a 1) Presupposition: the collection has been delivered
2) Results:
a) By implication the Achaians have accepted the Jerusalem saints
b) The Jerusalem saints will accept the Achaians as fellow Christians by conducting thanksgiving prayers
(1) The praise of God
(a) In recognition of the Achaians' submission
13b (b) In reccognition of the partnership and its benefits
14 (2) The intercession
(a) In recognition of the emotional relationship ("longing")
(b) In recognition of the theological relationship ("grace given to the Achaians")

15 E. Peroratio: Paul's prayer of thanksgiving

omitted [III. Epistolary postscript]

b. Commentary

■ 9:1–2: The Exordium (Introduction)

In terms of literary composition, the beginning of chapter 9 can easily be identified as the *exordium,* the introduction to the body of the letter.[1] If this identification is correct, the redactor has chosen once again to omit the epistolary prescript, as he did in chapter 8.[2] Consequently, one might expect that he left the body of the letter intact, so that the *peroratio* would still be found at the end of the chapter. As will be shown below, 9:15 does in fact constitute the *peroratio.*[3]

The question must then be raised whether the opening words, "regarding the charitable collection" (περὶ μὲν γὰρ τῆς διακονίας . . .), can be viewed as the introduction to the body of the letter, or whether the words merely mark the beginning of a new section within the same epistle. As scholars had already pointed out in the nineteenth century,[4] the construction which stands at the beginning, περὶ μὲν γάρ . . . , must not be confused with περὶ δέ . . . , which opens new sections, for example, in 1 Cor 7:1, 25; 8:1; 12:1; 16:1; 1 Thess 4:9; 5:1. The presence of the particle μέν means that γάρ ("for") need not refer to anything preceding. Rather, it refers to that which follows without connection to what has gone before. In fact, the δέ which one would expect to follow μέν is found in v 3.[5] In conclusion, it is likely that 9:1 constitutes the beginning of a new letter.[6]

This conclusion is supported by additional evidence. In ancient letters, it was customary to introduce the subject matter by means of the preposition περί ("regarding the matter of . . .").[7] The subject matter which Paul introduced is the official name of the collection for Jerusalem: "the charitable collection for the saints" (ἡ διακονία ἡ εἰς τοὺς ἁγίους).[8]

The next statement seems puzzling at first sight. Paul admitted that the collection for the Jerusalem saints was so familiar to the addressees that "it is redundant for me to write to you" (περισσόν μοί ἐστιν τὸ γράφειν ὑμῖν) about it. Why, then, did Paul write, if it was really superfluous for him to do so? In what sense is this a proper way to begin a letter?

Rhetoric seems to have dictated the type of introduction Paul chose for the epistle. Paul figured that his readers were so familiar with the subject of the collection that they had grown tired of hearing of it. Rhetorically speaking, the collection had become a matter of "boredom," or "weariness" (*taedium*).[9] To relieve the tiresomeness of the subject, Paul employed a contemporary epistolary tag,[10] a variation on the basic notion that "though I have nothing to say to you, I am writing to you all the same."[11] A denial of this kind was, and remains, one of the simplest devices for beginning a letter that introduces a subject which has grown tiresome to its

1 So correctly Windisch, p. 268: "V. 1 hat zweifelsohne den Charakter einer 'Einleitung'." Differently Heinrici, pp. 293–95; Plummer, pp. 257–58. For the nature of the *exordium* see the literature above, p. 41 n. 1.

2 See above, p. 38.

3 See below, pp. 126–28.

4 See above, pp. 5–6, 27–28.

5 Cf. also the μὲν γάρ in Acts 28:22 and Windisch's discussion, p. 269. Manuscript variants omitting either γάρ (C and some minuscles) or μέν (sah) are clearly attempts to improve the text. See Windisch, p. 269 n. 1.

6 So also Windisch, pp. 268–69, who provides a careful discussion of the problem.

7 There are parallels among the letters from antiquity, which introduce the body of the letter by περί (or Latin *de*) referring to the subject matter. See, e.g., Demosthenes *Ep.* 3.1; *Exord.* 15; Isocrates *Ep.* 7; Cicero *Ep. Fam.* 1.8; *Ep. ad Quint.* 3.9.1; *Ep. ad. Brut.* 21.1. Cf. Jude 3; *1 Clem.* 1.1; *2 Clem.* 1.1.

8 See above on 2 Cor 8:4.

9 For the handling of *taedium,* see Quintilian 4.1.48–49, and Lausberg, *Handbuch* 1, §§ 269–71. According to Aristotle *Rhet.* 3.14.12, p. 1415b33–40, an *exordium* is unnecessary in deliberative oratory because hearers are normally familiar with the subject, "except for the orator's own sake, or on account of his adversaries, or if the hearers attach too much or too little importance to the question according to his idea. Wherefore he must either excite or remove prejudice, and magnify or minimize the importance of the subject." Cf. also 3.13.3, pp. 1413a37–1414b3; Quintilian 4.1.72.

readers.[12]

Another reason for the choice of such an introduction may be reflected in the term "redundant" (περισσόν). The word occurs frequently in chapters 8 and 9, always with the meaning "abundant."[13] In this instance, however, Paul seems to have played with another meaning of the term. It is clear from Paul's letter that his readers were familiar, all too familiar, with the collection for Jerusalem. Other letters afford a glimpse of previous correspondence, visits, and delegations in relation to the endeavor.[14] Had the whole business become a nuisance, so that not only the letter, but the entire effort on behalf of the collection, began to appear redundant? Paul's conscious rhetorical attempt to overcome the *taedium* of the subject points in this direction. Thus Paul attempted to anticipate the reaction of the Achaians: "Oh, not another of those letters on the collection!" Using the same term that he used elsewhere, περισσός, the apostle resisted such a reaction by suggesting: "The collection is not redundant at all, but should be abundantly charitable!" Whatever the addressees felt that they knew about the collection before opening the epistle, careful study of its contents would convince them that it was by no means simply a restatement of what they had known all along, and thus was in no sense redundant.

Though these words alone would have served well as the *exordium,* Paul included a *captatio benevolentiae,* a complimentary statement designed to secure the good will of the readers. As appropriate as such a statement is to the *exordium,*[15] the element of "redundancy" is continued, giving to the compliment an ironic, perhaps even self-ironic, flavor.[16] Paul's statement in v 2, "For I know your willingness" (οἶδα γὰρ τὴν προθυμίαν ὑμῶν), appears to praise the Achaians without qualification, but on closer inspection, this phrase becomes more ambiguous. The words themselves present no difficulty; the phrase is known from other passages,[17] while the notion of willingness (προθυμία) has been discussed in connection with 2 Cor 8:11, 12, 19. But the narrative context of the statement raises questions.

As evidence of his enthusiasm on their behalf, Paul told his readers that he had praised them for their willingness among the Macedonians (ἣν ὑπὲρ ὑμῶν καυχῶμαι Μακεδόσιν). This must have been on the occasion of his recent visit to Macedonia, which he described in the letter of reconciliation (see especially 2 Cor 1:15–16; 2:13; 7:5ff). Paul disclosed what he had told the Macedonians during that visit, summing it up in the statement "Achaia has been prepared since a year ago" (Ἀχαΐα παρεσκεύασται ἀπὸ πέρυσι). Paul made no secret of his motives in spreading this information: he intended to use "your zeal" as a means of stimulating others (καὶ τὸ ὑμῶν ζῆλος ἠρέθισεν πρὸς πλείονας). It was a ploy that had evidently worked well.

10 Rhetorically, it is a *paraleipsis (praeteritio),* on which see BDF, § 495; BDR, § 495,3. For examples in letters see Cicero *Ep. Fam.* 2.4.2; 4.10.1; 4.13.1; 5.5.1; 6.4.1; *Ep. ad Quint.* 3.8.1; also Demosthenes *Exord.* 48.

11 Cicero *Ep. ad Attic.* 12.53, according to Malherbe's translation, "Ancient Epistolary Theorists," 24–25, where other examples can be found.

12 The same device is used in 1 Thess 1:8; 4:9; 5:1–2.

13 The position in 9:1 is anaphoric, indicating its importance. See BDF, § 399 (2); BDR, § 399,2. The term also occurs in 2 Cor 8:2, 7, 14; 9:8, 12; see also 1 Cor 8:8; 14:12; 15:58; 2 Cor 3:9; 4:15; 10:8; 1:5; 2:7.

14 It is first mentioned in 1 Cor 16:1–4, presuming prior familiarity with the collection; then in the four-chapter letter 2 Cor 12:14–18; the letter of reconciliation 2:13; 7:5–7; and the letter of chapter 8. For the prehistory see also above, pp. 41–49.

15 The *captatio benevolentiae* can be properly used in the *exordium.* See Lausberg, *Handbuch* 1, §§ 273–79; Martin, *Rhetorik,* 64ff; Kennedy, *Classical Rhetoric,* 186. In the NT epistles see, e.g., 1 Cor 1:5; 1 Thess 1:3ff; Phlm 5–7; cf. also Acts 17:22.

16 According to Aristotle *Rhet.* 3.14.4, p. 1415a5–7, the *exordium* can at once praise and blame and can function as *insinuatio* (on this see Lausberg, *Handbuch* 1, §§ 280–81). See also *Rhet. ad Her.* 1.6.10: "If the hearers have been fatigued by listening, we shall open with something that may provoke laughter—a fable, plausible fiction, a caricature, an ironical inversion of the meaning of a word, an ambiguity, innuendo, banter, a naivety, an exaggeration, a recapitulation, a pun. . . ."

17 Cf. Rev 2:2, 9, 19; 3:1, 8, 15; Matt 22:16; Mark 1:24; 12:14—to mention only some better-known parallel passages.

These observations bring to light an interesting piece of historical information: during his recent visit to Macedonia, Paul had evidently continued to muster support for the Jerusalem collection, though at that time the outcome of Titus's mission to Corinth was still unknown. Paul was convinced that, despite the interruption of the collection in Corinth, the Achaians had continued to raise funds, and that in fact they had been ready "since a year ago." The apostle then used this information to the interests of the Macedonians. The fact that Paul was able to boast about the Achaians at the moment when the future of the Corinthian collection was in doubt means that the affairs of Achaia must have been regarded as separate from those of Corinth. We may conclude that the crisis reflected in the Corinthian correspondence was limited to the church in that city, and that the other churches of the region experienced no interruption in their relationship to the apostle. This distinction between Achaia and Corinth had occasioned the present letter, with its tone of undisturbed confidence and its high regard for the Achaians' ability to expedite matters in Corinth.

How did Paul receive the information that "Achaia has been ready since a year ago"? How reliable was this information? Did it represent the state of Paul's knowledge before he met Titus in Macedonia? How could Paul be so optimistic when he was still uncertain about the outcome of his efforts in Corinth? Or did Titus bring the information directly from Corinth? In the letter of reconciliation, Paul explicitly stated that Titus had informed him about the "zeal" (ζῆλος) of the Corinthians (2 Cor 7:7). This seems to imply that Paul was told that the Achaians were ready, while the Corinthians were not, but that they had the zeal to get ready. This also corresponds to the situation reflected in chapter 8, where it is clear that the Corinthians had begun the collection, and had shown the willingness to complete it, but had yet to make the final effort.

How reliable was this information?[18] Did it reflect the real state of affairs, or was it nothing more than an expression of confidence—understandable but mistaken?[19] One could argue that, had Achaia really been ready over a year ago, it would have been unnecessary to write the letter of 2 Cor 9. Hence, the information must have been incorrect, or at least insufficient. Yet Paul gave no indication in chapter 9 that he had been mistaken about the state of the Achaians' preparedness.[20] Thus we must conclude that the information can no longer be understood by us today. The statement "Achaia has been ready since a year ago" does not include Corinth, nor does it imply that the collection has been completed.[21] What is implied is, rather, that Achaia was prepared to undertake the final phase of the collection, and, in particular, to be of service with respect to the difficulties being experienced in Corinth.[22] The verb *παρασκευάζειν* ("to prepare") reinforces this interpretation; it is, in the first place, a military term describing preparation for military action, but not its completion.[23]

What conclusions can be reached on the situation in Achaia and Corinth? It seems clear that Achaia was fully prepared, and had been since a year ago, to finish the collection. Because of their readiness, Paul could now turn to them for assistance with Corinth. Indeed, were it not for the crisis that had arisen in Corinth, all Achaia (including Corinth) would have completed the collection by this time.[24] The Corinthians had to be treated differently. They had made a start and had expressed their willingness to complete the collection, but they were not prepared and needed additional help from outside. First the crisis had intervened, and now confu-

18 See Windisch, pp. 270–72, with whom I am in substantial agreement.

19 In essence this is Klöpper's point of view, against whom Heinrici, pp. 296–97, argues that this would throw a bad light on Paul's character.

20 So rightly Klöpper, *ad loc.*

21 This is Heinrici's view, p. 296: "... *dass Achaia in Bereitschaft ist* [Unterstützungsgelder zur Beförderung abzugeben] *seit vorigem Jahre.*"

22 So rightly Windisch, p. 270 n. 3.

23 See also 1 Cor 14:8. Bauer, *s.v.* 2, renders the term "be ready." It is found frequently in administrative letters; see Welles, *Royal Correspondence*, nos. 1, line 68; 61, line 22; in addition Moulton and Milligan, *s.v.* *παρασκευάζω*; Preisigke, *Wörterbuch* 2, *s.v.* *παρασκευάζω*.

24 In the second apology 2 Cor 11:9–10 Paul in effect separates Macedonia and Achaia from the Corinthian crisis. One should also consider that Paul finds it necessary to include in a letter to Corinth a recommendation for Achaians (1 Cor 16:15–18). The letter of recommendation, preceding the letters of chapters 8 and 9, addresses the church of Corinth "together with all the saints in all of Achaia" (2 Cor

sion and disorganization prevailed.

If this interpretation is correct, then Paul's decision to dispatch Titus and two other envoys to Corinth, together with the letter of chapter 8, makes eminently good sense. What the Corinthians needed was help in organization and supervision, which they could not provide for themselves. Indeed, the difficulties seem to have been too great for the other churches of Achaia, so that experienced "trouble-shooters" had to be called in from outside. On the other hand, Paul could count on support from the Achaian churches, and he turned to them for help in writing the letter of chapter 9.

Consequently, there is no "psychological-ethical problem" in what Paul reported: he did not give different accounts in different places for purely pragmatic reasons.[25] If he had, he would indeed be open to charges as reflected in 2 Cor 1:17–18. But Paul made no effort to misrepresent the facts when he wrote chapter 9. He had told the truth, as he and the addressees knew it. The enthusiasm of the Achaians provoked the Macedonians (9:2), who, in turn, had become the model for the Corinthians (8:15). In 9:2, Paul made use of the same facts for enlisting the Achaians' support.

The verb "to arouse" or "to provoke" (ἐρεθίζειν) can be used in both a good and a bad sense. In the household code in Col 3:21, it is rejected as a method for educating children. But the term commonly refers to positive stimulation through competition, a method employed in the military, sports, and education.[26] Obviously, the method was used to good effect among the Macedonians.[27]

The expression οἱ πλείονες, however, poses a problem. Does it mean that at first only a minority supported Paul, but that after he had boasted about the Achaians, the majority of the Macedonian Christians gave their support to the collection?[28] Does it imply that a minority did not support the effort? Or does οἱ πλείονες simply refer to the members of all Paul's churches, except the Corinthians?[29]

The expression seems to imply that among the Macedonians there remained a skeptical minority.[30] This minority may also have insisted on sending a Macedonian representative to Corinth (8:18–21). That might account for Paul's willingness to expand the delegation from one to three. Even as Paul wrote chapter 9, he remained anxious that at the final stage, when he came with a delegation of Macedonians to collect the money for Jerusalem, things could still go wrong (9:3–5).

■ 9:3–5b: The Narratio (Statement of Facts)

The section vv 3–5b consists of a report by Paul justifying his inclusion of the two brothers in the delegation to Corinth. In terms of composition, the section is the *narratio,*[31] or "statement of facts."

Why did the apostle feel compelled to justify the appointment of the additional envoys? Why did he feel that he owed an explanation to the Achaians? These questions presuppose that Titus was not among the brothers of whom 9:3–5b speaks, but that these were the additional envoys. Commentators are, however, divided on this issue. Philipp Bachmann and Alfred Plummer,[32] for example, excluded Titus, while Hans Windisch[33] included him, owing to the verb συμπέμπειν ("to send someone along with") in 8:18 and 22. But two points speak in favor of the exclusion of Titus: (1) In 8:18–22, Paul provided reasons for the appointment of the two brothers, while no justification is needed for the appointment of Titus (8:6, 16–17, 23a). Thus Paul anticipated that the appointment of the two brothers would be viewed as exceptional, both in Corinth and in Achaia.

1:1).

25 Cf. Windisch, p. 270.

26 For references see LSJ, *s.v.;* Bauer, *s.v.;* Leonhard Goppelt, *TDNT* 8, *s.v.;* Spicq, *Notes de lexicographie* 1.288–91; Danker, *Benefactor,* 437–38.

27 The apostle uses the same method in 1 Thess 1:7–8, when he praises the Thessalonians as an example to the Macedonians. See also Phil 4:10–20.

28 See Bauer, *s.v.* πολύς II,2,a,α, γ: BDF, § 244(3); BDR, § 244,3.

29 So Ambrosiaster *ad loc.*

30 Is it accidental that Beroea is nowhere mentioned in the letters as a contributor, while the Thessalonians and the Philippians are (1 Thess 1:7–8; 4:10; cf. 2:2; Phil 4:10, 15–16)? Did Beroea come in at the end (cf. Acts 20:4, where a delegate from Beroea is named)? For οἱ πλείονες referring to a majority see also 2 Cor 2:6.

31 On the *narratio* see above, p. 54 n. 116.

32 Bachmann, p. 328; Plummer, p. 254.

33 Windisch, p. 271.

(2) In the description of a previous mission in 2 Cor 12:18 in which a certain brother took part, Titus is mentioned by name: "I appointed Titus, and sent the brother with him" (*παρεκάλεσα Τίτον καὶ συναπέστειλα τὸν ἀδελφόν*).

Like the reasons offered for sending the brothers in 8:20–22, those given in 9:3–5b appear precautionary in nature. All too familiar with the situation in Corinth, the Achaians might have begun to worry that the inclusion of the two brothers signaled a fresh outbreak of trouble. They might have feared that outsiders were becoming involved in the conflict, or that Paul's authority was in question, even in Macedonia. Thus the *narratio* is designed to dispel such fears and suspicions before they arise. But Paul's display of caution indicates that there was real cause for concern, and that all parties involved were aware of it.

In v 3, Paul accepted responsibility for the inclusion of the additional envoys. If *ἔπεμψα* ("I have sent") is to be taken as an epistolary aorist, on the analogy of *συνεπέμψαμεν* ("I have sent with him") in 8:18 and 22, we may conclude that Paul wrote two letters at about the same time, that is, when the envoys were about to leave for Corinth. The reason for sending *two* letters can only have been that they were intended for two different addressees and have two distinct purposes in mind.

It is noteworthy that the reason Paul gave for sending the brothers in 9:3–5b is stated somewhat differently than in 8:18–22, though the difference hardly amounts to contradiction. The differences are explained in part by the fact that 8:18–22 seeks to explain things to the Corinthians, while 9:3–5b is addressed to the Achaians.

Paul's way of formulating the matter in 9:3 makes it clear that what was at stake in the collection was his credibility and, by implication, that of the Achaians as well: "so that our boasting on your behalf may not be made void" (*ἵνα μὴ τὸ καύχημα ἡμῶν τὸ ὑπὲρ ὑμῶν κενωθῇ*).[34] What this boasting entailed is intimated in v 2, "in this particular point" (*ἐν τῷ μέρει τούτῳ*),[35] and then further spelled out: "so that, as I have said, you may be prepared" (*ἵνα καθὼς ἔλεγον παρεσκευασμένοι ἦτε*). The conjunction *ἵνα* ("so that") in v 3c picks up the same word found in v 3a, while the phrase *καθὼς ἔλεγον* ("as I have said") refers to vv 2 and 3, but hardly in the way Plummer (p. 254) suggested: "that, just as I repeatedly said [to the Macedonians]. . . ." Paul's boasting would be in vain if his claim did not conform to reality. He described how this could come about in v 4, where he sketched a hypothetical situation which he hoped to avert. It might happen, he explained, that he would arrive in Corinth, at the head of a delegation of Macedonians[36] on the way to Jerusalem, only to discover that the Achaians were unprepared, contrary to the assurances which both they and Paul had given. Dreading such a painful experience, Paul turned to the Achaians for help.

The situation envisioned in v 4 allows us to reconstruct the agenda in the mind of the author at the time of the composition of the letter: the completion of the collection in Corinth, and thus in all the churches of Achaia, the arrival of the delegation from Macedonia, and the transport of the funds to Jerusalem. Rom 15:25–28 indicates that Paul was able to adhere to his plans. From Corinth, where Romans was written, he reported that the collection had been completed in both Macedonia and Achaia, and that the delegation under his leadership was about to depart for Judea. Acts 20:2–4 speaks of a period of three months spent in Hellas, that is, Achaia and Corinth,[37] and provides a list of names, most probably those of the delegates who went to Jerusalem.[38]

In 2 Cor 9, the arrival of the Macedonians is still a thing of the future. The feared denouement would occur if, as Paul said, the delegation were to discover upon its arrival that the Achaians were "unprepared" (*ἀπαρασκεύαστοι*).[39] Such an embarrassment would effectively destroy not only Paul's, but also the Achaians' credibility.[40] That Paul could draw such a conclusion indicates that, while Corinth and Achaia were not

34 See Bauer, *s.v.* *κενόω*, 2 and 3, who translates "deprive of [its] justification," or "lose its justification."

35 The term comes from administrative language. See Moulton and Milligan, *s.v.;* Bauer, *s.v.* *μέρος*, 1,b, *θ*; Welles, *Royal Correspondence*, 348, with discussion.

36 Apparently, what remained only a possibility in 1 Cor 16:3–4 has now been decided: Paul will lead the delegation of Macedonians when they come to Corinth, whence they will go to Jerusalem. Differently Baur, "Beiträge zur Erklärung der Korinthierbriefe," 177, who assumes that the envoys in 1 Cor 16:3 are Corinthians, not Macedonians.

37 On the relationship between the names Hellas and Achaia see Haenchen, *Acts*, 581 with n. 2.

38 See above, pp. 50–52.

identical in his mind, the Achaians were nevertheless affected by the outcome of the present effort. What the relation may have been between Corinth and Achaia in terms of ecclesiastical organization remains unknown to us, but so much may be said: a fiasco in Corinth would have implicated the Achaian churches which, therefore, must have been responsible, at some level, for what happened at Corinth. Here, again, is another reason that Paul wrote a separate letter to Achaia.

The concluding words of v 4 are difficult to interpret: ἐν τῇ ὑποστάσει can be rendered "in this situation" or "in this frame of mind."[41] The whole context of the letter appears to support Helmut Koester's interpretation of ὑπόστασις in the classical sense of a "project" or "plan," referring specifically to the collection for Jerusalem.[42] This meaning fits very well in the context of an administrative letter.[43]

Verse 5 proceeds (οὖν) to report what measures Paul had taken to avert the situation envisioned in v 4. Again, Paul made use of language familiar from administrative letters: "I considered it necessary" (ἀναγκαῖον ἡγησάμην).[44] This expression, and ones like it, are found with considerable frequency in administrative letters and documents.[45]

The decision had been made "to commission the brothers" (παρακαλέσαι τοὺς ἀδελφούς)[46] as an advance team to organize affairs in Corinth. Were Paul simply reporting events as they occurred, Titus should have been mentioned by name, since he was the leader of the team. But Paul seems to have omitted reference to him. The reason must lie in the fact that the appointment of the two brothers alone needed explanation. Titus, on the other hand, was well known to the Achaians and needed no introduction.[47]

What was the task of the delegation according to 2 Cor 9? They were "to go ahead [of us] to you" (ἵνα προέλθωσιν εἰς ὑμᾶς)[48] to Corinth, where they were supposed "to get things ready in advance" (προκαταρτίζειν).[49] The emphasis here is clearly on their function as an advance team. It gives the impression that Paul felt that time was running out. Why was Paul in such haste? We do not know, but it may have been related to the escalation of tension in Jerusalem. In Rom 15:30–31, Paul seems to have expressed the fear that it is already too late, as indeed it was.

■ 9:5b–c: The Propositio (Proposition)

At 9:5b, the *narratio* passes over into the *propositio*. That this marks the point of transition is shown by the fact that Paul left off the report of past actions and turned to the tasks which remained to be done in the future. The purpose of the *propositio* is to set forth both the points of agreement and those which continue to be regarded as tasks or challenges. Thus 9:5b–c meets all the require-

39 The term refers to the opposite of the assurance given in vv 2b and 3c; it is commonly used in the context of military and business operations, on which see LSJ, *s.v.;* Bauer, *s.v.;* Preisigke, *Wörterbuch* 4/1 *s.v.* ἀπαράσκευος. Kypke, *Observationes sacrae* 2.260, refers to the parallels in Xenophon *Anab.* 1.5.9; *Cyr.* 7.5.25; Josephus *Ant.* 4.293; *BJ* 3.451.

40 The term καταισχύνομαι ("be put to shame") here refers to the opposite of v 3 καύχημα ("boasting"). Cf. also 2 Cor 7:14 and Bauer, *s.v.* καταισχύνω, 2.

41 These two meanings are given in Bauer, *s.v.* 2. Cf. 2 Cor 11:17.

42 See Helmut Koester, "ὑπόστασις," *TDNT* 8 (1972) 584–85 (C.1).

43 See ibid., 577–80 (A.4–5); also Windisch, p. 273; Spicq, *Notes de lexicographie* 2.910–12, who interprets ὑπόστασις as "'assurance' vraisemblablement dans II Cor. IX,4; XI,17. . . ."

44 Parallels to this epistolary expression are found in Phil 2:25; 2 Macc 9:21. See also Bauer, *s.v.* ἀναγκαῖος, 1. Bauer points to further parallels in *Pap. Fayyum* 111,19; Dittenberger, *Sylloge,* 867,9.

45 For instances of this usage see Moulton and Milligan, *s.v.* ἀναγκαῖος; Preisigke, *Wörterbuch* 1, *s.v.;* 4/1, *s.v.;* Welles, *Royal Correspondence,* nos. 1, lines 14–15; 7, line 10; 36, line 3; 58, line 11; 65, line 13; Smallwood, *Documents,* no. 370, line 5. On ἀναγκαῖος see also Spicq, *Notes de lexicographie* 1.77–80.

46 For the special meaning of παρακαλεῖν see above, p. 54 (on 8:6).

47 See on this point above, pp. 54–55.

48 The term is common in connection with the traveling of delegations. See Acts 20:5, 13; Ign. *Rom.* 10.2. On the notion see also Bauer, *s.v.* 3.

49 The term is a *hapax legomenon* in the NT, but καταρτίζω (see esp. 1 Cor 1:10; 2 Cor 13:11; Gal 6:1; 1 Thess 3:10; 1 Pet 5:10; Heb 11:3; 13:21), κατάρτισις (2 Cor 13:9), καταρτισμός (Eph 4:12) have an almost technical meaning. Bauer, *s.v.* προκαταρτίζω refers to the parallels in *SEG* 4, no. 449, line 13; see also Bauer, *s.v.* καταρτίζω κτλ.; Spicq, *Notes de lexicographie* 1.253–55 (ἐξαρτίζω, καταρτίζω).

ments of a *propositio*, which in any case follows the statement of facts.[50] It is in this section particularly that we should expect to learn why Paul wrote the letter.

Paul listed two points on which he believed there was agreement between himself and the addressees: (1) Not alone the church in Corinth, but the churches of Achaia as well had pledged to add to the collection (ἡ προεπηγγελμένη εὐλογία ὑμῶν).[51] (2) The collection was intended from the beginning to be a "gift of blessing" (εὐλογία). Given these two points, Paul's reasons for writing the letter are immediately clear.

As Paul saw it, two tasks lay before the Achaians: (1) The Achaians, in whose pledge Corinth was included, were responsible for successful completion of the collection in Corinth as well.[52] (2) Moreover, a question remained as to the character of their participation in the collection. Raising the money was one thing (ταύτην ἑτοίμην εἶναι),[53] but Paul was more concerned that the original, spiritual purpose of the collection did not get lost in the process. He was concerned that the collection "be made ready in such a way that it is indeed a gift of blessing and not greediness" (οὕτως ὡς εὐλογίαν καὶ μὴ ὡς πλεονεξίαν).

What is implied in the notion "gift of blessing" (εὐλογία) will be discussed below in greater detail; at this point, the juxtaposition of gift of blessing (εὐλογία) and greediness (πλεονεξία) needs explanation. The contrast is artificial, contrived for the sake of argument. Paul chose the term "greediness" for several reasons, not least of which was the cultural value which it expressed. In Hellenistic literature, the greedy man was a stock character, an antitype of public morality.

This character is vividly portrayed by Theophrastus, for whom he embodied parsimony (ἀνελευθερία). When a public contribution is voted by the assembly, he rises quietly and departs.[54] Isaeus told of a certain Dicaeogenes, who pledged three hundred drachmas under pressure, but then failed to make payment.[55] The names of such pledge-dodgers used to be published in the Athenian Agora.

Paul could count on the fact that the Achaians had no desire to become examples of such pledge-dodging.[56] What he did not take for granted, however, was that they had clearly understood what constituted a "gift of blessing." Did the Achaians really comprehend the dimensions of this concept? Apparently Paul did not want to take a chance on this point.

Both concepts, "gift of blessing" and "greediness," have an interesting background in Hellenistic philosophy and in folk wisdom in all of antiquity. This is true of the conception of the gift of blessing as one of generosity and liberality. Its opposite, greed, is the obsessive attempt to hold fast to what one possesses at any cost, and to acquire still more.[57] In the background are commonplace

50 On the *propositio* see above, p. 56.

51 The term προεπαγγέλλω is used here with a special meaning of "making a pledge." For ἐπαγγέλλομαι as "making a pledge for a public donation" see Demosthenes *De corona* 112, and Kuenzi, ΕΠΙΔΟΣΙΣ, 3. A related meaning is also that of ἐπαγγέλλομαι as "announcing a festival"; see Welles, *Royal Correspondence*, nos. 3, line 100; 29, line 3; 31, line 5; 32, line 5; 33, line 16; cf. also Welles's discussion, p. 334; Dittenberger, *Sylloge* 4, index *s.v.;* Dittenberger, *OGIS* 2, index *s.v.;* Preisigke, *Wörterbuch* 1, *s.v.;* Moulton and Milligan, *s.v.* προεπαγγέλλομαι; Bauer, *s.v.* προεπαγγέλλω also list a few instances where the rare word occurs. In the context of 2 Cor 9:5 the term must be seen in connection with the other verbs prefixed by προ-.

52 See 2 Cor 9:2–3.

53 The term ἕτοιμος ("ready") has, of course, a wide application. See LSJ, *s.v.;* Moulton and Milligan, *s.v.;* Bauer, *s.v.* For the special meaning in the context of law see Meyer, *Juristische Papyri*, nos. 67, line 20; 52, line 56; 62; 64.

54 Theophrastus *Char.* 22.3.

55 Isaeus 5.37–38. See also Dio Chrysostom *Or.* 31, in which Dio advises the Rhodians to fulfill their promise of setting up a statue for him instead of trying to engrave his name on another statue already standing there.

56 In the NT the story of Ananias and Sapphira in Acts 5:1–11 provides a good example.

57 On the whole concept see the article by Gerhard Delling, "πλεονέκτης κτλ.," *TDNT* 6 (1968) 266–74; moreover Bauer, *s.v.;* Heinz-Otto Weber, "Die Bedeutung und Bewertung der Pleonexie von Homer bis Isokrates" (Dissertation, Bonn, 1967); Betz, *Lukian*, 192 n. 1; idem, *PECL II*, index, *s.v.;* William C. Grese, *Corpus Hermeticum XIII and Early Christian Literature* (SCHNT 5; Leiden: Brill, 1979) 111; Spicq, *Notes de lexicographie* 2.704–6. In his commentary Martin L. West, *Hesiod, Works and Days* (Oxford: Clarendon, 1978) 238, also cites a parallel from ancient Egypt found in the *Instruction of Amen-em-Opet* 8.19–20: "Better is a bushel that God giveth thee than five thousand by force; they stay not a day

notions related to the custom of the exchange of gifts. Accordingly, prosperity was defined as the result of divine generosity, while wealth was thought to be obtained by injustice, violence, fraud, and selfishness.[58] As the proverb in John 3:27 relates: "No one can receive anything except what is given him from heaven" (*RSV*).

Thus by contrasting these two notions, Paul drew attention to two attitudes toward wealth. A gift of blessing is given in response to blessings received, while greed represents a failure to respond in kind, owing to one's failure to receive anything as a gift. "What do you have that you have not received?" (1 Cor 4:7). Greed is identical with ingratitude, and signifies stubbornness and immobility, in contrast to the whole chain of activities set in motion by the gift of blessing: receiving, enjoying, and giving.

But these general considerations only constitute the background to a more specific issue, indicated by the repeated reference to greed at various points in the Corinthian correspondence.[59] In 1 Cor 5:10; 6:10, the term is found in vice-catalogues, and is neither directly connected with concrete instances nor an integral part of the argument. All this has changed in the *peroratio* to the first apology (2 Cor 2:14—6:13; 7:2–4), where Paul denied three specific charges which he assumed have been made against him (7:2): "I have not offended anybody, I have not corrupted anybody, I have not taken financial advantage of anybody" (*οὐδένα ἀδικήσαμεν, οὐδένα ἐφθείραμεν, οὐδένα ἐπλεονεκτήσαμεν*). His denial is even more intense in the second apology (10:1—13:10), where the apostle asked in a highly sarcastic tone, "Did I, with the help of any of those I have sent to you, defraud you (ἐπλεονέκτησα)? I appointed Titus and sent the brother together with him—did Titus defraud you [ἐπλεονέκτησεν]?"[60] Finally, the letter of reconciliation (1:1—2:13; 7:5–16) raised the issue one last time, as Paul attempted to assure the Corinthians (2:11) that all he had ever been concerned about was "that we are not taken advantage of [μὴ ἐπλεονεκτηθῶμεν] by Satan." The recurrence of the issue of greed (πλεονεξία) in successive letter fragments, and the apostle's repeated denials, leave no doubt that someone in Corinth had accused Paul of such an offense, that is, of having initiated the collection for Jerusalem only in order to line his own pocket.[61] Paul's mention of the charge was not, therefore, mere rhetoric, but was a charge that had been formally made by someone in Corinth, in all probability by the person whom Paul called "the offender" (ὁ ἀδικήσας) in 2 Cor 7:12. If this is the case, then the long-standing problem as to the nature of his offense has been solved.[62]

Paul's final remark on the matter occurs in 9:6. The offense and the accusation were now things of the past, but Paul still showed a degree of apprehension when he employed the concept of greed (πλεονεξία), though now he turned it into a challenge to the Achaians.

---

in store and barn . . . a moment is their duration in the granary." That this kind of thought was also widespread in ancient Greece is shown by Xenophon *Oec.* 20.15, cited by West, *Hesiod, Works and Days,* 237: "Therefore, if a man will not dig and knows no other profit-earning trade, he is clearly minded to live by stealing or robbery or begging . . ." (ὁ δὲ μήτ' ἄλλην τέχνην χρηματοποιὸν ἐπιστάμενος μήτε γεωργεῖν ἐθέλων φανερὸν ὅτι κλέπτων ἢ ἁρπάζων ἢ προσαιτῶν διανοεῖται.). The translation is that of Marchant in the LCL edition.

58 So much can be concluded from Hesiod *Erga* 320–26, a section dealing with prudence in prosperity. The section does not contain the notion of πλεονέκτης κτλ., but the introductory maxim defines the issue:

> Goods are not to be grabbed; much better if God lets you have them.
>
> χρήματα δ' οὐχ ἁρπακτά· θεόσδοτα πολλὸν ἀμείνω

The text is cited according to West, *Hesiod, Works and Days*, 111; the translation is that of Richmond A. Lattimore, *Hesiod: The Works and Days* (Ann Arbor: University of Michigan, 1959).

59 See Seneca, *De ben.* 3.1.1; 6.30.1; *Ep.* 81.

60 My translation.

61 This language already figures prominently in 1 Thess 2:5; 4:6.

62 See also Betz, *Paulus,* 100ff, esp. 116.

Excursus: Paul's Agrarian Theology

As is clear from the passages of Hesiod, Xenophon, and Pliny frequently cited in connection with 9:14, Paul's argument in vv 6–14 is founded throughout upon presuppositions which belong to the realm of ancient agriculture. Ancient agriculture consisted not only of the farmer's work on his land, but also of the practical ideas connected with it, ideas which have their roots in folk wisdom, and which are reflected in a wide range of literary texts from the ancient world, products of Old Testament–Jewish as well as of Greco-Roman culture. In the Greco-Roman world, an entire literature dealing with agriculture evolved out of these ideas, that is, a literature concerned not only with the collection of useful observations, experiences, and advice, but also with genuine folk wisdom, embodied for the most part in proverbs and adages, and with religious rites and concepts. Indeed, ancient agriculture never confined itself to purely practical matters, but embraced the entire science of household economy, in which religion played a role that can hardly be overestimated. To this agrarian religion there also belonged a particular kind of "theology" which made use of reflections on such proverbial wisdom and of religious practices and the concepts connected with them. This complex of secondary reflection also played a role in ancient philosophy, and therefore was capable of being integrated into the philosophical systems of various schools. This agrarian theology is certainly pre-Christian and also pre-Jewish—in fact, it is simply the common possession of all of antiquity. But as Paul's use of these ideas demonstrates, they could also be easily integrated with Christian thought.

On the Jewish side, the integration took place along the entire length of Old Testament and post-biblical literature. The thought complex is made tangible in the rituals and laws connected with agriculture, as well as in wisdom literature and in metaphorical speech in general.

The earliest Greek material is contained in Hesiod's *Works and Days,* which most scholars today assume to have made liberal use of older sources, some of which may still be discerned within the text.[63] Xenophon's *Oeconomicus* is more systematic and comprehensive, and is also enriched by earlier sources.[64] The list of the later literature contains the names of a number of prominent authors,[65] among whom is M. Porcius Cato (243–149 B.C.), whose scientific work, *De agri cultura,* is the oldest prose work in all of Latin literature.[66] Then the following authors should be mentioned: M. Terentius Varro (116–27 B.C.),[67] P. Vergilius Maro (70–19 B.C.),[68] C. Plinius Secundus (A.D. 23/24–79),[69] Lucius Iunius Moderatus Columella (first century A.D.),[70] and Philo of Alexandria.[71]

The interconnections of which this literature gives evidence, not only within itself but also with ancient culture in general,[72] allow us to conclude that in their works the authors have collected current knowledge and combined it with their own ideas. As might be expected, this tradition also exercised a powerful influence on Hellenistic-Jewish literature. Thus, such

63 Hesiod *Erga* 354–60, 381–617. See West, *Hesiod, Works and Days,* 252ff. On the problem of composition and sources see Walter Nicolai, *Hesiods Erga: Beobachtungen zum Aufbau* (Heidelberg: Winter, 1964).

64 See the edition by Pierre Chantraine, *Xenophon, Economique* (Paris: Société d'Edition "Les Belles-Lettres," 1949); Hans Rudolf Breitenbach, "Xenophon," *PRE* 2. Reihe 9 (1967) 1837–71.

65 For lists of their predecessors see Varro *De reb. rust.* 1.1.4–10; Pliny *N.H.* 18.22–23; Columella *De re rust.* 1.1.7–14.

66 *M. Porcius Cato, De agri cultura liber* (ed. Georg Goetz; BT; Leipzig: Teubner, 1922); *Caton, De l' agriculture* (texte établi, traduit et commenté par Raoul Goujard; Paris: Société d'Edition "Les Belles-Lettres," 1975); *Marcus Porcius Cato, On Agriculture; Marcus Terentius Varro, On Agriculture* (tr. William Davis Hooper; Cambridge: Harvard University, 1934).

67 See the edition by Jacques Heurgon, *Varron, Economie rurale,* vol. 1 (Paris: Société d'Edition "Les Belles-Lettres," 1978); Hellfried Dahlmann, "M. Terentius Varro," *PRE.S* 6 (1935) 1172–1277, esp. 1183–1202.

68 See Friedrich Klingner, *Virgil: Bucolica, Georgica, Aeneis* (Zurich and Stuttgart: Artemis, 1967) 175–363.

69 Pliny *N.H.* bk. 18.

70 See Karl Ahrens, *Columella, Über die Landwirtschaft,* Ein Lehr- und Handbuch der gesamten Acker- und Viehwirtschaft aus dem 1. Jahrhundert u.Z., aus dem Lateinischen übersetzt, eingeführt und erläutert von Karl Ahrens (Schriften zur Geschichte und Kultur der Antike 4; Berlin: Akademie-Verlag, 1972).

71 Philo *De agricultura* and *De plantatione.* Like Paul, Philo is interested in agriculture only as it may provide metaphorical and allegorical material for spiritual interpretation.

72 A section in Aelius Aristides is also particularly close in thought, *Panathenaic Oration* 31–39, ed. and tr. Charles A. Behr, in the LCL edition.

works must have been current and popular in Hellenistic Judaism.

Seen in this way, it is hardly surprising that Paul appears to have been strongly influenced by such agrarian theology. Yet it is remarkable that he did so little to make these ideas Christian. In the entire section 9:6–14, which presents a unified train of thought, there is nothing which could be designated as specifically Christian. The concept "the gospel of Christ" (τὸ εὐαγγέλιον τοῦ Χριστοῦ) in v 13 constitutes the only exception, but this concept plays no role in the argument itself. Thus we must reckon with the fact that the entire complex derives essentially from pre-Pauline, Hellenistic-Jewish theology. If this is granted, then we may conclude that even at a later time Paul could still have recourse to complexes of thought which actually belonged to his pre-Christian period.

The principal component of this complex of thought is its emphasis on the religious aspect of sowing and reaping. In the ancient world, the act of sowing always meant a risk to the farmer, and one that could easily become a risk to his very life. Of course, one could be certain that scanty sowing could never lead to a rich harvest, but liberal sowing alone was no guarantee of plenty. The experience of the farmer from time immemorial is expressed in Jer 12:13:[73]

> They have sown wheat and have reaped thorns,
> they have tired themselves out but profit nothing.
> They shall be ashamed of their harvests
> because of the fierce anger of the Lord. (*RSV*)

The farmer knew the capriciousness of nature, inclemency and inconstancy of the weather, problems with the soil, diseases, and insects—all of these represented risks which were beyond the control of the ancient farmer. Thus the outstretched hand of the sower was a symbolic gesture of his risk and of his trust in the divine each time he cast the seed.[74]

The religious-spiritual dimension of agriculture was familiar to everyone in the ancient world. Thus, when Paul contrasted sowing "sparingly" (φειδομένως) with reaping "bountifully" (ἐπ᾽ εὐλογίας), he made reference to the presuppositions of an agrarian theology known to all. It was possible for him to pass back and forth between the material and spiritual aspects of the concept without expressly calling the transition to his readers' attention. Precisely what seems confusing to modern man was a self-evident fact of life for the ancients.

Now the complex of thought connected with agrarian theology, with which we have been dealing thus far, is closely bound up with the understanding of the concept "gift of blessing" (εὐλογία)[75] and its opposite, "greed" (πλεονεξία). By means of this contrast, Paul introduced another fundamental concept into his argument, the concept of the exchange of gifts. To be sure, this concept has its primary significance in the realm of social intercourse, but the connection with sowing and reaping, which goes back to remote antiquity, demonstrates its relation to the concept of sacrifice, to whose foundation it belongs.[76] The gift given to the divinity represents a thank-offering for blessings received, accompanied by the expectation of future blessings.[77] Regarded in this manner, the collection for Jerusalem, which was promised by the Christians of Macedonia and Greece as a gift of thanks (cf. the expressions προαγγέλλομαι, "promise beforehand" [9:5] and προενάρχομαι, "begin beforehand" [8:10]), bears a clear

73 See also Mic 6:15; Matt 13:27; cf. 1 Cor 15:36. Greek religion was familiar with this as well, as Hesiod *Erga* 483–85 testifies: "Yet still, the mind of Zeus of the aegis changes with changing occasions, and it is a hard thing for mortal men to figure" (ἄλλοτε δ᾽ ἀλλοῖος Ζηνὸς νόος αἰγιόχοιο, ἀργαλέος δ᾽ ἄνδρεσσι καταθνητοῖσι νοῆσαι). The translation is that of Lattimore, *Hesiod*. See also West, *Hesiod, Works and Days,* referring to parallels in Xenophon *Oec.* 17.4; *Geop.* 2.14.7. On the whole see Orth, "Getreide," *PRE* 7.1 (1910) cols. 1344–45.

74 The idea is stated succinctly in 1 Cor 3:7: "So neither he who plants nor he who waters is anything but only God who gives the growth."

75 The term εὐλογία ("gift of blessing") cannot be translated by any one word into English, but encompasses a variety of meanings, most of which figure in Paul's argument in 2 Cor 9:6–14. For further material and discussion see Hermann Wolfgang Beyer, "εὐλογέω κτλ.," *TDNT* 2 (1964) 754–63; Bauer, *s.v.* εὐλογέω, εὐλογία; Hermann Patsch, "εὐλογέω," *EWNT* 2 (1981) 198–201; Alfred Stuiber, "Eulogia," *RAC* 6 (1966) 900–928; idem, "Geschenk," *RAC* 11 (1977) 686–703; for further bibliography see Theobald, *Die überströmende Gnade,* 316–18; *ThWNT* 10.2 (1979) 1089–90. For the OT and Judaism see Josef Scharbert, "ברך *brk;* בְּרָכָה *b^erākhāh,*" *TDOT* 2 (1975) 279–308; Carl A. Keller and Gerhard Wehmeier, *Theologisches Handwörterbuch zum Alten Testament I* (1971) *s.v.* ברך *brk piel segnen.*

76 See on this point above, pp. 42, 47–48.

77 See also Plutarch's interpretation of the metaphor of seed in *Laud. ips.* 2, p. 539F (see Betz, *PECL II,* 385). See for further discussion Martin P. Nilsson,

relation to a votive offering.[78] If this assumption is warranted, then it is easy to understand why Paul placed this gift of thanks in the service of the poor in the Jerusalem community. Because for the whole of antiquity, but particularly for the Greeks and the Jews, the gift of thanks given to God was always bound up with the provision of social help to those who are in need and destitute.[79] Thus this connection must be regarded as pre-Christian as well. It represents a primal event in the history of the humanization of life, which Paul did not disdain, but which, on the contrary, he incorporated into his theology.

Bibliography:
Ferdinand Orth, "Landwirtschaft," *PRE* 12.1 (1924) 624–76; idem, "Getreide," *PRE* 7.1 (1910) 1336–52; Franz Dornseiff, "Hesiod's Werke und Tage und das alte Morgenland," *Philologus* 89 (1934) 397–415; rep. in his *Kleine Schriften* (Leipzig: Köhler & Amelang, ²1959) 72–95; Peter Walcott, "Hesiod and the Didactic Literature of the Near East," *REG* 75 (1962) 13–36; idem, "Didactic Literature in Greece and the Near East," in his *Hesiod and the Near East* (Cardiff: University of Wales, 1966) 80–104; idem, *Greek Peasants, Ancient and Modern: A Comparison of Social and Moral Values* (New York: Barnes & Noble, 1970); Alfred Hermann and Ilona Opelt, "Ernte," *RAC* 6 (1966) 275–306; Hans G. Kippenberg, *Religion und Klassenbildung im antiken Judäa. Eine religionssoziologische Studie zum Verhältnis von Tradition und gesellschaftlicher Entwicklung* (*SUNT* 14; Göttingen: Vandenhoeck & Ruprecht, 1978).

■ 9:6–14: The Probatio (Proofs)

If, as the *propositio* (9:5b–c) has shown, Paul's goal in the letter was to persuade the Achaians that help was needed in maintaining the original purpose of the collection, the *probatio* should be devoted to the explication of that purpose. This explication takes the form of an interpretation of the notion of the "gift of blessing" (εὐλογία) introduced in the previous section. This interpretation is developed in the form of an elaborate argument. The argument consists of an initial thesis (v 6) substantiated by five consecutive proofs (vv 7–14).[80] Thus the passage meets the requirements of a *probatio* in every respect, in that it sets forth the reasons which justify the author's concerns.[81]

Regarding the passage from the rhetorical point of view, what kind of rhetoric did Paul employ? Because Paul felt it necessary to justify the notion "gift of

Geschichte der griechischen Religion (HKAW 5.2.1–2; Munich: Beck, ²1955–61) 1.127ff; Walter Burkert, *Griechische Religion der archaischen und klassischen Epoche* (Stuttgart: Kohlhammer, 1977) 115ff.

78 On votive offerings see William H. D. Rouse, *Greek Votive Offerings* (Cambridge: Cambridge University, 1902); Burkert, *Religion,* 115ff; Danker, *Benefactor, passim.* See furthermore below, n. 234.

79 The general rule is stated in Matt 10:8: "Freely you have received, freely give." See also the constellation of ideas in Sir 35, esp. 35:10: "Give to the most High as he has given, and as generously as your hand has found." Similarly, Tob 4:7–11; Philo *Plant.* 126–31. For the background see Exod 23:10ff; Lev 23:9ff; Deut 26:1ff; Sir 35; Matt 7:7–11; etc.; on the Greek side see Hesiod *Erga* 354–60. For further references see Str-B 1.561ff; Friedrich Hauck, "θερίζω, θερισμός.," *TDNT* 3 (1965) 132–33; Siegfried Schulz and Gottfried Quell, "σπέρμα κτλ.," *TDNT* 7 (1971) 536–45. These ideas are found expressed in connection with the harvest festivals in the various religious traditions. See Pss 65:9ff; 67:6–7, and for further references Ernst Kutsch, "Feste und Feiern, II. In Israel," *RGG* 2³ (1958) 910–17. For the Greek side see Martin P. Nilsson, *Greek Popular Religion* (New York: Columbia University, 1940) 22ff; Orth, "Getreide," cols. 1347ff; Walter Burkert, *Homo necans: Interpretationen altgriechischer Opferriten und Mythen* (Berlin and New York: de Gruyter, 1972) 287ff; *Religion,* 166–67; furthermore Stephen Charles Mott, "The Power of Giving and Receiving: Reciprocity in Hellenistic Benevolence," *Current Issues in Biblical and Patristic Interpretation,* FS M. C. Tenney (Grand Rapids: Eerdmans, 1975) 60–72.

80 The unity and consistency of the passage has not escaped commentators. See Heinrici, pp. 299–300; Plummer, p. 257, remarks: "The paragraph is a closely united whole and is closely connected with what precedes. Having begged the Corinthians not to spoil his praise of them by exhibiting unreadiness now, but to give without further delay, he puts before them three motives for giving liberally and joyfully." Similarly Windisch, p. 275, who notes that the arguments contain little that is specifically Christian: "Auffallend ist dabei, dass die religiöse Wirkung nirgends auf Christus bezogen, nicht einmal . . . durch ihn vermittelt gedacht wird."

81 On the *probatio* see above, p. 60.

blessing,"[82] the individual proofs are argumentative in nature. Thus the argument as a whole employs what are called "artificial proofs" (*genus artificiale*).[83] As we shall demonstrate below, the apostle employed general didactic *loci*[84] related to the subject matter of the epistle; that is to say, he argued *a re.*[85] This type of rhetoric was discussed at length by Quintilian. He summed up his description as follows: "In all cases, however, in which we enquire into the nature and meaning of an act, and which can be considered by themselves apart from all considerations of persons and all that gives rise to the actual cause, there are clearly three points to which we must give attention, namely, Whether it is, What it is, and Of what kind it is."[86]

In terms of this type of rhetoric, Paul's interpretation of the notion "gift of blessing" is to be classified as *a finitione,* about which Quintilian remarked "Arguments, then, may be drawn from definition, sometimes called *finitio* and sometimes *finis*." One of the ways to proceed with this argument is by explication of the concept: "Further, we may define a word by giving its content as in the preceding instances, or by etymology."[87]

Cicero dealt extensively with the argument from definition. In his *Topica* 5.26ff, he stated: "A definition is a statement which explains what the thing defined is. Of definitions there are two classes, one defining things that exist, and the other, things which are apprehended by the mind."[88] The argument which Paul presented clearly belongs to the latter kind of definition. Consequently, the following statement by Cicero can be applied to 2 Cor 9:6–14: ". . . of these things there is no body but a clear pattern and understanding impressed on the mind, and this I call a notion. In the course of the argumentation this notion frequently requires definition."[89] Such definitions can be handled "partly by enumeration and partly by analysis."[90] Enumeration entails that "the thing which has been set up for definition is divided into its members as it were: for instance, if one should define the civil law as made up of statutes, decrees of the Senate, judicial decisions, opinions of those learned in the law, edicts of magistrates, custom, and equity."[91]

What Cicero meant by analysis is "all the *species* that come under the *genus* which is being defined: *Abalienatio* (transfer of property according to the forms of civil law) of a thing which is *mancipi* is either transfer with legal obligation (*mancipatio*) or cession at law (fictitious suit) between those who can do this in accordance with the civil law."[92] It appears that in 9:6–14 Paul made his argument by division, to employ Cicero's terms. He treated the gift of blessing (εὐλογία) as the *genus,* and divided it into its *species* or forms: the giver (δότης, v 7), grace and gift of grace or charitable gift (χάρις, vv 8 and 14), good work (ἔργον ἀγαθόν, v 8), provision (ἐπιχορηγεῖν, χορηγεῖν, v 10), thanksgiving (εὐχαριστία, vv 11 and 12), service (διακονία, vv 12 and 13), public service (λειτουργία, v 12), and partnership (κοινωνία, v 13). The whole is then characterized in v 15 as "the indescribable gift" (ἡ ἀνεκδιήγητος δωρεά), which amounts, in the words of Cicero, to "a deduction from a subdivision of a general head."[93]

82 See on this subject Lausberg, *Handbuch* 1, §§ 366ff.

83 See ibid., §§ 355ff.

84 See ibid., § 373.

85 See ibid., § 377.

86 Quintilian 5.10.53: "In rebus autem omnibus, de quarum vi ac natura quaeritur, quasque etiam citra complexum personarum ceterorumque ex quibus fit causa, per se intueri possumus, tria sine dubio rursus spectanda sunt, *An sit, Quod sit, Quale sit.*" See furthermore Lausberg, *Handbuch* 1, §§ 392–93.

87 Quintilian 5.10.55: "Praeterea finimus aut vi, sicut superiora, aut ἐτυμολογίᾳ. . . ."

88 *Top.* 5.26, according to the edition and translation by H. M. Hubbel in LCL: "Definitio est oratio quae id quod definitur explicat quid sit. Definitionum autem duo genera prima: unum earum verum quae sunt, alterum earum quae intelleguntur."

89 Ibid., 27: "quarum rerum nullum subest corpus, est tamen quaedam conformatio insignata et impressa intelligentia, quam notionem voco. Ea saepe in argumentando definitione explicanda est."

90 Ibid., 28: "Atque etiam definitiones aliae sunt partitionum aliae divisionum. . . ."

91 Ibid.

92 Ibid.: "Divisionum autem definitio formas omnis complectitur quae sub eo genere sunt. . . ." See also ibid., 2.9: "Sometimes a definition is applied to the whole subject which is under consideration; this definition unfolds what is wrapped up, as it were, in the subject which is being examined." Cf. also Cicero *De orat.* 2.39.164ff.

93 *De orat.* 2.40.168: "Ex parte autem ea, quae est subiecta generi. . . ." See also Lausberg, *Handbuch* 1, § 393.

■ 9:6: The Thesis

The *probatio* begins, as we have indicated, with the statement of the thesis in v 6. The entire argument of vv 6–14 having been set up, as Cicero termed it, *ex nota,* it is now introduced by a *sententia* which serves as the thesis. Quintilian suggested that this is a good way to begin, and Paul apparently agreed, if not with Quintilian, then with the thought behind his recommendation.[94] Paul's *sententia* is, however, quite complex. By definition, "Proverb and sententia provide a general statement of experience, which can be applied to specific instances."[95] Thus Paul's *sententia* was also based upon experience, but this experience was regarded as transparent. Thus it could lightly transform itself into metaphors. The whole is, of course, the product of succinct reflection and literary artistry.

Paul's *sententia* consists of two parallel lines, of which the first is a proverb, introduced by a citation formula τοῦτο δέ (something like "consider the following"). The proverb is drawn from the realm of agriculture:

> He who sows sparingly, sparingly will he also reap.[96]
> ὁ σπείρων φειδομένως φειδομένως καὶ θερίσει.

An even simpler form of this saying is found in Cicero *De oratore* 2.65.261:[97]

> As you sow, so shall you reap.[98]
> *Ut sementem feceris, ita metes.*

These proverbs belong to a whole family of proverbs built upon the contrast between sowing and harvesting.[99] The basic form cited by Cicero can be expanded by the addition of adverbs, etc., which introduce greater specification, as, e.g., in Aristotle *Rhetorica* 3.3, p. 1406b9–10:

> You sowed this shameful seed, and have reaped this evil harvest.[100]
> σὺ δὲ ταῦτα αἰσχρῶς μὲν ἔσπειρας, κακῶς δὲ ἐθέρισας.

If the opposite adverb is used, the opposite point is made, as is shown by an example from the *Greek Apocalypse of Baruch* (15:2):

> For those who have sown well will also harvest well.[101]
> οἱ γὰρ καλῶς σπείραντες καὶ καλῶς ἐπισυνάγουσιν.

---

94 For the role *sententiae* can play in the *probatio* see Quintilian 5.11.36–44, and Lausberg, *Handbuch* 1, § 426.

95 Hans Walther, *Proverbia Sententiaeque Latinitatis Medii Aevi: Lateinische Sprichwörter und Sentenzen des Mittelalters in alphabetischer Anordnung* (Göttingen: Vandenhoeck & Ruprecht, 1963) vol. 1, p. xv: "Sprichwort und Sentenz geben einen allgemeinen Erfahrungssatz, der sich auf Sonderfälle anwenden lässt." The literary side of the *sententia* has been discussed since antiquity. See esp. Aristotle *Rhet.* 2.21, p. 1394a19–29; Quintilian 8.5. See also Lausberg *Handbuch* 1, §§ 872–79; Betz, *Galatians,* 291ff. For modern literary investigations see esp. the journal *Proverbium: Bulletin d'information sur les recherches parémiologiques* 1 (Helsinki: Société de Littérature Finnoise, 1965–); Gerhard Neumann, ed., *Der Aphorismus: Zur Geschichte, zu den Formen und Möglichkeiten einer literarischen Gattung* (Darmstadt: Wissenschaftliche Buchgesellschaft, 1976); Wolfgang Mieder, ed., *Ergebnisse der Sprichwörterforschung = Europäische Hochschulschriften,* Reihe I, Band 192 (Bern: Lang, 1978); John D. Crossan, ed., *Gnomic Wisdom = Semeia* 17 (Chico, CA: Scholars, 1980).

96 My translation attempts to preserve the chiastic structure.

97 The commentary by August S. Wilkins, *M. Tulli Ciceronis De Oratore libri tres* (Oxford: Clarendon, 1892) 361 n. 4, mentions as parallels Aristotle *Rhet.* 3.3; 2 Cor 9:6; Gal 6:7.

98 My translation. Cf. Matt 6:26 par.; 25:24, 26; Luke 19:21; John 4:37.

99 For parallel proverbs see Job 4:8; 31:8; Ps 126:5; Prov 11:18; 22:8; Eccl 11:4, 6; Jer 12:13; Hos 8:7; Mic 6:15; Matt 6:26; 4:3–32 par.; Matt 25:24, 26; Luke 19:21; John 4:36–37; 1 Cor 15:36–44; Gal 6:7–8. See moreover August Otto, *Die Sprichwörter und sprichwörtlichen Redensarten der Römer* (Leipzig: Teubner, 1890) 221, no. 1104 *s.v.* "metere"; Reinhard Häussler, ed., *Nachträge zu August Otto, Sprichwörter und sprichwörtliche Redensarten der Römer* (Darmstadt: Wissenschaftliche Buchgesellschaft, 1968) 186, 240, 280; Victor Pöschl, ed., *Bibliographie zur antiken Bildersprache* (Heidelberg: Winter, 1964), *s.v.* "Säen und Ernten."

100 Cited according to the edition and translation of Richard C. Jebb, *The Rhetoric of Aristotle* (Cambridge: Cambridge University, 1909) 154. See also Job 4:8; Prov 22:8; Hos 8:7.

101 Cited according to the edition of J.-C. Picard, *Apocalypsis Baruchi Graece* (PVTG 2; Leiden: Brill, 1967) 95. My translation. I am indebted for the parallel to Str-B 3.524. See also Ps 126:5; Jer 12:13; Mic 6:15; Matt 13:29. Cf. Gal 6:7b–8, where another

Likewise, in Paul's proverb, the addition of "sparingly" (φειδομένως) lends a kind of cutting edge to the saying, which is intensified by the doubling of the lines and the chiastic structure. Was Paul himself responsible for composing the second line of the proverb? We cannot be sure, but Paul may be supposed to be the author of the saying because of the distinct character of the second line within the argumentation: it seems to have been created to fit the present argument:

> He who sows "upon blessings," "upon blessings" will he also reap.[102]
> ὁ σπείρων ἐπ' εὐλογίαις ἐπ' εὐλογίαις καὶ θερίσει.

The second line in 9:6b is constructed in antithesis to the first and introduces the notion of "gift of blessing" (εὐλογία) which is basic to the entire argument.[103] It takes a somewhat peculiar form, ἐπ' εὐλογίαις, so as to constitute the opposite of "sparingly" (φειδομένως).[104] Accordingly, it should be rendered "bountifully." It should be noted, however, that the Greek expression retains the meaning "blessing," which is lost in the English translation. Yet without this connotation (ἐπ' εὐλογίαις is literally "upon blessings"), Paul's entire argument remains incomprehensible.

The addition of this second line turns the whole *sententia* into a maxim, employing antithetical *parallelismus membrorum.* Of course, the maxim no longer speaks of agriculture but of the exchange of gifts in human society.

In terms of its rhetoric, the argument advanced in the proverb operates by way of consequences (*ex consequentibus*).[105] The addition of the second line in v 6b makes it an argument that works through its opposite (*ex contrario*).[106] If sowing sparingly results in a sparse harvest, the opposite must also be true: sowing bountifully leads to a bountiful harvest. Or does it?

The conclusion seems simple and self-evident, but the very form of the maxim should warn us that matters may not be as simple as they seem. We should also take account of the fact that Greek and Roman literature on agriculture engages in wide-ranging discussions on the proper amount of seed to be used in sowing. This literature advises the farmer to measure the amount of seed carefully, in accordance with the condition of the grain, the soil, and the climate. The subject was mentioned as early as Hesiod,[107] and was then discussed at length by Xenophon in his *Oeconomicus,* for example, 17.9: ". . . and I ask you whether you would give the same quantity of seed to both kinds, or to which you would give more?"[108] Similar deliberations are found in Pliny: "It is a well-known fact that some lands take more seed and others less, and this supplies farmers with a binding and primary augury: when the earth receives the seed more greedily, it is believed to be hungry and to devour the seed."[109] Pliny then proposed specific quantities of seed for different kinds of grain and soil, and concluded his discussion with a proverb: "Do not grudge the cornfield its seed."[110]

Whence did Paul have the proverb in v 6a? Commentators have often assumed Prov 11:24 to be the source,

version of the proverb is cited and then interpreted allegorically. See Betz, *Galatians,* 307–9.

102 My own translation attempts to preserve the untranslatable expression ἐπ' εὐλογίαις. See Bauer, *s.v.* ἐπί II,1,b, ζ: "of manner, corresponding to an adverb." See for this expression also Philo *Leg. all.* 3.210; *Mos.* 1.283.

103 So rightly Bauer, *s.v.* εὐλογία, 5: "Since the concept of blessing carries with it the idea of bounty, εὐλογία gains the meaning *generous gift, bounty. . . .*" For the background in ancient religion see also H. W. Pleket, "Religious History as the History of Mentality: The 'Believer' as Servant of the Deity in the Greek World," *Faith, Hope and Worship: Aspects of Religious Mentality in the Ancient World* (ed. H. S. Versnel; Studies in Greek and Roman Religion 2; Leiden: Brill, 1981) 183–84.

104 The term "sparingly" is certainly related also to the notion of "greediness" (9:5c).

105 Cf. on this point esp. Cicero *Top.* 12.53: "Nam coniuncta . . . non semper eveniunt; consequentia autem semper" ("For conjuncts . . . do not always happen, but consequents always do"). See also Lausberg, *Handbuch* 1, §§ 356,2; 371.

106 See on this conclusion Aristotle *Rhet.* 2.23.1, p. 1397a7–12; also Lausberg, *Handbuch* 1, §§ 377,3; 394; 395.

107 Hesiod *Erga* 467–82.

108 Translation by Edgar C. Marchant in the LCL edition of Xenophon's *Memorabilia* and *Oeconomicus,* p. 493.

109 Pliny *N.H.* 18.196, tr. H. Rackham in the LCL edition.

110 Ibid., 200: "Segetem ne defruges." So the text of

but this is far from evident.[111] In the first place, the text of Prov 11:24 is different, whereas content and context are similar. The Masoretic Text reads:

> A man may spend freely and yet grow richer;
> another is sparing beyond measure, yet ends in
> poverty.[112]

> יֵשׁ מְפַזֵּר וְנוֹסָף עוֹד
> וְחוֹשֵׂךְ מִיֹּשֶׁר אַךְ־לְמַחְסוֹר

The LXX reads somewhat differently:

> There are those who sow their own and do better;
> and there are those who collect and do worse.[113]

> *εἰσὶν οἱ τὰ ἴδια σπείροντες πλείονα ποιοῦσιν·*
> *εἰσὶν καὶ οἱ συνάγοντες ἐλαττοῦνται.*

Instead of translating the Hebrew text, the LXX appears to have replaced the Hebrew proverb with a similar Greek saying. It is interesting, too, that the whole group of sayings in Prov 11:23–31 has to do with the dangers of wealth among farming people. As has been repeatedly pointed out, many of these sayings have a strong background in the non-Israelite wisdom tradition.[114]

If these facts are taken into consideration, it begins to seem less likely that Paul quoted the proverb in 2 Cor 9:6a directly from the LXX. It may be that he was familiar with the whole cluster of sayings in Prov 11:23–31, where the term "gift of blessing" (*εὐλογία*) also occurs (v 26). Perhaps he was acquainted with similar proverbs, either individually or in groups. At any rate, it is more likely that the proverb quoted in v 6a came to him through oral tradition than through reading the text of Proverbs. Thus the history of the oral transmission of the proverb is illustrated by the preservation of three distinct versions of the saying: the Masoretic Text of Prov 11:24, the LXX version,[115] and the Pauline version. Other instances of proverbial material found in Paul would have to be treated in the same way, unless they explicitly state their dependence on the Book of Proverbs. As the Book of Proverbs drew on pre-Israelite wisdom, so did Paul. As Old Testament writers were capable of interpreting the saying in accordance with their own theologies,[116] Paul interpreted it in accordance with his. Taken by itself, the proverb gives expression to common ancient experience, and as such is neither specifically Jewish nor Christian. In specific contexts, it could be adapted to the needs of different communities, whether Jewish or Christian.

Originally, Paul's proverb may have been an old *Bauernregel.*[117] By the addition of the second line, he transformed it into a maxim, whose reflection remains at the pre-Christian level. Only its integration into the context of the letter makes it the bearer of specifically Christian thought.

For this reason, Windisch's suggestion that the future tense "he shall reap" (*θερίσει*) should be interpreted as a reference to the last judgment, making the saying as a whole an eschatological prediction, cannot be accepted.

Rackham. On the desirable quantity of seeds see also Cato *De agri cultura* 5.4; Varro *De reb. rust.* 1.44; Columella *De re rust.* 2.9. Cf. also the proverb of Plutarch stating the opposite, *Glor. Athen.* 4: *τῇ χειρὶ δεῖν σπείρειν, ἀλλὰ μὴ ὅλῳ τῷ θυλάκῳ* ("One should sow with the hand, not with the whole sack"); Seneca *Ep.* 81.1: "et post malam segentem serendum est" ("Also after a bad harvest one must sow"). On the whole subject see Orth, "Getreide," cols. 1342–43.

111 For a discussion of some of the problems in 2 Cor 9:6–9 cf. also Anthony T. Hanson, *Studies in Paul's Technique and Theology* (London: SPCK, 1974) 177–81; Theobald, *Die überströmende Gnade,* 318–31.

112 The translation is that of *NEB.*

113 My translation.

114 See Berend Gemser, *Sprüche Salomos* (HAT 1/16; Tübingen: Mohr, Siebeck, 1963) 57ff.

115 A similar process seems to have been followed by the Vg: "alii dividunt propria et ditiores fiunt alii rapiunt non sua et semper in egestate sunt." Cited according to the *Biblia sacra II* (Roma: Typis Polyglottis Vaticanis, 1957) 60.

116 Cf. Windisch, p. 276: "Es ist immerhin gut israelitische Spruchweisheit, was Paulus hier verkündet. . . ." He then refers to the parallels in Prov 11:25–26, 30; 22:8a; 19:14; Ps 36(= 37 MT):26; Deut 15:10; Hos 10:12.

117 Windisch, p. 276.

Parallel passages in Matt 13:39, Mark 4:29, Rev 14:15–16, and especially Gal 6:7–9[118] do not bear this out, particularly as their relationship to 2 Cor 9:6 cannot be demonstrated. Rather, these passages represent different interpretations of the same basic agrarian wisdom. As metaphors, "sowing" and "harvesting" are easy to interpret in eschatological terms, as Paul did in Gal 6:7–9; but this does not mean that the terms bear an eschatological sense everywhere they occur. 2 Cor 9:6 illustrates that the eschatological meaning does not predominate everywhere in Paul.

Against Windisch, the remarkable thing about the entire passage 9:6–14 is the lack of explicitly Jewish and Christian ideas.[119] Of course, Paul spoke of human needs and divine rewards, but he did so in this-worldly terms, and in keeping with the ancient concept of gifts and the giving of gifts in general.[120]

■ 9:7: The First Proof

The first proof focuses on the giver of the "gift of blessing." Once more (cf. v 6a), Paul began at the proverbial level, presenting what was the common view on the giver of gifts:

> Everyone [gives] as his heart has decided.[121]
> *ἕκαστος καθὼς προῄρηται τῇ καρδίᾳ.*

Antiquity believed, as indeed we do today, that gift-giving is a matter of the heart.[122] In the Old Testament, in Judaism and early Christianity,[123] and also in Greek philosophy after Chrysippus,[124] the heart was regarded as the place where plans and decisions were made.[125] As part of the emotional life, gift-giving was understood to be intimately related to the plans and decisions of the heart. When such decisions are made, they are usually not made without reason or motivation. Paul provided three such reasons, two negative and one positive. Gifts can be the result of internal distress (*λύπη*)[126] or external pressure (*ἀνάγκη*),[127] but gifts given under such circumstances cannot be regarded as gifts of blessing. Only gifts which result from a cheerful disposition (*ἱλαρός*)[128] can be properly called by that name.

As the parallels indicate, this point of view was a commonplace in antiquity. Paul justified his proof by what appears to be a quotation from Scripture, introduced by "for" (*γάρ*). But the quotation raises the same

118 In Gal 6:7–9 Paul interprets a non-eschatological proverb eschatologically. The fact that it is done here and in the Jewish tradition as well (see for references Str-B 3.524) does not mean that it is done everywhere. It is all the more remarkable that it is not done in 2 Cor 9:6.

119 Windisch, p. 276; cf. also Heinrici, pp. 300–301; Plummer, pp. 258–59.

120 On gift giving see above, p. 42.

121 My translation. The perfect form *προῄρηται*, represented by the better manuscripts, emphasizes that the decision of the heart has been made when the gift is given. The variant reading *προαιρεῖται* (D Ψ 048 𝔐) is a gnomic present and not different in meaning.

122 Hesiod's statement in *Erga* 357–60 is typical: "For when a man gives willingly, though he gives a great thing, yet he has joy of his gift and satisfaction in his heart, while he who gives way to shameless greed and takes from another, even though the thing he takes is small, yet it stiffens his heart" (*ὃς μὲν γάρ κεν ἀνὴρ ἐθέλων ὅ γε καὶ μέγα δώῃ, χαίρει τῷ δώρῳ καὶ τέρπεται ὃν κατὰ θυμόν· ὃς δέ κεν αὐτὸς ἕληται ἀναιδείηφι πιθήσας, καί τε σμικρὸν ἐόν, τό γ' ἐπάχνωσεν φίλον ἦτορ*). Citation according to the edition and translation of Lattimore, *Hesiod*, 61. For parallels to the statement see West, *Hesiod, Works and Days*, 247.

123 See Friedrich Baumgärtel and Johannes Behm, "*καρδία κτλ.*," *TDNT* 3 (1965) 606–7 (A.2), 609–11 (C), 612 (D.2.c).

124 See especially *SVF* 2.244ff; Seneca *De ben.* 6.10.2; *Ep.* 81.5–6; 81.30: "Nothing is more honorable than a grateful heart" ("nihil esse grato animo honestius"); for further passages cf. Baumgärtel and Behm, "*καρδία κτλ.*," *TDNT* 3 (1965) 608–9 (B); Hubert Martin, *PECL II*, 509.

125 Cf. Bauer's translation, *s.v.* *προαιρέω*, 2: "as he has made up his mind."

126 The use of the term with this meaning is rare in the NT, see Mark 10:22. The extensive discussion of *λύπη* ("distress") in the letter of reconciliation (2 Cor 2:1–7; 7:8–11) refers not to giving but to the effect of the previous letter, which is most probably identical with 2 Cor 10:1—13:10. On the whole concept see Rudolf Bultmann, "*λύπη κτλ.*," *TDNT* 4 (1967) 313–22; in addition *PECL II*, index, *s.v.;* Spicq, *Notes de lexicographie* 1.513–19.

127 Cf. the parallels Phlm 14; 1 Pet 5:2; other occurrences of the term in Paul are different; cf. 2 Cor 6:4; 12:10; etc. See Bauer, *s.v.*

128 See the parallels in Prov 17:22; Sir 35:8 LXX; Rom 12:8. On the concept of *ἱλαρός*, see Rudolf Bultmann, "*ἱλαρός κτλ.*," *TDNT* 3 (1965) 297–300.

question as was raised in regard to the proverb in v 6. Since the quotation is certainly a proverb, and since the introductory formula does not indicate specifically that what follows is a quotation from Scripture, the question remains whether Paul intended to quote a proverb or Holy Scripture. If the latter, which passage did he have in mind? The proverb is as follows:

> For God loves a cheerful giver.
> ἱλαρὸν γὰρ δότην ἀγαπᾷ ὁ θέος

In the Old Testament, only Prov 22:8a (LXX) comes close to Paul's wording:

> God blesses a cheerful man who is also a giver. . . .[129]
> ἄνδρα ἱλαρὸν καὶ δότην εὐλογεῖ ὁ θεός.

This proverb is Greek in character and seems to have replaced a Hebrew proverb found in the Masoretic Text (Prov 22:9):

> A good eye—it will be blessed.[130]
> טוֹב־עַיִן הוּא יְבֹרָךְ

The problem of the relationship between the Masoretic Text and the LXX of Prov 22 cannot be fully discussed here. It is evident, however, that the LXX did not, strictly speaking, translate the Hebrew proverb with its untranslatable idiom,[131] but substituted an equivalent Greek proverb.[132]

Paul's citation is sufficiently different from the LXX to make it likely that he quoted a proverb which he knew by heart because it circulated in his cultural environment, rather than that he quoted directly from the LXX.[133] Of course, this in no way excludes the possibility that Paul knew the "biblical" proverb from memory. The quotation simply provides another example of the transmission of proverbs like the one we have observed in v 6.

This verse also raises the question whether Paul took the proverb from a cluster of related sayings. It is part of such a group of sayings in Prov 22 dealing with the topic of rich and poor, including the giving of gifts. But there are similar collections which do not depend on one another textually.[134] After all, most proverbs are transmitted orally and recited from memory. If, on the other hand, Paul derived the proverb directly from Prov 22:8a (LXX), he changed the text in a characteristic way by replacing the phrase "he blesses" (εὐλογεῖ) with "he loves" (ἀγαπᾷ). All other quotations of Prov 22:8a (LXX) in ancient literature use, so far as we know, the term εὐλογεῖν/ברך ("bless"), a term that would fit well in Paul's argument in 2 Cor 9:7.[135] Then why did he change it?[136] Did he do so in anticipation of the next argument dealing with God's grace? Was he influenced

129 My translation.

130 My translation.

131 Cf. Kautzsch, *De Veteris Testamenti locis*, 58–59. The Hebrew proverb belongs to the category of ṭôḇ-min sayings. See Höver-Johag, "טוֹב," *TWAT* 3 (1982) 334–35.

132 On the tendency of LXX Prov to replace Hebrew by Greek proverbs see Gillis Gerleman, *Studies in the Septuagint*, vol. 3: *Proverbs* (Lunds Universitets Årsskrift, NF Avd. 1, Band 52, Nr. 3; Lund: Gleerup, 1956).

133 The proverb has many parallels in ancient literature. See Otto, *Die Sprichwörter*, 55, *s.v.* "beneficium"; also Häussler, *Nachträge zu August Otto*, 302, nos. 248–49. See also A. R. Hands, *Charities and Social Aid in Greece and Rome* (Ithaca, NY: Cornell University, 1968) 30 with n. 54.

134 For such a cluster see also Pseudo-Phocylides 22–30, 80–83; for more parallels see the commentary by van der Horst, *Pseudo-Phocylides*, 128ff, 168ff.

135 See also *Abot de Rabbi Nathan* A 13, according to the translation of Judah Goldin, *The Fathers According to Rabbi Nathan* (YJS 10; New Haven: Yale University, 1955) 73: "AND RECEIVE ALL MEN WITH A CHEERFUL COUNTENANCE: what is that? This teaches that if one gives his fellow all the good gifts in the world with a downcast face, Scripture accounts it to him as though he had given him naught. But if he receives his fellow with a cheerful countenance, even though he gives him naught, Scripture accounts it to him as though he had given him all the good gifts in the world." Cf. version B in Anthony J. Saldarini, *The Fathers According to Rabbi Nathan (Abot de Rabbi Nathan): Version B* (SJLA 11; Leiden: Brill, 1975) 143. See also the passages listed in Str-B 3.524.

136 Nestle-Aland 26th ed. takes ἀγαπᾷ to be due to Paul's change.

by Jewish hermeneutical principles? Or was he influenced by another proverb in Prov 22:11 (LXX) in such a way that he was led to combine the two sayings into one? Indeed, Prov 22:11 bears a remarkable similarity to 2 Cor 9:7:

> The Lord loves pious hearts.[137]
> *ἀγαπᾷ κύριος ὁσίας καρδίας.*

A decision as to the origin of Paul's proverb is made more difficult by the fact that it is bound up with two other unsolved problems: (1) the problem of how Paul quoted Scripture and of his textual sources; (2) the general problem of how proverbs are quoted in the Old and the New Testaments. If the conventional way of quoting proverbs was also employed by the authors of Scripture, it may be assumed that the actual wording of such proverbs differed, depending on the oral tradition with which an author was familiar. The main concern of the author in quoting a proverb was not to reproduce the exact words of the saying, but to make the point the proverb wanted to make.[138] Thus it seems most likely that in 2 Cor 9:7 Paul attempted to quote a scriptural proverb from memory.[139] Further, one can assume that certain proverbs were traditionally associated with certain topics, and that this is the reason why similar proverbs often turn up in the same thematic contexts. This phenomenon is confirmed by Seneca's reference to similar proverbs in his long essay *On Benefits* without, of course, being dependent on either Jewish or Christian tradition.[140] Both Paul and Seneca were concerned with the same group of ideas, but they treated them quite differently in both length and conceptuality. Seneca began book 2 by stating briefly what he will discuss (2.1.1–2):[141]

> Let us give in the manner that would have been acceptable if we were receiving. Above all let us give willingly, promptly, and without hesitation.
>
> Sic demus, quomodo vellamus accipere. Ante omnia libenter, cito, sine ulla dubitatione.

The first point, then, is this (2.1.2):

> No gratitude is felt for a benefit when it has lingered long in the hands of him who gives it, when the giver has seemed sorry to let it go, and has given it with the air of one who was robbing himself.
>
> Ingratum est beneficium, quod diu inter dantis manus haesit, quod quis aegre dimittere visus est et sic dare, tamquam sibi eriperet.

In giving his reasons, Seneca made the same point as Paul (2.1.2):

> For, since in the case of a benefit the chief pleasure of it comes from the intention of the bestower, he who by his very hesitation has shown that he made his bestowal unwillingly has not "given," but has failed to withstand the effort to extract it. . . .
>
> Nam cum in beneficio iucundissima sit tribuentis voluntas, quia nolentem se tribuisse ipsa cunctatione testatus est, non dedit sed adversus ducentem male retinuit; . . .

Later in the same book, Seneca offered sayings and examples to prove the points he had made. Among them is the following saying (2.7.1):[142]

> Fabius Verrucosus used to say that a benefit rudely given by a hard-hearted man is like a loaf of gritty bread, which a starving man needs must accept, but which is bitter to eat.
>
> Fabius Verrucosus beneficium ab homine duro aspere

137 My translation.

138 A similar impression is gained from rabbinic teaching, where Prov 22:9 may be explicitly quoted or not. In *Abot R. Nat.* A 13, it is quoted (see n. 135, above).

139 So also Plummer, p. 259.

140 See Cornelius a Lapide, p. 126; Wettstein, *ad. loc.;* Heinrici, p. 302; Plummer, pp. 259–60; Windisch, p. 277. See also J. N. Sevenster, *Paul and Seneca* (NovTSup 4; Leiden: Brill, 1961) 9ff.

141 Cited according to the text and translation of John W. Basore, LCL, 50–51.

142 Ibid., 60–61.

datum panem lapidosum vocabat, quem esurienti accipere necessarium sit, esse acerbum.

It should be emphasized that Seneca's essay has little to offer that is new, but is rather a collection of conventional wisdom drawn from his philosophical tradition.[143] This tradition rests upon earlier works, among which Aristotle's *Nicomachean Ethics* is the most important.[144]

The fourth book deals extensively with the giving and receiving (*δόσις καὶ λῆψις*), in particular with liberality (*ἐλευθεριώτης*) and the opposed vices, prodigality and stinginess (*ἀσωτία* and *ἀνελευθερία*).[145] These ethical concepts were discussed in dialogue with popular morality and religion, as Aristotle himself acknowledges (*EN* 5.5.7, p. 1133a3–6): "This is why we set up a shrine of the Graces [*Χάριτες*] in a public place, to remind men to return a kindness; for that is a special characteristic of grace [*χάρις*], since it is a duty not only to repay a service done one, but another time to take the initiative in doing a service oneself."[146]

Therefore, it is not surprising to find similar ideas in the quite-different context of Greek votive inscriptions. Of the many examples which could be given, the following, an inscription of particular prominence, will suffice.[147] It is a dedication to Demeter and Kore by a priestess of Demeter from the Eleusinion in Athens (ca. 455 B.C.):[148]

> O revered Demeter, Lysistrate, the attendant of your sacred rites and of your daughter's, has erected this offering of two crowns as an ornament of your forecourt. Of what she has, she is not sparing, but to the gods she is lavish to the extent of her means.
>
> ['Α]*ρρήτο τελετῆς πρόπολος σῆς, πότνια Δηοῖ, καὶ θυγατρὸς προθύρο κόσμον ἄγαλμα τόδε ἔστησεν στεφάνω Λυσιστράτη οὐδὲ παρόντων φείδεται ἀλλὰ θεοῖς ἄφθονος ἐς δύναμιν.*

143 Cf. also Matt 7:9, pointed out by Str-B 1.459. Clement of Alexandria *Quis dives salvetur* 31 quotes 2 Cor 9:6 and provides an interpretation in accordance with the wisdom conception of the time: "Now the Apostle's saying also is good, 'God loveth a cheerful giver,' one who takes pleasure in giving and sows not sparingly, for fear he should reap sparingly, but shares his goods without murmerings or dispute or annoyance. This is sincere kindness." (*καλὸς μὲν οὖν καὶ ὁ τοῦ ἀποστόλου λόγος· "ἱλαρὸν γὰρ δότην ἀγαπᾷ ὁ θεός," χαίροντα τῷ διδόναι καὶ μὴ φειδομένως σπείροντα, ἵνα μὴ οὕτως καὶ θερίσῃ, δίχα γογγυσμῶν καὶ διακρίσεως καὶ λύπης [καὶ] κοινωνοῦντα, ὅπερ ἐστὶν εὐεργεσία καθαρά.*) Text and translation according to G. W. Butterworth, LCL, 336–37. For further material from the church fathers see Cornelius a Lapide, p. 126.

144 Aristotle *EN* 4.1.1–45; pp. 1119b21–1122a18; cf. 2.7.4–5, p. 1107b9–15; *EE* 2.3, pp. 1221a5, 1231b27–1232a18; *MM* 1.22, pp. 1191b39–1292a20; also *Rhet.* 2.7.1–5, p. 1385a–b. See moreover Cicero *De off.* 1.14.42–49. On the whole subject See Bolkestein, *Wohltätigkeit,* index, *s.v. δικαιοσύνη*; Dihle, *Die Goldene Regel,* 21–22, 31–40; idem, "Gerechtigkeit," *RAC* 11 (1976) 234–60, esp. 258ff.

145 *EN* 4.1.13, p. 1120a27ff: the "right kind of giving" (*τῇ ὀρθῇ δόσει*) is giving "with pleasure" (*ἡδέως*) instead of "with pain" (*λυπηρῶς*). Cf. the concept "openhanded" (*δοτικός*) as opposed to "avaricious" (*φιλοχρήματος*) in *EN* 4.3, p. 1121b16.

146 The text and translation is that of Harris Rackham in the LCL edition.

147 I am indebted to Professor Walter Burkert for having called my attention to the votive inscriptions at this point. For further examples see Hermann Dessau, *Inscriptiones Latinae Selectae* 3.2 (Berlin: Weidmann, 1916) 793–95, especially the abbreviations VSLLM = *votum solvit laetus libens merito* ("an offering of acquittal from a vow, he made it cheerfully, willingly, deservedly"); *Thesaurus Linguae Latinae* 7.2, col. 1326; *CIL* 6, 7/3, pp. 3373–74; Werner Eisenhut, "Votum," *PRE.S* 14 (1974) 964–73, esp. 971.

148 *SEG* 10, no. 321. Cited here in the edition and translation of W. Kendrick Pritchett, "Greek Inscriptions," *Hesperia* 9 (1940) no. 18 (pp. 97–101). Heinrich Dörrie has shown in an essay on the cultic endowments of Kommagene how these attitudes are used for the education of the people by an enlightened Hellenistic ruler. According to this philosophy, piety (*εὐσέβεια*) toward the gods and the king is no longer to be based on "awe and fear" (*δεισιδαιμονία*) but on the imitation of the generosity of the god-king who through his endowments invited everyone to great festivals and sacrificial meals. See Heinrich Dörrie, "Das gute Beispiel—*καλὸν ὑπόδειγμα*. Ein Lehrstück vom politischen Nutzen sakraler Stiftungen in Kommagene und in Rom," *Studien zur Religion und Kultur Kleinasiens,* FS F. K. Doerner (EPRO 66/1; Leiden: Brill, 1978) 245–62.

In conclusion, the right kind of giver, from whom a gift of blessing can be expected, is the one who gives with a cheerful heart. His or her opposite is the person who may or may not give, depending on internal or external pressures.

■ 9:8: The Second Proof

The second proof is already announced in the concluding words of v 7: "God loves" (ἀγαπᾷ ὁ θεός). What does God's love have to do with the gift of blessing? In answer to this question, we must first of all pay attention to the presuppositions of Paul's argument. These presuppositions are not stated explicitly, since they were commonly held in antiquity. What Paul discussed were the applications of these presuppositions.

In the first place, the apostle referred to the notion that all human giving is in response to gifts received, the principle of *do ut des* ("I give to you, so that you may be willing to give to me").[149] Applied to religion, this principle implies that gifts offered as sacrifices are the human response to blessings received from the god,[150] and that the human response expresses the expectation of receiving still more.[151]

Applied to the case at hand, Paul asserted that "God is powerful" (δυνατεῖ δὲ ὁ θεός),[152] that is, that his gift is powerful enough to endow the Achaians richly with every kind of benefit (πᾶσαν χάριν περισσεῦσαι εἰς ὑμᾶς).[153] This cannot have been a new idea to the Achaians. They themselves have always been grateful that God's gifts came to them so abundantly. Therefore, Paul's purpose can only have been to remind them of things they knew from their own experience. Certainly the notions of grace (χάρις) and gifts of grace (χαρίσματα) must have been well known to them. They are indeed key terms in Paul's theology, and are discussed at length in 1 Corinthians.[154] In the letter fragments of 2 Corinthians, grace and gifts of grace are also fundamental notions underlying his arguments.[155] Starting from these basic assumptions, the apostle unfolded what he had to say.[156]

A second presupposition must also be spelled out, since it, too, underlies Paul's argument. It concerns the ancient principle of *do ut des* already mentioned. As Gerardus van der Leeuw has pointed out,[157] the various meanings of this principle are illustrated by the different translations, one of which runs as follows: "I give to you

149 Cf. the basic ideas as Hesiod states them, *Erga* 353–55: "Be a friend to your friend, and come to him who comes to you. Give to him who gives; do not give to him who does not give. We give to the generous man; none gives to him who is stingy" (τὸν φιλέοντα φιλεῖν καὶ τῷ προσιόντι προσεῖναι καὶ δόμεν ὅς κεν δῷ, καὶ μὴ δόμεν ὅς κεν μὴ δῷ· δώτῃ μέν τις ἔδωκεν, ἀδώτῃ δ᾽ οὐ τις ἔδωκεν). Text and translation are cited according to Lattimore, *Hesiod*, 61.

150 Aelius Aristides *Panathenaic Oration* 34 shows that these ideas have become commonplaces in oratory: "Thus having received gifts from the Gods, so well did they imitate the givers that they themselves became like Gods for other men and gave this first proof of the merited achievement of their needs, the proper employment of what they had. For they did not think that it was enough if they buried their gifts beneath the earth, but they were so far from fearing to make others their equals that they thought that they could not make a fairer demonstration of how superior they were to others than if they should be seen benefiting all men." Translation by A. Behr in the LCL edition, 33–34; see also Arthur Stanley Pease, *M. Tulli Ciceronis De natura deorum* (Darmstadt: Wissenschaftliche Buchgesellschaft, 1968) 2.689–90 on *De nat. deor.* 2.60.

151 See on the topic Gerardus van der Leeuw, "Die do-ut-des-Formel in der Opfertheorie," *ARW* 20 (1920) 241–53; Joseph W. Hewitt, "The Gratitude of the Gods," *Classical Weekly* 18 (1925) 148–51; Burkert, *Religion,* 115ff; a great amount of material is assembled in the article by Mott, "The Power of Giving and Receiving," 60–72; Danker, *Benefactor,* 436ff.

152 The question is whether 2 Cor 9:8 should read δυνατεῖ (P^{46} ℵ B C* D* F G 104 t vg Ambst) or δυνατός (C^{2} D^{2} Ψ 048). See on this question Kilpatrick, "The Text of the Epistles" (see above, p. 76 n. 296), 59 § 21. In Paul's theology, God's gift of grace is of course identical with his power, but the emphasis here is on the gift.

153 Windisch, p. 277, points to the allegorical feature of π-alliteration in vv. 8 and 11. On the notion of περισσεύειν, see above on 8:2.

154 See Hans Conzelmann, "χάρις κτλ.," *TDNT* 9 (1974) 393–96 (D.2), 403–6 (C.1–2).

155 See in 2 Corinthians the first apology 2:14; 4:15; 6:1; the second apology 12:9; the letter of reconciliation 1:11, 12, 15.

156 See 2 Cor 8:1, 4, 6, 7, 9, 16, 19; 9:8, 14, 15; cf. 1 Cor 16:3. For discussion see Windisch, pp. 277–78.

157 See above, n. 144.

so that your capacity of giving may be maintained." In the case at hand, Paul's conclusion is stated with reference to another important concept which he introduced at this point: the result of God's giving is human self-sufficiency (αὐτάρκεια). This situation was at present enjoyed by the Achaians: "so that you have full self-sufficiency in everything all the time" (ἵνα ἐν παντὶ πάντοτε πᾶσαν αὐτάρκειαν ἔχοντες). The term "self-sufficiency" (αὐτάρκεια) was chosen for a good reason. It has its origin in Greek philosophy, where it designates the precondition for human freedom.[158] The result of such self-sufficiency is that there is plenty left in reserve with which to do good works: "so that . . . you may have abundance for every good work" (ἵνα . . . περισσεύητε εἰς πᾶν ἔργον ἀγαθόν).

This chain of conclusions looks peculiar at first sight, and is certainly unique in the New Testament. But these ideas were generally held in the Greco-Roman world. The singular "good work" (ἔργον ἀγαθόν) looks more Hellenistic than Jewish.[159] More importantly, Paul seems to have disagreed with the Socratic tradition on the nature of self-sufficiency. In that tradition, self-sufficiency (αὐτάρκεια) was thought to be attainable by scaling down one's external needs to the point where, just like the gods, one has need of nothing. The deity is self-sufficient because he has no needs; humans can be self-sufficient to the degree that they can disengage themselves from human needs.[160]

Paul's view in 2 Cor 9:7 departs from the Socratic tradition and agrees with the mainstream of Greek thought as found in Greek religion—Plato, the Academy, the Peripatos, and the Stoa, to mention only the main representatives.[161] According to this line of thought, the possession of external goods with which to satisfy essential needs is indeed a precondition for self-sufficiency. Of course, it is not the only precondition; self-sufficiency depends in addition on what one considers to be the necessities of life, and how one consciously relates to external possessions. Paul agreed with this train of thought in that he based self-sufficiency on economic wealth obtained through the exchange of gifts. He disagreed with the mainstream of Greek philosophy, however, in that he did not regard man's "inner freedom" from possessions as the precondition for real self-sufficiency. It is at this point that Paul Wilpert's otherwise excellent article in *RAC* made Paul more "Christian" than he really is.[162]

For Paul, self-sufficiency is attainable because wealth can be accepted and used as part of God's grace. Wealth should be viewed as a gift of God's beneficence, rather than as the result of a purely human achievement. The expression "good work" (ἔργον ἀγαθόν) demonstrates how Paul carried these ideas further. The term "good work" must not be confused with the Jewish concept of the works of the Torah.[163] Rather, it represents a notion that was commonly held in antiquity and involved the following considerations: The recognition that wealth is a divine gift of blessing means ipso facto that it enables the human recipient to share with others. Divine gifts were believed to exceed what one needed for one's own use. The very act of receiving divine beneficence must, if done properly, lead to sharing the goods with those in

158 As Bauer, *s.v.* αὐτάρκεια, 1, points out, the term is used in 2 Cor 9:8 more as a description of someone who has had enough of everything. But this meaning should not be artificially separated from its philosophical background, from which it comes. See also the use of the adjective αὐτάρκης ("self-sufficient") in Phil 4:11. Cf. the long discussion by Chrysostom *In epist. II. ad Cor. Hom.* 19, *MPG* 61.574Aff. On the notion itself see Paul Wilpert, "Autarkie," *RAC* 1 (1950) cols. 1039–50.

159 See Betz, *Galatians,* on Gal. 6:4 and 6:10; Danker, *Benefactor,* 339–43.

160 See Socrates according to Xenophon *Mem.* 1.6.10; *Symp.* 4.35; *Oec.* 2.5ff; cf. Antisthenes according to Diog. L. 6.11. See Wilpert, "Autarkie," col. 1040.

161 For the complexities regarding ancient philosophy see Wilpert, "Autarkie," cols. 1040ff; Arthur W. A. Adkins, "'Friendship' and 'Self-Sufficiency' in Homer and Aristotle," *CQ* NS 13 (1963) 30–45.

162 Wilpert in his article, "Autarkie," col. 1045, states the apostle's position in idealistic terms: "Das Wort A. [*sc.* Autarkie] begegnet im NT nur in den paulinischen Briefen in der allgemeinen Bedeutung der Genügsamkeit, aber auch als Ausdruck der Haltung des Christen zur Welt. In innerer Freiheit, die ihm aus der Gnade Gottes fliesst . . . steht der Christ über den Werten dieses Lebens, doch nicht gleichgültig gegen sie." Likewise Meyer and Hofmann want to restrict self-sufficiency to "subjective conditions" ("subjective Verfassung") rather than objective realities; differently Heinrici, pp. 302–3, who correctly refers to the parallel in the Sermon on the Mount, Matt 6:25–26.

163 This concept occurs in Galatians but not in 2 Cor 8

need, in order to do good by giving freely. "Freely you have received, freely give"[164]—this saying was not originally Christian, but gives expression to what antiquity as a whole considered religiously proper. By contrast, one who received divine benefits and yet remained tightfisted and blind to the needs of others was considered sacrilegious and prone to divine retribution and punishment.[165]

These ideas must be very old, and must have constituted part of the generally accepted wisdom tradition in antiquity. Thus it is not surprising to find related wisdom ideas already contained in the Accadian "Councils of Wisdom":

> Give food to eat, beer to drink,
> Grant what is requested, provide for and
> treat with honor.
> At this one's god takes pleasure.
> It is pleasing to Shamash, who will
> repay him with favor.
> Do good things, be kind all your days.[166]

In conclusion: the second proof shows what makes a cheerful giver. Cheerful givers, we are told, are not so by nature. One becomes a cheerful giver when one realizes that great benefits have been bestowed on her or him by God. Those who have received God's benefits have both the material means and the inner disposition to become cheerful givers.

■ 9:9–11: The Third Proof

The third proof in vv 9–11 consists of a small compositional unit of three parts: (1) a proof from scripture (Ps 111:9 LXX); (2) an allegorical interpretation; and (3) ethical conclusions.

The scriptural passage is introduced in v 9a by a formula which clearly designates it as a quotation from Scripture: "as it is written" (*καθὼς γέγραπται*).[167] The text of Ps 111:9 agrees with the LXX,[168] which, in turn, corresponds to the Masoretic Text:[169]

> He scattered, he gave to the poor;
> his righteousness remains into eternity.

> *ἐσκόρπισεν, ἔδωκεν τοῖς πένησιν·*
> *ἡ δικαιοσύνη αὐτοῦ μένει εἰς τὸν αἰῶνα.*

The interpretation in v 10a and b takes up important points from the first (v 9a) and the second lines (v 9b) of the quotation respectively. The first term to be interpreted is "he scattered" (*ἐσκόρπισεν*); this is accomplished in v 10. Unlike the Psalm, which deals with the duties of the god-fearing man, Paul took God to be the subject: God is the one who scatters, and in this way he is the one who provides. The epithet "the one who provides" (*ὁ ἐπιχορηγῶν*) as applied to God is important not only in the New Testament, but in the Hellenistic world as a whole.[170] What is unusual about Paul's interpretation is that he combined the two epithets, the "one who scatters" and the "one who provides."[171] This combination calls to mind the ancient image of the deity as the divine sower who scatters the seed-grain, an image attested in Jewish and Christian literature.[172]

But when one considers that Paul did not employ these

and 9. See Betz, *Galatians,* 116.

164 Matt 10:8: *δωρεὰν ἐλάβετε, δωρεὰν δότε.*

165 See also 1 Tim 6:17–21.

166 *ANET,* Supplementary Volume (1969) 595.

167 This form of the quotation formula occurs also in 8:15. For references see above, p. 69.

168 Cited according to the edition of Alfred Rahlfs, *Septuaginta,* vol. 10: *Psalmi cum Odis* (Göttingen: Vandenhoeck & Ruprecht, 1931). See also Kautzsch, *De Veteris Testamenti locis,* 20.

169 Ps 112:9:

> פִּזַּר נָתַן לָאֶבְיוֹנִים
> צִדְקָתוֹ עֹמֶדֶת לָעַד

170 See Gal 3:5; *Herm. Sim.* 2.51.7; Phil 1:19; Col 2:19; Eph 4:16; 2 Pet 1:5. See Bauer, *s.v.; PGL, s.v.*

171 The image is also found in Matt 25:24, 26, where *διασκορπίζειν* ("scatter") is a synonym of sowing, the subject also being God. The usual understanding of God's scattering activity is that it is hostile and refers to the scattering of enemies. See Otto Michel, "*σκορπίζω κελ.*," *TDNT* 7 (1971) 418–22. The image of sowing as scattering seems to be proverbial (see Isa 28:25, where Aquila has *διασκορπίζειν*, while LXX has *σπείρειν*; see also Michel, "*σκορπίζω κτλ.*," 422 n. 17).

172 See esp. Isa 28:23–29, and on the whole image Gottfried Quell, "*σπέρμα κτλ.*," *TDNT* 7 (1971) 541–42 (B.3), 543–44 (C), 546 (D.2).

terms metaphorically, but spoke of God as the scatterer of seed-grain in a literal sense, then it becomes clear how rarely this notion is found in the Scripture.[173] When it is mentioned, it seems to reflect popular Israelite religion as it manifests itself above all in the seasonal festivals.[174]

In his commentary, Windisch rejected this realistic interpretation on the grounds that it does not fit in with Paul's concern for spiritual matters.[175] No doubt this concept of God as the scatterer of seed-grain is unusual in Paul; it is found nowhere else but in 2 Cor 9. But its rarity does not render it un-Pauline. Further, it should be noted that although Paul made use of a proof from Scripture, what he found in the quotation were not specifically Christian ideas, but notions drawn from ancient folk religion.

It is precisely at this point that Paul's language and thought seem very close to that of Greek religion, where the concept of God as provider was fundamental. Divine epithets such as "Bringer of fruit" (Ἐπικάρπιος) and "Fruit-giver" (Καρποδότης and Καρποδοτήρ) were connected with Zeus, especially in Asia Minor, where a number of older fertility deities had been Hellenized.[176] Dio Chrysostom explained the epithet "Bringer of Fruit" in this way: ". . . and as 'God of Wealth and Increase' since he causes all fruitage and is the giver of wealth and substance, not of poverty and want" (Κτήσιος δὲ καὶ Ἐπικάρπιος, ἅτε τῶν καρπῶν αἴτιος καὶ δοτὴρ πλούτου καὶ κτήσεως, οὐ πενίας οὐδὲ ἀπορίας).[177] Demeter was generally regarded as the deity who provided corn.[178] Thus at the time of sowing, the farmer was advised to pray to chthonic Zeus and to Demeter,[179] both of whom were honored at the harvest festivals.[180] According to the myth, Demeter had given the ears of grain to Triptolemus, the older of Metaneira's children, and he, ascending to heaven on the winged chariot, had sown the whole earth with it.[181]

It is in these texts that the deity is associated with scattering or sowing, and with threshing or the separation of the fruit from the chaff,[182] and with the filling of the barns. "The corn of Demeter" (Δημήτερος ἀκτή)[183] was a proverbial expression among the Greeks; it signified corn itself. And corn equaled wealth, so that her son was aptly called Plutos,[184] begotten on a thrice-plowed field. Plutos represented the storage bin full of grain, from which the seed-grain for the following year was to come.

173 See in the OT Gen 26:12; Ps 65:9; Isa 55:10–11; 62:8; 65:22; Deut 28:30–33; etc. Str-B 3.525 points out that in rabbinic literature Ps 112:9 is interpreted in terms of almsgiving by the righteous man, not the work of God.

174 See Exod 23:16ff; 34:22; Lev 23:15ff; Deut 16:9; Tob 2:1ff. For an overview of the matter see Alfred Hermann and Ilona Opelt, "Ernte," *RAC* 6 (1966) 275–306.

175 Cf. Windisch, pp. 279–80: "Gegen eine solche Erklärung spricht indes, dass man einen so realistischen Gedanken am wenigsten bei P. (i.e., Paulus) erwarten darf, der so ganz im Geistigen und Kirchlichen aufgeht (vgl. I.9.9f.), weiter dass in einer Handelsstadt wie Kor. (i.e., Korinth) der Wohlstand keineswegs allein vom Ausfall der Ernte abhängig war. . . ."

176 For references see Bolkestein, *Wohltätigkeit,* 19–20, 47–48, 173–74, 320; Hans Schwabl, "Zeus I. Epiklesen," *PRE* 2. Reihe, 19. Halbband (1972) 306–7, 311, 320; idem, "Zeus II. Nachträge," *PRE.S* 15 (1978) § 18; Nilsson, *GGR* 1.401ff.

177 Dio Chrysostom *De regno* 1.41; cf. Epictetus *Diss.* 1.19.12; 1.22.16.

178 See esp. Nilsson, *GGR* 1.456ff; G. Zuntz, *Persephone: Three Essays on Religion and Thought in Magna Graecia* (Oxford: Clarendon, 1971) 71ff, 100; Burkert, *Religion,* 247ff.

179 Hesiod *Erga* 465–66: "Make your prayers to Zeus of the ground and holy Demeter that the sacred yield of Demeter may grow complete and be heavy" (εὔχεσθαι δὲ Διὶ χθονίῳ Δημήτερί θ' ἁγνῇ ἐκτελέα βρίθειν Δημήτερος ἱερὸν ἀκτήν). Translation and text by Lattimore, *Hesiod,* 73. See West, *Hesiod, Works and Days,* 276 *ad loc.*

180 Theocritus *Thalys.* 7.3; 155.

181 *Homeric Hymn to Demeter* 153ff, 474ff; Aelius Aristides *Panathenaic Oration* 36–37. See A. B. Cook, *Zeus: A Study in Ancient Religion* (3 vols.; Cambridge: Cambridge University, 1914–40) 1.211ff; Friedrich Schwenn, "Triptolemos," *PRE* 2. Reihe, 13 Halbband (1939) 213–30; Neil J. Richardson, *The Homeric Hymn to Demeter* (Oxford: Clarendon, 1974) 194ff.

182 *Iliad* 5. 499–501.

183 Ibid., 13. 322; 21. 76; Hesiod *Erga* 466. For further references see LSJ, *s.v.* ἀκτή; Pease, *M. Tulli Ciceronis* 2.690–91 on *De nat. deor.* 2.60; p. 722 on *De nat. deor.* 2.67.

184 Hesiod *Erga* 126: πλουτοδότα. See West, *Hesiod, Works and Days,* 183 *ad loc.* For Πλουτοδότας as a personification see the Locrian vase painting published by Giuseppe Procopio, "Vasi a figure nere del Museo Nazionale di Reggio Calabria," *Archeologia*

If Paul's language and thought came so close to Greek religion, he simply reflected what was the common religious sentiment of antiquity. We might note, in addition, that Triptolemus was no stranger to Tarsus. Strabo, *Geography* 16.2.5, reports: "It is said that he [*sc.* Triptolemus] was sent by the Argives in search of Io, who disappeared first in Tyre, and that he wandered through Cilicia; and that there some of his Argive companions left him and founded Tarsus. . . ." One can assume that Paul was familiar with the Triptolemus myth, and thus with the myth of Demeter, from his childhood days in Tarsus, since these tales were part of Greek folk religion.

The closest parallel in the New Testament is the parable of the Rich Man in Luke 12:16–21. His foolishness and his sin are thus described: he is "one who gathers his harvest only for himself but is not rich toward God" (ὁ θησαυρίζων ἑαυτῷ καὶ μὴ εἰς θεὸν πλουτῶν).[185] He has amassed wealth without honoring God as the giver, taking it for granted that he has done it all by himself; thus he becomes the very impersonation of greed (πλεονεξία).[186]

The section "On Worrying" in the Sermon on the Mount (Matt 6:25–34) also has deep roots not only in Judaism but in ancient religion in general. Here we find the notion of God as a father who nourishes all his creatures (Matt 6:26, 32, 33).[187] Even that portion of the Lord's Prayer which contains the petition for daily bread (Matt 6:11; Luke 11:3; *Did.* 8.2), however central it may be to both Judaism and Christianity, is in basic agreement with ancient religious sentiment.[188]

Paul continued his interpretation of v 9a by explaining the nature of God's provisions and the manner in which he provides for the needy. Again, Paul made use of popular concepts which he saw no need to discuss in detail because he felt he could count on general assent. His reference to such notions takes what seems to be proverbial form. As in vv 6 and 7, we must ask whether Paul intended to refer to an oral proverb or to Scripture. In this instance, the saying is not introduced by a quotation formula, but is merely recited. Thus it is difficult to determine whether Paul intended to quote Scripture (Isa 55:10 LXX)[189] or whether he simply cited a proverb[190] current in his day:

> Seed for the sower and bread for consumption.[191]
> *σπόρον τῷ σπείροντι καὶ ἄρτον εἰς βρῶσιν.*

It must be understood that the proverb encapsulates the entire doctrine of the divine economy, in accordance with which God's provisions are twofold: (1) seed for the sower, (2) bread for consumption. In fact, three provisions are implied: (1) seed for this year's sowing, (2) seed for next year's sowing, (3) bread for present consumption. These provisions reflect ancient wisdom and practice, in accordance with which first consideration must be given at harvest time to the seed-grain needed for the next season. Only after a sufficient amount of such seed-grain has been set aside could the surplus be

---

classica 4 (1952) 153–61; furthermore Nilsson, *GGR* 1^{3}.860; George E. Mylonas, *Eleusis and the Eleusinian Mysteries* (Princeton: Princeton University, 1961) 210ff; Richardson, *Homeric Hymn,* 195.

185 Although the sentence is unusual and is missing in some manuscripts, it may well be original. See Nestle-Aland, *apparatus criticus;* Metzger, *Textual Commentary,* 160; Walter Grundmann, *Das Evangelium nach Lukas* (ThHNT 3; Berlin: Evangelische Verlagsanstalt, ^{2}1961) 258. Joachim Jeremias, *The Parables of Jesus* (New York: Scribner's, 1963) 106 n. 73, rightly refers to the parallel in Matt 6:19–21.

186 In Luke's interpretation, the parable in 12:16–21 exemplifies greed (πλεονεξία), for which he also provides an explanation (v 15).

187 For a more detailed discussion of this passage see my article, H. D. Betz, "Cosmogony and Ethics in the Sermon on the Mount," *Essays,* 89–123. See in addition Acts 14:17; 17:25. The tradition is also found in the *Codex Manichaicus Coloniensis,* 107, lines 4 and 16, for which see Albert Henrichs and Ludwig Koenen, *ZPE* 44 (1981) 214–15 with n. 361; 363–67.

188 See Theodor Klauser et al., "Brot," *RAC* 2 (1951) 611–20.

189 The wording of the LXX is slightly different: σπέρμα τῷ σπείροντι καὶ ἄρτον εἰς βρῶσιν .

190 Isa 55:10–11 sums up popular ideas about fertility: "For as the rain and the snow come down from heaven, and return not thither but water the earth, making it bring forth and sprout, giving seed to the sower and bread to the eater, so shall my word be. . . ."

191 My translation.

used for consumption.[192] Therefore, unless there was a plentiful harvest, a person had to choose whether to starve this year or next. On the other hand, the blessing of God becomes a manifest in the multiplication of grain which produces the surplus necessary and thus averts hunger. Hence God's provision takes the form of the multiplication of seed, that is, an increase which results in a surplus of the seed sown: *χορηγεῖν καὶ πληθύνειν τὸν σπόρον*.[193] Therefore God is not merely the "one who scatters" and the "one who provides." Rather, as scatterer and provider he becomes the "one who multiplies."[194] Again, the agricultural epithet was first of all at home in the cult of Demeter,[195] but was commonly employed in the Hellenistic world in general.[196]

While on the one hand Paul could speak literally of real, material matters, he was also capable of shifting his argument swiftly to the level of the metaphor. This shift is indicated by the future tense in the statement "he will provide and increase your seed" (*χορηγήσει καὶ πληθυνεῖ τὸν σπόρον ὑμῶν*). At present, the Corinthians' seed was their wealth, which served as the basis for their donation. At the same time, Windisch[197] was correct in saying that "seed" refers metaphorically to the money which the Corinthians were to contribute to the collection. It is not necessary when using metaphors to make a strict separation between the actual, or material, referent and its transferential application. Rather, it is in the nature of metaphors that they continue to interact with each other, thus keeping "things before the eyes."[198] That a transfer to the metaphorical has occurred is made clear by the final phrase of v 10b: "he will also increase the fruits of your righteousness" (*καὶ αὐξήσει τὰ γενήματα τῆς δικαιοσύνης ὑμῶν*). The phrase is meant to be an interpretation of the statement in v 9b: "his righteousness remains in eternity," and a corresponding change in the meaning of the term "righteousness" is also to be observed. In Paul's view, v 9b speaks of God's righteousness, v 10b of the righteousness of the Corinthians. They are related in the following way: God's righteousness provides for human righteousness by establishing its economic basis. To express this idea, Paul again had recourse to a notion which almost seems to be proverbial, but has its origin in Scripture. The notion "[the] fruits of righteousness" (*[τὰ] γενήματα δικαιοσύνης*) occurs in Hosea 10:12 (LXX), but there is no hint that Paul intended to refer to this scriptural passage.[199] Rather,

192 See Hesiod *Erga* 600–601: "Measure it [*sc.* the grain] by storing it neatly away in the bins. Then after you have laid away a good store of livelihood in your house, . . ." (*μέτρῳ δ' εὖ κομίσασθαιἐν ἄγγεσιν. αὐτὰρ ἐπὴν δὴ πάντα βίον κατάθηναι ἐπάρμενον ἐνδόθι οἴκου*, . . .). Translation and text by Lattimore, *Hesiod*, 89. See also *Erga* 473–76; Xenophon *Oec.* 17.15ff; Pliny *N.H.* 18.195ff; Columella *De re rust.* 2.11. On the keeping of the grain see Orth, "Getreide," cols. 1351ff.

193 The term *χορηγεῖν* ("provide") is a synonym of *ἐπιχορηγεῖν* . See Bauer, *s.v.* *χορηγέω*; Danker, *Benefactor*, 331–32. On God's activity as a multiplier see also *1 Clem.* 59.3; *Herm. Vis.* 1.1.6; *Sim.* 9.24.3; and furthermore Bauer, *s.v.* *πληθύνω*; Gerhard Delling, "*πληθύνω*," *TDNT* 6 (1968) 279–83.

194 The important term here is *αὐξάνω* ("increase"). See also 1 Cor 3:6–7; Bauer, *s.v.* *αὐξάνω*, *αὔξησις*; for the background see Gerhard Delling, "*ὑπεραυξάνω κτλ.*," *TDNT* 8 (1972) 517–19. The concept of the deity as a multiplier is basic to Israelite religion (see esp. Gen 1:22, 28; 8:17; 9:1, 7; 17:6, 20; 28:3; etc.), yet it is not unique to that religion but part of the widespread agrarian theology so often encountered in 2 Cor 9.

195 See esp. Hesiod *Erga* 392–94: ". . . if you wish to bring in the yields of Demeter all in their season, and so that each crop in its time will increase for you, . . ." (. . . *εἴ χ' ὥρια πάντ' ἐθέλῃσθα ἔργα κομίζεσθαι Δημήτερος, ὥς τοι ἕκαστα ὥρι' ἀέξηται*. . . .). Translation and text by Lattimore, *Hesiod*, 65.

196 For the Hellenistic theological idea see Pausanias 1.38.6: "They say that the plain called Rharium was the first to be sown and the first to grow crops [*αὐξῆσαι καρπούς*], and for this reason it is the custom to use sacrificial barley and to make cakes for the sacrifices from its produce" (tr. W. H. S. Jones, LCL); Plutarch *De E apud Delphos* 6, 386F: *ὁ θεὸς αὔξει* ("the god causes increase"); *Corp. Herm.* 1.18; Epictetus *Diss.* 1.14.4; 1.16.17; 3.22.5; 4.1.163; 4.8.36, 40; *PGM* 4.719, 2347, 2981; 7.763–764; 12.244; 13.65, 170, 438, 518 (cf. 4.601), 519, 575, 636. Auxesia was the name of the goddess of growth (Herodotus 5, 82–87. Cf. also the epithets *ὁ αὐξητής* ("the increaser") in *Orphic Hymns* 11.11; 15.8; *αὐξίτροφος* ("promoter of growth") in *Orphic Hymns* 10.17 (cf. 10.30); 51.13; see also 9.4; 13.3; 26.4, 10; 40.10; etc. The Athenians named one of the Graces "Auxo" (Pausanias 9.35.2; Pollux 8.106).

197 Windisch, p. 280.

198 Aristotle, *Rhet.* 3.11.2, p. 1411b23: *πρὸ ὀμμάτων ποιεῖν*. For the complexities of interpreting metaphors see Paul Ricoeur, *La métaphore vive* (Paris: du Seuil, 1975); ET: *The Rule of Metaphor* (Toronto: University of Toronto, 1979).

the notion belongs to a complex of agrarian metaphors popular both in Jewish ethics[200] and in Hellenistic morality. "Product" (*γένημα*)[201] is the general term; "fruit" (*καρπός*) is more frequent,[202] but both terms refer to the same thing.

It is remarkable that Paul could speak of human righteousness in a way not unlike that found in Jewish authors.[203] In fact, the same language is found in ancient popular morality outside Judaism. Also of note in v 10b is the absence of the doctrine of the spirit.[204]

The ideas that Paul expressed here correspond to an extraordinary degree to those found in Greek religion.[205] They were succinctly summarized by Xenophon, *Oeconomicus* 5.12, for example: "Yet again, the earth willingly teaches righteousness to those who can learn; for the better she is served, the more good things she gives in return."[206] Later, similar ideas were stated by Aelius Aristides in his *Panathenaic Oration* 45: ". . . that they not only have the seeds of wheat and barley, but that they also have from the Gods the seeds of justice and every other means of life and government."[207]

In v 11, Paul presented the conclusions that he wishes the Corinthians to draw from the preceding argument. At the same time, he continued to employ notions common to ancient religion. All together, Paul offered three conclusions:

1) First he summed up the results of God's care for human needs: "we are wealthy in every respect" (*ἐν παντὶ πλουτιζόμενοι*, v 11a). The statement is meant to be true in general, and not for the Corinthians alone. In fact, it is an anthropological statement which declares that humankind is poor (v 9a) in its absolute dependence on God's beneficence, but rich in God's abundant care. Therefore those who comprehend this truth will consider themselves not poor but rich. The term *πλουτίζειν* is used in v 11a in a peculiar way, to mean "to have received and therefore to be rich" and not in the sense of "to make others rich."[208] In addition, it is used here both in the literal, economic,[209] and in the figurative, spiritual sense.[210] Again, there is nothing specifically Christian about these ideas; all antiquity knew that whether one is rich or poor depends as much on economic realities as on one's perceptions and values. Consequently, wherever the language of wealth (*πλοῦτος*) and abundance (*περισσεία*) occurs in the text,

199 Windisch, p. 280, speaks of an allusion to Hos 10:12. Plummer, p. 263, takes it to be a quotation, but remarks: "Neither LXX nor Heb. give exactly the thought which St Paul has here, yet either might suggest the thought." Nestle-Aland, 26th ed., has correctly indicated that it is not a quotation.

200 For passages see Friedrich Hauck, "*καρπός κτλ.*," *TDNT* 3 (1965) 614–16; Str-B 1. 466–67; Bauer *s.v.* *καρπός*, 2, a.

201 The metaphor is unique in Paul. Cf. Luke 12:18. See Bauer, *s.v.* *γένημα*.

202 The NT expression is originally Jewish Christian (see Matt 7:15–20; 3:8; Jas 3:18 (3:17), but occurs also in Paul (Phil 1:11; Rom 6:21–22).

203 The whole idea is summed up in Prov 3:9–10: "Honor the Lord with your substance and with the first fruits of all your produce; then your barns will be filled with plenty, and your vats will be bursting with wine." The LXX has theologized v 9 further: "Honor the Lord from your righteous labors and give him the first fruits from your fruits of righteousness" (*τίμα τὸν κύριον ἀπὸ σῶν δικαίων πόνων καὶ ἀπάρχου αὐτῷ ἀπὸ σῶν καρπῶν δικαιοσύνης*).

204 Cf. Gal 5:22–23: *ὁ καρπὸς τοῦ πνεύματος* ("the fruit of the spirit"). See on this Betz, *Galatians*, 286.

205 Hesiod *Erga* 213ff has a series of sentences and exhortations concerning righteousness. See on these Walter Nicolai, *Hesiods Erga: Beobachtungen zum Aufbau* (Heidelberg: Winter, 1964) 56ff, 191ff; cf. Danker, *Benefactor*, 343–48.

206 *Ἔτι δὲ ἡ γῆ θέλουσα τοὺς δυναμένους καταμανθάνειν καὶ δικαιοσύνην διδάσκει· τοὺς γὰρ ἄριστα θεραπεύοντας αὐτὴν πλεῖστα ἀγαθὰ ἀντιποιεῖ.*

207 . . . *καὶ μὴ μόνον τῶν πυρῶν καὶ κριθῶν εἴη τὰ σπέρματα αὐτοῖς, ἀλλὰ καὶ δικαιοσύνης καὶ τῆς ἄλλης ἁπάσης διαίτης τε καὶ πολιτείας ἐκ θεῶν αὐτοῖς εἴη τὰ σπέρματα.* Cited according to the translation and text of Behr, LCL.

208 Cf. Plummer, p. 264; "Ye being enriched in everything." Turner, *Grammatical Insights*, 166, takes it to be an instance of the imperatival use of the participle: "be ye enriched in everything."

209 See also *1 Clem.* 59.3; *Herm. Sim.* 2.10.

210 Differently Bauer, *s.v.* *πλουτίζω*, 2, who thinks that

both the economic and spiritual realities are present, and are a part of the argument.[211] Finally, when Paul summed up his thoughts with the words "we are wealthy in every respect," he reiterated what he had already told the Corinthians in 1 Cor 1:5, and in 2 Cor 8:7. To be sure, the statement reflects not only the self-understanding of the Corinthians, but that of the Achaians as well.

2) Building on the previous conclusion, Paul stated that the Achaians' wealth was intended "for every kind of generosity" (εἰς πᾶσαν ἁπλότητα). Again, this view of wealth contains nothing specifically Christian but was generally held in the Hellenistic world. The notion of the "generosity of simple giving" (ἁπλότης) was a cultural ideal at the time.[212] It was common practice to leave some of the harvest to the poor. In Israel, this was even codified in the Torah (Lev 19:9–10):

> When you reap the harvest of your land, you shall not reap your field to its very border, neither shall you gather the gleanings after your harvest. And you shall not strip your vineyard bare, neither shall you gather the fallen grapes of your vineyard; you shall leave them for the poor and for the sojourner: I am the Lord your God.[213]

Rather than denouncing wealth as spiritually corrupting —the view commonly held in the New Testament[214]— Paul affirmed the common attitudes of his time regarding wealth: wealth is good and acceptable if it leads to generosity.[215]

3) The concluding statement in v 11b is rather difficult to interpret, and its meaning becomes clear only after its presuppositions have been spelled out: "which is such as to generate through us thanksgiving to God" (ἥτις κατεργάζεται δι᾽ ἡμῶν εὐχαριστίαν τῷ θεῷ).[216] In Paul's view, generosity produces thanksgiving among those who receive gifts; because this happens "through us," it is to our credit, and thus enhances our righteousness.

Again we are confronted by common Hellenistic ideas, so that "through us" (δι᾽ ἡμῶν) should not be taken to refer to Paul alone, but to all those who followed Paul's recommendations.[217] The term " produce" (κατεργάζεσθαι) is known from other Pauline passages.[218] It expresses his understanding of moral action as the result of external influences rather than innate abilities. Surely

Paul refers here as in 1 Cor 1:5; 2 Cor 6:10 to spiritual riches only.

211 See 2 Cor 8:2, 7, 9, 14; 9:1, 8, 12.

212 See above on 8:2.

213 See also Lev 23:22; Deut 24:19–22; Ruth 2:2–23; Isa 17:5–6. See Karl Elliger, *Leviticus* (HAT 1.4; Tübingen: Mohr, Siebeck, 1966) 257; Bolkestein, *Wohltätigkeit,* 470ff; Wilhelm Schwer, "Armenpflege," *RAC* 1 (1950) 689–98.

214 See esp. Mark 10:17–22 and the interpretation in Mark 10:23–31; Luke 6:20, 24–25; Jas 2:1ff; etc.

215 This agricultural ethic is very ancient, as the "Instruction of Any" from the Eighteenth Dynasty of Egypt shows: "One man is rich, another is poor. But food remains for him who shares it." Cited according to Miriam Lichtheim, *Ancient Egyptian Literature* (Berkeley and Los Angeles: University of California, 1976) 2.142. In the NT the same ethic is basic to the Sermon on the Mount, in which wealth is not denounced but only greed (6:19–21, 24; 7:7–11), and where fasting is treated lightly (6:16–18). Later Christian literature justifies wealth even more, if it is used to do good on behalf of the poor. See esp. *Herm. Sim.* 2.51.1ff, and Clement of Alexandria *Quis dives salvetur?* (on this work see L. William Countryman, *The Rich Christian in the Church of the Early Empire: Contradictions and Accommodations* [Texts and Studies in Religion 7; New York and Toronto: Mellen, 1980]). On the subject see Martin Dibelius, *James: A Commentary on the Epistle of James* (rev. Heinrich Greeven; ed. Helmut Koester; Hermeneia; Philadelphia: Fortress, 1976) 39ff; idem, *Der Hirt des Hermas* (HNT, *Ergänzungsband* 4; Tübingen: Mohr, Siebeck, 1923) 555–56; Carolyn Osiek, "Rich and Poor in the Shepherd of Hermas" (Dissertation, Harvard University, 1978). *CBQ* Monograph Series 15 (Washington, D.C.: The Catholic Biblical Association of America, 1983).

216 The translation is that of Plummer, p. 264. The ἥτις is textually uncertain; P⁴⁶ D* 326 b Ambst read εἴ τις. The difference may, as Nestle-Aland suggests, be due to itacism.

217 Differently Plummer, p. 264, who cites the dissenting view in a note: "Some understand δι᾽ ἡμῶν as meaning, 'through us weak mortals'. . . ." Windisch, p. 281, is unclear. Cf. Heinrici, p. 306; Cornelius a Lapide, p. 132, who cites patristic authorities.

218 See esp. 2 Cor 7:10–11; Phil 2:12; Rom 5:3; 7:18; and George Bertram, "κατεργάζομαι.," *TDNT* 3 (1965) 634–35.

any religious person in antiquity would have considered it a good thing to cause others to give thanks to God.[219] In Jewish thought above all it was regarded as meritorious.[220] "Through us" means, therefore, that it will be accredited to us, and thus our righteousness before God will be increased.

With this, the third argument, the interpretation of Scripture cited in v 9[221] reaches its conclusion. In this proof, Paul has shown that as a giver of gifts, one must first realize[222] that one is the recipient of God's beneficence, and that God's provisions encompass every kind of gift, both material and spiritual, in this world as well as in the world to come. At the end of the section, Paul, as he so often did in his arguments, introduced the key concept of the next section, the notion of "thanksgiving" (εὐχαριστία).[223]

■ **9:12: The Fourth Proof**

The fourth proof is brief by comparison. It continues the argument of v 11b in a different way. It provides the logical explanation for the ideas expressed in v 11b (ὅτι). How, then, is thanksgiving to God actually generated?

The answer lies in the identification of "charitable service" (διακονία), which is the name usually given to the collection for the saints in Jerusalem, as a λειτουργία or "public service performed by private citizens at their own expense."[224] Paul employed this familiar political and legal concept here in its secular, not in its metaphorical, religious sense.[225] Indeed, the collection for the poor in Jerusalem was, in accordance with the secular meaning of the term, a charitable donation by one group of people acting voluntarily on behalf of another. While originally such "liturgies" were carried out between cities, by the time of Paul it had become an acceptable practice to designate transactions between social groups by this term as well.[226] Paul's use of the term, however, raises additional questions. Does it imply that Christian

219 This was one of the purposes of votive inscriptions (see above, nn. 147–48). But see also the moral instructions of Epictetus *Diss.* 1.6.1ff; 1.16.15ff; 1.19.25; 4.4.14ff; Seneca *Ep.* 95.50. On the whole topic see Hans Conzelmann, "εὐχαριστέω κτλ.," *TDNT* 9 (1974) 408–9.

220 See on this esp. Philo *Plant.* 126ff, who in 136 sums up the matter in a formula reminiscent of Paul: "for the thanksgiver finds in thanksgiving itself an all-sufficient reward" (τῷ γὰρ εὐχαρίστῳ μισθὸς αὐτὸ τὸ εὐχαριστεῖν αὐταρκέστατος). On thanksgiving as a religious duty see esp. Deut 8:10; Pss 50:14, 23; 65:1ff; 79:13; 107:1ff; 116:1ff; Wis 16:28; Sir 51:1ff; Tob 12:20; 13:1ff; Josephus *Ant.* 8.111 (see also below, n. 254); Rom 1:21; Luke 17:16; etc. See also Conzelmann, "εὐχαριστέω κτλ.," 407–15; Günter Mayer et al., "ידה," *TWAT* 3 (1982) 455–74 (with further literature).

221 Differently Windisch, p. 280, who takes v 11 to belong with the following section.

222 Paul does not emphasize here the action of recognition presupposed. But recognition is specifically mentioned in Rom 1:21 and also in the interesting passage Luke 17:16, on which see Hans Dieter Betz, "The Cleansing of the Ten Lepers (Luke 17:11–19)," *JBL* 90 (1971) 314–28, esp. 318–19. Of course the cognitive aspect beomes the primary concern among the philosophers; see esp. Epictetus *Diss.* 1.6.1–2: "From everything that happens in the universe it is easy for a man to find occasion to praise providence, if he has within himself these two qualities: the faculty of taking a comprehensive view of what has happened in each individual instance, and the sense of gratitude [τὸ εὐχάριστον]. Otherwise one man will not see the usefulness [τὴν εὐχρηστίαν] of what has happened, and another, even if he does see it, will not be grateful therefor [οὐκ εὐχαριστήσει ἐπ᾽ αὐτοῖς]."

223 See also below on 2 Cor 9:12–14.

224 So the rendering in LSJ, *s.v.*

225 Cf. Bachmann, pp. 333–34; Bauer, *s.v.* λειτουργία, who does not recognize the secular usage in 2 Cor 9:12 which occurs also in Rom 15:27 (as a verb: λειτουργέω ["perform a public service"]). Heinrici's interpretation, p. 307, however, is correct: "eine gemeinsame öffentliche Angelegenheit für die Gläubigen." See also Plummer, p. 265: "Λειτουργία is used here in a sense closely akin to its classical meaning of the 'aids' which wealthy citizens had to render to the public in financing choruses for dramas . . . , fitting out triremes, training gymnasts, etc. These *publica munera* were enforced by law, but St Paul uses the word of voluntary service." Actually the voluntary nature of liturgies was always emphasized, even though it was often a farce. See on this point Kuenzi, ΕΠΙΔΟΣΙΣ, esp. 23ff. For the right interpretation see also Windisch, p. 280; Hermann Strathmann, "λειτουργέω κτλ.," *TDNT* 4 (1967) 226–27 (D.1); Spicq, *Notes de lexicographie* 1.479; Danker, *Benefactor*, 330–31.

226 The basic study is by Friedrich Oertel, *Die Liturgie: Studien zur ptolemäischen und kaiserzeitlichen Verwaltung Ägyptens* (Leipzig: Teubner, 1917). A subsequent collection of material was made by Naphthali Lewis,

churches in Greece and Jerusalem had some kind of official legal status? Did Paul regard the collection as more than a transaction between churches, that is, as involving the body politic as well?[227] The lack of historical evidence prevents us from reaching a clear answer. At least we may say that the term "liturgy" has a political overtone; to say more would amount to speculation.

For Paul, the purpose of the collection was achieved in two ways.

1) Most obviously, it served to "supply the wants of the saints" (*ἐστὶν προσαναπληροῦσα τὰ ὑστερήματα τῶν ἁγίων*).[228] If Paul limited this aspect of the collection by the phrase "not truly" (*οὐ μόνον*), it is not because he intended to minimize it, but only because he wished to emphasize the fact that this is the ordinary purpose of "liturgies." Therefore, his language is to be taken in its literal, secular sense as referring to the economic plight of the Jerusalem church.[229] This literal meaning is also found in parallel passages in 2 Cor 8:14, Gal 2:10, Rom 15:26–27, where Paul spoke even more concretely of the physical needs (*τὰ σαρκικά*) of the church in Jerusalem.[230]

2) In addition, the collection had a spiritual purpose, and for Paul this constituted an overriding concern: "but it is also abounding through many thanksgivings to God" (*ἀλλὰ καὶ περισσεύουσα διὰ πολλῶν εὐχαριστιῶν τῷ θεῷ*).[231] Whether the singular *εὐχαριστίαν* (P^{46} [d g r] Cyp Ambst) or the plural *εὐχαριστιῶν* represents the original reading is unclear.[232] In any event, the passage is an example of the peculiarly positive attitude which Paul had toward crowds in worship.

Paul's rather idiosyncratic ideas on thanksgiving were first expressed in 1 Thess 3:9, where he asked rhetorically: "For what adequate thanks can we return to God . . . ?" (*τίνα γὰρ εὐχαριστίαν δυνάμεθα τῷ θεῷ ἀνταποδοῦναι . . .*). All thanksgiving in Paul's terms is a response, a sacrificial gift due to God in return for beneficence received.[233] That is to say, thanksgiving is closely related to ancient votive offerings.[234]

Martin Dibelius has drawn attention to another unusual idea, which his student, George H. Boobyer, elaborated in his doctoral dissertation.[235] "Thanksgivings are the return of grace received from God to God; the more Christians [i.e., the more deeds of grace], the more thanksgivings, the more *δόξα θεοῦ* (II Cor 4:15)."[236] The doctrine is more fully stated in 2 Cor 4:13–15, where it is connected with the expression "the

Inventory of Compulsory Services in Ptolemaic and Roman Egypt (American Studies in Papyrology 3; New Haven and Toronto: American Society of Papyrologists, 1968). See also Johann Oehler, "Leiturgie," *PRE* 12 (1925) 1871–79; Moulton and Milligan, *s.v.*; Kuenzi, ΕΠΙΔΟΣΙΣ, *passim;* Andreas M. Andreades, *A History of Greek Public Finance* (rev. C. N. Brown; Cambridge: Harvard University, 1933) 1.130–33, 291ff; 349ff; Hands, *Charities,* 155; Spicq, *Notes de lexicographie* 1.475–81 (with additional biblio.).

227 See on this point especially Windisch, pp. 281–82, who emphasizes the role of the collection in establishing a social relationship between what is called ἐκκλησίαι. Does it matter that this originally secular and political term was used to describe the social entities created by the Christians? See on this point Wolfgang Schrage, "Ekklesia und Synagoge," *ZThK* 60 (1963) 178–202; Klaus Berger, "Volksversammlung und Gemeinde Gottes: Zu den Anfängen der christlichen Verwendung von 'ekklesia'," *ZThK* 73 (1976) 167–207; Jürgen Roloff, "ἐκκλησία," *EWNT* 1 (1980) 998–1011.

228 For the periphrastic construction see Moule, *Idiom Book,* 17.

229 On this term see also 2 Cor 11:9; Phil 4:10–20, and Bauer, *s.v.* προσαναπληρόω. See furthermore above on 2 Cor 8:14a.

230 οἱ ἅγιοι ("the saints") is here the name for the Christians in Jerusalem. See above on 2 Cor 8:4.

231 Plummer's translation, p. 265.

232 See Metzger, *Textual Commentary,* 582–83, where the author finds arguments against the singular as a case of scribal assimilation to the construction of v 11.

233 For the same concept see the great thanksgiving prayer 1 Chron 29:10ff, esp. v 14 (*RSV*): "But who am I, and what is my people, that we should be able thus to offer willingly? For all things come from thee, and of thy own have we given thee." That Greek ideas are not different at this point is shown by Philo *De vita Mosis* 2.239; *Quod Deus sit immutabilis* 7; *Plant.* 126; Epictetus *Diss.* 1.16.15–21.

234 See also Aelius Aristides *Panathenaic Oration* 189ff. For the various categories of votive gifts and current bibliography see F. T. van Straaten, "Gaven voor de goden," *Lampas* 12 (1979) 50–94; idem, "Gifts for the Gods," in Versnel, *Faith, Hope and Worship,* 65–151. See also above, n. 78.

235 George H. Boobyer, *"Thanksgiving" and the Glory of God in Paul* (Dissertation, Heidelberg; Borna-Leipzig: Noske, 1929). See also Gerhard Delling, *Worship in the New Testament* (Philadelphia: Westminster, 1962) 51–52, 123–24.

236 Martin Dibelius, *An die Thessalonicher I/II, an die*

spirit of faith" (τὸ πνεῦμα τῆς πίστεως). The upshot is the conclusion of v 15:

> in order that the grace which is bestowed on us, being augmented by the increasing number of those who believe with us and pray for us, may cause a greater volume of thanksgiving to rise both from us and from them to the glory of God.[237]

ἵνα ἡ χάρις πλεονάσασα διὰ τῶν πλειόνων τὴν εὐχαριστίαν περισσεύσῃ εἰς τὴν δόξαν τοῦ θεοῦ.

No less peculiar is the statement in the letter of reconciliation, 2 Cor 1:11, where Paul referred to the effect of the Corinthians' supplication on his behalf:

> . . . while you also join in helping on our behalf by your intercessions for us. And the blessed result of this will be that from many uplifted faces thanksgivings on our behalf will be offered by many for the mercy which has been shown to us.[238]

συνυπουργούντων καὶ ὑμῶν τῇ δεήσει, ἵνα ἐκ πολλῶν προσώπων τὸ εἰς ἡμᾶς χάρισμα διὰ πολλῶν εὐχαριστηθῇ ὑπὲρ ἡμῶν.

Giving thanks to God, therefore, is not merely a demonstration of recognition due him, but more important, it is a manifestation of God's power. "The prayer of praise and thanks of a continually-growing Church of Christ is the real purpose of all apostolic activity."[239] The more thanksgiving occurs, the more grace has been bestowed and received, the greater is the testimony, and the greater the power of God. Paul's goal, therefore, was to increase the number of worshipers, for thereby the manifestation of God's power would increase. Since the collection for the saints in Jerusalem served this spiritual purpose, the apostle recommended it with such incessant fervor.

As Windisch[240] reminded us, this argument is based on a rather primitive concept of God. Paul's view of prayer and worship may indeed be archaic, but it is deeply rooted in the Old Testament psalms,[241] and seems to have been popular in Judaism of the Hellenistic period.[242]

As a rule, early Christian tradition was critical toward this concept of worship. In the introduction to the Lord's Prayer in Matt 6:7–8, such ideas are even called pagan, a judgment shared by Luke when he depicted large pagan crowds and the ineffectual character of their religious "power."[243] It is all the more remarkable, then, that Paul's judgment on this "speculative 'thanksgiving' theory"[244] was positive. Does this understanding lie behind the statement which occurs so frequently in his

Philipper (HNT 11; Tübingen: Mohr, Siebeck, [3]1937) 18: "Dankgebete sind eine Wiedergabe der von Gott kommenden Gnade an Gott; je mehr Christen (d.h. je mehr Begnadigungen), desto mehr Dankgebete, desto mehr δόξα θεοῦ (II Cor 4[15])." So also Martin Dibelius and Hans Conzelmann, *The Pastoral Epistles* (Hermeneia; Philadelphia: Fortress, 1972) 35–36; Conzelmann, "εὐχαριστέω κτλ.," 412–13 (b).

237 The paraphrase of this untranslatable sentence is Plummer's, p. 123; see also his discussion of other translations, pp. 134–35.

238 Plummer's paraphrase, p. 6; see also his commentary, pp. 20ff; Windisch, pp. 48ff.

239 Delling, *Worship,* 124.

240 Windisch, p. 50, referring to Friedrich Heiler, *Das Gebet* (3d ed.; Munich: Ernst Reinhardt) 179–80. See also J. H. Quincey, "Greek Expressions of Thanks," *JHS* 86 (1966) 133–58; H. S. Versnel, "Van oderen . . . : Antiek gebed in kelderlicht," *Lampas* 12 (1979) 7–49, esp. 31ff; idem, "Religious Mentality in Ancient Prayer," in Versnel, *Faith, Hope and Worship,* 1–64, esp 42ff.

241 The magic power of the name of Yahweh is one of the fundamental concepts of Israelite worship. See esp. Pss 22:27–28; 24:1; 33:8; 49:1; 89:1ff; 96:1; etc. See Otto Eissfeldt, "Jahwe-Name and Zauberwesen," *Kleine Schriften* (6 vols.; Tübingen: Mohr, Siebeck, 1962–79) 1.150–71.

242 See especially the great hymn of praise Dan 3:52–90 LXX. Further passages are to be found in Conzelmann, "εὐχαριστέω κτλ.," 410–11 (c). Philo is important for Hellenistic Jewish ideas; see esp. *De ebr.* 105–7; *Her.* 199–200, 226; *Leg. Gai.* 284. On the whole doctrine and for further literature see Jean Laporte, *La doctrine eucharistique chez Philon d'Alexandrie* (Théologie historique 16; Paris: Beauchesne, 1972).

243 A paradigm of this idea is the Demetrius episode in Acts 19:23–40.

244 Cf. also Paul Schubert, *Form and Function of the Pauline Thanksgiving* (BZNW 20; Berlin: Töpelmann, 1939) 92, who, however, seems to reject Dibelius's interpretation. Günther Harder, *Paulus und das Gebet*

letters, "I give thanks *always*"?[245] Conversely, the failure to give thanks to God, as he pointed out in Rom 1:18ff, results in religious and moral corruption.[246] This critique draws heavily on ideas at home in Hellenistic philosophy. It suggests that the view Paul expressed here may have connections with Hellenistic philosophy, specifically with Euhemerist theories on the origin of religious power.[247]

■ 9:13–14: The Fifth Proof

The question which remains at the end of v 12 concerns how the increase of thanksgiving will take place. The answer is signaled by the transition from singular "thanksgiving" (εὐχαριστία) to the plural "thanksgivings" (εὐχαριστίαι),[248] that is, thanksgiving prayers, in v 12. A more explicit answer is then provided in vv 13–14 by presenting to the readers a preview of the situation which would ensue when the collection was delivered to the Jerusalem church. The participles in vv 13–14 are therefore to be taken as descriptive rather than imperative in force.[249] The language used in these statements is drawn from the areas of worship and law. Mention of "the evidence of this charitable gift" (δοκιμῆς τῆς διακονίας) in v 13 assured the Achaians that when the collection was turned over to the Jerusalem church, it would constitute undeniable evidence (δοκιμή)[250] of God's grace. When they had received the gift, the Jerusalem Christians would respond in the way of all religious people on such occasions; they would offer prayers of thanksgiving (εὐχαριστίαι) to God. This could take place in private or in the public worship services of the church.

In light of the fact that our knowledge of what actually went on in the worship services of early Christian churches is extremely limited, Paul's description of what he thought would occur in Jerusalem gains added significance for the history of early Christian worship. In any event, Paul's statements are among the oldest on this form of early Christian prayer.

As the apostle saw it, the prayer of thanksgiving has two parts: praise offered to God (v 13: δοξάζειν τὸν θεόν), and intercession (v 14: δέησις ὑπὲρ ὑμῶν) on behalf of others. Extant liturgical material reflecting Jewish and early Christian prayers warrants the conclusion that Paul's statements are historically reliable: most known thanksgiving prayers consist of these two parts at least.

Although it could take different forms, the old Jewish *berakhah* seems to have consisted of the three parts: praise, thanksgiving, and petition.[251] This order is found in the prayer commonly used at table after meals, the *birkat ha-mazon.*[252] Its oldest form, as reconstructed by Louis Finkelstein, consists of three *berakhot:* an expression of praise that God feeds the whole world with goodness, grace, and mercy; a thanksgiving for the land,

(Gütersloh: Bertelsmann, 1936) 132 n. 1; 138–51, and Delling, *Worship,* 124 n. 4, also argue against Dibelius.

245 See the adverbs πάντοτε ("always") and ἀδιαλείπτως ("incessantly") in Paul's epistolary thanksgivings (1 Thess 1:2; 2:13; 3:10; 1 Cor 1:4; Phil 1:4; Phlm 4; Rom 1:10; etc). See the exhibit in Schubert, *Thanksgiving,* 54–55. On the whole concept see Rudbert Kerkhoff, *Das unablässige Gebet: Beiträge zur Lehre vom immerwährenden Beten im Neuen Testament* (Munich: Zink, 1954).

246 Failure to give thanks to the deity was condemned by all antiquity, especially in the Jewish and Christian tradition. See Ps 78:1; Isa 43:1; Hos 11:1; Wis 14:26; 16:29; Philo *Op.* 169; *Sacr.* 58; *Her.* 226, 302; *Mos.* 1.58; *Virt.* 165; *Leg. Gai.* 60, 118; *Deus* 48, 74; *Jos.* 99; *Spec. leg.* 1.284. In the NT see esp. Luke 6:35; 17:11–19 (see on this Betz, "Cleansing"); 2 Tim 3:2, and for further passages Bauer, *s.v.* ἀχάριστος. The tradition continues in the Apologists (see Justin *Apol.* 1.13.1–4; *Dial.* 117–18). See also Schubert, *Thanksgiving,* 106ff; Danker, *Benefactor,* 440–42.

247 See on this point Betz, *Galatians,* 214–15.

248 For the textual problem see above, n. 232.

249 On the imperatival force cf. Moule, *Idiom Book,* 30–31, 179; Turner, *Grammatical Insights,* 166.

250 On this difficult term see 2 Cor 8:2; 13:3; 2:9; also Betz, *Paulus,* 132–37. The verb δοκιμάζειν occurs in 2 Cor 8:8, 22; Gal 6:4. See Betz, *Galatians,* 302.

251 On the history of the thanksgiving prayer see Adolf Wendel, *Das freie Laiengebet im vorexilischen Israel* (Ex Oriente Lux 5/6; Leipzig: Pfeiffer, 1931) 170ff, 195ff; Arthur Spanier, "Zur Formengeschichte des altjüdischen Gebetes," *MGWJ* 77 (1934) 438–47; C. W. Dugmore, "Jewish and Christian Benedictions," *Paganisme, Judäisme, Christianisme: Influences et affrontements dans la monde antique. Mélanges offerts à Marcel Simon,* ed. A. Benoit et al. (Paris: Boccard, 1978) 145–52; Cesare Giraudo, *La struttura letteraria della preghiera eucaristica. Saggio sulla genesi letteraria di una forma: Toda veterotestamentaria, b'raka giudaica, anafora cristiana* (AnBib 92; Rome: Biblical Institute, 1981); H. A. J. Wegman, "Une anaphore incomplète? Les fragments sur Papyrus Strasbourg Gr. 254,"

the Torah, life, and food; and an intercession for the people of Israel and the city of Jerusalem:[253]

> 1)
> Blessed art Thou, O Lord, our God, King of the Universe, Who feedest the whole world with goodness, with grace, and with mercy. Blessed art Thou who feedest all.
> 2)
> We thank Thee, O Lord, our God, that Thou hast caused us to inherit a goodly and pleasant land, the covenant, the Torah, life, and food. For all these things we thank Thee and praise Thy name forever and ever. Blessed art Thou, O Lord, for the land and for the food.
> 3)
> Have mercy, O Lord, our God, on Thy people Israel, and on Thy city Jerusalem, and on Thy Temple and Thy dwelling-place and on Zion Thy resting-place, and on the great and holy sanctuary over which Thy name was called, and the Kingdom of the dynasty of David mayest Thou return to its place in our days, and build Jerusalem soon. Blessed art Thou, O Lord, who buildest Jerusalem.[254]

The Eighteen Benedictions (*Shemone esre*) also have three parts, but they follow a different order. They begin with praise (1–3), continue with petitions (4–15), and conclude with thanksgiving (16–18).[255]

The early Christian thanksgiving prayer in *Did.* 10 is very similar to the Jewish prayers but differs in that it first has a thanksgiving in two parts, then an intercession for the church, each part concluding with a doxology.[256] The prayer in *Did.* 10 cannot be discussed fully here, but at least it should be pointed out that it is a mixture of older Jewish and younger Christian elements. The doctrines underlying the prayer appear to go back to the early church; one indication of this is that they closely resemble Paul's ideas in 2 Cor 9:13–14. Here, too, we encounter a rather unusual notion of thanksgiving (*Did.* 10.3–4):

> You, Lord Almighty, have created the universe for the sake of your name, and you have given food and drink to the people for their enjoyment, so that they may give thanks to you, but to us you have granted spiritual food and drink and life eternal through your servant. Above all we give thanks to you because you are powerful. To you be the glory into eternity.[257]

> *σύ, δέσποτα παντοκράτορ, ἔκτισας τὰ πάντα ἕνεκεν τοῦ ὀνόματός σου, τροφήν τε καὶ ποτὸν ἔδωκας τοῖς ἀνθρώποις εἰς ἀπόλαυσιν, ἵνα σοὶ εὐχαριστήσωσιν, ἡμῖν δὲ ἐχαρίσω πνευματικὴν τροφὴν καὶ ποτὸν καὶ ζωὴν αἰώνιον διὰ τοῦ παιδός σου. πρὸ πάντων εὐχαριστοῦμέν σοι, ὅτι δυνατὸς εἶ· σοὶ ἡ δόξα εἰς τοὺς αἰῶνας.*

Though the relationship of the prayers which Paul included in his epistles to those employed in early Christian worship is far from clear, the occurrence of the sequence—thanksgiving, intercession, doxology—in Pauline and Deutero-Pauline letters is evidence of their

Studies in Gnosticism and Hellenistic Religions, presented to Gilles Quispel on the Occasion of his 65th Birthday (ed. R. van den Broek and M. J. Vermaseren; EPRO 91; Leiden: Brill, 1981) 432–50.

252 See the basic article by Louis Finkelstein, "The Birkat Ha-Mazon," *JQR* NS 19 (1928–29) 211–62; furthermore Joseph Heinemann, *Prayer in the Talmud: Forms and Patterns* (StJud 9; Berlin: de Gruyter, 1977) 194–96.

253 Finkelstein, "The Birkat Ha-Mazon," 218ff, refers also to the thanksgiving prayers in Jub 22:6–9; Sir 36:17–19. Cf. also Willem C. van Unnik, "Eine merkwürdige liturgische Aussage bei Josephus," *Josephus-Studien, FS O. Michel*, ed. Otto Betz, Klaus Haacker, and Martin Hengel (Göttingen: Vandenhoeck & Ruprecht, 1974) 362–69, who calls attention to Josephus *Ant.* 8.111–17.

254 Cited according to Finkelstein, "The Birkat Ha-Mazon," 215–16.

255 On this prayer see Kaufmann Kohler, "The Origin and Composition of the Eighteen Benedictions. With a Translation of Corresponding Essene Prayers in the Apostolic Constitutions," *HUCA* 1 (1924) 387–425; Ismar Elbogen, *Der jüdische Gottesdienst in seiner geschichtlichen Entwicklung* (Hildesheim: Olms, 1962) 27ff, 582–83; Elias Bickerman, "The Civic Prayer for Jerusalem," *Studies in Jewish and Christian History* (2 vols.; Leiden: Brill, 1976–80) 2.290–312.

256 See also Martin Dibelius, "Die Mahlgebete der Didache," *Botschaft und Geschichte* (2 vols.; Tübingen: Mohr, Siebeck, 1956) 2.117–27.

257 My translation.

liturgical background (cf. Rom 1:8–10; Phil 4:18–20; Col 1:3–11; Eph 1:3–14; 3:14–21; 2 Thess 1:3–12). A similar pattern can be found in early Christian liturgies which have taken over and modified Jewish prayers. On the basis of this material, one must conclude that the phrase "they praise God" (*δοξάζοντες τὸν θεόν*)[258] does not refer to doxologies in the formal sense of the term,[259] but to the opening words of a thanksgiving prayer.

Such a prayer of praise is found in the thanksgiving prayer of the so-called Clementine Liturgy in the Eighth Book of the *Apostolic Constitutions.*[260] The prayer is addressed to God in praise as the one who is truly God, and the provider of all good things. The similarity between the epithet "the provider of every good" (*ὁ παντὸς ἀγαθοῦ χορηγός*) in this praise, and that found in 2 Cor 9:10, can hardly be incidental.[261] An intercessory prayer follows, beginning with a petition on behalf of the worldwide church.[262] This petition is in keeping with Paul's assumption in v 14 that the Jerusalem church will pray for the Achaians.

The same two sections are also found in thanksgiving prayers from the liturgies of St. James[263] and St. Mark,[264] in a liturgy from Palestine (St. Cyril, fourth century)[265] and from Antioch (St. Chrysostom, fourth century).[266] The constancy of this pattern of praise and intercession in liturgies which are otherwise quite different, and its continuity with prayers used in contemporary Judaism, allow us to conclude that the pattern may have already existed in the time of Paul. If this was the case, then the apostle had every right to assume that it existed in Jerusalem as well. Thus Paul expected that the thanksgiving prayer used by the church in Jerusalem would first praise God for his beneficence in general terms. The very existence of the donation provides concrete evidence of divine benevolence in this particular instance.

But the collection was also evidence of something else. Paul did not hesitate to predict that the church in Jerusalem would regard the donation as a sign of the submission of the Achaians. When they gave thanks to God, it would be for their submission. Paul was extremely brief, but to the point: "for the submission" (*ἐπὶ τῇ ὑποταγῇ*) specifies the reason for the Jerusalem Christians' praise to God. The key terms which Paul employed are, in the first place, legal administrative, and have only been Christianized secondarily. In fact, the terms belong to the language of politics.[267] In administrative and legal terms, the expression *ἡ ὑποταγὴ τῆς ὁμολογίας ὑμῶν* means that the donors have entered into a contractual agreement (*ὁμολογία*)[268] by means of their donation, the substance of which is their submission (*ὑποταγή*) to Jerusalem. Against W. Bauer,[269] whose opinion is shared by many commentators, the term

258 For this term see also Gal 1:24; 1 Cor 6:20; Rom 1:21; 15:6; Matt 5:16; 9:8; Mark 2:12; Luke 17:15; etc.

259 See Gal 1:5 and Betz, *Galatians,* 43. The question of what is and what is not a doxology is to a certain extent a matter of definition. See Eric Werner, "The Doxology in Synagogue and Church, A Liturgico-Musical Study," *HUCA* 19 (1945–46) 275–351, also in his *The Sacred Bridge* (London: Dobson, 1959) 273–312; Heinemann, *Prayer,* 77ff, 135ff, 285.

260 The following quotations from the liturgical sources are from F. E. Brightman, *Liturgies Eastern and Western,* vol. 1: *Eastern Liturgies* (Oxford: Clarendon, 1896). For surveys see also Anton Baumstark, "Anaphora," *RAC* 1 (1950) 418–37; Otto Michel and Theodor Klauser, "Gebet II (Fürbitte)," *RAC* 9 (1976) 1–36.

261 Brightman, p. 14, lines 25–31: *῎Αξιον ὡς ἀληθῶς καὶ δίκαιον πρὸ πάντων ἀνυμνεῖν σε τὸν ὄντως ὄντα θεόν, τὸν πρὸ τῶν γενητῶν ὄντα, ἐξ οὗ πᾶσα πατριὰ ἐν οὐρανοῖς καὶ ἐπὶ γῆς ὀνομάζεται, τὸν μόνον ἀγέννητον καὶ ἄναρχον καὶ ἀβασίλευτον καὶ ἀδέσποτον, τὸν ἀνευδεῆ, τὸν παντὸς ἀγαθὸν χορηγόν, τὸν πάσης αἰτίας καὶ γενέσεως κρείττονα, τὸν πάντοτε κατὰ τὰ αὐτὰ καὶ ὡσαύτως ἔχοντα, ἐξ οὗ τὰ πάντα καθάπερ ἔκ τινος ἀφετηρίας εἰς τὸ εἶναι παρῆλθεν.*

262 Ibid., p. 21, lines 15–19: *῎Ετι δεόμεθά σου Κύριε καὶ ὑπὲρ τῆς ἁγίας σου ἐκκλησίας τῆς ἀπὸ περάτων ἕως περάτων ἣν περιεποιήσω τῷ τιμίῳ αἵματι τοῦ Χριστοῦ ὅπως αὐτὴν διαφυλάξῃς ἄσειστον καὶ ἀκλυδώνιστον ἄχρι τῆς συντελείας τοῦ αἰῶνος, καὶ ὑπὲρ πάσης ἐπισκοπῆς τῆς ὀρθοτομούσης τὸν λόγον τῆς ἀληθείας.*

263 Ibid., pp. 50, lines 12ff (thanksgiving); 54, lines 24ff (intercession).

264 Ibid., pp. 125, lines 21ff (thanksgiving); 126, lines 11ff (intercession).

265 Ibid., pp. 465, line 13 (thanksgiving); 466, lines 4ff (intercession).

266 Ibid., pp. 474, lines 4ff (thanksgiving); 474, lines 26ff (intercession).

267 Apparently the connection between religion and politics is part of the complex of ideas connected with the gifts of the deity. Another instance of this connection is Aelius Aristides *Panathenaic Oration* 21,

ὁμολογία does not mean in this instance what it means elsewhere in the New Testament:[270] it does not mean "confession" as a ritual act, but is to be understood in its legal sense as a public act involving a document which codifies the transaction. In legal terms, of course, the collection for Jerusalem was a *donatio* ("donation"),[271] so that ὁμολογία is the name of the legal process by which such a donation is made.[272] In Hellenistic law, a donation of this kind would have been accompanied by a document which could also be called by the name ὁμολογία. Thus it is likely that Paul referred to this document as well. Once this is assumed, other details fall into place.[273] One of the purposes of such a document was to state the signers' intent to establish personal relations.[274] There were even donations for the sole purpose of establishing a community, for instance a community for worship.[275] Thus the donation was then only a part of the commitment made by the partners to one another.[276] If this interpretation is applied to 2 Cor 9:13–14, the donation by the Achaians would signify their obligatory submission (ὑποταγή)[277] to the Jerusalem church. On this basis, the difficult genitive construction can also be explained. Is τῆς ὁμολογίας a *genitivus subiectivus* or *obiectivus*? Has the contract been subjected or is it an expression of subjection? Only the latter option makes sense in legal terms: Jerusalem would regard the donation as the evidence of the Achaians' submission.

If Paul had a specific document in mind, we must ask whether the somewhat stilted phrase "the submission expressed by the contractual agreement to the gospel of Christ" (ἡ ὑποταγὴ τῆς ὁμολογίας εἰς τὸ εὐαγγέλιον τοῦ Χριστοῦ) is part of the wording of such a document. Did Paul know the actual stipulations of a document accompanying the donation? Are these stipulations reflected in Paul's brief statement? Several reasons may be adduced in support of such a supposition:

1) The legal and political terminology employed is just

where the city of Athens is called a "seed of gratitude toward the gods" (σπέρμα τῆς χάριτος τῆς πρὸς τοὺς θεούς). Included in this gratitude are the city's reception of exiles, the establishment of colonies, its military history, and its cultural achievements.

268 The correct interpretation is found in Erasmus *In Novum Testamentum Annotationes* (Basel: Frobenius, 1542 [first ed. 1519] 578: "non solum confessionem significat, verum etiam consensum."

269 Bauer, *s.v.* ὁμολογία, 1, who assigns the meaning "*confessing* as an action" and applies it to 2 Cor 9:13: "*the subjection of your confession to the gospel* [= your confessing the gospel finds expression in obedient subjection to its requirements]." Similarly Otto Michel, "ὁμολογέω κτλ.," *TDNT* 5 (1967) 215–16.

270 See 1 Tim 6:12, 13; Heb 3:1; 4:14; 10:23. See Bauer, *s.v.* 2. The verb ὁμολογέω occurs more often in the legal sense; see Bauer, *s.v.* 3.a.

271 See on this legal concept Rudolf Leonhard, "Donatio," *PRE* 10. Halbband (1905) 1533–40; Erich Ziebarth, "Δόσις," *PRE* 10. Halbband (1905) 1598–1603; idem, "Stiftungen," *PRE.S* 7 (1940) 1236–40.

272 See for instance the *protocol* and *homologia* in *Pap. Grenf.* 2,71 (in Mitteis and Wilcken, *Grundzüge und Chrestomathie,* 2/2, no. 190 [A.D. 244–48]; *Pap. Grenf.* 2,70 (Mitteis and Wilcken, *Grundzüge und Chrestomathie,* 2/2, no. 191 [A.D. 270]; *Papiri della società italiana* 12, no. 1256 (3d century A.D.). On the concept see the study by Heiko Freiherr von Soden, *Untersuchungen zur Homologie in den griechischen Papyri Ägyptens bis Diokletian* (Graezistische Abhandlungen 5; Cologne and Vienna: Böhlau, 1973) esp. 25–26.

273 The term εὐδοκέω ("give approval") in Rom 15:27 seems to occur there as well with its legal meaning. See Otto Gradenwitz, *Einführung in die Papyruskunde,* 1 Heft: *Erklärung ausgewählter Urkunden,* nebst einem Konträr-Index und einer Tafel in Lichtdruck (Leipzig: Hirzel, 1900) 62–63, 71, 160–62; von Soden, *Untersuchungen,* 110–11; Moulton and Milligan, *s.v.*

274 See on this point the study by Anneliese Mannzmann, *Griechische Stiftungsurkunden: Studie zu Inhalt und Rechtsform* (Münster: Aschendorff, 1962) 24–25.

275 See ibid., 136ff.

276 See Mannzmann's description of ὁμολογία, *Stiftungsurkunden,* 81: ". . . das Wesen der Homologie besteht eben darin, dass einseitig Rechtsfolgen festgelegt werden, die jeweils für die *festsetzende* Partei verbindlich sind. Die Parteien können nicht gemeinsam homologieren, jeder muss sich selber binden. Erst durch Addition zweier Selbstbindungen kommt ein Erfolg zustande, der dem 'Con-sens' entspricht. . . . Es müssen Erklärungen in bestimmten Formen abgegeben werden, die mit sich selber identisch bleiben, weil der Erklärende—ursprünglich durch den Eid—unauflöslich an seine Erklärung gebunden ist."

277 So correctly Ferdinand Christian Baur in his article, "Beiträge zur Erklärung der Korinthierbriefe," 180–81. The term ὑποταγή is certainly political in origin. See LSJ, *s.v.;* Dittenberger, *Sylloge* 4, *s.v.; OGIS, s.v.* ὑποτάττω; Moulton and Milligan, *s.v.* ὑποταγή, ὑποτάσσω; Preisigke, *Wörterbuch* 2, *s.v.;* Bauer, *s.v.*

as unique in Paul[278] as it is common in Hellenistic documents.

2) Paul's words explain why the donation should be regarded as useful to the recipients. This is in keeping with what one would expect of a document attached to the donation: it would provide a formal statement of why the donation should be welcomed by the recipients.

3) The situation which Paul described flatly contradicts his lifelong opposition to submission to the Jerusalem authorities. His attitude in the letter to the Galatians, with its description of the Jerusalem conference (Gal 2:4–5),[279] is unmistakable in this regard. Why should the apostle give his approval to a situation in 2 Cor 9:13–14 to which he was so utterly opposed?[280] In fact, his words "to [for the purpose of] the gospel of Christ" (*εἰς τὸ εὐαγγέλιον τοῦ Χριστοῦ*)[281] are, like all good diplomatic language, ambiguous. The Jerusalem Christians would presumably take the words to refer to themselves, and thus conclude that the Achaians have submitted to them.[282] Others, Paul included, would take the words to refer to the gospel of Christ, which transcended both Jerusalem and Achaia. Submission to that gospel did not mean submission to Jerusalem, but the submission of all Christians to the gospel of Christ. This interpretation of Paul's phrase would not be unlike that of the formula of collaboration agreed upon at the Jerusalem conference many years before.[283] Even at present Paul would have had no problems with this notion of submission. As long as the terms were sufficiently ambiguous, Paul could speak of Jerusalem with reverence; in Rom 15:27, he spoke of debts owed to Jerusalem.[284] But none of these gestures implies that he compromised his theology. Furthermore, in the situation which Paul described, the submission of the Achaians would not be the only reason for the church in Jerusalem to give thanks. They would also give thanks for "partnership" (*κοινωνία*).[285] The following is to be interpreted in the same way as the preceding construction: "and [for] the generosity of the partnership benefiting them and all" (*καὶ ἁπλότητι τῆς κοινωνίας εἰς αὐτοὺς καὶ εἰς πάντας*). In legal terms, the financial donation of the kind the Achaians were going to make would establish a partnership between the communities involved.[286] The term generous giving (*ἁπλότης*) plays an important part in both 2 Cor 8 and 9, so it is not a surprise to find it here as well.[287] Taken together, submission and generosity

ὑποταγή, ὑποτάσσω; Gerhard Delling, "*ὑποτάσσω, ὑποταγή*," *TDNT* 8 (1972) 39–47; Spicq, *Notes de lexicographie* 2.913–16.

278 The metaphorical usage of subjection to God, Christ, or within the family hierarchy, which is often found in early Christian literature is a special application of the political meaning, but religious and political meanings should be kept separate.

279 See on this point Betz, *Galatians*, 91.

280 One should not minimize the contradictions between Paul's resistance to subjection elsewhere and his apparent willingness to subject here. Cf. Gerhard Delling, "*ὑποταγή*," *TDNT* 8 (1972) 47, who harmonizes Paul's statements when he says that Paul had to overcome a certain inner resistance but did so because of the unity of Christendom.

281 The preposition *εἰς* can also be interpreted in the legal sense ("for the purpose of"). See, e.g., Mannzmann, *Stiftungsurkunden*, 41, lines 40–44: . . . *περὶ τοῦ ἀργυρίου, οὗ ἔδωκαν τᾶι πόλει καὶ τῶι Διονύσωι εἰς τὰν τῶν τεχνιτᾶν μίσθωσιν* . . . ("... regarding the money which they have given to the city and to Dionysos for the purpose of hiring *technitae* . . .").

282 If this strategy was indeed that of the Jerusalem church it is confirmed by Acts, in which the various mission fields are all brought under the control of Jerusalem. See esp. Acts 1:8 (programmatically); 8:4ff, 14ff; 9:32ff. On the view of history expressed in Acts see Haenchen, *Acts*, 98ff.

283 See Gal 2:8–9; and Betz, *Galatians*, 97–101.

284 Paul's remark in Rom 15:27 has an interesting parallel in the *exordium* of Aelius Aristides' *Panathenaic Oration*, LCL edition of *Aristides* 1.7: "The Greeks, and, I think, most of the barbarians, have an old custom, to pay back, as far as they can, every debt of gratitude [*χάρις*] to their foster-fathers. But, it seems to me at least, it is not easy to find persons whom anyone, who could somehow be apparently classified as a Greek, would regard as foster-fathers before you, O men of Athens. . . ." The initial statement is then elaborated in §§ 1–7 of the speech. See also Plutarch *Glor. Athen.* 2.

285 See for this concept above on 2 Cor 8:4 (p.46). For passages from documents see von Soden, *Untersuchungen*, 25 (see above, n. 272).

286 See also Gal 2:9; 6:6; Rom 12:13; 15:26–27; Phil 1:5.

287 See on 2 Cor 8:2; 9:11 (above, pp. 44–45, 115–17).

constitute the attitude expected of Gentiles friendly to Judaism and Christianity. Examples of such an attitude abound in the prototypical figures of the Gospels and Acts.[288] Thus the entire phrase states that the generosity evidenced by the donation was to be regarded as the fruit of the partnership which the two communities enjoyed. Again, the language is reminiscent of legal documents, as is the concluding phrase: "benefiting them and all" (εἰς αὐτοὺς καὶ εἰς πάντας).[289]

For all the reasons given above, we may conclude that Paul's language reflects the language of a document which would have to be called a *homologia*. Was such a document already in existence when he wrote 2 Cor 9? Did he quote from it here? Or did he merely envision what such a document would say? Unfortunately, the lack of evidence does not allow us to do more than raise the question.

In v 14, Paul turned to the second element[290] of the thanksgiving prayer, the intercession:[291] "petition on your behalf" (δέησις ὑπὲρ ὑμῶν).[292] Again, the sentence structure presents difficulties. Paul used a participle instead of a finite verb; and instead of the nominative in v 13, he chose the genitive. Plummer was probably right in treating the construction as a genitive absolute, translating: "Also in their prayer for you they long for you . . ." (καὶ αὐτῶν δεήσει ὑπὲρ ὑμῶν ἐπιποθούντων ὑμᾶς).[293] But how is the motif of longing (ἐπιποθεῖν, ἐπιπόθησις) related to the prayer of intercession, and how are both related to the epistolary motif which scholars call the πόθος-motif?[294] By such a motif, the writer expressed his longing for the addressee. But the expression can also be part of a prayer which Paul included in the epistle.[295] 2 Cor 9:14 employed the motif differently: Paul did not speak of his own longing, but of the intercessory prayer of the church in Jerusalem as the expression of their longing for the Achaian Christians. Thus v 14 represents Paul's interpretation of a prayer that would be offered in Jerusalem.[296]

288 See the prototypical figures in the NT: the centurion in Matt 8:5–13 par.; the royal official in John 4:46–54; and above all the centurion Cornelius in Acts 10:1ff. As Gerhard Delling has shown in his article "Alexander der Grosse als Bekenner des jüdischen Gottesglaubens," *JSJ* 12 (1981) 1–51, even the great Macedonian was cast in Jewish literature as a prototype of the proselyte who was submissive to the one God and generous in his support of the Jewish religion. On the "Profile of the Benefactors" see Danker, *Benefactor,* 317–92. One should not interpret the collection for Jerusalem merely in terms of Jewish proselytism as Klaus Berger does in his article "Almosen für Israel. Zum historischen Kontext der paulinischen Kollekte," *NTS* 23 (1977) 180–204. At least Paul did not think in those terms, because he never says that the gift was collected "for Israel," but for the Christian congregation of Jerusalem, or that the donation had propitiatory purposes (cf. ibid., 182). For further discussion see the appendix "Gentile Participation in Worship at Jerusalem," in Emil Schürer, *The History of the Jewish People in the Age of Jesus Christ (175 B.C.—A.D. 135)* [rev. Geza Vermes, Fergus Millar, and Matthew Black; 2 vols.; Edinburgh: Clark, 1979] 2.309–13.

289 See Gal 6:10 and Betz, *Galatians,* 311; also Danker, *Benefactor,* 336–39.

290 καί seems to refer to the second element in comparison with the praise in v 13. Differently Windisch, p. 285, who places it alongside Rom 1:11 ("like myself").

291 On Paul's prayer of intercession see the study by Gordon P. Wiles, *Paul's Intercessory Prayers* (SNTSMS 24; Cambridge: Cambridge University, 1974) esp. 248–53.

292 On this term see also 2 Cor 1:11; Phil 1:4, 19; 4:6; Rom 10:1; and Bauer, *s.v.* δέησις; Wiles, *Paul's Intercessory Prayers,* 19–20.

293 Plummer, p. 267; also Windisch, p. 285; differently Bachmann, pp. 334–35, who takes καὶ αὐτῶν δεήσει to belong together with δοξάζοντες or even περισσεύουσα (v 12) and regards ἐπιποθούντων to be in apposition to αὐτῶν. Cf. Plummer's translation, p. 267: "While they themselves also, with supplication on your behalf, long after you."

294 For this epistolary motif see 2 Cor 7:7, 11; Phil 1:8; 2:26; 4:1; 1 Thess 3:6; Rom 15:23. For discussion see the studies by Gustav Karlsson, *Idéologie et cérémonial dans l'épistolographie byzantine* (Uppsala: Almqvist & Wiksell, ²1962) 57ff; Klaus Thraede, *Grundzüge griechisch-römischer Brieftopik* (Zetemata 48: Munich: Beck, 1970) 162ff; idem, "Flügel (Flug) der Seele II (Briefmotiv)," *RAC* 8 (1972) 65–67.

295 See Rom 1:11 as part of a prayer; so also Phil 1:8 (cf. 1:9); 2 Tim 1:4; *Barn.* 1.3.

296 So also Wiles, *Paul's Intercessory Prayers,* 248, who treats the passage as a prayer report, albeit an exceptional one: "instead of describing actual prayers it anticipates future ones." His translation, however, obscures the matter: "While they long for you and pray for you. . . ."

The cause of the longing of the Jerusalem church is stated at the end of the sentence: "on account of the exceeding grace of God [bestowed] on you" (διὰ τὴν ὑπερβάλλουσαν χάριν τοῦ θεοῦ ἐφ' ὑμῖν).[297] It is necessary to recall that the grace of God (χάρις τοῦ θεοῦ) is the main theme of the entire argument of vv 6–14, explaining the notion of gift of blessing (εὐλογία). The notion of grace was last mentioned in v 8 as the basis of all human giving.[298] The root of the word may also be heard in εὐχαριστία (thanksgiving), in vv 11, 12.

Outside the present context, the theme of grace (χάρις) is basic to the entire Corinthian correspondence, and was no doubt one of the key concepts in the Corinthians' own self-understanding. That God has given abundantly of his grace was a fact well known to the Achaians.[299] The notion is merely restated programmatically in the letters of chapters 8 and 9.[300]

The proof in vv 13–14 answers the question of the ultimate purpose of the collection, which, in Paul's view, was spiritual, not merely financial. But by stating it in legal and administrative terms, Paul insisted that the spiritual aspect of the collection was not to be divorced from the ecclesiastical and political aspects. This was rightly pointed out by Ferdinand Christian Baur at the beginning of scholarly debate on the various parties in early Christianity: "These were the deeper motivating reasons which the Apostle had for the collection and the journey to Jerusalem. The attempt was to be made to bridge the gap which still existed between the Jewish Christians and the gentile Christians, to obtain recognition for Pauline Christianity from the Jerusalem church, a recognition that had thus far been denied him."[301]

■ 9:15: The Peroratio (Peroration)

The final sentence of the chapter, and presumably of the epistle, is a brief prayer: "Thanks be to God for his indescribable gift" (χάρις τῷ θεῷ ἐπὶ τῇ ἀνεκδιηγήτῳ αὐτοῦ δωρεᾷ).[302] Can this prayer constitute the *peroratio* of the letter, and if so, how does it function? What kind of prayer did Paul intend it to be?

We shall begin with the last question first. The prayer is composed of two parts: first, the well-known formula, "Thanks be to God" (χάρις τῷ θεῷ), which occurs elsewhere in Paul;[303] second, a final reference to God's gifts. This last reference is unusual on account of its terminology. The term "gift" (δωρεά) is not found elsewhere in 2 Cor 9; however, it is a common New Testament term used to describe God's gift of salvation to the Gentiles, in particular the gift of the spirit.[304] More important, δωρεά appears repeatedly in the thanksgiving prayers of the early church.[305]

The same is true of the term "indescribable" (ἀνεκδιήγητος).[306] Why is this term used here? How could Paul say that God's gift is indescribable, when he had

297 My translation. Cf. similarly Plummer, p. 267.

298 On χάρις see above on 8:1 (p. 42 nn. 9, 11, 12, 13).

299 The expression ἐφ' ὑμῖν ("upon you") suggests again the notion of gift. See 1 Cor 1:4; 3:10; 15:57; 2 Cor 8:1, 16; Gal 2:9. Cf. εἰς ὑμᾶς 2 Cor 8:6, 14; 9:8.

300 ὑπερβάλλω occurs only here in 2 Cor 8 and 9. But other notions are περισσεύω κτλ (8:2, 7, 14; 9:8, 12), πλεονάζω (8:15), πλούσιος (8:9), πλουτέω (8:9), πλουτίζω (9:11), and πλοῦτος (8:2).

301 "Beiträge zur Erklärung der Korinthierbriefe," 181–82. The full German text is given here as follows: "Diess waren also die tiefern Beweggründe, welche der Apostel bei der Beisteuer und der Reise nach Jerusalem hatte. Es sollte der Versuch gewagt werden, die noch immer bestehende Kluft zwischen den Judenchristen und den Heidenchristen aufzuheben, dem paulinischen Christenthum bei der Gemeinde in Jerusalem die Anerkennung zu verschaffen, die man ihm immer noch versagte. Um beide Theile einander näher zu bringen, musste vor allem das Vorurtheil beseitigt werden, das auf der Seite der jerusalemischen Christen einer engern Anschliessung an die Heidenchristen entgegenstand, indem sie die letzteren wegen ihres paulinischen Ursprungs noch gar nicht als ächte ebenbürtige Christen anerkennen wollten. Diess ist es, was der Apostel im Auge hat, wenn er die Christen in Jerusalem von der aufrichtigen Anhänglichkeit der Christen seiner Gemeinde an das von ihnen bekannte Evangelium Christi überzeugen zu können hofft. Dieses Misstrauen und Vorurtheil, das auf judenchristlicher Seite noch immer stattfand und seinen Grund nur in den alten Verhältnissen haben konnte, glaubte der Apostel durch den Eindruck der Liebesgabe brechen zu können, welche die heidenchristlichen Gemeinden der jerusalemischen, zum Beweis ihrer brüderlichen Einheit, darbrachten. Wie sehr täuschte er sich aber in dieser Hoffnung! Welche Ursache hatte er, zu der verhängnissvollen Reise sich nur mit zögerndem Entschluss anzuschicken!"

302 The Vg translates: "gratias deo super inenarrabili dono eius." Ambrosiaster interprets: "super ineffabili dono eius" (CSEL 81/2, p. 271).

303 For references see above on 8:16 (p. 70 n. 254).

described it in detail in the preceding sections of the epistle? In seeking an answer to this question, it is worthwhile to consider the origin of the term.[307] It may have its origin in rhetoric, but the sources in which it is found are late and uncertain.[308] Hesychius[309] gave its meaning as *ἀνεκλάλητον, ἄρρητον*, synonyms which have probably influenced the renderings in LSJ "indescribable, ineffable."[310] These synonyms designate matters that are "incapable of expression by speech."[311] In later patristic texts, *ἀνεκδιήγητος* is found in hymns describing God's gifts, especially the gift of the spirit.[312] Less clear are references in the Apostolic Fathers[313] and the Apologists,[314] but they are also suggestive of hymnic language. In an informative note, Windisch[315] pointed to Old Testament parallels[316] and concluded that the sentiment expressed here is similar to that found in Rom 11:33–36.

On the basis of these observations, we may conclude that the term derives from the rhetoric of hymns.[317] In the hymnic context, it affirms, paradoxically, that all attempts to sing the great deeds of God[318] are bound to fail in the final analysis. The human mind is too limited and the human tongue too clumsy to render an adequate account of God's benefits. Thus the phrase "for his indescribable gift" recalls hymns which contain aretalogical lists of divine gifts. These lists are introduced by *ὅτι* ("for"), and prefaced by the claim that God's gifts surpass humanity's ability to describe them. It was also common practice in ancient Christian prayers of thanksgiving to summarize God's gifts, rather than to describe them at length. Thus, for example, a thanksgiving prayer in the liturgy of St. James praises God in the following way: "God who has shown consideration on account of your great and inexpressible love of humankind . . ." (*ὁ θεὸς ὁ διὰ πολλὴν καὶ ἄφατον φιλανθρωπίαν συγκαταβάς*),[319] while the Byzantine Liturgy of the ninth century addresses God as follows: "for you are God, unutterable, incomprehensible, invisible, ungraspable . . ." (*σὺ γὰρ εἶ θεὸς ἀνέκφραστος ἀπερινόητος ἀόρατος ἀκατάληπτος . . .*).[320]

This suggests that in v 15, Paul actually cited the first line of an early Christian prayer of thanksgiving. If this is the case, further conclusions may be drawn. Placing the opening line of a thanksgiving prayer in the peroration of the letter gives the letter a special function in worship. One can assume that the letter, with its brief concluding

304 See Acts 2:38; 8:20; 10:45; 11:17; also Rom 5:15, 17; Eph 3:7; 4:7; Heb 6:4.

305 Brightman, pp. 49, line 34 (St. James); 474, line 5 (Antioch). See also *PGL, s.v.* *δωρεά*.

306 The term is a *hapax legomenon* in the NT, but it occurs in *1 Clem.* 20.5; 49.4; 61.1. See Bauer, *s.v.*

307 Cf. the related terms *ἀνεκλάλητος* 1 Pet 1:8; Ign. *Eph.* 19.2; Pol. *Phil.* 1.3; *ἄρρητος* 2 Cor 12:4 (for the interpretation see Betz, *Paulus*, 92; Bauer, *s.v.* *ἄρρητος*); *ἀνεξεραύνητος* and *ἀνεξιχνίαστος* Rom 11:33; Eph 3:8; *1 Clem.* 20.5. For more references see Bauer, *s.v.*

308 The text cited by Bauer, *s.v.* as *Rhet. Gr.* III, 747, 8, ed. Walz, is a Byzantine Anonymous entitled *Ἔκθεσις ῥητορικῆς*; it speaks of *πειθανάγκη ἄρρητος τε καὶ ἀνεκδιήγητος* ("compulsory persuasion, ineffable and undescribable").

309 *Lexicon*, ed. Adler, *s.v.*

310 LSJ, *s.v.*

311 So Plummer, p. 268.

312 See, e.g., Cyril of Jerusalem *Catech.* 7.11 (ed. Reischl; 1848) 1.220: *πιστεύομεν τοίνυν εἰς ἕνα θεὸν πατέρα, τὸν ἀνεξιχνίαστον καὶ ἀνεκδιήγητον* ("We believe in one God the Father, the inscrutable and indescribable"). Epiphanius *Adv. haer.* 69.69 (GCS, p. 218,6) speaks of the indescribable divine *φιλανθρωπία*. God's gift of salvation, in particular the holy spirit, is characterized by the same term in Origen *Expos. in Prov.* 18.4 (*MPG* 17.204A); Gregory of Nyssa *De spiritu sancto* (*MPG* 46.697B); Chrysostom *In epist. II. ad Cor. Hom.* 20 *MPG* 61.597Eff: *ἀπόρρητα ἀγαθά*; *Hom. 51.1 in Jo.* (*MPG* 59.300A–B with the synonym *ἄφατος*). For more references see *PGL, s.v.* *ἀνεκδιήγητος*.

313 *1 Clem.* 20.5; 49.4; 61.1 (in the great intercession).

314 Athenagoras *Leg.* 10.1; Justin *Dial.* 43.3; 76.2; *Apol.* 1.51.1. Cf. also *Constitutiones apostolicae* 2. 25. 7, ed. Funk: *κλέος ἀνεκδιήγητον ἐν δόξῃ* .

315 Windisch, p. 286.

316 Isa 53:8 LXX: *τὴν γενεὰν αὐτοῦ τις διηγήσεται*; (quoted in Acts 8:33); Sir 42:17; *οὐκ ἐξεποίησεν τοῖς ἁγίοις κυρίου ἐκδιηγήσασθαι πάντα τὰ θαυμάσια αὐτοῦ*. . . . Cf. also Philo's theology of thanksgiving in *Plant.* 127ff.

317 See also Gen 15:5; Sir 18:4–6; 43:27–33; Eccl 6:12; 10:14; also 8:1ff; etc. See Delling, "Alexander der Grosse" (above, n. 288) 17–18.

318 See, e.g., Ps 117:1ff, esp. v 17; Sir 42:15–16; Luke 8:39.

319 Brightman, p. 65, lines 25–27. My translation.

320 Ibid., 322, lines 2–4. My translation.

prayer in v 15, would be conveyed to Achaia, where it would be read in the course of the worship. The reading of the letter would thus conclude with the intonation of the first line of the thanksgiving prayer. Presumably, the congregation would continue the prayer. This presupposes, in addition, that the Achaians would be able to recognize the prayer and recite it from memory.

How does v 15 function as the peroration? We may recall that it is the function of the *peroratio* to sum up the content of the letter, to restate its main concerns, and to include whatever final emphasis the author wishes to give.[321]

Verse 15 certainly suffices as a final summary of the letter. Throughout the epistle, Paul had dealt with various aspects of the "gift of blessing" as the concept which properly describes the purpose of the collection for Jerusalem. In conclusion, Paul assured his readers that, in the final analysis, no one can render an adequate account of every aspect of the divine gift of salvation, of which the collection for the saints was but a small part. Paul was not concerned to give a point-by-point description, but to make the readers respond to the gift in appropriate ways.[322] He wished to motivate them, as potential donors and collaborators in the collection for Jerusalem, to complete the task. Therefore, he had to seek to move his readers to go beyond reading and argumentation to action.[323] How did the apostle bring this about? In order to understand his strategy, we must consider the nature of letter-writing in general. According to ancient epistolary theory, letters are regarded as both oral and written texts.[324] But they are viewed as primarily oral, with the written text serving as a substitute for a conversation made impossible by the physical separation of the partners. In v 15, Paul moved from the written to the oral level, in anticipation of the day when the letter would be read in the worship service.[325] Thus the first line of the prayer turns the worshipers into active participants. By reciting the first line of the prayer, Paul assumed the role of liturgist leading the congregation in prayer, which they were encouraged to continue on their own. His prayer had become their own, and hence their answer to all the things he had said in the letter.[326] Thus the letter set in motion a thanksgiving service in the Achaian churches. Rather than waiting for the church in Jerusalem to begin the thanksgiving prayer, Paul initiated the great liturgy at the moment of writing the letter. By sending the letter to the churches, he extended the liturgy and included them in it. Through their response, it would be extended to Jerusalem as well.[327] Once these epistolary implications have been realized, it is difficult to think of a more appropriate peroration for the letter of chapter 9.

321 On the *peroratio* see above on 8:24.

322 This speaks against Kennedy's hypothesis, *Hermathena* 12 (1903) 365–66 (see above, pp. 13–14), who regards the δέ inserted after χάρις by ℵ^3 C^2 D^{2,3} E K L P *syr copt arm* as original and as an indication that the end of the letter has been lost, in which Paul had explained what the indescribable gift was. Cf. the discussion of this hypothesis by Plummer, p. 269; Windisch, p. 286.

323 See on this point Malherbe, "Ancient Epistolary Theorists" (see above, p. 17 n. 140).

324 In his letter to the Galatians, Paul achieved a similar effect through the inclusion of a curse and a blessing. See Betz, *Galatians,* 23–25.

325 That Paul's letters were written to be read in the worship service is known from 1 Thess 5:27; Col 4:16; and in general from the liturgical endings of the letters, and particularly from the Amen found in many manuscripts. See Bauer, *s.v.* ἀμήν, 1.

326 These implications seem to have been well understood by Ambrosiaster in his comments on 2 Cor 8:7 (CSEL 81/2, pp. 270–71).

327 It should also be noted that the epistolary thanksgivings in the *exordia* of most of Paul's letters are different in form and content. See 1 Thess 1:2 (imitated in 2 Thess 1:3); 1 Cor 1:4; Phil 1:3; Phlm 4; Rom 1:8; also Col 1:3; Eph 1:16. These passages are part of descriptive prayer reports concerned with Paul's daily practice. 2 Cor 1:3 is different; it begins with a *berakhah* which employs performative language.

Chapter IV: The Literary Genre and Function

The detailed analysis of 2 Corinthians 8 and 9, presented in chapters 2 and 3, has already laid the foundation for the attempt to answer the question of the literary genre and function of both letters under consideration. But more is involved in the discussion of this question than a summary of what has already been said. The high literary quality of Paul's letters[1] resulted from the fact that on the one hand he was able to make masterly use of a wealth of rhetorical possibilities,[2] while on the other he exhibited a tendency toward highly original combi-

1 At present there is nevertheless no agreement in the evaluation of the literary quality of the Pauline letters. The differing judgments of earlier scholarship still stand in unmediated opposition to one another, though they should have been revised long ago. Ulrich von Wilamowitz-Moellendorff, *Die Griechische Literatur des Altertums* (Die Kultur der Gegenwart Teil 1, Abteilung 8; Berlin and Leipzig: Teubner, 1905, ²1907, ³1912) 232–33; and Martin Dibelius in his *Geschichte der urchristlichen Literatur* (Leipzig: Teubner, 1926; Munich: Kaiser, ²1975) 95–100, appraised them rather highly. But the influential, opposed theses of Franz Overbeck ("Über die Anfänge der patristischen Literatur," *Historische Zeitschrift* 48 [1882] 417–72; rep. Basel: Schwabe, n.d.) and the standard works which were influenced by Paul Wendland, *Die urchristlichen Literaturformen* (HNT 1.1; Tübingen: Mohr, Siebeck, ²⁻³1912) 342–43, and Eduard Norden, *Die antike Kunstprosa* (2 vols.; Leipzig: Teubner, 1898; Darmstadt: Wissenschaftliche Buchgesellschaft, ⁵1958) 2.451–510 have prevailed despite the fact that their problematic is temporally limited. This is still true of Philipp Vielhauer's *Geschichte,* which attempts to embark on new paths (see my review in *SEÅ* 43 [1978] 128–32, as well as my remarks in *Galatians,* 14–15.

2 There is also no unanimity in scholarship with respect to the rhetoric of Paul, although one is more than ever inclined today to admit that the apostle made use of small rhetorical forms. This concession is the result of important works from the end of the nineteenth and the beginning of the twentieth century, among which the following especially deserve to be mentioned: Johannes Weiss, "Beiträge zur paulinischen Rhetorik," *Theologische Studien,* Bernhard Weiss zu seinem 70. Geburtstag dargebracht (Göttingen: Vandenhoeck & Ruprecht, 1897) 165–247, and the dissertation of his student Rudolf Bultmann, *Der Stil der paulinischen Predigt und die kynisch-stoische Diatribe* (Göttingen: Huth, 1910). But Paul's use of rhetoric is not limited to the diatribe and other small forms (see on this work Stanley K. Stowers, *The Diatribe and Paul's Letter to the Romans* [SBLDS 57; Chico, CA; Scholars, 1981]). Reference should also be made to older works in which valuable material may be found collected, and whose utilization is to be hoped for: Karl Ludwig Bauer, *Rhetoricae Paullinae, vel, Quid oratorium sit in oratione Paulli* (2 vols.; Halae: Impensis Orphanotrophei, 1782); Herman Johan Royaards, *Disputatio inauguralis De altera Pauli ad Corinthios epistola, et observanda in illa apostoli indole et oratione* (Trajecti ad Rhenum: Altheer, 1818) esp. 99–152; Christian Gottlob Wilke, *Die neutestamentliche Rhetorik, ein Seitenstück zur Grammatik des neutestamentlichen Sprachidioms* (Dresden and Leipzig: Arnold, 1843). That these older works have been largely forgotten today has many causes, hardly one of which can be justified scientifically. The harsh attack of Eduard Norden in his work *Die antike Kunstprosa* 2.474–75, 493ff, on Georg Heinrici had a disastrous effect. In his study *Das zweite Sendschreiben des Apostels Paulus an die Korinthier* (Berlin: Hertz, 1887), Heinrici made full use of citations of parallels from classical literature. Norden's emotional and heavily biased attack was refuted by Heinrici in the appendix to his commentary ("Zum Hellenismus des Paulus," *Der zweite Brief an die Korinther* [KEK 6; Göttingen: Vandenhoeck & Ruprecht, ²1900] 436–58) and met with little approval in general, a fact which Norden was obliged to recognize (see the *Nachträge* to the second volume of his work *Die antike Kunstprosa,* 3–4; further Paul Schmiedel, "Paulinische Briefe 1," *ThR* 4 [1901] 507–10; Adolf Deissmann, "Die Sprache der griechischen Bibel [Septuaginta, Neues Testament und Verwandtes]," *ThR* 5 [1902] 65–69; idem, *Light from the Ancient East* [Grand Rapids: Baker, 1978] 3–4). In point of fact, the problems still stand today at the point that had been reached at the beginning of the century; strictly speaking, they remain at the point attained by Gregory of Nyssa (see his exegesis of 1 Cor 15:28 [*MPG* 44.1303–26, esp. 1304A–B]), Augustine (*De doctrina Christiana* 4.7.11–18 [CSEL 80, 1963, pp. 124–32; see Kennedy, *Classical Rhetoric,* 153–57; Gerald A. Press, "The Content and Argument of Augustine's De Doctrina Christiana," *Augustiniana* 31, 1981, 165–82]) and Melanchthon (see the information in Betz, *Galatians,* 14). On the problem see also Erich Fascher, "Der Logos-Christus als göttlicher Lehrer bei Clemens von Alexandrien," *Studien zum Neuen Testament und zur Patristik,* Erich Klostermann zum 90. Geburtstag dargebracht (TU

nations.[3] Thus in dealing with the letters of the apostle, we shall always have to consider these two aspects: on the one hand his epistles must be investigated in terms of how they correspond to the relevant literary genres, while on the other we must always bear in mind that they go their own way in respect to form. We may note in passing that the apostle's literary versatility corresponds precisely to the creativity of his theological thinking, which makes it possible for him to adopt terms and concepts from the Jewish, Christian, and even pagan environment, only to make something totally new out of them.[4]

We can come to grips with the problem of the literary genre of Paul's epistles only by drawing upon existing literary parallels. In the process, difficulties which arise from the nature of this comparative material must be considered. The material for comparison must necessarily be drawn from ancient epistolary theorists and their handbooks on the one hand, and from the extant letter-collections of ancient authors on the other. To these sources must be added the rhetorical handbooks and the corresponding works of rhetoric by Greek and Latin authors.[5] But between all these texts there exists neither methodological unanimity nor objective agreement. On the contrary: the material that has been transmitted represents nothing more than a collection of random excerpts from a rich literary tradition, which was in itself many-sided and full of controversies. Complexity and controversy are, in themselves, nothing surprising in the literary world, but rather the norm. To this world belong the conventions no less than attempts to break through them, the disputes no less than attempts to establish a consensus.

The descriptions of letter-types and the collections of examples by epistolary theorists represent attempts to capture what was conventional praxis in the lifetimes of the respective authors and to bring it into a system which makes it easier for persons of average needs to deal with those very conventions. It can hardly be surprising that attempts of this nature, from different times and by different authors, should differ from one another; rather, what is remarkable is the high degree of similarity. The same may be said of the relationship of these theoretical works to the extant letters: life itself is always richer than attempts to systematize it. Yet the proximity of existing letters to epistolary theory should not be overlooked.

On the whole one can say that the more literary a letter-writer is, the freer he is in the use he makes of the conventions. But in making this statement we should not assume that freedom in this instance means arbitrariness; it only means that one convention is violated in the name of another. For literary conventions are nothing more than indicators of literary possibilities and limitations. The more literary an author is, the greater are the possibilities with which he works, and the wider are the horizons of what is acceptable. By the same token, the more conventional the authors, the more alike are the texts of their letters—a principle which can be demonstrated by innumerable examples from the papyrus letters.

These methodological insights must be kept in mind in undertaking the comparative analysis of the Pauline epistles. The theorists' descriptions of the various letter-types and their collections of examples must be drawn upon in determining literary genre. But in regard to the letters of Paul, we should expect them to provide little more than general criteria for the identification of individual types.[6] In comparison with the letter-types discussed by epistolary theorists, the letters of Paul are

77; Berlin: Akademie-Verlag, 1961) 193–207.

3 As Vielhauer, *Geschichte*, 58–70, observes, research into this dimension of Paul's letter-writing remains in its infancy.

4 The refusal to concede to the apostle a means of argumentation that is shaped by contemporary rhetoric and must be taken earnestly goes hand in hand with the popular notion: Paul "ist Gelegenheitsdenker, kein Systematiker" (Erich Fascher, "Paulus [Apostel]," *PRE.S* 8 [1956] 453). An unsystematic, occasional thinker is, of course, no thinker at all but a scatterbrain!

5 See the text in Valentin Weichert, *Demetrii et Libanii qui feruntur* ΤΥΠΟΙ ΕΠΙΣΤΟΛΙΚΟΙ *et* ΕΠΙΣΤΟΛΙΜΑΙΟΙ ΧΑΡΑΚΤΗΡΕΣ (BT; Leipzig: Teubner, 1910); Malherbe, "Ancient Epistolary Theorists," 3–77. For further bibliography see also Betz, *Galatians*, xiii–xv, 14–25; also the informative review of the work by David E. Aune, *Religious Studies Review* 7 (1981) 322–28.

6 Naturally one can also turn this logic around: because the handbooks and the illustrative texts are not identical, and because no exact parallels to Paul can be found, Paul cannot be interpreted within the

altogether literary. This literary quality manifests itself in two characteristic phenomena: the "mixture" of letter-types and the internal rhetorical design of the letters. Here it should be observed that the mixture of letter-types was a risk for the writer of conventional, non-literary letters, something which he could hope to achieve only with difficulty, and which was therefore better avoided. But precisely this risk suggested new possibilites of expression to the more literary letter-writer. The same may be said of the appropriation of the devices of professional rhetoric. The conventional letter-writer wisely limited himself to so-called natural rhetoric, the kind which comes to expression in the conventional letter. For the literary letter-writer, on the contrary, professional rhetoric opened up new, creative possibilities, the kind which one who knew how to make use of rhetoric would not wish to let escape. Consequently, literary letters naturally bear a strong individual stamp which makes their comparison with one another all the more difficult.

The task is rendered still more difficult by the fact that literary letters are in part influenced by recognized, classical models which in many cases have not been preserved. The best-known instances of this problem are the letters of Seneca and those which they were designed to imitate, the letters of Epicurus. These letters had a great literary influence in the ancient world, despite the fact that only a few have survived.[7] The loss of the letters of Epicurus sets a clear limit to all work on the epistolary literature of the subsequent era, to which also belong the letters of Paul. If we only had the letters of Epicurus, many literary phenomena in the Corpus Paulinum would no doubt be easier to understand.[8]

In contrast to work of an unscientific nature, true scholarship cannot allow itself to be deterred by such complications. It must take hold of the problems methodologically, so as to make the phenomena more precise and their investigation more fruitful. So much must be said over against a seemingly scientific minimalism which, having the appearance of being critical, declares itself content with what has ostensibly been achieved, appoints itself the guardian of this small sum, and defends it against uncomfortable inquiries. It must be admitted that those who hold this outlook have it far easier, and that their position appears more respectable in educational establishments, where what is pursued above all is caretaking and instruction. But one should not await new insights from this quarter.

The opposite problem prevails among those who are fond of theories such as are currently in vogue, and which attempt to evade methodological control. But methodological rigor can be achieved only through criticism of one's own ideas. While such self-criticism is guided by one's own conceptions, it is helped by analogies, that is, in this case, by literary parallels. The search for such parallels is always tiresome, but it is indispensable if one does not wish to renounce altogether the task of understanding the text. Scientific facts can only be recognized and demonstrated through comparison with existing parallels.

1. The Letter of Chapter 8

As scholars have already recognized, chapter 8 falls into two parts which seem to have little in common with one another from a formal point of view. The first part, up to v 15, consists of arguments; the second part, from v 16 on, is devoted to matters of business.[9] The change affects the content, form, and function of the letter. In addition, it makes unavoidable the question how both parts could have belonged to the same letter, and if they did not,

framework of ancient literature. For this conclusion cf. Wayne A. Meeks in his review of my *Galatians* commentary in *JBL* 100 (1981) 304–7; 306: "Betz does not inspire confidence in his thesis, though, by referring almost exclusively to rhetorical and epistolary *theory* rather than to specific examples of real apologies and real letters from antiquity. He does not offer us a single instance of the apologetic letter with which one can compare Galatians. We are therefore asked to interpret Galatians as an example of a genre for which no other example can apparently be cited." But as Meeks views things, there are no precise analogies, e.g., for Plato's *Apology of Socrates* or for his *Letter VII*. Does he therefore wish to deny the existence of the literary categories of these texts?

7 See the editions of Peter von der Mühll, *Epicuri epistulae tres et ratae sententiae a Laertio Diogene servatae; accedit Gnomologium Epicureum Vaticanum* (BT; Leipzig: Teubner, 1922); Graziano Arighetti, *Epicuro. Opere: Introduzione, testo critico, traduzione e note* (Florence: Einaudi, ²1973).

8 Cf. Vielhauer, *Geschichte*, 61–62.

9 See Heinrici, p. 286: "Das Geschäftliche. Was über

how the text came to be in its present form. Hans Windisch[10] suggested that the letter contains an ongoing narrative interrupted in v 6 and taken up again in v 16. He found that the "paraenetic section" (vv 9–15) looks like an insertion, something which he termed "strange" and "quite puzzling."[11] Windisch suggested that two pages of the letter may have been exchanged by accident, giving rise to confusion.[12] But such a radical solution as that of a *Blättervertauschung* is hardly called for. One can point to a number of close connections between the different sections of the letter, and in any case, we have provided an explanation for the compositional unity of the letter which did not occur to Windisch. Furthermore, Windisch's concept of narrative[13] is misleading in that he worked from the assumption that a continuous narrative determines the composition of the letter. There is, of course, a certain sense in which there is a narrative behind 2 Corinthians: the course of events as reported in the various sections. But this narrative emerges from a variety of literary forms; to reestablish the original continuity of events would require rearranging the components of the letter. Focusing on 2 Cor 8 alone, we have found that there are elements of narrative in the *exordium* (vv 1–5), in the *narratio* (v 6), in the *propositio* (vv 7–8), and so forth. In other words, the narrative which runs through the letter fragments is not identical with the surface structure or with any one of its literary forms.

What are the connections between the various parts of the letter of chapter 8? On the whole, its rhetoric is advisory. In the first part, Paul advised his readers about the collection; the second part of the commendation constitutes advice regarding the envoys. The parties participating in the collection are considered in turn, first the Macedonians (vv 1–5), then the Corinthians (vv 6–15), then the envoys. In narrative terms, Paul took the readers from the past history of the collection through the present situation to the immediate future. That future would be determined by the success or failure of the envoys' mission in Corinth. Titus had been mentioned in the *narratio* (v 6), but not the other envoys. Finally, in terms of function, v 16 moves from theory to practice, from the analysis of the problem to its solution.

Do the commendations on behalf of the envoys in the second part of the letter make the whole work a letter of recommendation? There are certainly close parallels between 2 Cor 8 and many letters of recommendation, but the differences should not be overlooked. The typical letter of recommendation has as its core a request and a petition[14] on behalf of the recommended person. No such petition, however, is found in 2 Cor 8.[15] On the other hand, letters of recommendation carry no legal authorizations such as that found in 2 Cor 8.[16] These differences show that 2 Cor 8 must be compared with

Titus (V. 6) und die anderen Abgeordneten zu sagen ist." Similarly Plummer, p. 246: "In what follows we have the business arrangements respecting the collection for the fund. It is a kind of ἐπιστολὴ συστατική (iii.1) for the officials." Windisch, p. 260, apparently follows Plummer: "Eine ἐπιστολὴ συστατική für Titus und zwei (ungenannte) Brüder, die mit der Einbringung der Kollekte in Kor. [Corinth] beauftragt sind V. 16–24." Bultmann, p. 257, notes Paul's concern for formal exactitude.

10 Windisch, p. 260, following Heinrici, p. 286.

11 Windisch, p. 260: "Es ist wohl seltsam, dass sich im vorliegenden Text zwischen die Mitteilung, dass P. [Paul] den T. [Titus] ersucht habe, sich der Sache in Kor. [Corinth] anzunehmen (V. 6), und der dankerfüllten Erzählung, dass T. dem Gesuch entsprochen und sich auf die Reise nach Kor. begeben hat (V. 16f.), ein paränetisches Stück, das den Eifer der Kor. erwecken soll, wie eine Einlage einschiebt. Die Einlage ist zwar hier nicht so störend, wie die zwischen 2_{14} und 7_4, aber doch verwunderlich genug."

12 Ibid.; see also 268.

13 Ibid.

14 See Chan-Hie Kim, *Form and Structure of the Familiar Greek Letter of Recommendation* (SBLDS 4; Missoula, MT: Society of Biblical Literature, 1972) 61ff; John L. White, *The Form and Structure of the Official Petition: A Study in Greek Epistolography* (SBLDS 5; Missoula, MT: Society of Biblical Literature, 1972).

15 Petitions are not found in 2 Cor 9 or in the letter in Acts 15:23–29.

16 On the other hand, they are not without legal force. See Cicero's remark in *Ep. Fam.* 13.6.3: "But as for the recommendation I have been willing to sign in this letter, I would have you know that it is more important than any . . ." ("Sed hanc commendationem quam his litteris consignare volui, scito esse omnium gravissimam").

letters of appointment given to envoys. Such letters are mentioned in the New Testament in Acts 9:12; 22:5, where the subject is the letters of authorization given to Paul empowering him to persecute Christians in Damascus. The letter included in Acts 15:23–29 had similar legal force but served a more peaceful purpose.

If the second part of the letter contains both commendation and authorization, does this make the entire letter a letter of recommendation (ἐπιστολὴ συστατική)? Or is the composite nature of the epistle an advisory section (vv 1–15) plus an administrative part (vv 16–23), concluded by a *peroratio* (v 24) indicative of a "mixed" type? Or should the commendations be regarded as advisory, and the arguments given in vv 1–15 as part of a letter of administration?

Commendations such as those found in vv 16–23 have significant parallels in epistolary literature from the Hellenistic era. Yet a note of caution must be sounded here. The history of Greek letter-writing remains to be written; as yet there is neither a classification system nor a literary analysis which can claim to be completely adequate to the demands of scholarship. Yet in spite of the lack of sufficient studies in the field, some observations on the commendations in 2 Cor 8:16–23 may still be made.

The commendations suggest that 2 Cor 8 should be compared with that type of official letter which Friedrich Schroeter, in his important dissertation,[17] called a letter of commendation meant to accompany royal envoys. It should be obvious that 2 Cor 8 does not belong to the category of the private letter of recommendation, for such letters were exchanged between private persons in the context of family and friends.[18] But the classification of the epistle remains a problem. Recent discussion has shown that the distinction between "true letters" and "epistles," introduced by Adolf Deissmann,[19] is unworkable in light of the variety of existing letters. In the title of his dissertation, Chan-Hie Kim promised to deal with "the familiar Greek letter of recommendation," but in fact he limited himself to what he called the "private letters." For Kim, "private letters" are "non-literary" but not necessarily "non-official."[20] Yet the equation of "private" with "non-literary" seems out of place. Hannah Cotton, on the other hand, distinguished "documentary" from "non-documentary" letters of recommendation, assigning "private correspondence" to the former category and the letters of Cicero, Pliny, and Fronto to the latter.[21] Yet it is hard to see why Cicero's letters, for example, should be termed non-documentary or public simply because he is a member of a different social class than most of the authors of papyrus letters. The fact that Cicero's letters were written in high style and subsequently published in no way lessens their documentary value or does away with their privacy.

Cotton recognized that not all of the letters of recommendation by Cicero,[22] Pliny,[23] and Fronto[24] can be

17 Fridericus Schroeter, *De regum hellenisticorum epistulis in lapidibus servatis quaestiones stilisticae* (Dissertatio inauguralis; Leipzig: Teubner, 1931) 20–23: *Epistulae commendaticiae a legatis regum perlatae.* From his collection Schroeter puts into this category nos. 1, 7, 13, 33, 39, 40 (they correspond to nos. 1, 5, 14, 49, 50 in Welles's collection).

18 For a collection of papyrus letters and bibliography see Kim's dissertation (see above, n. 14); furthermore Hannah Cotton, *Documentary Letters of Recommendation, in Latin from the Roman Empire* (BKP 132; Königstein: Hain, 1981). Cotton also adds more papyrus letters to Kim's collection (pp. 53–54).

19 See Deissmann, *Light,* 227–54. For a critique of Deissmann see William G. Doty, "The Classification of Epistolary Literature," *CBQ* 31 (1969) 183–99; idem, *Letters in Primitive Christianity* (Philadelphia: Fortress, 1973) 1ff.

20 Kim, *The Familiar Greek Letter of Recommendation,* 3–4.

21 Cotton, *Documentary Letters of Recommendation,* 4–5.

22 Letters of recommendation are found throughout Cicero's correspondence, but *Epistulae Familiariae* book 13 is a collection of just this category of letters. See the historical commentary by D. R. Shackleton Bailey, *Cicero: Epistulae ad Familiares* (2 vols.; Cambridge: Cambridge University, 1977). See also Friedrich Lossmann, *Cicero und Caesar im Jahre 54: Studien zur Theorie und Praxis der römischen Freundschaft* (Hermes, Einzelschriften 17; Wiesbaden: Steiner, 1962) 10ff.

23 Pliny *Ep.* 1.14; 2.13; 3.2; 3.3; 4.4; 10.4; 10.12; 10.58; etc. For an attempt at classification see A. Nicholas Sherwin-White, *The Letters of Pliny: A Historical and Social Commentary* (Oxford: Clarendon,

designated private, because they often involved other individuals, statesmen, groups, and cities. Most of the time they played a part in contemporary political events, so that the "private" language and the air of friendship and intimacy are deceptive. In fact, the hackneyed expressions of family loyalty, love, and friendship generally constitute a political artifice. Letters such as these are in part private, in part public and official.[25] These ambiguities illustrate the need for a better system of classification within the genre.

2 Cor 8 presents us with a different case still: it is an official letter sent by an individual writing in an official capacity to a corporate body, the church at Corinth, along with officially appointed envoys. The letter is concerned with the administration of financial transactions which involve a number of communities in different lands.

The term "official" may be appropriately applied to the letter because of the status of the individuals involved in their respective communities. Here church officials function in much the same way as the heads of the various community organizations, clubs, and religious groups. This official class played an important role in ancient society,[26] just as it does today. Naturally, this social officialdom must be distinguished from the governmental system which presided over the state, provinces, and cities.

With respect to ancient letters of recommendation, we may assert that they can be divided into different subtypes by function. But they also share many of the same terms, formulae, etc. Consequently, while 2 Cor 8 bears comparison with a specific letter subtype, it also has language and formulae in common with other epistolary subtypes. The letters with which 2 Cor 8 deserves primarily to be compared are found among the correspondence of rulers of cities, provinces, and countries. How can this comparison be justified?

In the first place, only this "royal" correspondence managed to survive to any great extent, while most of the exchanges between smaller units within the society have disappeared. Royal correspondence was preserved largely because it was published, often in stone, or because it was deposited in archives and later quoted in other documents. Naturally, formal differences between this royal correspondence and the letters of Paul must be taken into account. But as the letters vary greatly among themselves, similarities between these letters and those of Paul will vary accordingly. In any case, formal parallels are great enough to warrant comparison.

What gives rise to these parallels is their common setting in legal and administrative practices of the day. Comparative studies of law have shown that language born in this context exhibits an intrinsic tendency toward uniformity, continuity, and expansion. Its standards are most often established by the royal court and then filter down to city officials and private attorneys. As part of the correspondence of a religious community within the larger society, Paul's letters share the administrative practices and legal terminology of the day. Naturally, the extent to which Paul's epistles conformed to current usage depends upon particular issues, concerns, etc. But in fact, as we shall see, the integrity and credibility of the churches as administrative agencies depended to a great degree in these early years on the extent to which they were able to conform to current practices in the conduct of official business.

The administrative purpose of the letters of 2 Cor 8 and 9 also helps to explain why the letters are relatively short. It seems that for practical reasons business letters must usually be kept short. Typically, little time is

1966) 42–45.

24 M. Cornelius Fronto, *Epistolae ad amicos* (ed. Samuel Adrianus Naber; Leipzig: Teubner, 1867) 172–201.

25 Cf. Cotton, *Documentary Letters of Recommendation*, 4–5: "Like their non-documentary counterparts (i.e., the letters of recommendation of Cicero, Pliny, and Fronto), the documentary ones also fall within the sphere of private correspondence, as is shown by their mood and formal aspect. However, in view of the fact that each and every one of them involves persons connected in one way or another with the government (*qua* being soldiers or officials), it is not impossible that the vague requests contained in them impinge upon some official capacity vested in the addressee. If this is the case, it might be suggested that the fact that they are cast in the form of private communications faithfully reflects the Roman preference for relying on personal ties and for using private forms of address even when transacting official or semi-official business."

26 For the background and bibliography see John F. Matthews, "Gesandtschaft," *RAC* 11 (1977) 635–85, esp. 669, 672–78.

available for their planning and composition, and they must achieve their effect without delay or circumstance. Related matters, doctrinal or ideological, must be kept to an absolute minimum.

Clearly, 2 Corinthians 8 and 9 conform to these conditions. In light of this fact, the length of Paul's letters is one of the factors which must be considered in any future discussion. Thus with respect to length and purpose, the Letter to Philemon and, one may assume, the letter fragment in Rom 16:1–23 come closest to 2 Cor 8 and 9. By contrast, 1 Corinthians, Galatians, and Romans bear no resemblance to business letters.

In 1 Cor 16:3, Paul himself mentioned the type of letter represented by 2 Cor 8. Looking forward to his arrival in Corinth, he spoke of his plans for the future: "When I arrive, I will send people of whom you approve, provided with letters to bring your gift to Jerusalem" (ὅταν δὲ παραγένωμαι, οὓς ἐὰν δοκιμάσητε, δι' ἐπιστολῶν τούτους πέμψω ἀπενεγκεῖν τὴν χάριν ὑμῶν εἰς Ἰερουσαλήμ).[27] These letters, had they been written, would have been letters of introduction and authorization similar to 2 Cor 8. But, in fact, they were never sent;[28] the crisis interrupted the collection which, as 2 Cor 8 and 9 indicate, had to be reorganized. But still another change was made in Paul's plans. In 1 Cor 16:4, Paul mentioned the possibility that "if it is worthwhile that I should also go, then they shall go with me" (ἐὰν δὲ ἄξιον ᾖ τοῦ κἀμὲ πορεύεσθαι σὺν ἐμοὶ πορεύσονται).[29] It seems that when Paul finally arrived in Corinth, it was decided that he should lead the delegation to Jerusalem himself, making the letters obsolete.[30] Yet the change in plans is a vivid reminder of the fact that the letters would have served as a substitute for the apostle's personal presence, a function which was also served by 2 Cor 8.

The assumption that 2 Cor 8 conforms to the conventions of Hellenistic epistolography is supported by similar letters in Cicero's *Epistulae Familiariae.* As Cicero himself acknowledged, he made use of handbooks, probably of Greek origin.[31] Among these letters there are several which were written not on behalf of individuals but on behalf of communities. *Ep. Fam.* 13.9 is addressed to P. Furius Crassipes on behalf of a Bithynian company of *publicani.* It begins with an *exordium* and a *narratio* (13.9.1), then presents reasons for the request that follows (13.9.2–3), and concludes with a *peroratio.*

Ep. Fam. 13.11 is written to M. Brutus on behalf of the municipality of Arpinum. The *exordium* takes the form of a *captatio benevolentiae* (13.11.1), while the *narratio* reports that a delegation of three men has been sent to Gaul to collect outstanding debts for the people of Arpinum: "To visit those estates, to call in the moneys still owed by the tenants, and to investigate and arrange for the management of the whole business, we have sent a commission of Roman knights—Q. Fufidius the younger, M. Faucius the younger, and Q. Mamercus the younger."[32] There follows a request to treat the commission well and to help them carry out their assignment effectively (13.11.2). Thereafter, Cicero provided reasons for his commendation, and concluded with the following *peroratio* (13.11.3): "Now you will have done due honour to them and to myself in particular, if it turns out that the public business of the township has

27 My translation. For the meaning of δοκιμάζειν ("approve") see above, pp. 56–60, 78 n. 317.

28 For other early Christian letters of recommendation see Kim, *The Familiar Greek Letter of Recommendation,* 119ff. Kim differentiates between references to the practice of writing such letters (1 Cor 16:3; 2 Cor 3:1–2; Acts 9:2; 18:27; 22:5), passages of commendation within letters of a different genre, and exemplars of the genre itself. He thus identifies commendations within Pauline letters (Rom 16:1–2; 1 Cor 16:15–16, 17–18; Phil 2:29–30; 4:2–3; 1 Thess 5:12–13a; Philemon) and in other early Christian epistles (3 John 12; Heb 13:17; Pol. *Phil.* 14.1), but he does not consider the macrostructure of the letters and their literary-critical problems. 2 Cor 8 has been overlooked completely, when he says (p. 120): "Only 2 Corinthians and Galatians lack recommendations."

29 My translation. Cf. Conzelmann, *1 Corinthians,* 294 with n. 5.

30 See 2 Cor 9:4; Rom 15:25–28; Acts 20:1ff.

31 *Ep. Fam.* 13.15.3: "I have adopted a new style of letter writing to you, so that you may understand that this is no stereotyped recommendation" ("Genere novo sum litterarum ad te usus, ut intellegeres, non vulgarem esse commendationem"). Part of the new form is the inclusion of quotations from Homer and Euripides. See also 13.6.3; 35.1. Texts and translation are those of the LCL edition by W. Glynn Williams.

32 Ibid., 11.1: "Ad ea visenda pecuniasque, quae a colonis debentur, exigendas totamque rem et cognoscendam et administrandam legatos equites Romanos misimus, Q. Fufidium, Q. F., M. Faucium,

been, thanks to your zealous assiduity, well-managed. And this is what I earnestly and again and again beg you to do."[33]

In light of the relationship between 2 Cor 8 and 9, it is interesting to note that the following letter, *Ep. Fam.* 13.12, addressed to the same M. Brutus, is a special recommendation for the leader of the delegation, Q. Fufidius. This second letter makes explicit reference to the first, and provides a detailed description of the character of the one being recommended along with the reason for his request to add Q. Fufidius to his circle of friends.

A useful collection of royal letters from the Seleucid and Attalid kingdoms of Asia, and the Ptolemaic Kingdom of Egypt, spanning the period from the late fourth century B.C. to the early first century A.D., was made by C. Bradford Welles, published in 1934 under the title *Royal Correspondence in the Hellenistic Period. A Study in Greek Epigraphy.*[34] All the letters in Welles's collection were published subsequently, many being inscribed on stone. Publication involved a certain amount of editorial activity, both on the letters themselves and on the collections, but unfortunately, little is known of the editorial process. It is uncertain, for example, to what extent publication entailed revision and improvements on stylistic grounds. It makes things more difficult still if epistolography is regarded systematically as a subcategory of rhetoric. Welles stated the problems in this way: while "the literary letter-form developed in the philosophical schools during the fourth century B.C., it is clear that the official letter like the private letter was evolved first as a purely practical instrument of communication. Its development was as far as can be determined uninfluenced by the rhetorical schools. It is true of course that its style may at times show the rhetorical training of the royal secretaries, but there is no indication that its forms were prescribed in the handbooks of any system."[35] Thus if Welles was correct, official letters came under the influence of rhetoric only secondarily. Though Welles's statement provides for the complexity of the situation,[36] it is possible that it is greater than even he has realized. It seems best to judge each letter on its own terms.

In addition to the letters collected by Welles, other official correspondence must be taken into account, particularly in light of the fact that in time the production of such official correspondence fell to the Romans. Extant Roman letters, however, are no older than the second century B.C. Work on these letters was begun by Paul Viereck in his Göttingen dissertation of 1888,[37] and was carried on by Leon Lafoscade in his Paris dissertation of 1902.[38] Taking up Viereck's work in particular, whose *Nachlass* was placed at his disposal, Robert K. Sherk published a collection of letters in 1969 under the title, *Roman Documents from the Greek East: Senatus Consulta and Epistulae to the Age of Augustus.*[39]

Other collections of special importance are as follows: H. Idris Bell, *Jews and Christians in Egypt,*[40] which contains the text and commentary on the famous letter of Claudius to the Alexandrians, written in A.D. 41.[41] Then there are the collections of documents begun by Victor Ehrenberg and A. H. M. Jones,[42] and continued

M. F., Q. Mamercum, Q. F."

33 Ibid., 3: "Quos cohonestaris in primisque me, si res publica municipi tuo studio, diligentia, bene administrata erit. Quod ut facias, te vehementer etiam atque etiam rogo."

34 (New Haven: Yale University, 1934). Welles is critical of Schroeter's classification: see his remarks on the problem pp. xliii–xlv. See further Adolf Wilhelm, *Griechische Königsbriefe* (Klio. Beiheft 48 [NF 35]; Leipzig: Dietrich, 1943).

35 Welles, *Royal Correspondence,* xlii, who also discusses the problem of how these letters are related to the epistolary handbooks (pp. xlii–xliii).

36 Welles, *Royal Correspondence,* xlvi–l.

37 Paul Viereck, *Sermo graecus quo senatus populusque romanus magistratusque populi romani usque ad Tiberii Caesaris aetatem in scriptis publicis usi sunt examinatur* (Dissertation und Preisschrift Göttingen; Göttingen: Officina academica Dieterichiana, 1888).

38 Leon Lafoscade, *De epistulis (aliisque titulis) imperatorum magistratuumque romanorum quas ab aetate Augusti usque ad Constantinum graece scriptas lapides papyrive servaverunt* (Thesis Parisiensis; Insulis: Le Bigot, 1902).

39 Robert K. Sherk, *Roman Documents.* On Sherk's relationship to Viereck see the preface, p. V.

40 Bell, *Jews and Christians in Egypt.* The letter is also included in C. C. Edgar and A. S. Hunt, *Select Papyri,* LCL no. 212; Tcherikover and Fuks, *CPJ* 2, no. 153; Smallwood, *Documents* (1967) no. 370 (see below, n. 44).

41 Bell, *Jews and Christians in Egypt,* 1–37.

42 Victor Ehrenberg and A. H. M. Jones, *Documents Illustrating the Reigns of Augustus and Tiberius* (Oxford:

by M. McCrum and A. G. Woodhead,[43] and by E. Mary Smallwood.[44]

In comparing these letters with 2 Cor 8, it is important to keep the difficulty and complexity of the task in mind.[45] Whereas little work has been done on the literary structure and composition of the letters,[46] much more is known about epistolary formulae. Both Welles and Sherk called attention to the phenomenon of the mixture of genres. This is particularly clear when legal documents are transmitted in epistolary form. Of course, it is also possible to document epistolary formulae from a wide variety of epigraphical and papyrus letters, as well as from those contained in literary works. In addition, legal and administrative terms are not restricted to letters alone, but can be found in many other texts as well.[47]

By way of illustration, a small number of letters which bear comparison with 2 Cor 8 will be discussed in what follows. It will be necessary, however, to limit discussion to those aspects which are of significance for the analysis of Paul's letter.

A relatively simple letter is found in Schroeter's collection (p. 80, no. 33), dated ca. 201 B.C.; it was sent by Philip V to the inhabitants of the island of Nisyri.[48]

1 King Philip to the Nisyrians, greetings.
2 I have sent Callias to you,
3 who is both my friend and your
4 citizen. Knowing that he is
5 friendly to the city and that he has
6 often negotiated on your behalf with
7 me, I have ordered him to report
8 to you what I want you to know.[49]

1 Βασιλεὺς Φίλιππος Νισυρίοις χαί
2 ρειν· ἀφέσταλκα καλλίαν πρὸς
3 ὑμᾶς, ὄντα καὶ ἡμῖν συνήθη καὶ ὑ
4 μέτερον πολίτην· εἰδὼς δὲ αὐτ
5 ὸν εὔνουν ὄντα τῇ πόλει καὶ πολλ
6 άκις ὑπὲρ ὑμῶν διειλεγμένον πρὸ
7 s ἐμέ, ἐντέταλμαι αὐτῶν ἀναγγεῖλα
8 ι ὑμῖν ἅ ἠβουλόμην ὑμᾶς εἰδῆσαι

The literary structure may be outlined as follows:

1–2 I. Epistolary prescript
1. Sender, with his title
2. Addressees
3. Salutation
2 II. Narratio: "I have sent . . ."
III. Commendation
1. Name
3–4 2. Relationships
a. To the sender
b. To the addressees
4–6 3. Qualifications
a. Disposition toward the addressees
b. Evidence
7–8 4. Assignment

In Welles's collection, three letters in particular bear comparison with 2 Cor 8. Though more complex than Schroeter's no. 33, they resemble 2 Cor 8 even more closely in structure.

Clarendon, 1949, ^{2}1955, ^{3}1976).

43 M. McCrum and A. G. Woodhead, *Select Documents of the Principates of the Flavian Emperors Including the Year of the Revolution A.D. 68–96* (Cambridge: Cambridge University, 1961).

44 E. Mary Smallwood, *Documents Illustrating the Principates of Nerva, Trajan and Hadrian* (Cambridge: Cambridge University, 1966); idem, *Documents Illustrating the Principates of Gaius, Claudius and Nero* (Cambridge: Cambridge University, 1967).

45 Welles's comment (*Royal Correspondence,* xlii) is as true today as it was in his time: ". . . much yeoman service will have to be done before we can deal with Greek epistolography on a broad basis. . . ."

46 See also Wilhelm Schubart, "Bemerkungen zum Stile hellenistischer Königsbriefe," *Archiv für Papyruskunde* 6 (1920) 324–47; Welles, *Royal Correspondence,* xli–l; Sherk, *Roman Documents,* 186–209.

47 Works investigating the sending of envoys and the institutional practices connected with it include some important older dissertations. See Franciscus Poland, *De legationibus Graecorum publicis* (Dissertatio inauguralis Lipsiensis; Leipzig: Teubner, 1885); Georg Friedrich Schömann, *De comitiis Atheniensium libri tres* (Gryphiswaldiae: Sumptibus Ernesti Mauritii, 1819). See also Anton von Premerstein, "Legatus," *PW* 12.1 (1924) 1133–49; Allan C. Johnson, Paul R. Coleman-Norton, Frank C. Bourne, *Ancient Roman Statutes* (Austin: University of Texas, 1961); John F. Matthews, "Gesandtschaft," *RAC* 11 (1977) 635–85.

48 Also in Dittenberger, *Sylloge,* 3d ed., no. 572, but not in Welles, *Royal Correspondence.*

49 My translation.

The first is a letter of Antigonus to the city of Scepsis in Asia, dated 311 B.C. The beginning is now lost, and the extant letter opens with a *narratio* (lines 1–51). The *narratio* is rather long and discloses the main purpose of the letter. It consists of a detailed and self-serving account of the actions taken by Antigonus on behalf of the city up to the moment of the sending of the envoys. It is really little more than a piece of propaganda, designed to demonstrate Antigonus's "zeal" (*σπουδή*)[50] for the freedom of the Greeks.[51] In lines 51–56 follows the *propositio,*[52] introduced by *ἴστε οὖν* . . . and containing the following announcement (lines 51–54): "Know then that the truce has been established and that peace is made." Provision is made in the treaty that all Greeks shall swear an oath to protect their liberty (lines 54–56). Lines 56–70 appear to be the *probatio,* in which two reasons are given for the necessity of the oath: (1) to safeguard the freedom and autonomy of the Greeks in the future (lines 56–61); (2) to protect the present treaty with all its provisions (lines 62–65). Then follows the request that the recipients of the letter take the oath as well (lines 65–69).

The commendation, by comparison, is short and formulaic (lines 69–72).[53] It consists of a reference to the present letter and to the sending of an envoy, whose name is given and whose assignment is described. The letter concludes with a greeting.

Also of interest from the point of view of 2 Cor 8 is Welles's no. 49.[54] It is a letter of Eumenes II to a Carian city, dated spring, 182 B.C. The extant text begins with a short *narratio* (line 1), which is followed by the commendation of the two envoys (lines 2–5). The commendation of the first envoy contains his name, his place of birth, his relationship to the sender, and his qualifications (line 2). The second envoy is said to have the same status (*ὁμοίως*) as the first. His name and place of birth are also given, followed by his qualifications (lines 3–5). While the first envoy had been appointed by Eumenes,[55] the second had been appointed by the city,[56] and joined in the delivery of the message: "[and who has been chosen] by his city because it joins us in this proclamation" ([*καὶ προκεχειρισμένον*] *ὑπὸ τῆς πόλεως διὰ τὸ καταγγέλλειν μεθ' ἡμῶν τ*[*αῦτα*]).[57] Lines 5–10 contain the request, and the letter concludes in line 11 with a final greeting and subscription.

Welles's no. 50 is very similar. Again, it is a letter of Eumenes II, in this instance to Cos, also dated in the spring, 182 B.C.[58] The extant text begins with a *narratio* (lines 1–4), followed by the commendation of a delegation of five envoys (lines 4–12).[59] Eumenes is represented by three of his courtiers, while two additional envoys have been chosen by the city of Pergamum. The names of the first three delegates are given, along with their qualifications. The first is of high official rank, while the other two are friends (*φίλοι*) of the king. Next come the representatives of Pergamum, their names, qualifications, and the source of their appointment: "men by us [considered excellent and who as] citizens have attained [everything] suitable [to their age], and who have been selected [by their city] because it [joins with us] in proclamation of the Nicephoria."[60] Lines 12–22 contain the request, which concludes with a

50 Cf. Paul's references to "zeal" (*σπουδή*), on which see above, pp. 58–59, 70.

51 See Welles's comment, *Royal Correspondence,* 11: "The letter is not a special communication to Scepsis. Nothing, except the heading and the name of the envoy at the end, need have been changed before it could have been sent to any other Greek city. Undoubtedly copies of it were sent out widely; otherwise a town of the comparative insignificance of Scepsis would hardly have received one. It was intended to be read throughout the Greek world, and everywhere to win public opinion for Antigonus. As a state paper of the first importance, then, great care must have been taken with its form as with its content."

52 The following analysis differs to some extent from that of Welles, *Royal Correspondence,* 11–12.

53 Beginning with *ὑπὲρ τούτων* (cf. 2 Cor 8:23).

54 See his commentary, pp. 199–202; also Wilhelm, *Königsbriefe,* 41ff.

55 Being his "friend" (*φίλος*) he represents the king. Cf. 2 Cor 8:22.

56 Representing the city. See Welles, *Royal Correspondence,* 201.

57 Text and translation are Welles's. Cf. 2 Cor 8:18–19.

58 See Welles's commentary, pp. 204–5.

59 The usual number was three envoys, as in 2 Cor 8:16–23.

60 The translation is that of Welles. Cf. 2 Cor 8:18–19. Also of interest for comparison is a list of requirements for becoming an official found in an Egyptian papyrus. See Hubert Metzger, "Zur Stellung der liturgischen Beamten Ägyptens in frührömischer Zeit," *MH* 2 (1945) 54–92,

final greeting (line 22).

In conclusion we may state that in 2 Cor 8 a letter fragment of the so-called mixed type is to be found. The first part contains arguments which aim at making the resumption and the successful conclusion of their part in the collection for Jerusalem a matter of concern to the Corinthians. The second part (vv 16–23) contains the authorization of the delegation which accompanied the letter to Corinth in order to reorganize the collection. Each part has a different aim in view: vv 1–15 is advisory; vv 16–22 administrative. Yet these two objects are clearly related to one another: the argumentative section deals with the problem of the administration of the collection; the administrative section contains the implicit advice to recognize the delegation and support it in its task, advice which is made explicit in the *peroratio* (v 24), where it appears as a demand that they receive the delegation in an appropriate manner.

On the basis of their common concern it is clear that the two parts of the letter belong together. Without doubt the major portion of the epistle is administrative in nature, but the intended task and function of the letter is advisory. In determining the type and function of the letter, both aspects must be discussed as part of the same literary situation.

With respect to its epistolary type and function, 2 Cor 8 belongs to the administrative correspondence of Paul. We may suppose that this correspondence was once much more extensive, and can only regret the fact that of these letters only two fragments have been preserved in 2 Cor 8 and 9, to which perhaps we should also add the fragment of a letter of thanks in Phil 4:10–20. The rhetoric is advisory, or deliberative, in the first part (vv 1–15) and administrative, or juridical, in the second part (vv 16–23). In keeping with this, the principal parallels to the first section come from rhetorical and philosophical literature, while the formulae and terms of the second part are mainly drawn from Hellenistic administrative language. Yet both administrative and philosophical letters have shown that both kinds of rhetoric are found and combined elsewhere as well. Nevertheless, the separation of these linguistic spheres has proven important in ascertaining the content and purpose of the letter.

2. The Letter of Chapter 9

In comparison with chapter 8, it is far easier to determine the literary form and function of the letter fragment of chapter 9. The fragment is of one piece and contains no inner tensions. The text-type is that of an advisory letter; the rhetoric is correspondingly deliberative.[61]

The aim of the composition is again—as in chapter 8—the conclusion of the collection for Jerusalem which remains outstanding. But the letter of chapter 9 has another task than that of the letter of chapter 8. Parallels and differences between the two letters may be explained by the fact that despite differences in function they share a common goal—to bring the collection for the saints in Jerusalem to a successful conclusion. The addressees of the letters also differ from one another. Chapter 8 can only have been addressed to the community in Corinth, for only Corinth could have been the recipient of the authorizations contained in 8:23.[62] Chapter 9 by contrast is addressed to the Christians of Achaia, who are even named in 9:2–5a.[63] Both letters make clear in different ways that the apostle dealt with the Christian community in Achaia differently than the community in Corinth, which in fact belonged to Achaia but occupied a special position within it.[64] This peculiar state of affairs

col. V, p. 57.

61 For details see above, chap. 3.

62 The other letters are all addressed to the Corinthians: on the lost letter which preceded 1 Corinthians see 1 Cor 5:9; for 1 Corinthians see the address in 1:1; for the first apology see 2 Cor 6:11. That the second apology (2 Cor 10:1—13:10) was likewise written to Corinth is clear from the letter of reconciliation (2 Cor 1:23), when Paul calls God to witness that "it was to spare you that I refrained from coming to Corinth," but instead wrote the letter of 2 Cor 10:1—13:10, which he then terms "a letter of tears" (2 Cor 2:4; 7:8).

63 See also above, pp. 91–98.

64 When Paul in 1 Thess 1:7–8; Rom 15:26 speaks of "Macedonia and Achaia" and in 1 Cor 16:15 of Achaia alone (cf. v 17), this includes Corinth. On the other hand the apostle can presuppose an unbroken relationship between himself and the Achaians in 2 Cor 11:10, but without doubt this excludes the Corinthians. Cf. also Windisch, pp. 34–36.

underlies the often-discussed address of the letter of reconciliation (2 Cor 1:1), in which "the church of God which is in Corinth" (ἡ ἐκκλησία τοῦ θεοῦ ἡ οὔσῃ ἐν Κορίνθῳ) is distinguished from "all the saints who are in the whole of Achaia" (σὺν τοῖς ἁγίοις πᾶσιν τοῖς οὖσιν ἐν ὅλῃ τῇ ʼΑχαίᾳ). But this distinction is not to be explained, as Walter Schmithals thought,[65] by a later interpolation, but by the apostle's intention to address both Christian organizations in common which were affected by the crisis in Corinth. In 2 Cor 8 and 9, on the other hand, he once again addressed the Corinthians and the Achaians separately, and here his aim was that they recognize and carry out their own parts in the common collection.

Chapter 9 deals with the special role which the Achaians were called upon to play in the resumption and successful conclusion of the collection. Thus the Achaians did not actually need to be admonished to complete the collection; rather, Paul explained to them what role they should assume in bringing the Corinthian collection to a conclusion. This includes in essence three points: First, the Achaians should provide a good example, just as they have done before, which can be imitated by the Corinthians (vv 1–2).[66] Then Paul regarded it as necessary to explain the sending of two additional envoys in order to prevent any objections against these brothers from arising from the very beginning.[67] But most of all the apostle entrusted to the Achaians the task of seeing to it that the spiritual aspect of the collection, which ought to be a "gift of blessing," was safeguarded. For this reason he explained to them in vv 6–15 what is to be understood by such a "gift of blessing."[68] Despite his joy over the resolution of the conflict with the community in Corinth, the apostle believed that only the Achaians, not the Corinthians, have the spiritual maturity to make the Corinthian collection a real "gift of blessing."

65 Schmithals, *Gnosticism*, 89 n. 13; followed by Schenke and Fischer, *Einleitung* 1.112.

66 See above, pp. 90–93.

67 See above, pp. 93–95.

68 See above, pp. 96–128.

In conclusion, we must deal with the question of how the letters of chapters 8 and 9, which we have reconstructed, are related to the rest of the apostle's correspondence, and where these letters are to be placed in its history. In respect to this question, we must distinguish between direct references to the letters and those parallel texts which are of indirect significance.

All direct references to the reconstructed letters occur in the context of the collection for Jerusalem. Of great importance here are Paul's remarks in the account of his travel plans in Rom 15:25–32. Chronologically, this section followed immediately upon the situation presupposed in 2 Cor 8 and 9. There it was assumed that the collection was still unfinished; Paul's journey to Corinth was only just being contemplated. But the Letter to the Romans indicates that Paul had arrived in Corinth, whence he wrote to Rome saying that the collection had been brought to a successful conclusion and that his departure for Jerusalem was imminent.[1]

The terminology used in Rom 15:25–32 is throughout reminiscent of 2 Cor 8 and 9. His imminent journey to Jerusalem (Rom 15:25) was being undertaken "in the service of the saints" (διακονῶν τοῖς ἁγίοις). "Service of the saints" (ἡ διακονία ἡ εἰς τοὺς ἁγίους) is also the name given to the collection in 2 Cor 8:4; 9:1.[2] Paul had to first explain to the Romans that Macedonia and Achaia had consented to take part in the collection for the poor among the saints in Jerusalem, for he could not assume that they already knew about it (Rom 15:26). In his explanation, Paul made use of the same administrative language found in 2 Cor 8 and 9. That Macedonia and Achaia had "consented" (εὐδοκεῖν)[3] to the collection is also presupposed in 2 Cor 8 and 9, though there he spoke more concretely of pledges (2 Cor 8:4–6, 10–12; 9:2–5). According to 2 Cor 8 and 9, the collection in Macedonia had already been brought to a successful conclusion, and Achaia's collection was also complete—with the exception of Corinth, where the collection activity had been interrupted on account of the great crisis. Thus the Letter to the Romans makes clear that the purpose for which 2 Cor 8 and 9 were written had been fully achieved.

In Rom 15:27, Paul began to speak about the significance of the collection. As in 2 Cor 9:13–14,[4] the apostle conceived of the gift of the Gentile Christians as a return gift to their Jewish brethren: "For if the Gentiles have come to be partners in their spiritual things, they are obliged to be of service to them in material things." Thus it was a matter of the payment of a "debt" (ὀφειλέται εἰσὶν αὐτῶν) owed to the Jewish Christians. When Paul said in Rom 15:28 that he would bring the collection "to a conclusion," he did not mean the collection in Corinth, but the journey to Jerusalem and the delivery of the funds. The expression "to bring to completion" (ἐπιτελεῖν) is often used in 2 Corinthians,[5] while the term "to seal" (σφραγίζειν), as an expression for the delivery of the collection, appears only in Rom 15:28.[6] That the entire collection was a kind of "fruit" (καρπός) is expressed in another manner, with the aid of the agricultural metaphor, in 2 Cor 9:6–11.

Paul brought the account of his travel plans in Romans to a close in 15:30–32 with an important glimpse of the situation which awaited him in Jerusalem, and of how he expected to deal with it. Clearly the apostle had few illusions about the problems which prevailed there, if he appealed to the Romans to pray for his "deliverance" from the "agōn" (ῥύομαι, συναγωνίζομαι). He obviously feared that the "unbelievers in Judea" (οἱ ἀπειθοῦντες ἐν τῇ Ἰουδαίᾳ) would make it impossible for the "saints in Jerusalem" to accept the collection. If the account in Acts

1 Thus rightly Hans Lietzmann, *An die Römer* (HNT 8; Tübingen: Mohr, Siebeck, [5]1971) 123, who also contends that the Epistle to the Romans "hinter II Cor 8, 10f. fällt."
2 See above, pp. 46, 90.
3 On this expression see above, p. 123 n. 273.
4 Lietzmann, *An die Römer,* 123, emphasizes the distinction: "a different motivation." See also above, pp. 120–26.
5 2 Cor 8:6, 11; cf. also 7:1.
6 This administrative *terminus technicus* is found only here in the NT. On the sealing of sacks of money see Tob 9:5; Job 4:17. See Ludwig Radermacher, "σφραγίζεσθαι: Römer 15, 28," *ZNW* 32 (1933) 87–89; Bauer, *s.v.* σφραγίζω, 5; differently Gottfried Fitzer, "σφραγίς κτλ.," *TDNT* 7 (1971) 948, who fails to recognize the administrative use of the term.

is trustworthy, what Paul feared actually occurred. The author of Acts was familiar with the collection, but he knew nothing of its fate in Jerusalem (cf. Acts 21:15–26; 24:17; cf. 11:29).[7] In any case, we can infer from Luke's scanty reports that Paul's great hopes for a reconciliation between Jewish and Gentile Christians were not fulfilled. To be sure, the Jerusalem Christians gave glory to God (Acts 21:20) as Paul had expected (2 Cor 9:13), but the accusation against Paul that he preached apostasy from Judaism (Acts 21:21) cast a shadow over everything. One cannot help but wonder whether it would have been better had Paul remained by his original plan not to undertake the journey to Jerusalem himself (1 Cor 16:4).

At the beginning of the collection activity in Corinth stood, of course, Paul's First Epistle to the Corinthians. The section of 1 Corinthians which makes reference to it, 16:1–4, presupposes that the collection had already begun,[8] so that the "resolution" of the Corinthians (Rom 15:26, 27) and the first visit of Titus, who organized the collection[9] originally (2 Cor 8:6), are no longer mentioned. What Paul offered in 1 Cor 16:1–4 were additional directions for the completion of the collection, which correspond to those enjoined upon the Christians in Galatia (1 Cor 16:1). It is possible that the necessity for these additional directions already hints at the coming crisis, though Paul seemed as yet to have had no presentiment of what was coming at the time of the completion of 1 Corinthians. As we have already discussed,[10] the plans for the delivery of the collection as presented in 1 Cor 16:3–4 were later changed. The direction to always set aside a certain amount in savings on the first day of the week was surely suspended by the crisis. Whether the practice was later resumed cannot be gathered from 2 Cor 8:11–12, but the statements in these passages do not necessarily stand in contradiction to one another. Many points of contact between 1 Corinthians and 2 Cor 8 and 9 may be found in addition to the directions for the collection.[11] But between these letters there lay the great crisis and its resolution.

That the crisis interrupted the progress of the collection may be inferred first of all from the fact that after its resolution and reconciliation, a new beginning had to be made. For this reason, the delegation under the leadership of Titus was sent to Corinth with the letters of chapters 8 and 9.

Consequently, the resumption of the collection in Corinth presupposed the reconciliation between the community and its apostles. This reconciliation is described in the so-called letter of reconciliation, which is completely preserved in 2 Cor 1:1—2:13; 7:5–16; 13:11–13, and which provides the redactional frame for the epistle.[12] This letter, which cannot be further investigated here, immediately precedes the letters of chapters 8 and 9. In the letter of reconciliation itself, there is as yet no discussion of the collection; on the contrary, the collection was only set in motion again later at the instigation of the Macedonians (2 Cor 8:6). The letter of reconciliation constitutes the apostle's reaction to the conciliatory offer which Titus had brought from Corinth to Macedonia (2 Cor 7:5–7).

Thus the second visit of Titus to Corinth preceded the letter of reconciliation and brought the crisis to an end, a

7 Cf. on this point the thoughts of Haenchen, *Acts*, 606–14; Georgi, *Kollekte*, 88–90.

8 See on this point Conzelmann, *1 Corinthians*, 364–66.

9 Paul used the business term λογεία as a designation for the collection in 1 Cor 16:1, 2. See on this matter Bauer, *s.v.;* Georgi, *Kollekte*, 40–41. This designation is not repeated later, but is replaced by other concepts (see above, p. 42). Luke's own judgment seems to be contained in Acts 24:17 where the collection is included in the category of Jewish offerings, ἐλεημοσύνη καὶ προσφορά, which are known to the redactor (Acts 3:2, 3, 10; 9:36; 10:2, 4, 31; 21:26). But the sacrificial concept is also found in Paul himself (cf. the sacrificial concept in 2 Cor 8:5, the concept "acceptable," εὐπρόσδεκτος, in 2 Cor 8:12, and above all the term "gift of blessing," εὐλογία.

10 On this point see above, p. 135.

11 For details the reader is referred to chaps. 2 and 3.

12 Semler had already seen that 2 Cor 13:11–13 cannot have belonged to the same letter as 10:1—13:10 (see also Windisch, p. 426; Strachan, pp. xx, 145–46; Betz, *Paulus*, 44). Bornkamm, *Vorgeschichte* (= *Gesammelte Aufsätze* 4.187): "Die Frage, zu welchem Brief die Schlussverse 13, 11–13 ursprünglich gehört haben, ist nicht mit Sicherheit zu entscheiden. Am besten wird man sie dem zugrunde gelegten Versöhnungsbrief zuweisen, doch ist auch ihre Zugehörigkeit zu 2 Kor 10—13 keineswegs unmöglich."

crisis which had reached its climax in the fragment preserved in 2 Cor 10:1—13:10. This apologetic letter[13] is commented on at length in the letter of reconciliation, and a revised judgment is reached (cf. esp. 2 Cor 2:2–4; 7:8–9).[14] But before his second apology in 2 Cor 10:1—13:10, Paul had written another apology, at least part of which is preserved in the fragment 2:14—6:13; 7:2–4.[15] This first apology already attempted to refute the charges which had been raised against the apostle, but it appears to have achieved the opposite result in Corinth. For this reason, Paul wrote the second apology, whose biting sarcasm constitutes a commentary on the failure of the first attempt.[16] As Paul reported in the letter of reconciliation, this second apology had the desired effect in Corinth and brought about a change of heart (*μετάνοια*) in the community (2 Cor 7:9).

Of what did the charges directed against Paul consist? It is necessary to distinguish different points in the opponents' critique of Paul.[17] In each case, we must keep in mind at what point in time the criticism arose, by whom it was being advanced, and in what connection the individual charges stand to one another. Taken together, the charges clearly amount to a denial of the "legitimacy of the apostle," to use the title of Ernst Käsemann's famous essay.[18] Paul already had to defend himself against the suspicion of illegitimacy in 1 Corinthians.[19] But in subsequent letter fragments, the point of controversy always recurred in connection with the collection.[20] In the first apology, Paul already dismissed the notion that he, like so many religious charlatans of his day, "peddled the word of God" (2 Cor 2:17).[21] The same charge had to be refuted in the second apology as well (2 Cor 12:14–18).[22]

Finally, if the letter of reconciliation also provided for the reconciliations of the "wrongdoer" (*ὁ ἀδικήσας*, 7:12), we can assume that the charge that Paul wished to enrich himself by means of the collection had been advanced, above all, by the wrongdoer.[23] But we should not therefore conclude that this was the only accusation against Paul. The opposition certainly included a number of other persons who, in order to discredit Paul, pressed every available charge into their service. The details of the whole controversy can only be guessed at. In the letter of chapter 8 itself, Paul undertook precautionary measures on the advice of his co-workers in order to avoid a repetition of the charge of corruption (8:20–

13 See on this point my study *Paulus, passim,* as well as the reviews by Albert Henrichs, *JBL* 94 (1975) 310–14, and Thomas Meyer, *ThLZ* 100 (1975) 757–61; Barrett, pp. 243ff; A. T. Lincoln, "Paul the Visionary: The Setting and Significance of the Rapture to Paradise in II Cor. 12:1–10," *NTS* 25 (1979) 204–22; Klaus Döring, *Exemplum Socratis: Studien zur Sokratesnachwirkung in der kynisch-stoischen Popularphilosophie der frühen Kaiserzeit und im frühen Christentum* (Hermes, Einzelschriften 42; Wiesbaden: Steiner, 1971).

14 The phenomenon of Paul's self-interpretation within the Corinthian correspondence, which has received far too little consideration methodologically, must, above all, be applied to the problem of whether what is called the "letter of tears" in 2 Cor 2:4 is identical with the fragment 10:1—13:10. Cf. Betz, *Paulus,* 4–9, 42.

15 On this first apology see Bornkamm, *Vorgeschichte* (= *Gesammelte Aufsätze* 4.177–79, 191–92); Georgi, *Gegner,* 22–24, 225ff; Vielhauer, *Geschichte,* 150–55; J. Collange, *Enigmes de la deuxième épître de Paul aux Corinthiens: Etude exégètique de 2 Cor. 2, 14–7, 4* (SNTSMS 18; Cambridge: Cambridge University, 1972); Koester, *Einführung,* 486, 561–63, 570–72; idem, *Introduction to the New Testament* (2 vols.; Hermeneia: Foundations and Facets; Philadelphia: Fortress, 1982) 2.53–54, 126–29, 135–37.

16 Rightly Koester, *Einführung,* 563; idem, *Introduction* 2.129: "The events following the receipt of this letter suggest that it did not remove the doubts of the Corinthians and probably only provoked his opponents' mockery."

17 See on this point Betz, *Paulus,* 43ff.

18 Ernst Käsemann, "Die Legitimität des Apostels. Eine Untersuchung zu II Korinther 10—13," *ZNW* 41 (1942) 33–71; rep. in the series Libelli 33 (Darmstadt: Wissenschaftliche Buchgesellschaft, 1956); also in the collection of essays *Das Paulusbild in der neueren deutschen Forschung* (ed. Karl Heinrich Rengstorf; Darmstadt: Wissenschaftliche Buchgesellschaft, 1964) 475–521.

19 See esp. 1 Cor 4:1–12; 9:1–27; 15:8–11. To these passages should be added the earliest letter of Paul, 1 Thessalonians (esp. 2:1ff) which confirms the fact, which Paul himself never attempted to keep secret, that his apostolic office was in doubt from the very beginning.

20 See Betz, *Paulus,* 100ff.

21 Cf. also 2 Cor 4:2; 6:3; 7:2. See also Bornkamm, *Vorgeschichte* (= *Gesammelte Aufsätze* 4.167–68); Collange, *Enigmes,* 37–39; Bultmann, pp. 72–73.

22 See Betz, *Paulus,* 116–17.

23 See ibid., 7, 10–12, 13.

21).[24] Even if this charge was not the only one brought against Paul, it must, nevertheless, have been one of the principal arguments of Corinthian anti-Paulinism.

24 See above, pp. 76–78.

Bibliography
Indices

Ambrosiaster
Ambrosiastri qui dicitur commentarius in epistulas Paulinas, Pars secunda: In epistulas ad Corinthios, recensuit Henricus Josephus Vogels, CSEL 81/2 (Vindobonae: Hoelder, Pichler, Tempsky, 1968).
Augustine
De doctrina Christiana, CSEL 80 (Vindobonae: Hoelder, Pichler, Tempsky, 1963).
David E. Aune
Review of Hans Dieter Betz, *Galatians, RSR* 7 (1981) 322–28.
Philipp Bachmann
Der zweite Brief an die Korinther, KNT 8 (Leipzig: Deichert, [4]1922).
Fridericus Balduinus
Apologia apostolica; hoc est, S. Apostoli Pauli epistola posterior ad Corinthios, commentario . . . illustrata; . . . cum textu Graeco-Latino . . . (Wittenberg: Sumtibus haeredum Samuelis Selfichij, 1620).
Johannes Marinus Simon Baljon
De tekst der brieven van Paulus aan de Romeinen, de Corinthiërs en de Galatiërs als voorwerp van de conjecturalkritiek beschouwd (Utrecht: J. van Boekhoven, 1884).
C. Kingsley Barrett
A Commentary on the Second Epistle to the Corinthians, Black's New Testament Commentaries (London: Black, 1973).
Karl Ludwig Bauer
Rhetoricae Paullinae, vel, *Quid oratorium sit in oratione Paulli,* 2 vols. (Halae: Impensis Orphanotrophei, 1782).
Siegmund Jacob Baumgartens Auslegung der beiden Briefe St. Pauli an die Corinthier, mit Anmerkungen und einer Paraphrasi M. Johann August Nösselts, . . . nebst einer Vorrede herausgegeben von Johann Salomon Semler (Halle: Gebauer, 1761).
Ferdinand Christian Baur
Paulus, der Apostel Jesu Christi: Sein Leben und Wirken, seine Briefe und seine Lehre, ein Beitrag zu einer kritischen Geschichte des Urchristenthums (Stuttgart: Becher & Müller, 1845, [2]1866).
Ferdinand Christian Baur
"Beiträge zur Erklärung der Korinthierbriefe." *Theologische Jahrbücher* 9 (1850) 139–85.
Ferdinand Christian Baur
"Die Einleitung in das Neue Testament als theologische Wissenschaft. Ihr Begriff und ihre Aufgabe, ihr Entwicklungsgang und ihr innerer Organismus," *Theologische Jahrbücher* 9 (1850) 463–566.
Hans Dieter Betz
Der Apostel Paulus und die sokratische Tradition: Eine exegetische Untersuchung zu seiner "Apologie" 2 Kor 10—13, BHTh 45 (Tübingen: Mohr, Siebeck, 1972).
Hans Dieter Betz
Review of Philipp Vielhauer, *Geschichte der urchristlichen Literatur, SEÅ* 43 (1978) 128–32.
Hans Dieter Betz
Galatians: A Commentary on Paul's Letter to the Churches in Galatia, Hermeneia (Philadelphia: Fortress, 1979).
Theodorus Vezelius Beza
Annotationes Majores in Novum Dn. Nostri Iesu Christi Testamentum, 2 parts in 1 vol. (sine loco, 1594).
Gustav Billroth
Commentar zu den Briefen des Paulus an die Corinther (Leipzig: Weidmann, 1833).
Friedrich Bleek
"Erörterungen in Beziehung auf die Briefe Pauli an die Korinther." *ThStKr* 3 (1830) 614–32.
Friedrich Bleek
Einleitung in das Neue Testament, ed. Wilhelm Mangold (Berlin: Reimer, [3]1875).
Günther Bornkamm
Die Vorgeschichte des sogenannten Zweiten Korintherbriefes, SHAW.PH 1961, 2. Abhandlung (Heidelberg: Winter, 1961); rep. with an addendum in his *Geschichte und Glaube II, Gesammelte Aufsätze IV* (Munich: Kaiser, 1971) 162–94.
Günther Bornkamm
"The History of the Origin of the So-Called Second Letter to the Corinthians." *NTS* 8 (1962) 258–63; rep. in: *The Authorship and Integrity of the New Testament,* Theological Collections 4 (London: SPCK, 1967) 73–81.
Wilhelm Bousset
"Der zweite Brief an die Korinther." In *Die Schriften des Neuen Testaments,* vol. II (Göttingen: Vandenhoeck & Ruprecht, [3]1917) 167–223.
Rudolf Bultmann
Der Stil der paulinischen Predigt und die kynisch-stoische Diatribe (Göttingen: Huth, 1910).
Rudolf Bultmann
Exegetische Probleme des zweiten Korintherbriefes. Zu 2. Kor 5,1–5; 5,11—6,10; 10—13; 12,21, Symbolae Biblicae Upsalienses 9 (Uppsala: Wretman, 1947); rep. *Exegetica,* 298–322.
Rudolf Bultmann
Exegetica. Aufsätze zur Erforschung des Neuen Testaments, ed. Erich Dinkler (Tübingen: Mohr, Siebeck, 1967).
Rudolf Bultmann
Der zweite Brief an die Korinther, ed. Erich Dinkler, KEK 6. Abteilung, Sonderband (Göttingen: Vandenhoeck & Ruprecht, 1976); ET: *The Second Letter to the Corinthians,* tr. Roy A. Harrisville (Minneapolis: Augsburg, 1985).
William Burkitt
Expository Notes with Practical Observations on the New

Testament, 2 parts (London: Thomas Parkhurst, 1703).
Robert Smith Candlish
The Duty of Laying By for Religious and Charitable Uses a Stated Proportion of Our Income: An Analysis of 2 Cor. viii.ix (London: Nisbet, 1862).
John Chrysostom
In secundam ad Corinthios epistolam commentarius, MPG 61, 381–610.
John Chrysostom
Sancti Patris Nostri Joannis Chrysostomi archiepiscopi Constantinopolitani in Divi Pauli Epistolam ad Corinthios posteriorem homiliae XXX. Editio nova, (Oxonii: T. Combe, 1845).
Samuel Clarke
The New Testament of Our Lord and Saviour Jesus Christ: with annotations, containing I. An Interpretation of all difficult phrases and words; II. Parallel scriptures, both as to matter and words (London: Thomas Simmons, 1683).
Patrick Cleary
"The Epistles to the Corinthians." *CBQ* 12 (1950) 10–33.
Carl Clemen
Die Chronologie der paulinischen Briefe aufs neue untersucht (Halle: Niemeyer, 1893).
Carl Clemen
Die Einheitlichkeit der paulinischen Briefe, an der Hand der bisher mit bezug auf die aufgestellten Interpolations- und Compilationshypothesen geprüft (Göttingen: Vandenhoeck & Ruprecht, 1894).
Carl Clemen
Paulus, sein Leben und Wirken (Giessen: Ricker [Töpelmann], 1904).
Carl Clemen
Review of James Houghton Kennedy, *The Second and Third Epistles of St. Paul to the Corinthians, ThLZ* 25 (1900) 703–6.
J. -F. Collange
Enigmes de la deuxième épître de Paul aux Corinthiens: Etude exégétique de 2 Cor. 2:14—7:11, SNTSMS 18 (Cambridge: Cambridge University, 1972).
Hans Conzelmann
Der erste Brief an die Korinther, KEK 5. Abteilung (Göttingen: Vandenhoeck & Ruprecht, [12]1981).
Hans Conzelmann
1 Corinthians: A Commentary on the First Epistle to the Corinthians, Hermeneia (Philadelphia: Fortress, 1975).
Paul-Louis Couchoud
"Reconstitution et classement des lettres de Saint Paul." *RHR* 87 (1923) 8–31.
Nils Astrup Dahl
Studies in Paul (Minneapolis: Augsburg, 1977).
Gerhard Delling
Worship in the New Testament (Philadelphia: Westminster, 1962).
Martin Dibelius
Geschichte der urchristlichen Literatur (Leipzig: Teubner, 1926; Munich: Kaiser, [2]1975).
Martin Dibelius
A Fresh Approach to the New Testament and Early Christian Literature (New York: Scribner's, 1936).
Martin Dibelius
An die Thessalonicher I/II, an die Philipper, HNT 11 (Tübingen: Mohr, Siebeck, [3]1937).
A. J. Dickinson
"The Genetic History of I and II Corinthians." *The Review and Expositor* 14 (1917) 32–39.
Albrecht Dihle
Die Goldene Regel: Eine Einführung in die Geschichte der antiken und frühchristlichen Vulgärethik (Göttingen: Vandenhoeck & Ruprecht, 1962).
Albrecht Dihle
"Goldene Regel." *RAC* 11 (1981) 930–40.
Erich Dinkler
"Korintherbriefe." *RGG* 4 ([3]1960) 17–23.
Charles Harold Dodd
New Testament Studies (Manchester: Manchester University, 1953).
William G. Doty
"The Classification of Epistolary Literature." *CBQ* 31 (1969) 183–99.
William G. Doty
Letters in Primitive Christianity (Philadelphia: Fortress, 1973).
Richard Drescher
"Der zweite Korintherbrief und die Vorgänge in Korinth seit Abfassung des ersten Korintherbriefes." *ThStKr* 70 (1897) 43–111.
Ismar Elbogen
Der jüdische Gottesdienst in seiner geschichtlichen Entwicklung (Hildesheim: Olms, 1962).
Christian August Gottfried Emmerling
Epistola Pauli ad Corinthios posterior graece perpetuo commentario illustravit (Leipzig: Barth, 1823).
Desiderius Erasmus
Paraphrasis in duas epistolas Pauli ad Corinthios (Lovanii, 1519); also in his *Opera Omnia,* vol. 7 (Lugduni Batavorum: Petrus van der Aa, 1706).
Desiderius Erasmus
In Novum Testamentum Annotationes, ab ipso auctore iam postremum recognitae (Basel: Apud Io. Frobenium, 1542).
Heinrich Ewald
Die Sendschreiben des Apostels Paulus (Göttingen: Dieterich, 1857).
Paul Feine
Einleitung in das Neue Testament (Leipzig: Quelle & Meyer, 1913).
Paul Feine
Einleitung in das Neue Testament, rev. Johannes Behm (Leipzig: Quelle & Meyer, [8]1936).
Paul Feine and Johannes Behm
Einleitung in das Neue Testament, rev. Werner

Georg Kümmel (Heidelberg: Quelle & Meyer, [12]1963).

Johann Friedrich von Flatt
Vorlesungen über die beyden Briefe Pauli an die Corinthier, 2 vols.; Nach seinem Tode herausgegeben von seinem Sohne, M. Christian Daniel Friedrich Hoffmann (Tübingen: Fues, 1827).

Karl Friedrich August Fritzsche
De nonnullis posterioris Pauli ad Corinthios epistolae locis dissertationes duae (Leipzig: Reclam, 1824).

Victor P. Furnish
II Corinthians, tr. with Introduction, Notes, and Commentary, AB 32A (Garden City, NY: Doubleday, 1984).

Johann Philipp Gabler
Dissertatio critica de capitibus ultimis IX–XIII posterioris epistolae Pauli ad Corinthios ab eadem haud separandis (Göttingen: apud Vidvam Abr. Vandenhoek, 1782).

Johann Philipp Gabler
Review of Michael Weber, *De numero . . . Pars I, Neues Theologisches Journal* 12/4 (1798) 405–10.

Dieter Georgi
Die Gegner des Paulus im 2. Korintherbrief: Studien zur religiösen Propaganda in der Spätantike, WMANT 11 (Neukirchen-Vluyn: Neukirchener Verlag, 1964).

Dieter Georgi
Die Geschichte der Kollekte des Paulus für Jerusalem, ThF 38 (Hamburg-Bergstedt: Reich, 1965).

Dieter Georgi
"Second Letter to the Corinthians." *IDBSup* (1976) 183–86.

Dieter Georgi
Review of Walter Schmithals, *Die Gnosis in Korinth* in *Verkündigung und Forschung* 1958/59 (1960) 90ff.

Eduard Golla
Zwischenreise und Zwischenbrief, Biblische Studien 20/4 (Freiburg: Herder, 1922).

Gregory of Nyssa
Exposition of 1 Cor 15:28, MPG 44, pp. 1303–26.

Hugo Grotius
Annotationes in Novum Testamentum, 3 vols. (Paris: Sumptibus authoris, 1641, 1646, 1650).

H. Hagge
"Die beiden überlieferten Sendschreiben des Apostels Paulus an die Gemeinde zu Korinth." *Jahrbücher für protestantische Theologie* 2 (1876) 481–531.

Anton Halmel
Der Vierkapitelbrief im zweiten Korintherbrief des Apostels Paulus (Essen: Baedeker, 1894).

Anton Halmel
Der zweite Korintherbrief des Apostels Paulus (Halle: Niemeyer, 1904).

Anthony T. Hanson
Studies in Paul's Technique and Theology (London: SPCK, 1974).

Günther Harder
Paulus und das Gebet, Neutestamentliche Forschungen 1/10 (Gütersloh: Bertelsmann, 1936).

Adolf Hausrath
Der Vier-Capitel-Brief des Paulus an die Korinther (Heidelberg: Bassermann, 1870).

Adolf Hausrath
Neutestamentliche Zeitgeschichte, 4 vols. (Heidelberg: Bassermann, [2]1875–1879).

Carl Friedrich Georg Heinrici
Das zweite Sendschreiben des Apostels Paulus an die Korinthier (Berlin: Hertz, 1887).

Carl Friedrich Georg Heinrici
Der zweite Brief an die Korinther, KEK 6. Abteilung (Göttingen: Vandenhoeck & Ruprecht, [8]1900).

Matthew Henry
An Exposition of the Old and New Testament, vol. 5 (London: Knapton, [4]1738).

Hans-Eberhard Hess
Theologie und Religion bei Johann Salomo Semler: Ein Beitrag zur Theologiegeschichte des 18. Jahrhunderts, Inaugural Dissertation, Kirchliche Hochschule Berlin, 1974 (Augsburg: Blasaditsch, 1974).

Adolf Hilgenfeld
"Die Christusleute in Korinth." *ZWTh* 3 (1865) 241–42.

Adolf Hilgenfeld
Historisch-kritische Einleitung in das Neue Testament (Leipzig: Fues [R. Reisland], 1875).

Johann Christian Karl von Hofmann
Die heilige Schrift neuen Testaments zusammenhängend untersucht, 2. Theil, 3. Abteilung: *Der zweite Brief Pauli an die Korinther* (Nördlingen: Beck, [2]1877).

Carl Holsten
Zum Evangelium des Paulus und des Petrus: Altes und Neues (Rostock: Stiller [H. Schmidt], 1868).

Carl Holsten
Das Evangelium des Paulus, 2 vols. (Berlin: Reimer, 1880, 1898).

Carl Holsten
"Einleitung in die Korinthierbriefe." *ZWTh* 44 (1901) 324–69.

Heinrich Julius Holtzmann
"Das gegenseitige Verhältniss der beiden Korintherbriefe." *ZWTh* 22 (1879) 455–92.

Gottfried Hornig
Die Anfänge der historisch-kritischen Theologie: Johann Salomo Semlers Schriftverständnis und seine Stellung zu Luther (Göttingen: Vandenhoeck & Ruprecht, 1961).

Nils Hyldahl
"Die Frage nach der literarischen Einheit des Zweiten Korintherbriefes." *ZNW* 64 (1973) 289–306.

Robert Jewett
"The Redaction of I Corinthians and the Trajectory of the Pauline School." *JAAR* 44 (1978) 389–444.

Robert Jewett
A Chronology of Paul's Life (Philadelphia: Fortress, 1979).

Sherman E. Johnson
"A New Analysis of Second Corinthians." *ATR* 47 (1965) 436–43.

Adolf Jülicher
Einleitung in das Neue Testament (Tübingen: Mohr, Siebeck, [1.2]1894, [5.6]1906, [7]1931).

Ernst Käsemann
"Die Legitimität des Apostels. Eine Untersuchung zu II Korinther 10—13." *ZNW* 41 (1942) 33–71; rep. Darmstadt: Wissenschaftliche Buchgesellschaft, 1956; also in *Das Paulusbild in der neueren deutschen Forschung,* ed. Karl Heinrich Rengstorf (Darmstadt: Wissenschaftliche Buchgesellschaft, 1964) 475–521.

Ernst Käsemann
Commentary on Romans (Grand Rapids: Eerdmans, 1980).

Aemilius Fridericus Kautzsch
De Veteris Testamenti Locis a Paulo Apostolo allegatis, Dissertatio critica (Leipzig: Metzger & Wittig, 1869).

J. B. G. Keggemann
Dissertatio historico-hermeneutica De duplici epistolae ad Romanos appendice capite XV, XVI (Halae Magdeburgicae, 1767). Johann Salomo Semler, *Paraphrasis epistolae ad Romanos,* cum notis, translatione vetusta, et dissertatione de appendice cap. XV. XVI (Halae Magdeburgicae: Hemmerde, 1769) 277–311.

James Houghton Kennedy
"Are There Two Epistles in 2 Corinthians?" *The Expositor* 6 (1897) 231–38, 285–304.

James Houghton Kennedy
The Second and Third Epistles of St. Paul to the Corinthians (London: Methuen, 1900).

Chan-Hie Kim
Form and Structure of the Familiar Greek Letter of Recommendation, SBLDS 4 (Missoula, MT: Scholars, 1972).

Albert Klöpper
Exegetisch-kritische Untersuchungen über den zweiten Brief des Paulus an die Gemeinde zu Korinth (Göttingen: Vandenhoeck & Ruprecht, 1869).

Albert Klöpper
Kommentar über das zweite Sendschreiben des Apostel Paulus an die Gemeinde zu Korinth (Berlin: Reimer, 1874).

Erich Klostermann
Review of Hans Windisch, *Der zweite Korintherbrief, ThLZ* 52 (1927) 341–42.

Helmut Koester
"Häretiker im Urchristentum." *RGG* 3 ([3]1959) 17–21.

Helmut Koester
Einführung in das Neue Testament (Berlin: de Gruyter, 1980).

Helmut Koester
Introduction to the New Testament, 2 vols., Hermeneia: Foundations and Facets (Philadelphia: Fortress, 1982).

Karl König
"Der Verkehr des Paulus mit der Gemeinde zu Korinth." *ZWTh* 40 (1897) 481–554.

Max Krenkel
Beiträge zur Aufhellung der Geschichte und der Briefe des Apostels Paulus (Braunschweig: Schwetschke, 1880, [2]1895).

Werner Georg Kümmel
Introduction to the New Testament, tr. Howard C. Kee (Nashville: Abingdon, [2]1975).

Kirsopp Lake
The Earlier Epistles of St. Paul: Their Motive and Origin (London: Rivingtons, 1911, [2]1914).

Cornelius a Lapide
The Great Commentary of Cornelius a Lapide: II. Corinthians and Galatians, tr. and ed. W. F. Cobb (London: Hodges, 1897).

Jean Laporte
La doctrine eucharistique chez Philon d'Alexandrie, Théologie historique 16 (Paris: Beauchesne, 1972).

Johannes Georgius Fridericus Leun
Pauli ad Corinthios epistula secunda graece, perpetua annotatione illustrata (Lemgo: Meyer, 1804).

Hans Lietzmann
An die Römer, HNT 8 (Tübingen: Mohr, Siebeck, [5]1971).

Hans Lietzmann
An die Korinther I/II, HNT 9 (Tübingen: Mohr, Siebeck, 1909, [4]1949 [ed. Werner Georg Kümmel]).

Andreas Lindemann
Paulus im ältesten Christentum, BHTh 58 (Tübingen: Mohr, Siebeck, 1979).

Heinrich Lisco
Die Entstehung des zweiten Korintherbriefes (Berlin: Schneider, 1896).

John Locke
A Paraphrase and Notes on the Epistles of St. Paul to the Galatians, I & II Corinthians, Romans, Ephesians, To which is Prefix'd, An Essay for the Understanding of St. Paul's Epistles, by Consulting St. Paul Himself (London: Awnsham and John Churchill, 1707): in this volume: *A Paraphrase and Notes on the Second Epistle of St. Paul to the Corinthians* (1706).

Eduard Lohse
Colossians and Philemon: A Commentary on the Epistles to the Colossians and to Philemon, tr. William R. Poehlmann and Robert J. Karris, ed. Helmut Koester; Hermeneia (Philadelphia: Fortress, 1971).

Alfred Loisy
"Les épîtres de S. Paul." *Revue d'histoire et de littérature religieuses* 7 (1921) 76–125, 213–50.

Gerd Lüdemann
Paulus, der Heidenapostel, I. Studien zur Chronologie, FRLANT 123 (Göttingen: Vandenhoeck & Ruprecht, 1980).
Wilhelm Lütgert
Freiheitspredigt und Schwarmgeister in Korinth, Beiträge zur Förderung christlicher Theologie 12/3 (Gütersloh: Bertelsmann, 1908).
Adalbert Maier
Commentar über den zweiten Brief Pauli an die Korinther (Freiburg: Wagner, 1865).
Thomas W. Manson
"St. Paul in Ephesus, 3: The Corinthian Correspondence." *BJRL* 26 (1941/42) 101–20, 327–41; rep. as "The Corinthian Correspondence" (1) and (2) in his *Studies in the Gospels and Epistles* (Manchester: Manchester University, 1962) 190–209, 210–24.
Willi Marxsen
Einleitung in das Neue Testament (Gütersloh: Mohn, 1963).
Willi Marxsen
Introduction to the New Testament (Oxford: Blackwell, 1968).
Michel Mauduit
Analyse des épîtres de Saint Paul, et des épîtres canoniques, avec les dissertations sur les lieux difficiles, 2 vols. (Lyon: Briasson, [3]1710).
Allan Menzies
The Second Epistle of the Apostle Paul to the Corinthians (London: Macmillan, 1912).
Eduard Meyer
Ursprung und Anfänge des Christentums, 3 vols. (Stuttgart and Berlin: Cotta, [4.5]1924); rep. Darmstadt: Wissenschaftliche Buchgesellschaft, 1962.
Heinrich August Wilhelm Meyer
Der zweite Brief an die Korinther, KEK 6. Abteilung (Göttingen: Vandenhoeck & Ruprecht, 1840, [5]1870) [Title of the first edition of 1840: *Kritisch-exegetisches Handbuch über den zweiten Brief an die Korinther*].
Johann David Michaelis
Einleitung in die göttlichen Schriften des Neuen Bundes, 2 Theile (Göttingen: Vandenhoeck & Ruprecht, [2]1765).
Wilhelm Michaelis
Einleitung in das Neue Testament (Bern: Haller, [3]1961 [with Ergänzungsheft]).
Wilhelm Michaelis
"Teilungshypothesen bei Paulusbriefen. Briefkompositionen und ihr Sitz im Leben." *ThZ* 14 (1958) 321–26.
J. H. A. Michelsen
"'T Verhaal vaan Paulus' vlucht uit Damaskus, 2 Kor. XI:32,33; XII:1,7a een interpolatie." *Theologisch Tijdschrift* 7 (1873) 421–29.
James Moffatt
An Introduction to the Literature of the New Testament (New York: Scribner's, 1910, [3]1918).
Johann Lorenz von Mosheim
Erklärung des zweiten Briefes des heiligen Apostel Pauli an die Gemeinde zu Corinthus (Flensburg: Korten, 1762).
Stephen Charles Mott
"The Power of Giving and Receiving: Reciprocity in Hellenistic Benevolence." *Current Issues in Biblical and Patristic Interpretation,* FS M. C. Tenney (Grand Rapids: Eerdmans, 1975) 60–72.
Stephanus Le Moyne
Varia Sacra, seu *Sylloge variorum opusculorum Graecorum ad rem ecclesiasticam spectantium,* 2 vols. (Lugduni Batavorum: Daniel à Gaesbeeck, 1685).
Wolfgangus Musculus
In ambas Apostoli Pauli ad Corinthios epistolas, Commentarij, 2 vols. (Basel: per I. Hervagium, 1559, [2]1566).
Albrecht Oepke
Der Brief des Paulus an die Galater, ed. Joachim Rohde, ThHK 9 (Berlin: Evangelische Verlagsanstalt, [3]1973 [[1]1937, [2]1957]).
Wolf-Henning Ollrog
Paulus und seine Mitarbeiter. Untersuchungen zu Theorie und Praxis der paulinischen Mission, WMANT 50 (Neukirchen-Vluyn: Neukirchener Verlag, 1979).
Hermann Olshausen
Die Briefe des Apostels Paulus an die Korinther (Königsberg: Unzer, 1837, [2]1840).
Johann Ernst Osiander
Commentar über den zweiten Brief Pauli an die Korinthier (Stuttgart: Basser, 1858).
Franz Overbeck
"Über die Anfänge der patristischen Literatur." *Historische Zeitschrift* 48 (1882) 417–72; rep. Basel: Schwabe, n.d.
Norman Perrin and Dennis C. Duling
The New Testament: An Introduction (New York: Harcourt Brace Jovanovich, [2]1982).
Otto Pfleiderer
Das Urchristentum, seine Schriften und Lehren in geschichtlichem Zusammenhang beschrieben, 2 vols. (Berlin: Reimer, 1887, [2]1902).
Johannes Piscator
Analysis logica epistolarum Pauli (London: Impensis Georg. Bishop, 1591).
Johannes Piscator
Analysis logica utriusque epistolae Pauli ad Corinthios; una cum scholiis et observationibus locorum doctrinae, . . . (Herbornae Nassoviorum: Typis Christophori Corvini, 1593).
Alfred Plummer
A Critical and Exegetical Commentary on the Second Epistle of St Paul to the Corinthians, ICC (Edinburgh: Clark, 1915).
Matthaeus Polus [Matthew Poole]
Synopsis criticorum aliorumque S. Scripturae interpretum, Vol. IV, pars posterior, complectens

Epistolas universas & Apocalypsin (London: apud Carolum Smith, 1676).
Matthaeus Polus
Annotations upon the Bible. Wherein the sacred text is inserted, and various readings annex'd, Together with Parallel Scriptures. The more difficult Terms in each Verse are Explained. Seeming Contradictions Reconciled. Questions and Doubts Resolved. And the Whole Text Opened. Vol II, Being a Continuation of Mr. Pool's Work by certain Judicious and Learned Divines (London: Parkhurst, 1688).
Herbert Preisker
"Zur Komposition des zweiten Korintherbriefes," *Theologische Blätter* 5 (1926) 154–57.
Julius Ferdinand Räbiger
Kritische Untersuchungen über den Inhalt der beiden Briefe des Apostels Paulus an die korinthische Gemeinde mit Rücksicht auf die in ihr herrschenden Streitigkeiten (Breslau: Morgenstern, 1847, ²1886).
Gerald Henry Rendall
The Epistles of Paul to the Corinthians (London: Macmillan, 1909).
James M. Robinson and Helmut Koester
Trajectories Through Early Christianity (Philadelphia: Fortress, 1971).
Herman Johan Royaards
Disputatio inauguralis De altera Pauli ad Corinthios epistola, et observanda in illa apostoli indole et oratione, . . . (Trajecti ad Rhenum: Altheer, 1818).
Leopold Immanuel Rückert
Der zweite Brief Pauli an die Korinther (Leipzig: Köhler, 1837).
Wolfgang Schenk
"Der 1. Korintherbrief als Briefsammlung." *ZNW* 60 (1969) 219–43.
Hans-Martin Schenke
"Das Weiterwirken des Paulus und die Pflege seines Erbes durch die Paulusschule." *NTS* 21 (1974/75) 505–18.
Hans-Martin Schenke and Karl Martin Fischer
Einleitung in die Schriften des Neuen Testaments, vol. 1: *Die Briefe des Paulus und die Schriften des Paulinismus* (Berlin: Evangelische Verlagsanstalt, 1978).
Paul Wilhelm Schmiedel
Hand-Commentar zum Neuen Testament, vol. 2 (Freiburg: Mohr, Siebeck, 1891, ²1892).
Paul Wilhelm Schmiedel
"Paulinische Briefe I." *ThR* 4 (1901) 498–522.
Walter Schmithals
Die Gnosis in Korinth: Eine Untersuchung zu den Korintherbriefen, FRLANT 66 (Göttingen: Vandenhoeck & Ruprecht, 1956, ²1965, ³1969).
Walter Schmithals
Gnosticism in Corinth, tr. John E. Steely (Nashville: Abingdon, 1971).
Walter Schmithals
Paulus und die Gnostiker. Untersuchungen zu den kleineren Paulusbriefen, ThF 35 (Hamburg-Bergstedt: Reich, 1965).
Walter Schmithals
Paul and the Gnostics, tr. John E. Steely (Nashville: Abingdon, 1972).
Walter Schmithals
"Zur Abfassung und ältesten Sammlung der paulinischen Hauptbriefe." *ZNW* 51 (1960) 225–45.
Walter Schmithals
"On the Composition and Earliest Collection of the Major Epistles of Paul." *Paul and the Gnostics,* 239–45.
Walter Schmithals
Review of Dieter Georgi, *Die Geschichte der Kollekte, ThLZ* 92 (1967) 668–72.
Walter Schmithals
"Die Korintherbriefe als Briefsammlung." *ZNW* 64 (1973) 263–88.
Paul Schubert
Form and Function of the Pauline Thanksgiving, BZNW 20 (Berlin: Töpelmann, 1939).
Emil Schürer
The History of the Jewish People in the Age of Jesus Christ (175 B.C.—A.D. 135), rev. Géza Vermès, Fergus Millar, and Matthew Black, 2 vols. (Edinburgh: Clark, 1973, 1979).
Albert Schweitzer
Geschichte der paulinischen Forschung von der Reformation bis auf die Gegenwart (Tübingen: Mohr, 1911).
Nicolaus Selneccerus
In omnes epistolas D. Pauli Apostoli Commentarius plenissimus. . . . Post auctoris obitum nunc primum in lucem editus, studio filij Georgii Selnecceri (Leipzig: Sumptibus Iacobi Apelii Bibliop., 1595).
Johann Salomo Semler
Commentatio ad 2 Corinth. VIII,9. Nomine publico in natalium Domini Nostri Iesu Christi memoriam prodita (Halae: Litteris Hendelianis, 1758).
Johann Salomo Semler
Paraphrasis epistolae ad Romanos, cum notis, translatione vetusta, et dissertatione de appendice cap. XV. XVI (Halae Magdeburgicae: Hemmerde, 1769).
Johann Salomo Semler
Abhandlung von freier Untersuchung des Canon, 4 parts (Halle: Hemmerde, 1771–75).
Johann Salomo Semler
Paraphrasis II. epistolae ad Corinthios. Accessit Latina Vetus traslatio et lectionum varietas (Halae Magdeburgicae: Hemmerde, 1776).
J. N. Sevenster
Paul and Seneca, NovTSup 4 (Leiden: Brill, 1961).
Karl Staab
Pauluskommentare aus der griechischen Kirche, NTA 15 (Münster: Aschendorff, 1933).
A. M. G. Stephenson
"Partition Theories on II. Corinthians." *Studia*

Evangelica II, TU 87 (Berlin: Akademie-Verlag, 1964) 639–46.

Stanley Kent Stowers
The Diatribe and Paul's Letter to the Romans, SBLDS 57 (Chico, CA: Scholars, 1981).

Robert Harvey Strachan
The Second Epistle of Paul to the Corinthians, MNTC (New York and London: Harper, 1935).

Hermann Strathmann
"Die Krise des Kanons der Kirche. Joh. Gerhards und Joh. Sal. Semlers Erbe." *Das Neue Testament als Kanon,* ed. Ernst Käsemann (Göttingen: Vandenhoeck & Ruprecht, 1970).

Alfred Suhl
Paulus und seine Briefe: Ein Beitrag zur paulinischen Chronologie, StNT 11 (Gütersloh: Mohn, 1975).

Michael Theobald
Die überströmende Gnade: Studien zu einem paulinischen Motivfeld, Inaugural Dissertation (Bonn: Rheinische Friedrich-Wilhelms-Universität, 1980).

G. A. van den Bergh van Eysinga
Die holländische radikale Kritik des Neuen Testaments: Ihre Geschichte und ihre Bedeutung für die Erkenntnis der Entstehung des Christentums (Jena: Diederichs, 1912).

G. A. van den Bergh van Eysinga
Radical Views About the New Testament, tr. S. B. Black (London: Watts, 1912).

Willem Christiaan van Manen
Paulus, vol. 3: *De Brieven aan de Korinthiërs* (Leiden: Brill, 1896).

H. S. Versnel, ed.
Faith, Hope and Worship: Aspects of Religious Mentality in the Ancient World, Studies in Greek and Roman Religion 2 (Leiden: Brill, 1981).

Philipp Vielhauer
Geschichte der urchristlichen Literatur (Berlin: de Gruyter, 1975).

Marvin R. Vincent
"The Integrity of Second Corinthians." *Essays in Modern Theology and Related Subjects,* gathered and published as a testimonial to Charles Augustus Briggs (New York: Scribner's, 1911) 185–89.

Daniel Völter
Paulus und seine Briefe: Kritische Untersuchungen zu einer neuen Grundlegung der paulinischen Briefliteratur und ihrer Theologie (Strassburg: Heitz, 1905).

Michael Weber
De numero epistolarum ad Corinthios rectius constituendo, P. I: *Paulus, Apostolus non duas, sed quinque epistolas ad Corinthios scripsit, Neues Wittenbergisches Wochenblatt* 6 (1798) 143.

Michael Weber
De numero epistolarum Pauli ad Corinthios rectius constituendo, Programmschriften I–XII (University of Wittenberg, 1798–1807).

Walther Weber
Wieviele Briefe hat der Apostel Paulus an die Korinther geschrieben? Programm des Königlichen Gymnasiums zu Wetzlar (Wetzlar: Schnitzler, 1899).

Johannes Weiss
Review of Anton Halmel, *Der Vierkapitelbrief, ThLZ* 19 (1894) 513–15.

Johannes Weiss
"Beiträge zur paulinischen Rhetorik." *Theologische Studien,* B. Weiss zu seinem 70. Geburtstag dargebracht (Göttingen: Vandenhoeck & Ruprecht, 1897) 165–247.

Johannes Weiss
Der erste Korintherbrief, KEK 5. Abteilung (Göttingen: Vandenhoeck & Ruprecht, [9]1910; rep. 1970).

Johannes Weiss
Das Urchristentum, ed. Rudolf Knopf (Göttingen: Vandenhoeck & Ruprecht, 1917).

Johannes Weiss
The History of Primitive Christianity, tr. Frederick C. Grant (New York: Wilson & Erickson, 1937); republished as *Earliest Christianity,* ed. Frederick C. Grant, 2 vols. (New York: Harper, 1959).

Christian Hermann Weisse
Philosophische Dogmatik oder Philosophie des Christenthums, 3 vols. (Leipzig: Hirzel, 1855–62).

Christian Hermann Weisse
Beiträge zur Kritik der paulinischen Briefe an die Galater, Römer, Philipper und Kolosser, ed. E. Sulze (Leipzig: Hirzel, 1867).

Karl Heinrich von Weizsäcker
Das apostolische Zeitalter der christlichen Kirche (Freiburg: Mohr, 1886, [2]1892).

Paul Wendland
Die urchristlichen Literaturformen, HNT 1/1 (Tübingen: Mohr, Siebeck, [2.3]1912).

Daniel Whitby
A Paraphrase and Commentary on the New Testament, 2 vols. (London: Awnsham and John Churchill, 1703, [2]1706).

John L. White
The Form and Structure of the Official Petition; a Study in Greek Epistolography, SBLDS 5 (Missoula, MT: Scholars, 1972).

Gordon P. Wiles
Paul's Intercessory Prayers, SNTSMS 24 (Cambridge: Cambridge University, 1974).

Christian Gottlob Wilke
Die neutestamentliche Rhetorik, ein Seitenstück zur Grammatik des neutestamentlichen Sprachidioms (Dresden and Leipzig: Arnold, 1843).

Hans Windisch
Der zweite Korintherbrief, KEK 6. Abteilung (Göttingen: Vandenhoeck & Ruprecht, [9]1924; rep. 1970).

Thomas Wittaker
The Origins of Christianity, with an Outline of van

Manen's Analysis of the Pauline Literature
(London: Watts, 1904, ²1909).
Werner Carl Ludwig Ziegler
Theologische Abhandlungen, 2 vols. (Göttingen:
Vandenhoeck & Ruprecht, 1791–1804).
Euthymius Zigabenus
*Commentarius in XIV epistolas sancti Pauli et VII
Catholicas,* ed. Nicephorus Calogeras, vol. I
(Athens: Perri, 1887).

Indices*

1. Passages

a / Old Testament and Apocrypha

*Numbers in parentheses following page citations for this volume refer to footnotes.

b / Old Testament Pseudepigrapha and Other Jewish Literature

c / New Testament

d / Early Christian Literature and the Ancient Church

2. Greek Words

3. Subjects

4. Modern Authors

In the design of the visual aspects of *Hermeneia*, consideration has been given to relating the form to the content by symbolic means.

The letters of the logotype *Hermeneia* are a fusion of forms alluding simultaneously to Hebrew (dotted vowel markings) and Greek (geometric round shapes) letter forms. In their modern treatment they remind us of the electronic age as well, the vantage point from which this investigation of the past begins.

The Lion of Judah used as visual identification for the series is based on the Seal of Shema. The version for *Hermeneia* is again a fusion of Hebrew calligraphic forms, especially the legs of the lion, and Greek elements characterized by the geometric. In the sequence of arcs, which can be understood as scroll-like images, the first is the lion's mouth. It is reasserted and accelerated in the whorl and returns in the aggressively arched tail: tradition is passed from one age to the next, rediscovered and re-formed.

"Who is worthy to open the scroll and break its
seals . . ."
Then one of the elders said to me
"weep not; lo, the Lion of the tribe of David,
the Root of David, has conquered,
so that he can open the scroll and
its seven seals."
Rev. 5:2, 5

To celebrate the signal achievement in biblical scholarship which *Hermeneia* represents, the entire series will by its color constitute a signal on the theologian's bookshelf: the Old Testament will be bound in yellow and the New Testament in red, traceable to a commonly used color coding for synagogue and church in medieval painting; in pure color terms, varying degrees of intensity of the warm segment of the color spectrum. The colors interpenetrate when the binding color for the Old Testament is used to imprint volumes from the New and vice versa.

Wherever possible, a photograph of the oldest extant manuscript, or a historically significant document pertaining to the biblical sources, will be displayed on the end papers of each volume to give a feel for the tangible reality and beauty of the source material.

The title-page motifs are expressive derivations from the *Hermeneia* logotype, repeated seven times to form a matrix and debossed on the cover of each volume. These sifted-out elements will be seen to be in their exact positions within the parent matrix. These motifs and their expressional character are noted on the following page.

Horizontal markings at gradated levels on the spine will assist in grouping the volumes according to these conventional categories.

The type has been set with unjustified right margins so as to preserve the internal consistency of word spacing. This is a major factor in both legibility and aesthetic quality; the resultant uneven line endings are only slight impairments to legibility by comparison. In this respect the type resembles the handwritten manuscripts where the quality of the calligraphic writing is dependent on establishing and holding to integral spacing patterns.

All of the type faces in common use today have been designed between 1500 A.D. and the present. For the biblical text a face was chosen which does not arbitrarily date the text, but rather one which is uncompromisingly modern and unembellished so that its feel is of the universal. The type style is Univers 65 by Adrian Frutiger.

The expository texts and footnotes are set in Baskerville, chosen for its compatibility with the many brief Greek and Hebrew insertions. The double-column format and the shorter line length facilitate speed reading and the wide margins to the left of footnotes provide for the scholar's own notations.

Kenneth Hiebert

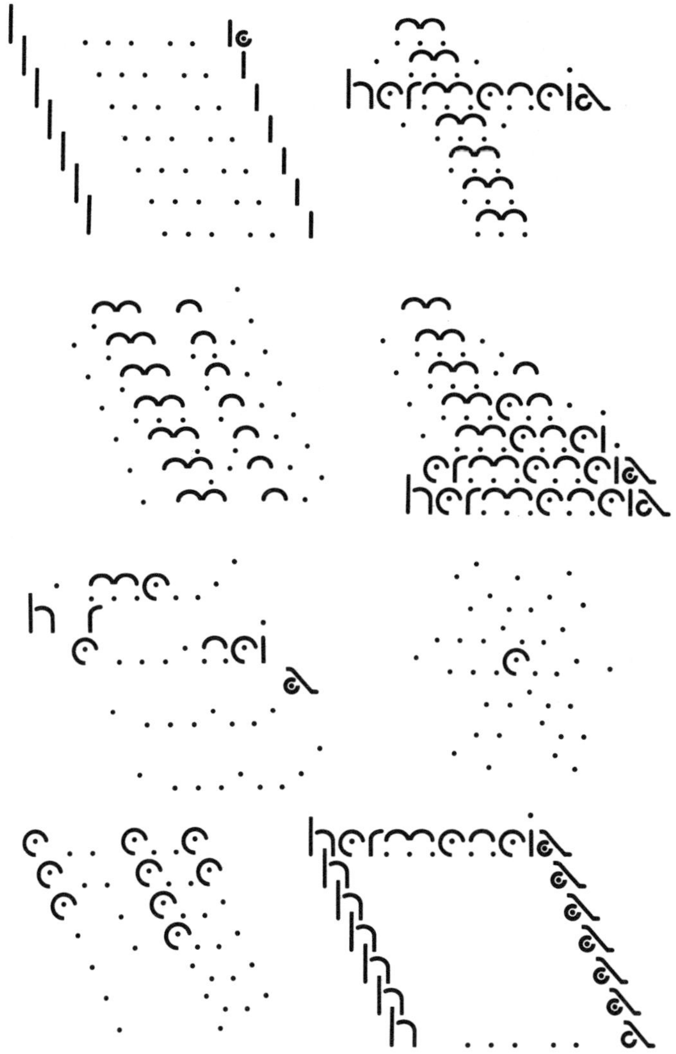

Category of biblical writing,
key symbolic characteristic,
and volumes so identified.

1
Law
(boundaries described)
- Genesis
- Exodus
- Leviticus
- Numbers
- Deuteronomy

2
History
(trek through time and space)
- Joshua
- Judges
- Ruth
- 1 Samuel
- 2 Samuel
- 1 Kings
- 2 Kings
- 1 Chronicles
- 2 Chronicles
- Ezra
- Nehemiah
- Esther

3
Poetry
(lyric emotional expression)
- Job
- Psalms
- Proverbs
- Ecclesiastes
- Song of Songs

4
Prophets
(inspired seers)
- Isaiah
- Jeremiah
- Lamentations
- Ezekiel
- Daniel
- Hosea
- Joel
- Amos
- Obadiah
- Jonah
- Micah
- Nahum
- Habakkuk
- Zephaniah
- Haggai
- Zechariah
- Malachi

5
New Testament Narrative
(focus on One)
- Matthew
- Mark
- Luke
- John
- Acts

6
Epistles
(directed instruction)
- Romans
- 1 Corinthians
- 2 Corinthians
- Galatians
- Ephesians
- Philippians
- Colossians
- 1 Thessalonians
- 2 Thessalonians
- 1 Timothy
- 2 Timothy
- Titus
- Philemon
- Hebrews
- James
- 1 Peter
- 2 Peter
- 1 John
- 2 John
- 3 John
- Jude

7
Apocalypse
(vision of the future)
- Revelation

8
Extracanonical Writings
(peripheral records)

ἤρξασθε ἀπὸ πέρυσι. Νυνὶ δὲ καὶ τὸ ποιῆσαι ἐπιτελέσατε· ὅπως καθάπερ ἡ προθυμία τοῦ θέλειν, οὕτω καὶ τὸ ἐπιτελέσαι ἐκ τοῦ ἔχειν. Εἰ γὰρ ἡ προθυμία πρόκειται, καθὸ ἐὰν ἔχῃ τις, εὐπρόσδεκτος, οὐ καθὸ οὐκ ἔχει. Οὐ γὰρ ἵνα ἄλλοις ἄνεσις, ὑμῖν δὲ θλῖψις· ἀλλ' ἐξ ἰσότητος, ἐν τῷ νῦν καιρῷ τὸ ὑμῶν περίσσευμα εἰς τὸ ἐκείνων ὑστέρημα· Ἵνα καὶ τὸ ἐκείνων περίσσευμα γένηται εἰς τὸ ὑμῶν ὑστέρημα, ὅπως γένηται ἰσότης· Καθὼς γέγραπται· Ὁ τὸ πολὺ, οὐκ ἐπλεόνασε· καὶ ὁ τὸ ὀλίγον, οὐκ ἠλαττόνησε· Χάρις δὲ τῷ Θεῷ τῷ διδόντι τὴν αὐτὴν σπουδὴν ὑπὲρ ὑμῶν ἐν τῇ καρδίᾳ Τίτου· Ὅτι τὴν μὲν παράκλησιν ἐδέξατο· σπουδαιότερος δὲ ὑπάρχων, αὐθαίρετος ἐξῆλθε πρὸς ὑμᾶς. Συνεπέμψαμεν δὲ μετ' αὐτοῦ τὸν ἀδελφὸν, οὗ ὁ ἔπαινος ἐν τῷ εὐαγγελίῳ διὰ πασῶν τῶν ἐκκλησιῶν· (Οὐ μόνον δὲ, ἀλλὰ καὶ χειροτονηθεὶς ὑπὸ τῶν ἐκκλησιῶν συν-

προενήρξασθε] ἐνήρξασθε D a prima manu. F. πέρυσι] πέρσυ D a prima manu. FG.
11. τὸ prius] τοῦτο 26. προθυμία] + ὑμῶν W. Musculus. τοῦ prius] τὸ D a prima man
τὸ posterius] τοῦ Versio *Vulg.* 12. ἐὰν] ἂν D a prima manu.
τις] — CDEFG 10. 11. 17. 21. 26. 39. 46. Editio *Colinaei*. Versio *Vulg*. *Syra* prior, posterior vero hab cum asterisco. *Damascenus*. *Clemens* Str. II. p. 296. *Theodoretus*. probante *J. Millio* prol. 633.
εὐπρόσδεκτος] + καὶ Versio *Syra* posterior.
οὐ καθὸ οὐκ ἔχει] — Versio *Æthiop*. probante *J. Millio* prol. 1215.
13. δὲ] — 33. 35.
ἔχει] + τις DEFG.
ab ὑστέρημα ad ὑστέρημα] — 3.
ἀλλ'] — 30. νῦν] — F.
14. ὁ prius] ὁ 13. 26. a prima manu. 38. 48. Editio *Complut*. Codices *Latini*. ὅτι 14. ὃ 39.
ὁ posterius] — FG 1. 2. 14. ὁ 26. a prima manu. 38. 48. Editio *Complut*. Codices *Latini*.
16. διδόντι] — Editio *Haultini*. δόντι CDEFG 1. 3. 4. 6. 8. 9. 11. 18. a prima manu. 19. 20. a prima manu. 21. 22. 28. 29. 30. 33. 39. 41. 47. *Chrysostomus*, *Theophylactus*. probante *J. Millio* prol. 884.
διδόντι 26. + ὑμῖν C. αὐτὴν] τοιαύτην 2. Editio *Erasmi* 1. *Ald*. αὐτοῦ 38.
ὑπὲρ ὑμῶν] — 2. ὑπὲρ ἡμῶν 23. καρδίᾳ] παρουσίᾳ 2.
17. αὐθαίρετος] αὐθαιρέτως 46. 18. μετ' αὐτοῦ] αὐτῷ 31. 37. Editio *Colinaei*.
ἀδελφὸν] + ἡμῶν 10. Versio *Syr*. *Hilarius*, *Pelagius*. ὁ] — Editio *Complut*.
ἔπαινος] + ὁ 2. 19. ὑπὸ] ἐπὶ P. *Junius*. ἡμῶν prius] + ἐγένετο DE
σὺν τῇ] ἐν C. ἐν τῇ 6. 10. 17. 31. 37. 39. 47. Editio *Colinaei*. Versio *Vulg*. *Syr*. *Copt*. *Æthiop*. *Damascenus*, *Augustinus*, *Hilarius*.
ab ὑφ' ἡμῶν ad ὑφ' ἡμῶν comm. 20.] — 21.
ἡμῶν posterius] ὑμῶν C.
αὐτοῦ] — CD a prima manu. FG 23. 31, 39. Editio *Colinaei*. Versio *Copt*. *Vulg*. *Hilarius*, *Augustinus*. αὐτὸν 6.

vel δώσειν, daturum esse. *Phil*. II. 13. *Rom*. VII. 18.

πέρυσι] *Demosthenes*. αἱ πέρυσι πρεσβεῖαι. πέρυσι ἐπιδημῶν. *Theophrastus* H. P. III. 12. διαμένει δ' εἰς ἐνιαυτὸν, εἶθ', ὅταν ἄλλος ἐπιφύῃ, ὁ περύσινος ἀποπίπτει. *Philostratus* in Heroic. I. p. 670. εἶδον αὐτὸν πέρυσι.

11. Ut promte & alacriter promisistis: ita & praestetis.

13 ἄνεσις] *Bereschith R*. XXXVIII. 16. Non venit afflictio homini, in qua non sit postremo remissio.

ἐξ ἰσότητος] *Anthol*. IV. 12. 92. ὡς ἰσότης πάντων ἐστὶ δικαιοτάτη.

ἐν τῷ νῦν καιρῷ] *Aristophanes* Plut. 50. σφόδρ' ἐστὶ συμφέρον τὸ μηδὲν ἀσκεῖν ὑγιὲς ἐν τῷ νῦν καιρῷ.

Xenophon. ἃ ἂν ἴδω περιττὰ ὄντα τῶν ἐμοὶ ἀρκούντων, τούτοις ταῖς ἐνδείαις τῶν φίλων ἐξαρκοῦμαι. *Livius* VI. 15. 9. ex eo, quod affluit opibus vestris, sustinendo necessitates aliorum.

15. ὁ τὸ πολὺ] *Lucianus* in fugitiv. 29. ὁ τὴν κιθάραν. Gallo 14. ὁ τὰ ῥάκια τὰ πιναρά. Bis accus. 14. ὁ τὴν σύριγγα. — ἡ τὰ ποίκιλα sub. ἔχων & ἔχουσα.

17. σπουδαιότερος] *Augustinus* princip. Dialect. A virtute non potest dici virtuosus, sed moderatus & industrius. Nec in graeco quidem ἀπὸ τῆς ἀρετῆς ἀρετὸς dicitur, sed σπουδαῖος. *Aristoteles* Categor. VIII. 21. ἀπὸ τῆς ἀρετῆς, ὁ σπουδαῖος, τῷ γὰρ ἀρετὴν ἔχειν σπουδαῖος λέγεται. — φαῦλον καὶ σπουδαῖον contraria sunt. Sentent. *Antagorae* μηδενὸς ἄξιος & σπουδαῖος ἄνθρωπος. *Demosthenes* Philipp. III. ἀνδράποδον σπουδαῖον. *Plut*. Pericle p. 152. E. Ἀντισθένης ἀκούσας, ὅτι σπουδαῖός ἐστιν αὐλητὴς Ἰσμηνίας, ἀλλ' ἄνθρωπος, ἔφη, μοχθηρός. *Pausanias* Messen. 4. ταῦτα μὲν οὖν ἑκάτεροι λέγουσι, θέσθω δὲ, ὡς ἔχει τις εἰς τοὺς ἑτέρους σπουδῆς. *Cic*. de Invent. I. 25. Studium est animi adsidua & vehemens ad aliquam rem applicata magna cum voluntate occupatio, ut philosophiae, poetices, geometriae, literarum.

19. χειροτονηθεὶς] Lucam intelligunt. *Jos*. A. … 8. 1. ἑβραῖοι δὲ — συνῄνουν τῇ τοῦ Θεοῦ χειροτονίᾳ. … 4. 2. & 13. 9. ὑπὸ τοῦ Θεοῦ βασιλεὺς κεχειροτονημένος … XIII. 2. 2. χειροτονοῦμέν σε — ἀρχιερέα. 7. 1. πρὸς στρατιώτας, εἰ βασιλέα χειροτονήσουσιν αὐτόν. *Philo* sac… *Cic*. pro Flacco. 6. Sic sunt expressa ista praec…ra, quae vocantur, Psephismata, non senten… neque autoritatibus declarata, nec jurejurando co…stricta, sed porrigenda manu profundendoque c…more multitudinis concitatae. *Aristophanes* Co… 266. χειροτονητέον ἐξωμισάσαις τὸν ἕτερον βραχίονα. *De…mosthenes* in Timocr. προσῆλθε τῇ βουλῇ, προβούλευ… ἐγράφη, μετὰ ταῦτα γενομένης ἐκκλησίας προυχειροτόνει ὁ δῆμος. *Thucydides* III. 49. ῥηθεισῶν τῶν γνωμῶν τ… — οἱ ἀθηναῖοι — ἐγένοντο ἐν τῇ χειροτονίᾳ ἀγχώμαλοι … IV. 38. ἱππάρχου ἐφῃρημένου. *Sch*. ἀντὶ τοῦ μετ' ἐκεῖνον … μένου καὶ χειροτονηθέντος. *Polyaenus* p. 52. Γέλων Συ…κούσιος — στρατηγὸς αὐτοκράτωρ χειροτονηθείς. p. 4… ὅτῳ δοκεῖ ὑπὲρ καὶ ἀγαθοκλεῖ, αἰρέτω τὴν χεῖρα. *Dio* p… ἐπὶ τοὺς καταποντιστὰς ἄλλον χειροτονήσατε. *Libanius* XII. p. 389. ἡ πόλις αἰσχύνεται ἠδικηκυῖα, καὶ το…κεκώλυται πέμψαι πρός σε πρεσβείαν, ἐγὼ δὲ ἐμαυ… χειροτονήσας ἥκω.

20. στελλόμενοι] *Hesychius*. στέλλεται, φοβεῖται. Gl… sae *Phrynichi* Arabii. στείλασθαι τὸ πρόσωπον, αὐτὸ συστρέψαι καὶ σκυθρωπάσαι· ἡ μεταφορὰ ἀπὸ τῶν ἱστίων